COLIN READ is assistant professor at Huron College, University of Western Ontario.

In December 1837 assemblyman Dr Charles Duncombe of Burford led a rebellion in south-western Upper Canada, gathering 500 men near Brantford. Historians have assumed that Duncombe acted in concert with William Lyon Mackenzie, leader of the revolt near Toronto. Professor Read finds this supposition wrong, though acknowledging that Duncombe was induced to promote rebellion by the erroneous report that Mackenzie and his men had taken Toronto.

To better define the events of the period, Read examines the state of society in the western area of the Gore district and much of the London district, including settlement and the national and religious backgrounds of the inhabitants, and the types of society and economy they evolved. He looks at their political culture and its development, clearly indicating the battle lines drawn between Reformers and Tories in the pre-rebellion period – lines which grew increasingly rigid as the rebellion neared, hardened by a number of issues, some provincial in nature, others purely local.

Read describes the mustering of the rebels, the crushing of the rebellion by 'loyalist' forces, and the subsequent detention and imprisonment of the rebels, assessing the role of the authorities in their punishment and defining its nature.

The author concludes that the rebels were mostly American or Upper Canadian and broadly representative of the members of a reasonably prosperous agrarian community, not of a rural proletariat, nascent or otherwise. He suggests that the Duncombe rising and its attendant troubles were precipitated, not by a broadly based movement aimed at producing fundamental social change, but by a narrowly centred movement which sought political reforms.

COLIN READ

The Rising in Western Upper Canada, 1837–8: The Duncombe Revolt and after

UNIVERSITY OF TORONTO PRESS
Toronto Buffalo London

© University of Toronto Press 1982
Toronto Buffalo London
Printed in Canada
Reprinted in 2018
ISBN 0-8020-5498-6 (cloth)
ISBN 978-0-8020-6495-0 (paper)

Canadian Cataloguing in Publication Data

Read, Colin Frederick, 1943–
  The rising in western Upper Canada, 1837–8

  Bibliography: p.
  Includes index.
  ISBN 0-8020-5498-6 (cloth); ISBN 978-0-8020-6495-0 (paper)

  1. Canada – History – Rebellion, 1837–1838.
  2. Ontario – History – 1791–1841.* 3. Duncombe,
  Charles, 1794–1875. I. Title.

  FC454.R43   971.03'8   c81-095047-2
  F1032.R43

To Jackie and Geoffrey
(Robbie and Audie)

Contents

MAPS ix

ACKNOWLEDGMENTS xi

1
Introduction 3

2
The Setting – People and Places 11

3
Political Discontents 47

4
The Revolt 82

5
Repercussions 107

6
Consequences 133

7
Rebels and Loyalists 164

8
Conclusion 205

APPENDICES 213

Introduction 215

1
The Rebels 220

2
Those who Aided the Rebels 233

3
Suspected Traitors 238

4
Bayham Loyalists 241

5
Bayham Rebels 244

6
Those Bound Over in the Rebel Area in December 1837 for Reasons Unknown 246

7
Those Charged with Offences Unconnected with the Duncombe Rising 247

8
Those Bailed or Imprisoned Suspected of Being Implicated in the Duncombe Rising on Evidence that Now Seems Insufficient or Contradictory 248

9
Norwich Men 251

NOTES 253

BIBLIOGRAPHY 295

INDEX 309

Maps

1
Central and western Upper Canada, 1837 2

2
Reference map 13

3
Dates of settlement 15

4
National settlement 22

5
Religious activities, 1834–7 28–30

6
Distribution of rebels in 1837 167

7
Bayham township 200

Acknowledgments

This work has been in preparation for a relatively long time. It began as a doctoral thesis under the supervision of Professor J.M.S. Careless at the University of Toronto. Only he and I know how much effort he expended to ensure that a worthwhile result came from my labours. To him I am deeply indebted.

Over the years many have contributed to this book. Among them are various individuals who allowed me to examine their private collections of archival material and archivists throughout the province who guided me to and through virtual mountains of material. The staff of both the Ontario Archives and the Public Archives of Canada, Mr Ed Phelps of the Regional History Collection at Western's Weldon Library, and the Reverend Glenn Lucas of the United Church Archives deserve particular mention and thanks for affording me, over extended periods and with remarkable patience and good grace, their expertise.

Several people have read and commented throughtfully upon my thesis or on one of its revisions. Professor J.K. Johnson of Carleton, Mr Dan Brock of London and editors Jean Houston and Barbara Sutton of the University of Toronto Press have been especially keen and kind as has Professor Fred Armstrong of the University of Western Ontario, who has been an invaluable source of advice and encouragement.

I owe thanks to various bodies, institutions, and their representatives – to the old, unreconstructed Canada Council for supporting me in my graduate school career, to Huron College, and to the editors of *Histoire sociale – Social History* for giving me permission to reproduce the maps I published in their May 1976 issue. This book has been published with the help of a grant from the Social Science Federation of Canada, using funds provided by the Social Sciences and Humanities Research xii Acknowledgments

Council of Canada, and a grant from the Andrew W. Mellon Foundation to the University of Toronto Press.

To Professor Donald Forster of the University of Guelph, who prompted me to seek publication of this work, I owe a great deal. I am deeply grateful to my wife, Jackie, who has helped me through much of the drudgery involved in producing this book. She and our son, Geoffrey, are responsible for whatever degree of equilibrium I have been able to maintain throughout.

Ultimately, of course, I must accept full responsibility for the book's shortcomings myself.

COLIN READ

THE RISING IN WESTERN UPPER CANADA,

1837–8: THE DUNCOMBE REVOLT AND AFTER

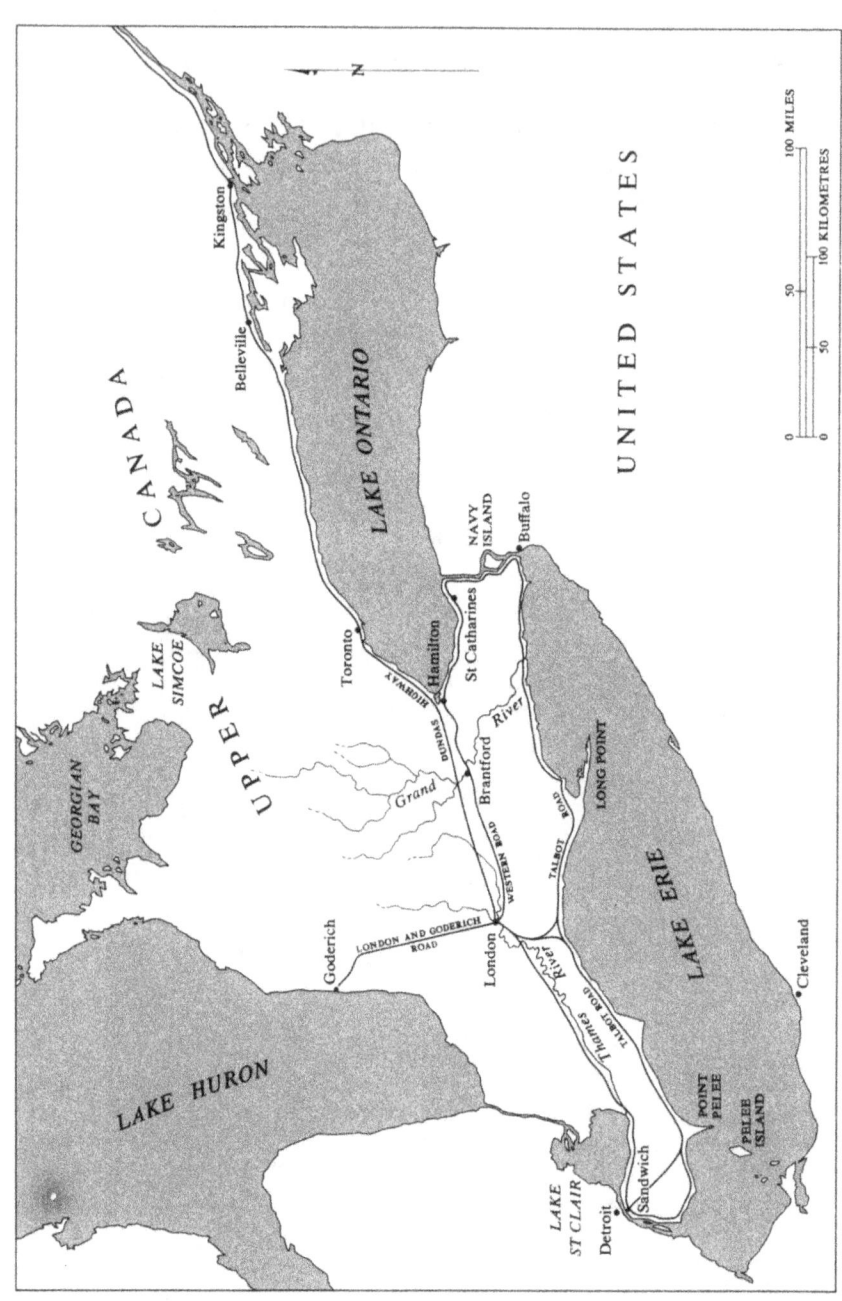

Map 1. Central and western Upper Canada, 1837

1
Introduction

The Duncombe rising was the western aspect of one of the most celebrated events of Upper Canadian history – the rebellion of 1837. Both manifestations of the rebellion – the revolt directed by William Lyon Mackenzie at Toronto and that led by Charles Duncombe near Brantford – were quickly crushed, but both were comparatively dramatic. Each saw men shoulder arms in an effort to secure changes in the system of government, only to be confronted by men equally anxious to prevent the violent change of that system. Each provides the stuff of drama, though it has been peculiarly the Mackenzie rising, which was the initial as well as the central expression of rebellion in Upper Canada, which has attracted the attention of historians and popular writers alike.

Many have seen the Mackenzie rising, and by implication the Duncombe revolt which was inspired by it, as the logical culmination of Upper Canada's political development. The argument according to this view is that the ordinary people of Upper Canada had accumulated legitimate grievances against the government and their spokesmen were the Reformers, whose efforts to achieve change were obstructed by an unfeeling, unprincipled Tory oligarchy. Eventually, an exasperated William Lyon Mackenzie, the acknowledged leader of the Reformers, decided upon an armed rebellion to secure by force what he and his colleagues could not achieve by peaceful means. Hence he inspired both the rebellion at Toronto and that near Brantford which was led by Charles Duncombe, one of his Reform colleagues in the house of assembly.

The classic articulation of this thesis was provided by Charles Lindsey in his two-volume study of his father-in-law, *The Life and Times of William Lyon Mackenzie*. Though several of the main tenets of the 'Lindsey interpretation' have been persuasively challenged by Aileen Dunham in *Political Unrest in Upper Canada, 1815–1836* and Gerald M. Craig in *Upper Canada: The Formative Years, 1784–1841* it has had remarkable durability, particularly in popular literature and in student essays. A reason for its longevity is that one of its central propositions, that by 1837 many people had grievances against the government, is sound, as a brief account of Upper Canadian history will show.

Upper Canada, like New Brunswick, another of Britain's North American colonies, owed its creation to the United Empire Loyalists, who fled the America of the revolution. By 1791 perhaps as many as 10,000 had settled in what is now southern Ontario, which in that year became Upper Canada. The Constitutional Act of the same year gave the colony its governmental structure, supplying in the process many of the grievances which were to bedevil the Upper Canadian political scene. Under that Act Upper Canada had a lieutenant-governor, appointed by the British government and answerable to it. The chief executive officer of the colony, he had wide decision-making powers, among the most important the filling of certain offices. In particular, he appointed the members of two vital bodies, the executive and legislative councils. These, respectively, helped frame administrative policy and initiate and pass legislation. The lieutenant-governor (or governor, as he was commonly known) and the members of the two councils represented monarchy and aristocracy in a government designed to blend the elements of King, Lords, and Commons.

The positions of the lieutenant-governor and his councillors were all appointive. The appointive principle in government was extended by legislation establishing the mechanisms of local government. While that principle at first might have ensured that the best qualified among the province's small population filled the most important offices of government, it had very obvious limitations. It did help ensure that, in time, at least some functionaries, safe from the necessity of accounting to the common people, were emboldened to exercise power arbitrarily and corruptly. Also, it meant that the governors, who came and went with some regularity, were in constant need of advice from trusted advisers on a host of matters, including the question of whom to appoint to vacant offices. Certain high-ranking officials at the provincial capital of York, by gaining the confidence of the governors, were thus in a position to secure the naming of friends and relatives to those offices. Hence the appointive principle promoted the development of a network of interests. By the late 1820s, known as the 'Family Compact,' that network was fully established

5 Introduction

and was headed by such notables as the archdeacon of York, Dr John Strachan, and his former pupil, attorney-general John Beverley Robinson. But even before then, not every man who had the ability and desire to hold office found his wishes accommodated, his talents used. Amongst such men a sense of grievance grew, as it did among that still larger body of settlers who objected to the near-uniformity of belief among officials regarding the necessity of close imperial ties and the wisdom of preserving government forms.

If the monarchical and aristocratic sides of Upper Canada's government, of which the appointive principle was a part, created discontent, so too did its 'democratic' component – the assembly created by the Constitutional Act. The difficulty was not that the assembly's franchise was a propertied one, for even as late as 1837 few Upper Canadians advocated universal manhood suffrage, but that the assembly's powers were exceedingly limited. Although the assembly could initiate legislation and was, indeed, the main legislative body in the province, its bills could be rejected by the legislative council or the lieutenant-governor or the British government. Hence, from the outset, the possibility was that a particular house of assembly would be at loggerheads with other centres of governmental authority, engaged in a struggle it could not hope to win. That possibility was realized very early, indeed before the War of 1812–14. Thereafter, reform-dominated houses sometimes found their bills turned back with such regularity that they were in danger of becoming little more than forums for debate.

Aside from establishing a contentious framework of government, the Constitutional Act created the Clergy Reserves. They, and the Crown Reserves devised in 1792, provided another rich source of discontent. Each type of reserve accounted for one-seventh of the lots of every surveyed township in the province. The revenues acquired from the eventual sale or lease of the Crown Reserves were to help defray the costs of government, and those from the Clergy Reserves were to support the Church of England clergy. Although certain other denominations acquired access to a portion of the Clergy Reserve revenues in 1820, those reserves remained the most spectacular, if just one of the many, ways in which the government favoured the Church of England in the colony. Non-Anglicans could legitimately object to the Clergy Reserves and settlers generally could complain that both the Clergy and the Crown Reserves hindered progress and prosperity by creating a checkerboard system of lots in each township withheld, for a time at least, from occupation. Certainly, the two sets of reserves helped produce a dispersed pattern of settlement. That they were a source of grievance was demonstrated by Robert Gourlay, a Scot who arrived in Upper Canada in 1817. Interested in promoting the emigration of Britons to the colony, he decided to canvass the settlers already there about their satisfactions and discontents. The responses he received revealed that the reserves bulked large among the latter.

Gourlay had arrived in the province just after the War of 1812–14, which had been fought between Britain, her colonies, and the United States. On the eve of the war Upper Canada had had a population of less than 100,000, the largest component being Americans who had not participated in the original United Empire Loyalist influx into the province. During the course of the war, which ended in a stalemate, officials both in Britain and in Upper Canada became alarmed at the extent of disaffection and disloyalty on the part of the American-born in the colony. Those of the western peninsula were particularly suspect.[1] Suspicion of the American settlers, and the fact that post-war Britain had a surplus population which could be encouraged to emigrate to Upper Canada, led to the decision to bar Americans from the province. They were no longer needed. Legal means were found to prevent their taking the oath of allegiance and, because anyone wishing to secure full legal title to land had to take that oath, this action did much to discourage American immigration. It also created consternation among many Americans already resident in the province. These, and large landholders wishing to sell land to incoming Americans, opposed this decision, as did Robert Gourlay. He raised the issue while in Upper Canada from 1817 to 1819 when he crusaded against the various abuses, Crown and Clergy Reserves included, which he felt hindered the settlers and retarded the growth of their province. Expelled from the colony in 1819 for his activities, he did not witness the implementation of the settlement of 1828. In general, under it Americans living in the province could, after meeting certain residence requirements, take the oath of allegiance and secure the full privileges of British subjects, including the right to hold land. This settlement made no provision for Americans who entered the province after 1828; thus it did not completely end the controversy which remained, in muted form, to trouble the political life of the province to 1837 and beyond.

In the years before the rebellion the agitation over the alien question helped give rise to the Reform party as did the controversies surrounding the system of government, the Crown and Clergy Reserves, and the many privileges of the Church of England. Various other issues also favoured the rise of that party. Some – the close alliance between the Family Compact and various enterprises, notably the Bank of Upper Canada, the Welland Canal Company, and the Canada Company – bulked very large. Others – the tearing down of a private fence on a military reserve at Niagara Falls, the rebuke and punishment of an assemblyman, Captain Matthews, a retired British army officer on half-pay who had toasted a touring company of American players by calling for 'Hail Columbia' – did not. A variety of issues, many of which concerned ordinary settlers, explain the rise of the Reform party, which began taking shape in the 1820s. Indeed, so extensive had the catalogue of grievances become by then that, quite possibly, the only people completely satisfied with the status quo were Anglicans of Loyalist or British origin who had the ear of the governor.

To argue that many Upper Canadians harboured this or that grievance is not to suggest that all the aggrieved were dissatisfied with the general situation and in the camp of the Reformers. It is revealing to look at the four elections to the assembly in the period from 1828 to 1836, after the emergence of the Reformers as a recognizable political entity. They were far from uniformly successful, winning the contests of 1828 and 1834, but losing those of 1830 and 1836 to the Tories. Rather than proving that in the years leading up to the rebellion the Reformers grew from strength to strength until they had the mass of the electorate behind them, these results show that the electorate wavered in its support of the Reformers and Tories, favouring first one, then the other. They also show that the large influx of British immigrants into the colony after the Napoleonic wars had helped provide the Tories with a solid constituency.

Another popular misconception about the rebellion era, one that Charles Lindsey also helped foster, is that in the years before 1837 William Lyon Mackenzie was the acknowledged leader of the Reformers. Certainly, Mackenzie's career was both a celebrated and a colourful one. In 1820 he had emigrated from Scotland and from 1824, as a newspaper editor, had taken up the cudgels on the Reform side of politics. In 1826 his flagging financial fortunes were retrieved and his career as a Reformer advanced by a group of Tory youths who wrecked his shop and his press. This incident served to widen the circulation of his paper, once re-established, for it earned him a reputation as a Reform martyr, a reputation enhanced by the vendetta leading Tories conducted against him in the assembly in 1831–4, when they expelled him repeatedly for allegedly libelling that body. Despite his notoriety and his undeniably effective agitation, he was not the leader of the Reform party. Steadier

8 The Rising in Western Upper Canada

and more moderate men, individuals such as Marshall Spring Bidwell, Dr William Warren Baldwin and his son, Robert, had better claim to that honour, particularly in light of the divergence in the thirties between Mackenzie and many others in the Reform camp.

Increasingly, moderate Reformers were attracted to the Baldwins, who advocated responsible government. According to that theory, the dominant party in the assembly should select the executive councillors who should, after taking office, be answerable to the assembly. If implemented, responsible government would achieve at a single stroke a great and significant change in government, one that would diffuse power downward and one that was in accord with the parliamentary practice then evolving in Great Britain.

Though Mackenzie also advocated, on occasion, the institution of responsible government, his advocacy was at odds with his argument that Upper Canadians should forsake British political institutions and procedures for American ones.[2] In his view, American norms and devices not only would offer the ordinary settler a far greater voice in government than he then had, but also would quickly improve the economic state of the colony. American democracy and prosperity went hand in hand, for American government was inexpensive, yet effective.[3]

Mackenzie's position could readily be branded as disloyal and the Tories were only too ready to do so. In the process they saw no reason to make fine distinctions between moderate and radical Reformers – all were American by inspiration and treasonable by intent. The Tories took this position with startling effect in the elections of 1836 when they swept most provincial ridings. Consequently, many moderate Reformers, Robert Baldwin among them, withdrew from politics in disgust. Mackenzie had also been checked at the polls; embittered, he was not prepared to retire from the fray.

In 1837 Mackenzie and his allies organized an agitation aimed at recouping Reform fortunes. They sought to mobilize Reformers in political unions and hold a great convention in Toronto to seek redress of their many grievances. The aim was heightened agitation, not rebellion. But rebellion broke out at Toronto in December 1837 because Mackenzie, acting independently, decided on it.[4] The haphazard organization of his revolt suggests the haste with which it was planned, as does his failure to co-ordinate his actions with those of radical colleagues elsewhere. It was not the case, as virtually everyone who has touched upon the subject has implied, that Mackenzie and Duncombe had previously concocted a plot in which the two would launch simultaneous and co-ordinated risings.

9 Introduction

Indeed, Duncombe made an instantaneous decision to lead an insurrection on hearing the rumour that Mackenzie had gathered a force near Toronto and had taken the provincial capital. Similarly, the speed with which both risings were crushed and the failure of either to attract the support of many leading Reformers demonstrate that they were decidedly not the product of the labours of a united group of Reformers who had the near-uniform backing of the province's ordinary settlers. In sum, several misconceptions about the causes and the movements to rebellion in Toronto and the west exist. Neither the abundance of writing on the Mackenzie rising nor the relative lack of it on the Duncombe revolt has prevented these misconceptions.

The Duncombe revolt has received little attention from historians. Lindsey devotes only a few pages to it as do J.C. Dent and E.C. Guillet, in the other two standard studies of the rebellion, *The Story of the Upper Canadian Rebellion* and *The Lives and Times of the Patriots*. A number of studies have appeared, however, containing information of a local nature not available in any of the three studies. James Young's *Reminiscences of the Early History of Galt and the Settlement of Dumfries*, Warner and Beers' *History of the County of Brant, Ontario*, R.C. Muir's *The Early Political and Military History of Burford*, and F.D. Reville's *History of the County of Brant* provide some detail about the rebellion as it affected the settlers of the Brantford area. That area was not the only one which supplied men for Duncombe's cause. Rebels mustered from a region extending approximately from Brantford in the east to St Thomas in the west. In 1887 a former rebel, Lewis Adelbert Norton, published in Oakland, California, a diverting, if highly coloured, account of the rebellion and his role in it. His *Life and Adventures of Col. L.A. Norton*, W.A. and C.L. Goodspeed's *History of the County of Middlesex, Canada*, and C.O. Ermatinger's *The Talbot Régime* offer further glimpses of the events of the rebellion in the area directly affected by the Duncombe rising.

No work published thus far has adequately moved beyond the general treatment of the Duncombe rebellion set out by Lindsey, Dent, or Guillet or successfully synthesized and expanded upon the relevant narratives available in works of local interest. No study has yet provided a comprehensive, coherent assessment of the western revolt and its widespread repercussions. The best account is Fred Landon's 'The Duncombe Uprising of 1837 and Some of Its Consequences' which appeared in the *Proceedings and Transactions of the Royal Society of Canada* for 1931. That article did tie together a number of loose threads, but it was too brief to do much more than that, consisting of only sixteen pages, over half of which comprised primary documents. Landon, however, had an abiding interest in the effects of the Duncombe revolt and of the rebellion of 1837 generally. Ten years after his article appeared he published *Western Ontario and the American Frontier* in which he devoted some twenty-seven pages to the rebellion era.

Though Landon was more aware than most earlier writers of the difficulties faced by the loyalists in dealing with Reformers, rebels, and 'patriots' (those invading the province from the United States after the rebellion), he shared their essential attitudes. He was at one with them in decrying the way in which the Tories had crushed the revolts and allegedly instituted 'a veritable reign of terror.'[5] Basically, he believed, as others did, that many Tories were self-seeking, unprincipled men, ready to take advantage of the opportunity presented them by the ill-fated risings to grind not just rebels, but all Reformers, into the dust. Some Tories were bent upon vengeance and eager to harass and jail rebels and Reformers alike, of course, but others were not. After the rebellion the Tories were exposed to the turbulent, aggressive population which had gathered on the frontiers of the States during the depression of the later thirties. This population in conjunction with fleeing Upper Canadian rebels was a threat to the province. As authorities in the province were keenly aware, should the patriots invade the colony with any success, some still resident within the colony would likely rise in support. Hence the treatment the Tories meted out to traitors, real or merely suspected, was conditioned as much by fear as by malice, fear which was in large measure justified.

On the whole, the little that has been written about the Duncombe rising has suffered from certain limitations, some of which also apply to the writing about the Mackenzie revolt. Certainly, room exists for a new study examining in detail the nature of western Upper Canadian society, the agitation in the west prior to the rebellion, the mustering of the Duncombe rebels, the rallying of the loyalists, and the crushing of the rising, as well as the complex of events that followed. This study attempts to provide such a many-sided examination and also probes some of the assumptions long held about the social, national, and religious characteristics of the Duncombe rebels. The more we know about those rebels, about the western rising and why it occurred, the better we understand the repercussions of that revolt and, ultimately, the richer our insight into the politics and society of contemporary western Upper Canada.

2

The Setting – People and Places

The men who marched in arms under the banner of rebellion hoisted by Dr Charles Duncombe and Eliakim Malcolm in December 1837, those who mustered to suppress their treasonable insolence, and indeed those who merely watched the two contending groups were all, in part at least, products of the communities in which they lived. Those communities possessed certain definite national, religious, and economic characteristics which help explain why the rebels harboured certain grievances while the loyalists shared certain satisfactions.

The Duncombe rebels who gathered at Oakland in December 1837 drew their forces from sixteen townships of western Upper Canada in a rough arc from Dumfries in the north-east to Southwold in the south-west. The townships were spread over five counties – Halton, Wentworth, Oxford, Norfolk, and Middlesex – and two districts – Gore and London. In Halton, however, the rebellion touched only Dumfries and in Wentworth only Brantford. These two townships, Dumfries and Brantford, were the only ones of the Gore district directly involved in the revolt, and they formed part of that district's western extremity. Moreover, the insurgents from Dumfries and Brantford came primarily from the western sections of those townships, and appear to have been oriented not eastward to Hamilton but westward to the settlements of the London district.

By and large, the population of the Gore district, which extended eastwards around the head of Lake Ontario, was remarkably free from the contagion of revolt. The Gore men who were infected were caught up primarily in the whirl of events about Toronto, conspiring and mustering with Mackenzie and the Home district insurgents. The people of the Western district and of the northern section of the London district,

Huron county, became embroiled in the Patriot troubles of 1838, but were relatively unaffected by the rebellion itself. The one known rebel from Huron, Anthony Van Egmond, was drawn not south to Duncombe's men but eastward down the Huron road to Guelph and on to Toronto and death in a cold, damp jail cell.

The sixteen townships involved in the Duncombe revolt were primarily western in character – rural, agricultural, and somewhat remote from Toronto and the provincial centres of power. The townships were Oakland, Burford, Brantford, Dumfries, Blenheim, East Oxford, West Oxford, Norwich, Dereham, Southwold, Yarmouth, Malahide, Bayham, Windham, Townsend, and Woodhouse. Repercussions from the rebellion affected most of the other nineteen townships of Middlesex, Oxford, and Norfolk counties – Houghton, Dorchester, Middleton, Charlotteville, Walsingham, Blandford, Zorra, North Oxford, Nissouri, London, Westminster, Delaware, Caradoc (then spelled Carradoc), Ekfrid, Mosa, Lobo, Adelaide, Aldborough, and Dunwich. The events which followed the rebellion, as well as the geographical proximity of these latter townships to the 'rebel' region, provide two reasons why they form part of the study area.

Also, as indicated, the nineteen 'non-rebel' townships along with the sixteen 'rebel' ones did have a rough sort of administrative unity. All except two were in the London district and encompassed within the counties of Middlesex, Oxford, and Norfolk. (See map 2.) Perhaps more notably, in terms of settlement they constituted a geographic unit; for in 1837 Oxford was bounded on the north, and Middlesex on the north and west, by zones of lightly settled townships. In addition, the easternmost townships of Norfolk and Oxford were flanked by Indian lands which stretched northwestward along the Grand River from Lake Erie to Brantford township. In the northeast, the German Mennonite settlers of Waterloo, who had overflowed into the adjacent townships of Wilmot, Blenheim, and Dumfries, formed an ethnic frontier for the primarily American, Upper Canadian, and British inhabitants of the western townships. For a number of reasons, then, the study area consists of thirty-five townships in Upper Canada's western peninsula.

I

Those who took up land in the western section of the province in the years prior to the rebellion were confronted, as perhaps no other Upper Canadian settlers were, with a bewildering variety of tracts closed to

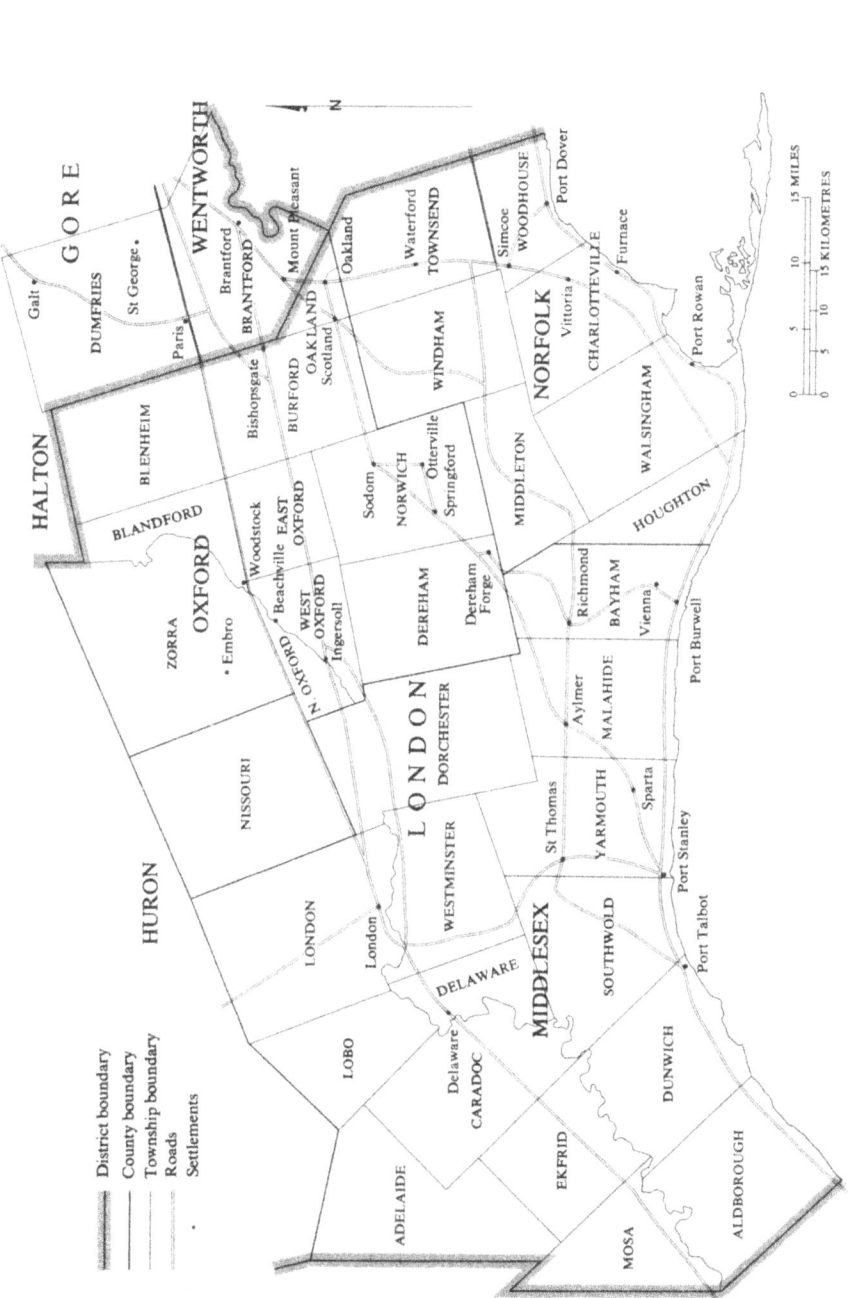

Map 2. Reference map

occupation for one reason and another. As well, they found an excessive number of bodies or individuals exercising jurisdiction over settlement. By the thirties, prospective inhabitants in the area were discovering that the government had already disposed of much of the public domain. The basic land policy adopted at the creation of the province involved the issuance of free grants of 200 acres to bona fide settlers, who received their patents, conveying full legal title to their properties, only on the completion of settlement duties and on the payment of patent fees. Aside from the grants available to the ordinary settler, free lands were given to those people officially categorized as United Empire Loyalists (refugees from the American Revolution who had entered Upper Canada before 28 July 1798 and were registered as Loyalists before 15 December 1798), to their offspring, to discharged veterans of the imperial army or navy, to militiamen, and, generally, to people favoured by the provincial or British governments.

The multiplication of grants meant that large blocks of land were lost to the Crown. By 1800 settlers in significant numbers had moved into sections of the Oxford county townships of East, West, and North Oxford, Oakland, and Blenheim, into the Norfolk townships of Townsend, Windham, Woodhouse, Charlotteville, and Walsingham, and into Delaware in Middlesex, and Brantford in Wentworth. (See map 3.)[1] Areas of Norwich in Oxford county, and of Yarmouth, Malahide, Dorchester, Westminster, Dunwich, and Mosa in Middlesex had been occupied in the succeeding decade. Even though genuine settlers, reluctant to pay the necessary fees, were often slow to take out patents on their properties, and even though most of the aforementioned townships had been settled in small part only, by 1810 most of the lots in Oakland, Burford, Blenheim, East, West, and North Oxford in Oxford county, in Woodhouse, Windham, Townsend, Charlotteville, and Walsingham in Norfolk, and in Delaware in Middlesex county had been patented.[2] By 1820 most of the land in Dorchester and in the south half of Dereham had been patented but there was very little settlement in Dorchester and none in Dereham; in these two townships absentee owners had acquired large holdings.

In 1826, in an attempt to create revenue and to facilitate development, a sales policy, repealing the system of free grants, was instituted for Crown lands. At public sales a minimum of 100 acres, a maximum of 1,000, was to be sold on credit to the highest bidder. The 1826 act, however, was doomed to failure, for it did not dispose of all the outstanding grants allotted earlier to various claimants. In any event, it was too late by the mid-twenties to alter radically the pattern of land

Map 3. Dates of settlement. Sources: travellers' accounts, settlers' letters, local histories, etc.

acquisition in the longer settled portions of the province. In 1838 reportedly a mere 250 acres, exclusive of the Clergy Reserves established by the Constitutional Act of 1791, remained to be disposed of by the Crown in the rebel townships. A further 6,500 acres, 6,000 in Dunwich alone, remained in the other townships surveyed.[3] The fact that tracts had not yet been opened to settlement by 1837 in Southwold, Dorchester, Aldborough, Dunwich, Mosa, Ekfrid, Caradoc, Delaware, and Adelaide in Middlesex county, in Dereham, Norwich, East, West, and North Oxford, in Blenheim, Blandford, and Zorra in Oxford county, and in Charlotteville, Walsingham, Houghton, and Middleton in Norfolk county suggests that by that date large holdings were tied up in various reserves or were in the hands of private individuals.

Many of those people who had accumulated large blocks of land simply held on to them, hoping that the development of surrounding areas would increase their value. This may explain why in the years before the rebellion Blenheim and Dorchester developed so slowly. In some instances, however, such as Yarmouth and Dumfries – which, aside from its southern gore, belonged to William Dickson, a Niagara district merchant – aggressive and enlightened management ensured rapid development of the lands.

In the west one man, Colonel Thomas Talbot, combined the roles of government land agent and private speculator. Talbot, an Irishman who had been an aide-de-camp to Lieutenant-Governor Simcoe, in 1803 acquired a grant of 5,000 acres in Dunwich and Aldborough townships. He was to receive 200 acres for himself for every 50 acres of his own land upon which he located bona fide settlers. Talbot ignored this stipulation, retaining for himself his original grant and adding to his own holdings a further 200 acres for each head of household established in the lands under his superintendence. As the townships entrusted to his care increased in number, his private holdings assumed awesome proportions, and were estimated, probably conservatively, in 1838 at 48,520 acres.[4] By 1836 he had located settlers in twenty-seven townships, thirteen in the Western district and fourteen in the London district.[5] Eight of the townships in the latter extended along the Lake Erie shore from Houghton and Middleton in the east to Dunwich in the west, the other six townships stretching westward along the Thames from London to Mosa.

Talbot's achievements in helping develop the huge demesne under his control were not always appreciated. His sharp practice in acquiring lands to which he was not entitled earned him censure from several quarters, particularly from provincial officials, who resented not only his obliquity but also the fact that he and the territory under his care were largely exempt from provincial land legislation. His own settlers were not always enamoured of him either. As the area under his administration was simply too great to be dealt with adequately by one man, an element of arbitrariness crept into his dealings, an element magnified by his own irascibility. Stories abounded that the peevish colonel 'rubbed out' settlers – that is, removed their names from the maps he kept denoting the location and owners of the lots under his control, thereby depriving those 'rubbed out' of their lands. Such action was often taken by Talbot, it was rumoured, for merely whimsical reasons or because those erased held political principles he found personally obnoxious.

The despotic nature of Talbot's inclinations and administration have not endeared him to most historians and it has often been said that his settlement grew so rapidly because it lay in the path of the western immigrant. It has also been charged that the colonel's character and the administration of his lands served to deter settlers, not to attract them.[6] Talbot's eccentricities, amusing as they may be, cannot excuse the shortcomings of his rule. He must be censured for adopting the worst methods of the land speculator in refusing to open his own private holdings in Dunwich and Aldborough to the settler until the settlement and development in surrounding areas had much inflated their value.

With respect to land policies the main grievances of the western settler centred on the tracts acquired by private individuals and on the Crown and Clergy Reserves. In 1817 in response to a questonnaire circulated by Robert Gourlay, who was canvassing the state of the province, the residents of Bayham, Yarmouth, Delaware, Dorchester, Southwold, Aldborough, and Dunwich in Middlesex county, of Burford and Norwich in Oxford, of Woodhouse, Charlotteville, Walsingham, and Middleton in Norfolk, and of Dumfries in Halton county expressed objections either to the existence of Crown and Clergy Reserves or to the holdings of absentee landowners in their townships.[7]

In 1827 the provincial government made the Crown and Clergy Reserves available to settlement. In that year the province, in return for various considerations, handed over 1,322,010 acres in the Huron Tract bordering Lake Huron north of Middlesex and Oxford counties to a private concern, the Canada Company. The company also secured the right to assume the ownership of those Crown Reserves then being leased in those townships which had been surveyed before 1 March 1824. It was hoped that the company would actively promote the settlement of all of the lands it had acquired. It had, in fact, been given so much property to dispose of that its actual prosecution of sales, at least in the early years of its existence, must inevitably have disappointed provincial officials, even though it had undertaken a reasonably vigorous campaign to attract settlers.

In 1827 as well, an imperial statute allowed for the sale of one-quarter of the Clergy Reserves. These had hitherto been available solely for lease. In an effort to ease accumulated grievances and to facilitate purchases, credit was extended. By 1836, 364,428 of the 2,254,668 acres comprising the Reserves had been sold,[8] and in 1838 Robert Baldwin Sullivan, the commissioner of Crown lands, reported that almost all of the Clergy Reserves offered to the public had been sold, people having been anxious to acquire the lots because they had been scattered through the settled areas.[9]

Many acres in 1837–8 were still tied up in the Clergy Reserves, and it was maintained by some in those years that the Reserves continued to hinder settlement and communications. Such indeed was the opinion not only of Commissioner Sullivan[10] but also of the great Reform inquisitor Lord Durham.[11] Alan Wilson has suggested that the Reserves may in fact have helped induce the rebels, who came from rural areas and who were presumably adversely affected by them, to take up arms.[12] Wilson's proposition is a difficult one to prove or to disprove, but it should be noted that in 1838 there were 107,550 acres of Clergy Reserves in fifteen of the rebel townships and proportionately even more acres, 169,069, in the nineteen non-rebel townships.[13]

It is not clear to what extent the Clergy Reserves extant in 1837–8 were a bar to settlement. Although the system of leasing the Reserves had been discontinued in 1834, three years later there were still 361,000 acres under lease in the province, all presumably in some state of improvement.[14] Thus by 1837–8 the number of original Clergy Reserve lots leased or sold in any one township may have meant that the effects of the Reserves on local development had been diminished. In Bayham township, for example, forty-two lots had been set aside originally as Clergy Reserves and an additional forty-two as Crown Reserves.[15] In 1839–40 there were twenty, or 47.6 per cent, of the former and sixteen, or 38.1 per cent, of the latter unassessed. Seventy-seven, or 29.7 per cent, of the remaining 259 lots in the township were also unassessed.[16] If it is assumed that the assessed lots had been improved to some extent and that the unassessed lots had not, then it appears that in Bayham, at least, the Clergy and Crown Reserves approximated the condition of the general run of properties.

19 The Setting – People and Places

If the Clergy Reserves were not a serious barrier to settlement in the west in 1837, they appear to have been so regarded, however. Critics of the whole system of land reserves could certainly point to specific instances where reserves had delayed local development. In Norfolk county, for example, most of the lots of Houghton and Middleton formed part of various reserves from which settlers were barred until some future date. Similarly, in the ranges south of the Longwoods road in the townships of Mosa, Ekfrid, and Caradoc in Middlesex county, King's College lots were clustered, impeding settlement there. If the settlers and the critics of the province's land administration exaggerated the burdens inflicted upon the colony's inhabitants by a reputedly callous government which mismanaged and misappropriated Upper Canada's public domain, there were none the less very real hardships inherent in the land policies pursued by the various levels of government.

II

The western peninsula became home for people of various nationalities, most of whom in the years prior to the rebellion tended to regard fellow settlers of different national origins with a jaundiced eye. Yet, however much the white settlers were distrustful of each other, all were particularly wary of the Indian inhabitants of the area; for by 1837 the natives had acquired little more than a veneer of civilization. Thus in 1837 the rebel leaders in raising recruits were able effectively to convince the Reformers that the Indians were going to be unleashed.

In 1837 there was a reserve for the Six Nations Indians southeast of the town of Brantford. The initial grant to those Iroquois under Joseph Brant who had fled north with their defeated British allies at the close of the American War of Independence involved 570,000 acres about the Grand River. This reserve was, however, constantly eroded by a succession of land transfers in the years 1798 to 1835, and in 1837-8 the 2,000[17] Mohawks, Oneidas, Senecas, Onondagas, Cayugas, and Tuscaroras, who shared the land with a few Indians from other tribes and with several adopted negro families,[18] found themselves with only 187,000 acres left along the river.

Essentially, government policy towards the Indians involved sheltering them from the evil and exposing them to the good aspects of white culture, while weaning them from their ancient economy to a new and better one. By 1837 this approach had enjoyed but indifferent success among the Six Nations. For one thing, surrounding whites were not prepared to leave the Indians alone, coveting their lands and their revenues, taking possession of the first by squatting and illegal purchase and bargain and acquiring the second by the normal process of trade and by carrying on an illicit liquor traffic with them,[19] as well as by persuading the Indian Department to sink the Six Nations' monies into unprofitable investments. Both the Wesleyan Methodists and the Church of England brought Christianity to the reserve. One suspects that, though George Petrie, an Anglican missionary, reported in 1839 that two-thirds of the Indians about the Grand were professing Christians,[20] their religious observance was more often than not nominal and that the statement that only the Mohawks and Tuscaroras had embraced the Lord[21] was a more accurate reflection of the spiritual state of the Indians. The efforts to convert the Six Nations' economy to an entirely agrarian one had not been wholly successful either. The Indians practised agriculture only on the alluvial flats beside the Grand. Their crops were thus inadequate to their needs and, in 1838, Indian agent Marcus Blair recorded that they spent much of the year 'in a state of most miserable distress, bordering upon starvation.'[22] Hunting supplemented their meagre rations and in the 1830s Six Nations' warriors in search of game roamed in the fall of the year over Norwich, Zorra, Dereham, Windham, and Blenheim.[23]

In Delaware and neighbouring Caradoc in Middlesex county were to be found Muncies (or Munceys), who had entered the area in 1800, and Chippewas, who had settled about 1830. In 1837–8 the Indians of Delaware and its area, together with the Moravians downstream at New Fairfield, numbered 775.[24] The Muncies and Chippewas, like the Six Nations, were ministered to by the Wesleyan Methodists and by the Church of England. As late as 1841 the Anglican priest serving the Indians around Delaware, the Reverend Richard Flood, insisted that the majority of them were still pagans.[25] The Muncies and Chippewas did not settle down to a completely agricultural existence either, continuing to supplement their food supplies with game.

Upper Canada, however, was destined to be a white man's preserve. Most noticeably, in the years prior to the rebellion, Americans, Scots, English, and Irish flocked into the province and into its western peninsula. Of the groups in the west, the Americans were the most numerous and, in official circles at least, the most controversial. By 1800 settlers from across the line had entered the Norfolk townships of Walsingham, Charlotteville, Woodhouse, Townsend, and Windham, and the Oxford townships of Oakland, Burford, Blenheim, and the Oxfords. In addition, they had found their way into Delaware in Middlesex and

21 The Setting – People and Places

Brantford in Wentworth. (See map 4.) By 1810 they had established themselves in Norwich in Oxford county and in Yarmouth, Malahide, Mosa, Westminster, and Dorchester in Middlesex.

As indicated earlier, American penetration into Upper Canada after the war was regarded with an unfriendly eye by the Colonial Office. The instructions of Bathurst, the Colonial Secretary, in 1815 prevented non-Loyalist Americans from taking the oath of allegiance without specific authorization from York. The oath had to be taken to ensure property holders secure land tenure. For a time at least the influx of 'Yankees' into the province was thus stemmed, with the notable exception of the Talbot domain, for Thomas Talbot was virtually excused by the imperial government from observing the regulations of 1815. For several years the alien question furnished the province with one of its most contentious and divisive issues. Finally, in 1828 legislation decreed that all persons who had received grants of land from the government, or who held public office, or who had taken the oath of allegiance could be admitted to the privileges of British citizenship if they had been resident in the province before 1820.[26] Other aliens could become citizens after completing seven years' residence, as long as they took the oath of allegiance within three years after assent was given to the act.

The 1828 statute did not entirely settle the alien issue, as it left the question of the citizenship of American settlers entering the province after 1828 untouched. Although authority could be found in existing British statutes for endowing 'Yankee' immigrants with the rights of citizens, the situation in the province after 1828 was that recent American settlers were, in effect, disenfranchised and barred from purchasing public land. None the less, some individuals from the south continued to enter the province and to acquire holdings, either by squatting on government land or by purchasing property from private owners. In either case, security of land tenure did not exist. Legislation, supported strongly by the western part of the province, to regularize the land titles of aliens failed to gain the acceptance of the legislative council in 1836 and again in 1837.[27] Lord Durham was to claim, on rather flimsy evidence, that uncertainty over their land titles led many American settlers either to participate in the rebellion of 1837 or to adopt an attitude of neutrality towards the insurgents.[28]

It is difficult to gauge the extent of American immigration into the province after the War of 1812 or to estimate the number of 'Yankees' who entered the west under the protective covering of Colonel Talbot's authority. Former Lieutenant-Governor Colborne may well have been

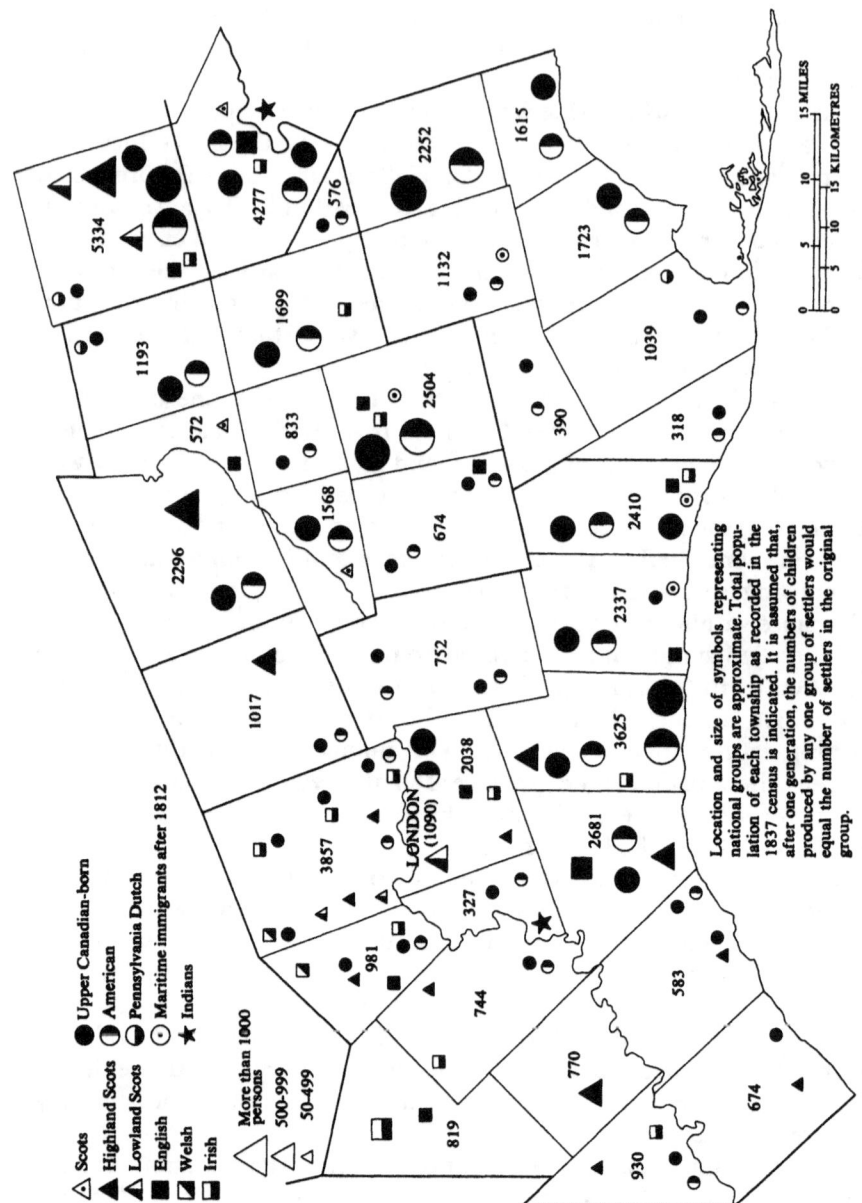

Map 4. National settlement. Sources: travellers' accounts, settlers' letters, local histories, theses, etc.

right when he claimed in 1838 that most of the settlers of the London district were American-born.[29] Cumulative evidence suggests that, in the thirty-five townships examined, natives of the United States and their Upper-Canadian-born progeny formed in 1837 the dominant national element in seventeen of the nineteen townships into which they had gained entry by 1810.[30] In addition, they likely constituted the single largest segment of the populations of Bayham township in Middlesex, of Dereham in Oxford, and of the townships of Houghton and Middleton in Norfolk county.

The Scots probably formed the second largest national group in the area. Large numbers of Scots had found their way into the western peninsula in the second decade of the nineteenth century. In this period Highlanders entered Aldborough and Dunwich in Middlesex and Dumfries in Halton County by way of the United States. The succeeding ten years saw Highlanders settle in the Oxford townships of Zorra and Nissouri and in the Middlesex townships of London, Lobo, Caradoc, Ekfrid, and Mosa, while Lowlanders settled in Dumfries, Westminster, and London townships. In the 1830s Highlanders continued to settle in the townships of Middlesex, moving into Yarmouth, Westminster, and Southwold, while in the east Scots appeared in Brantford, likely from the Lowland settlement to the north. Virtually all of the Scots in the area were Protestants – Baptists and Presbyterians of various stripes.

The English settlers appear to have constituted the third largest national group by 1837 in the thirty-five townships. It is not known precisely how the British influx into the province, which had begun after the War of 1812, broke down into its English, Scottish, Welsh, and Irish components, but it is certain that in the thirties England was sending far more emigrants to Upper Canada than ever before. Doubtless, a sizable proportion of the 260,089 immigrants from Great Britain who arrived at Quebec in the years 1829 to 1838, of whom 175,390 travelled on to the western province, were English.[31]

The English came largely on their own initiative and were unaided, although the Petworth emigration committee in England in the early thirties helped establish small groups of immigrants in the Middlesex townships of Southwold and Malahide and in the Oxford township of Blandford. The dearth of assisted or group English immigration meant that the English settlers tended, to a far greater extent than their Scots or Irish counterparts, to be scattered throughout the province and to be interspersed with Upper Canada's North American population. None the less, by 1837 identifiable English communities existed in the towns of

Brantford, Paris, and Woodstock, in the Oxford townships of Norwich and Dereham and in the Middlesex townships of Bayham, Southwold, Malahide, and Lobo. While most of the English settlers were drawn from the lower orders of society in England, a significant proportion had claims to social position and to pride of place, claims which, even though not strong enough to merit recognition and deference in their native land, they were prepared to push upon the inhabitants of the infant province. In Woodstock, for example, a little community of half-pay officers formed the nucleus of a society which, if not polite, was at least respectable – which had, if not a salon, at least a cricket club.

In 1837 then, Americans, Scots, and English – and their native-born offspring – composed the three principle nationalities in the thirty-five townships. In 1818 Richard Talbot led a group of Irish settlers into London township in Middlesex, and in the 1830s a colony of comparatively well-to-do Irishmen and their 'servants' located in Adelaide in the same county. As well, by 1837 Irish settlements, both Protestant and Catholic, could be found in the towns of Paris, Brantford, St Thomas, and London and in the Oxford townships of Burford and Norwich, and the Middlesex townships of Bayham, London, Westminster, Lobo, Adelaide, Caradoc, and Mosa. In the early twenties Welsh immigrants settled in the northwest corner of London township and in the adjacent section of Lobo. Nova Scotians, many of whom were United Empire Loyalists or their descendants, moved into Bayham and Malahide in Middlesex and probably into Norwich in Oxford and Townsend in Norfolk in the years 1811–20, and apparently continued to filter into the area. It is not clear, however, if the Maritimers establishing themselves in the western part of the province in the 1830s were of the same national background as those who had settled earlier, for a Presbyterian observer noted in 1833 that 'a good many people' who had lately entered the London district from Nova Scotia were all Highlanders.[32]

A few German Mennonite settlers lived in the northern sections of the neighbouring townships of Blenheim and Dumfries who had moved there from the old settlement of Waterloo in the north. Other Mennonites had wandered farther afield – into the south of Walsingham in Norfolk county, for example. The Mennonites were a clearly identifiable group, preserving their language and dress, and famed for their industry and farming ability. However, those who were prepared to move some distance away from Waterloo were not beyond severing themselves from their brethren; a resident of North Oxford township, Alexander Whalley Light, noted in 1837 that the 'Dutch' settlers in his neighbourhood considered themselves Britons, 'despising to be called what they really are, whilst the Dutch language is forgotten.'[33]

It would have been surprising had such a variety of nationalities been able to settle together without friction and tension developing, and friction and tension there were, particularly between the two largest groups, the Americans and their offspring on the one hand, and the British settlers on the other. As Patrick Shirreff, a Scotsman who toured the province in the mid-thirties, noted, most inhabitants of Upper Canada, particularly the late arrivals from Great Britain, were 'filled with inveterate prejudice' against their southern neighbours, regarding them as 'a band of cheating and lying democrats.'[34] This attitude, combined with the fact that many American settlers in the province were involved in Upper Canada's commerce, craft, and service trades, led naturally to a suspicion, not always undeserved, concerning the purity of the 'Canadian Yankee's' financial morals. In 1837 a disgruntled newcomer from Bayham, James Martin, bitterly complained that 'British Emigrants have a great many enemies to contend with,' as the North Americans 'take every advantage to defraud us. I find this daily in paying my family expences. And there is not one lot of land that I go to see in this Township but some of the Inhabitants pretends to have some claim on – with the intention to get money from strangers.'[35] Thus in the province there was considerable sympathy for Mahlon Burwell's denunciation of Upper Canada's 'Yankee' settlers as 'a contemptible, speculating, wooden-pump-kin-seed-peddling posse of Americans.'[36] It did not go unnoticed by his critics, however, that Burwell, a prominent Port Talbot resident and the son of a United Empire Loyalist, had himself been born in New Jersey.[37]

In part, the dislike among Americans, native-born Upper Canadians, and arrivals from Great Britain was caused simply by different attitudes to the ordering of the affairs of everyday life. This was particularly true of native North Americans and those British settlers who had some pretensions to breeding and sophistication. The turbulent nature of the province's inhabitants quite appalled Alexander Whalley Light, who observed that when he first arrived 'any trifling dispute among these people, was always settled by a blow or a kick, exclusively enjoyed by the weakest.'[38] Apparently, this practice continued until the appointment of an active magistracy. The egalitarian attitudes of North Americans were not always appreciated. One obviously well-to-do immigrant complained bitterly of 'the great incivility and rudeness of the lower classes ... their assumption not of equality only but even of superiority is very galling, and I consider it by far the most trying and disagreeable thing, as a gentleman, you have to encounter.' The same individual went on to note the existence of 'a considerable number of Yankees' in the west of the province, adding, 'I *reckon* this is a great drawback. I would certainly shun Canadian Yankees.'[39]

The dislike of some British settlers for the province's North American population could be warmly reciprocated. In 1833 a British preacher, George Marchen, wrote from the township of Townsend in Norfolk that he was surrounded by 'an immoral and irreligious people,' most of whom were from the Republic. They had, he complained, rejected his application to run the local school, as 'I should not give satisfaction as a Teacher because the pronunciation, manner and Prejudices of the people would operate against me.'[40] In January 1837, when the union achieved in 1833 between the majority of Upper Canada's Methodists and the British Wesleyans was already straining under the weight of tensions, native-born John Ryerson instructed his brother and fellow preacher, Egerton, not to return to the colony from England with any more English ministers in train. Objecting to the attitudes of those already in the province, he related that one Wesleyan, the Reverend Mr Steer, who was appointed to the Grimsby circuit, on finding that in some of his various lodgings chamber pots had not been provided by his hosts, 'thought he would teach them *british Manners* not in word but in *Deed* – by pissing on the floor whenever he had occation to Discharge his [urine?] & he wrote to me saying as he was diseased he had occation to do this once – twice & three times of a night; he now goes by the name of the *pissing* Preacher especially among the wicked.' John related that his brother William had asked him to accept Steer on John's circuit, 'but I told him the people here were too vulger to be taught in that *stile*, that such *classical* flights would carry him in a [region?] quite beyond their capacities.'[41]

In outlining the extent of the animosity prevailing between North Americans and newcomers to the province one should not forget that very real differences existed even within the latter group. The Scottish Highlanders, for example, who clustered together, who perpetuated their customs, religion, and tongue, and who generally resisted the process of acculturation, were frequently criticized for their narrow exclusiveness. Thomas Talbot, probably mindful of the difficulties he, an Irishman, had experienced with Scots in Aldborough and Dunwich, advised a prospective colonizer, John Elmsley, to exclude Highlanders from his proposed settlement.[42] The Reverend William Proudfoot, a Presbyterian (United Secession Church) minister at London and a Lowland Scot, although sure that his Lowland brethren were warmly

27 The Setting – People and Places

regarded in Upper Canada for their intelligence, sobriety, and religious disposition, felt that 'the Highland Scotch are not very well liked in this country. They are very selfish, very greedy, and very ignorant.' Proudfoot's own opinion of the Highlanders was so low – perhaps because of the obstinacy with which they clung to the Church of Scotland or, in some instances, to the Baptist faith – that he could not denigrate them enough. He declared on one occasion that 'these Highlanders are a stiff necked race. They will not understand anything that is not spoken in the Gaelic, and they will not understand any thing which requires thought.'[43] Later he noted that 'there is an obstinacy, a fastness about the Gaelic mind, into which nothing can be driven that is not sharpened and oiled by Gaelic – They are an ignorant race in general ... They are fit for nothing but driving cattle, which is a calling that admits of no improvement.'[44]

III

As the Reverend Mr Proudfoot's bitter comments about the Highlanders, who were compatriots but not co-religionists of his, suggest, some of the conflicts involving different nationalities were in part precipitated by sectarian struggles. In the west there was a multiplicity of religious groups, most of which were successful in appealing to particular national constituencies. Thus in 1833 an itinerant Methodist preacher, Samuel Rose, noted that the country north of Lake Erie 'surpasses all for parties and sects.'[45] Map 5 shows the wide range of religious groups active in the area in the period 1834–7, demonstrating the truth of Rose's comment. Table 1 suggests that many different denominations and sects did appeal, with varying degrees of success, to the settlers of the region.

Table 1 is based on the first religious census of the area, that of 1839.[46] Hence it provides no more than a very rough guide to the rankings of the various religious groups as they existed in 1837. The census was taken two years after the rebellion year, and some shifts had occurred in the population of the area in those two years. Further, the religious census of 1839 did not cover everyone. In that year 58,935 people lived in the thirty-five townships but the affiliations of only 45,186 were recorded. The inhabitants of Norfolk county, a centre of Baptist strength, were canvassed hardly at all and those of Brantford, a Church of England stronghold, not at all. In addition, the census takers of the Gore district used fewer categories than their counterparts elsewhere, creating problems of classification.[47] Nevertheless, when taken in conjunction with other evidence, Table 1 allows the drawing of certain well-founded conclusions.

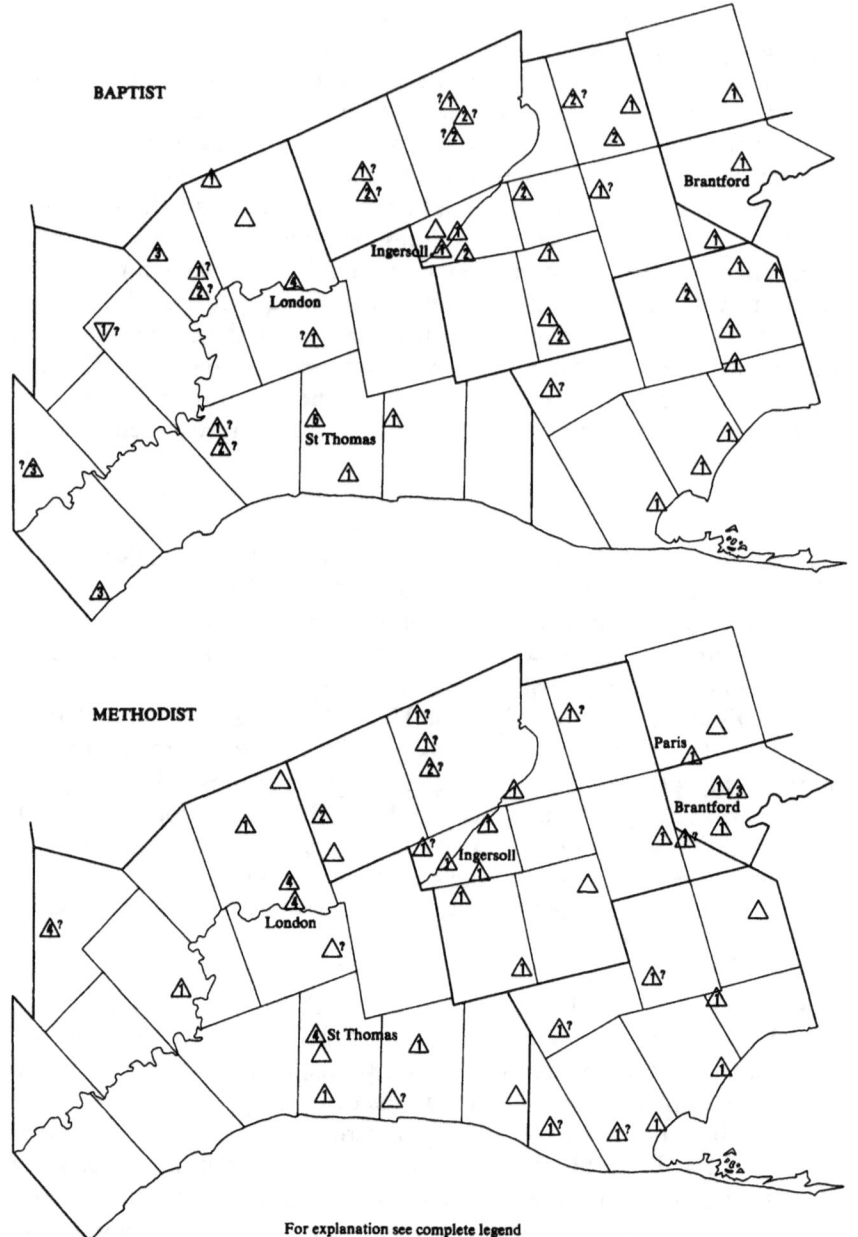

Map 5. Religious activities, 1834–7. Sources: church records, settlers' letters, church histories, etc.

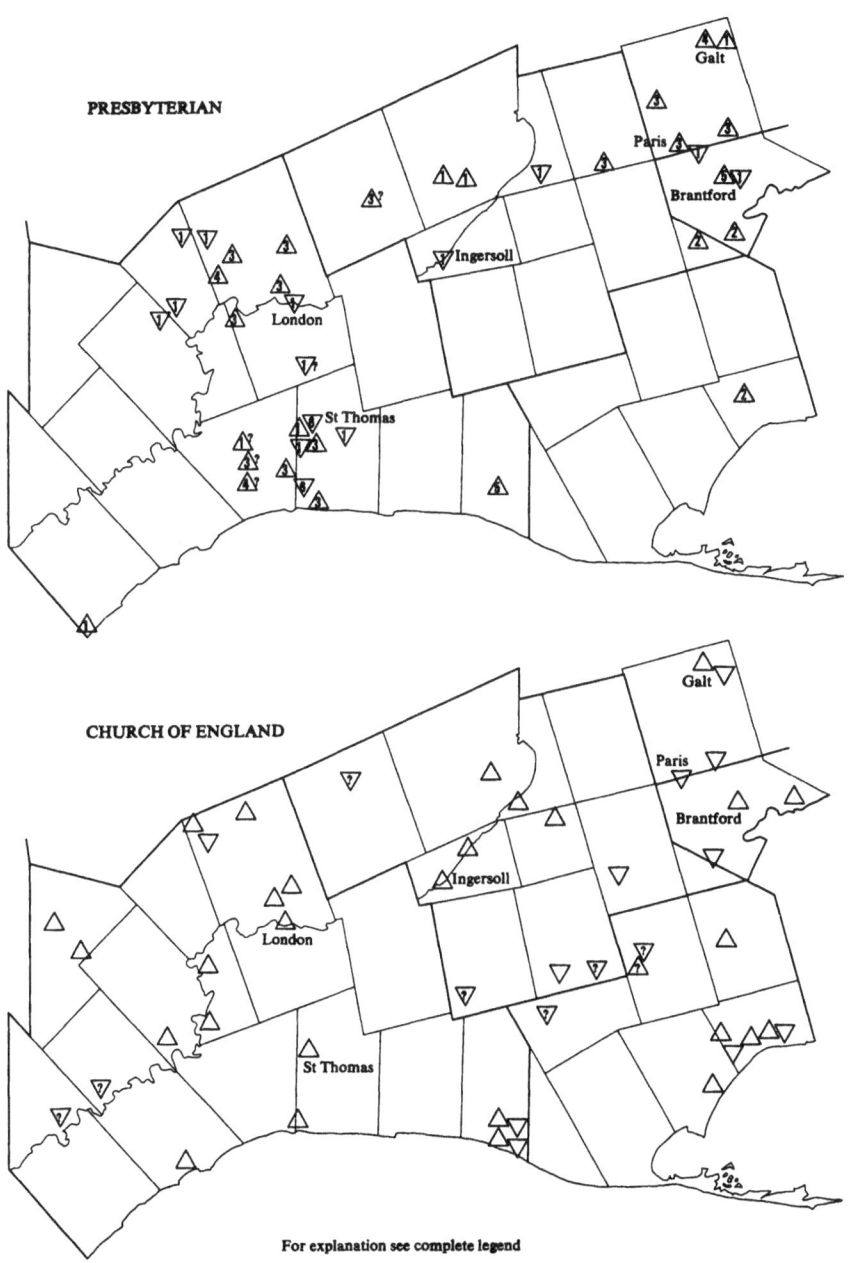

For explanation see complete legend

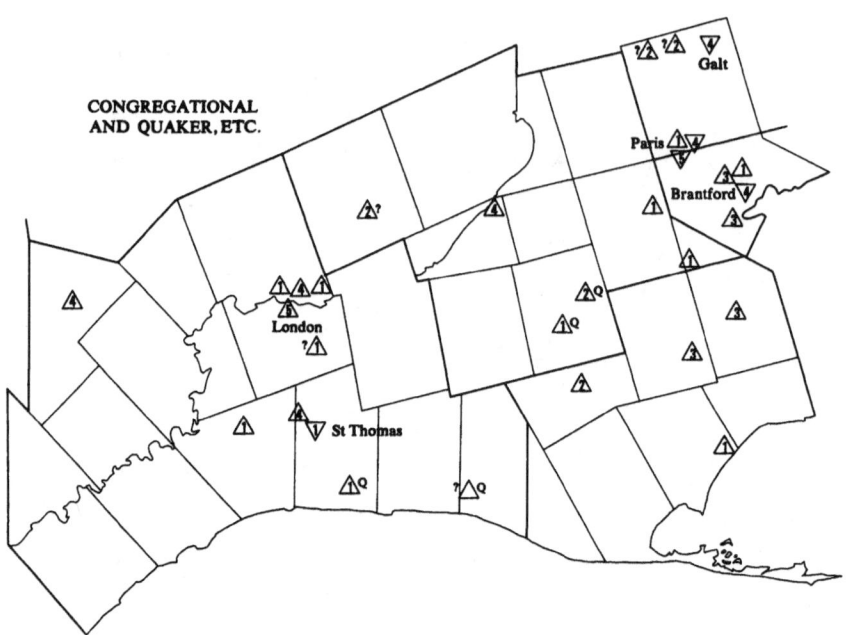

CONGREGATIONAL AND QUAKER, ETC.

△ Established congregation with regular preaching
?△ Established congregation with regular preaching, but precise location unknown
▽ Itinerant preacher
?▽ Itinerant preacher, precise location unknown

BAPTIST
Baptist
1 Regular or Closed Communion
2 Open Communion
3 Scotch
4 Freewill
5 Regular, African

METHODIST
Methodist
1 Wesleyan
2 Episcopal
3 Coloured
4 Ryanite or Canadian Wesleyan

PRESBYTERIAN
Presbyterian
1 Church of Scotland
2 United Synod
3 United Secession Church
4 United Associate Synod
5 Niagara Presbytery
6 Associate Reformed Church

CONGREGATIONAL, ETC.
1 Congregational
2 Christian
3 Mormon
4 Roman Catholic
5 Universalist

CHURCH OF ENGLAND
Church of England

QUAKER
Quaker
1 Hicksite
2 Conservative

Symbols without numbers indicate sect unknown

TABLE 1
Religious affiliations of the population of the study area, 1839

Affiliation	Number	Percentage of 45,186	Percentage of 58,935
Presbyterian	10,444	23.1	17.7
Church of Scotland	5,716		
Other Presbyterians	4,728		
Methodist	9,054	20.0	15.4
Wesleyan	3,999		
Episcopal	2,910		
Ryanites	2,145		
Church of England	7,542	16.7	12.8
Baptists	6,109	13.5	10.4
Closed Communion	4,087		
Open Communion	1,367		
Free Will	655		
Roman Catholics	1,474	3.3	2.5
Quakers	1,141	2.5	1.9
Congregationalists	292	0.6	0.5
Others	781	1.7	1.3
No affiliation	8,349	18.5	14.2
Total known	45,186	100.0	76.7
Total unknown	13,749	–	23.3
Total population	58,935	–	100.0

Presbyterians constituted one of the major components of the religious population of the thirty-five townships. By far the largest of the various Presbyterian sects was the Church of Scotland. Although one partisan, Mr Romanes of Hamilton, proudly asserted that members of the Kirk were 'generally of respectable character and station in society, and many of them occupy the most influential station in their respective neighbourhoods,'[48] the Church of Scotland in the west drew its support largely from the Highland communities, which were most often agrarian in character and poor in pocket. The Church of Scotland formed the single largest denomination in the townships of southwest Middlesex, in Dumfries in Halton county, and in Zorra in Oxford. It maintained resident ministers in all of these regions.

A variety of other Presbyterian sects was active in the area, chief of which was the United Secession Church. In 1832 ministers of that body arrived in the province and, after a brief association with the United

Synod, established in December 1834 the First Presbytery of the Missionary Presbytery of the Canadas. By 1837 the church, which was voluntaryist, had 1,400 *members*, as distinct from adherents, in Upper Canada.[49] Its main strength was in Toronto and in the western peninsula. Around London, at least, it was most successful among the Scots Lowlanders and the congregation in London was deemed 'most respectable.'[50] The church's statistics for 1837 suggest that small, but none the less significant, segments of the populations of London town and township, of the townships of Westminster and Southwold in Middlesex, and of the townships of Dumfries in Halton and Blenheim in Oxford supported the Missionary Presbytery.[51]

Among the other Presbyterian groups was the United Synod, which was created in 1831 by the members of an earlier organization whose ministers had been ordained in Upper Canada. The Synod declared its doctrines to be identical with those of the Kirk.[52] The Synod had but one settled minister – in Brantford township, and he was to desert the Synod after 1837 for the fold of the Church of Scotland.

Two American Presbyterian churches had entered the region. The Associated Synod Church of North America had only two ministers in the province, one of whom had in 1837 a congregation at Galt which boasted 250 communicants.[53] A congregation in London township was languishing, as were two others in the province, for lack of supply.[54] The other American Presbyterian ministers active in the area were those of the Niagara Presbytery.[55] In favour of voluntaryism and temperance, members of the Niagara Presbytery churches numbered only 807, and were clustered primarily about the western end of Lake Ontario. In 1837 a resident minister tended to a congregation of twenty members in the town of Brantford and evidently supplied a second charge at Vienna in Bayham consisting of only eighteen persons.[56]

Though not Presbyterians themselves, the Congregationalists, who were small in number, were closely akin to the Niagara Presbyterians. The type of Congregationalism in Upper Canada was the English rather than the New England variety, and the main point at issue between the members of the Niagara Presbyterian and the Congregational or Indepedent churches was the refusal of the latter to espouse the cause of temperance. In addition, the two groups could not unite because, according to two observers, the Reverend C.E. Furman and the Reverend Edward Marsh of the Niagara Presbyterians, 'there is a national difference which renders it probably unpleasant to both English and Americans to meet together.'[57] It is noteworthy that the records of the Oakland

Congregational church do not indicate that those associated with it, several of whom were leading spirits in the rebellion, were primarily British in origin. Of the thirteen Congregational ministers in the province supported by the parent British Colonial Society, two were located in what was to become the rebel area – one in the township of Oakland and one in the town of Brantford. A third minister was resident in the town of London, and individual congregations existed in the Middlesex townships of London, Westminster, and Southwold, in Charlotteville in Norfolk county, and in the village of Paris in Dumfries township.

The Methodists were one of the largest denominations and probably were at least as numerous as the Presbyterians. The character of Methodism's appeal, its use of revivalist techniques, its denominational organization, and the energy of its ministers, who were admitted to be 'conspicuous' for their zeal 'and diligence,'[58] all struck responsive chords among the largely rural, American population of the western peninsula, and among some of the more recent lower- or lower-middle-class arrivals from industrial Britain as well. A somewhat uncharitable observer, Mr Romanes of Hamilton, noted that the Methodists of the province 'consist chiefly of the ignorant and uneducated; their adherents are principally the natives of the country, settlers from the United States, and emigrants from England.'[59] In 1837 the Methodists constituted the largest denomination in Oxford county and possibly in eastern Middlesex and in Norfolk as well. In most of the west Middlesex townships they formed the second largest religious group. Of the area considered in this study, only in southwest Middlesex do they appear to have been inconsequential.

In the west the Methodist constituency was divided among three sects – the Canadian Wesleyan Methodists or Ryanites, the Wesleyan Methodists, and the Episcopal Methodists. The Methodist Church in Upper Canada was originally an adjunct of the American one. In 1824 Henry Ryan, an obstreperous Upper Canadian elder, began an agitation for the establishment of a separate provincial organization. In 1827 he severed his connection with the official Methodist body, after losing his position as an elder and being threatened with removal as a circuit rider for publishing pamphlets attacking church officials. Ryan died in 1833, but not before he had organized his own followers, who were mostly conservative Irish Methodists,[60] into the Canadian Wesleyan Methodist Church. Ryan's death, however, removed one of the sect's *raisons d'être*, and in 1837 its membership was only 1,916,[61] down dramatically from the 2,544 recorded in 1835,[62] the date of the earliest surviving membership survey. Still, in the rebellion year the Ryanites were the dominant

Methodist group in some of the Oxford townships, and were generally entrenched in the north of Oxford county and in Norwich township, in northwest and southeast Middlesex, and in Norfolk as well.

The main body from which the Ryanites seceded severed its own ties with the American Methodists in 1828 to become the Methodist Episcopal Church. In 1833, challenged by the British Wesleyans who had come into the province with educated preachers and a comparatively sophisticated service to minister to the British immigrants and to make inroads into the few urban centres, the Methodist Episcopal Church negotiated a union with the Wesleyans in which the two groups united as the Wesleyan Methodist Church. In 1837 this Methodist sect was by far the largest in the province, reporting a membership of 14,530 whites and 923 Indians.[63] The Wesleyans were the strongest of the three Methodist bodies in Norfolk, in the eastern half of Middlesex, and in all but one or two of the seven townships in the south of Oxford county. They were relatively weak in west Middlesex and in the northern section of Oxford county, but were still the most influential Methodist group in the area examined.

In 1833 not all Methodist Episcopals had agreed to enter the union with the British Wesleyans. Some objected that those negotiating the merger had not consulted the various societies in the province and that the agreement reached ended the episcopal character of the church's organization. Furthermore, they suspected that anyone allying with the conservative Wesleyans must be prepared to abandon voluntaryist principles, which demanded that there be a complete separation of church and state lest either be corrupted by its association with the other. Voluntaryism was largely a North American phenomenon, for British practice and tradition accepted the marriage of church and state. Those opposing the union consequently formed their own church or, rather, simply continued the organization of the Methodist Episcopal one. The members of this church increased in number from 1,243 in 1835 to 3,522 in 1837,[64] their strength lying in the western peninsula.[65] Thus the Episcopal Methodists vied with the other Methodist bodies for primacy in the eastern and north central portions of Middlesex, in the eastern sections of Oxford county, and in the townships of Nissouri and Dumfries.

Although the Church of England appealed particularly to the urban, the propertied, and those holding office[66] – especially the British – Anglicans formed one of the major religious groups in the thirty-five townships. In fact, there was considerable squabbling about the precise strength of the Church in the area. Thomas Green, an Anglican itinerant, argued that Churchmen constituted the London district's most numerous religious body,[67] but Lord Durham noted that the Anglicans in calculating their strength laid claim to all those who indicated that they had no particular denomination.[68] In any event, the Anglicans were a major religious force in the region, being particularly numerous in Dereham township, in the eastern half of Oxford county, in all of Middlesex county except for some scattered areas in the southwest, in all of Norfolk county, and in Brantford township.

The Baptists, another leading religious group, resembled the Methodists in several respects. The two denominations utilized revivalist techniques and allowed those who simply answered the 'call' to become preachers. This latter fact caused some embarrassment to the Baptists, particularly to their more sophisticated British members, who had been entering the province since 1820. In 1837 the Reverend John Gilmore lamented that Baptist churches were seldom built 'in towns, villages, &c., but always in some remote country place. The reason assigned for this was, that our ministers were not qualified for occupying such stations.'[69] Similarly, it was reported that the preachers of one Baptist association about Lake Erie 'are all made to labour for their own support, and are extremely deficient in useful information and sound religious knowledge: they are generally good and zealous people, and chiefly Americans.'[70] In the west the Baptist constituency, with some notable exceptions, was indeed American. The Baptists were very strong in Norfolk county, in the southeast of Middlesex, in much of the north of Oxford county, and in the Oxford townships of Oakland and Norwich and had various areas of support in much of Middlesex as well.[71]

The regular or Calvinistic Baptists, who clung to the doctrine of the elect and who admitted only church members to their communion – and hence were known as Closed Communionists – were the largest of the four Baptist sects. They maintained twenty-six separate congregations in twenty different townships, and were the dominant Baptist group in Norfolk county, in the town of Brantford, in the majority of the Oxford townships, and in most of the townships of Middlesex except those along the county's northern perimeter.

There were also Open or Free Communion Baptists, who belonged to a sect that had originated in England in the early seventeenth century. Although they did not accept the doctrine of predestination and were concerned that nothing should 'infringe the rights of independent government and discipline of individual churches,'[72] a conference in 1837 on Baptist union declared that the only thing separating the Open and

Closed groups was the question of communion.[73] It may be, however, that the two bodies were also divided by nationality, the Open Communionists being mainly British and their Closed brethren mainly North American.[74] In the period from 1834 to 1837 the Open Communionists had twelve established congregations in ten of the thirty-five townships. Their greatest strength was in Oxford county, notably in an east-west band running through the central portion of the county. In addition, they had pockets of support in Townsend and Windham in Norfolk, and in Southwold and Caradoc in Middlesex.

Still other Baptist sects practised in the region. The Free Will Baptists were similar to the Open Communionists in that they too denied the doctrine of predestination and admitted non-members to communion. They had originated in the United States. Although in 1837 they formed a small portion of the religious population of the area examined, they were concentrated in several townships in the western parts of Middlesex, and maintained a congregation in the town of London. The remaining Baptists were Scotch Baptists, who doctrinally were quite distinct from the rest of their Baptist brethren; for example, they maintained a baptism of total immersion. They had congregations in Middlesex county among the Scots of Mosa, Aldborough, and Lobo.

One of the smaller groups was the Roman Catholic Church. Throughout the province the Catholics drew their support from the Scottish Highlanders, the southern Irish, and the French Canadians,[75] but the relatively few Catholics in the region examined appear to have been Irish. They were, in the opinion of priest Daniel Downie, extremely poor.[76] In the period from 1834 to 1837 Catholic itinerants tracked through various townships, the town of London alone having a resident priest. In 1837 only in the townships of Yarmouth, London, Ekfrid, and Adelaide in Middlesex and in the townships of North and West Oxford and of Dumfries were Catholics assembled in any considerable strength.

Entrenched in certain sections of the townships were the Friends or Quakers who were primarily of American birth or descent. The pietistic Society of Friends was noted for its avowed and unyielding pacifism. In 1828–9 a split between the followers of Elias Hicks and the Conservative Quakers rent the Friends. Hicks, who reportedly believed that Christ had been a mortal man,[77] insisted that the traditional freedom of Quakers from being obliged to adhere to any particular creed must be preserved. The Conservative Quakers were not prepared to extend their tolerance to Hicks' peculiar doctrines, however, and a split occurred. The Hicksites were the larger of the two parties in what were to be the rebel townships, maintaining meeting houses in Bayham and Yarmouth in Middlesex, and in Norwich in Oxford. The Conservatives had a solitary place in Norwich. Quakers, whether Hicksite or Conservative, formed the preponderant religious sect in Norwich and in the south of Yarmouth, and constituted small minorities of the religious populations of Bayham and Malahide.

Three other groups active in a minor way in the townships were the Christians, the Universalists, and the Mormons. These sects deviated from contemporary religious norms and were objects of general denunciation. The Christians, an ecumenical group which made no doctrinal statements and which spoke of 'Religion without Bigotry – Zeal without Fanaticism – Liberty without Licentiousness,'[78] had congregations in 1834 in three widely separated townships: Dumfries, Nissouri, and Middleton. All three, though, were evidently defunct by 1837. The Universalists, like the Christians an American sect, maintained the doctrine that all men would achieve eternal bliss and, 'embracing these expansive views of universal benevolence and charity,'[79] held very little other doctrine. Like the Christians, the Universalists drew their support largely from former Methodists and Baptists, but had only one society, at London, comprising individuals scattered over a number of townships. Finally, there were the Mormons, a new sect which believed that God had revealed his purpose and design to their founder, Joseph Smith. The Mormons had been active around Brantford in the early thirties, and had organized two congregations in Brantford township and one each in the nearby Norfolk townships of Windham and Townsend.

Of course, not every settler maintained ties to formal religion. In fact, in 1839 8,349 or 18.5 per cent reported that they were of no particular religious persuasion.[80] Daniel Allan, a Church of Scotland missionary, had calculated earlier that over one-quarter of those living in the London district did not belong to any denomination.[81] Common report placed the figure for specific locales even higher. For instance, in 1834, the Reverend William Proudfoot recorded a rumour that only one in every two people in Bayham professed a religious affiliation.[82] (If true, the situation had improved by 1839 when only one in four in that township was non-professing.)[83] If contemporary comment can be trusted, the inhabitants of the study area were not peculiarly 'irreligious.' For instance, in 1838 a Kirk committee reported that 'vast numbers' of the Western district's approximately 12,000 people were 'of no religious profession,'[84] while the editor of the *Canadian Christian Examiner and Presbyterian Review* calculated that, in the long-settled Niagara district, only about one in ten of the 33,000 residents attended services of a Sunday.[85]

Most people, however, were adherents of some particular persuasion and, in the west, belonged to a bewildering array of denominations and sects. Just as the many different nationalities in the area gave rise to a good deal of prejudice, so too did the excessive number of religious groups. No group was too small to escape censure from some quarter. The Mormons were described as 'a sect of the wildest fanatics,'[86] the Universalists were said to be 'propagating ... pernicious doctrines,'[87] the Baptists were derided for making 'immersion ... the great vital essence of Christianity,'[88] the ministers of the United Secession Church found themselves depicted 'as Wolves in sheep's clothing,'[89] and one enthusiastic Anglican denounced all others, insisting that the various denominations 'are devastating this fine country as with a moral pestilence.'[90] Catholic priests could not always be assured of admittance to inns,[91] and at least one discovered as late as 1839 that, although he had won entrance to a public house, his stabled horse had been severely mutilated.[92]

Sectarian strife was often most intense in relations between various bodies of the same denomination. By 1837 the dislike of Wesleyan and Episcopal Methodists for each other was manifest, with Egerton Ryerson deriding his Episcopal brethren as being 'insignificant and worthless.'[93] In 1838 a report from Bayham stated that the Anglicans had been offered the use of the Methodist chapel at Vienna by the church trustees because the intensity of strife among the three Methodist sects (Wesleyans, Ryanites, and Episcopals) prevented its use by any of them.[94] Considerable bitterness also characterized Presbyterian rivalries. One Church of Scotland minister feared that the churches of the Niagara Presbytery, 'corrupted ... both in point of doctrine & worship,' would undermine the spiritual welfare of the entire Niagara area.[95] Reputedly, J. Strang, the minister of the Associated Synod Church in Galt, censured severely the missionary efforts of his United Secession Church colleagues.[96] Peace could not be preserved even among the Quakers, the Conservative Friends in Norwich charging at the time of the Hicksite separation that the teachings of Elias Hicks were 'Anti-Christian & subversive of Christian principles.'[97]

IV

While the religious and national diversity of the area divided the settlers, economic concerns unified them. The major livelihood of the inhabitants was farming, as indeed it was in the province as a whole. In 1838 an estimated nine-tenths of Upper Canada's population were farmers.[98] Travellers through the Canadas and prospective settlers were, therefore, intensely interested in the climate, vegetation, waterways, topography, and soil of a region.

Even impartial observers praised the topography and soil of the western townships. For example, Samuel Rose described the land north of Lake Erie as being 'of the best quality, and the most level part of the country that is in Canada.'[99] Flat land, of course, was of supreme importance, not only because it was easily ploughed but also because it facilitated the development of roads and communications.[100] 'Level' or 'flat' were terms applied by contemporaries to the Oxford county townships of Dereham, Norwich, Burford, and Oakland, to Middleton and Charlotteville in Norfolk, and to Southwold, Dunwich, Ekfrid, and Mosa in Middlesex. Windham in Norfolk county and the Middlesex townships of Yarmouth, Aldborough, Westminster, Malahide, and Delaware were 'nearly' or 'generally' level. Oxford East in Oxford county, Townsend and Woodhouse in Norfolk, and the southern part of Dumfries in Halton were 'rolling' or 'undulating.' The latter characteristics were acceptable because the slight agricultural inconveniences they connoted were offset by aesthetic considerations. The Lord Bishop of Quebec, for one, noted in 1828 that the countryside about Woodhouse reminded him more of England than did any other part of Upper Canada, 'the clearings being large, the copses and forest thus more or less widely dispersed, and the ground undulating.'[101] Although Woodhouse's inhabitants preferred to describe their township as 'level' rather than 'undulating,'[102] no one could apply that adjective to the hilly sections of Bayham, Houghton, and Middleton.

For soil the magic word was 'loam,' a soil of clay and sand containing a generous mixture of humus. 'Loam' or 'loamy' soils conjured up visions of rich vegetable mould in which virtually anything would grow and grow with abundance. The Middlesex townships of London, Westminster, Caradoc, and Ekfrid were evidently 'loamy,' while Blenheim in Oxford county and Dumfries in Halton, it was suggested, contained loam and very little else. Loam and clay were commonly found in most of the townships of Oxford county and in the Middlesex townships of Malahide, Bayham, Dunwich, Aldborough, Delaware, Mosa, and Adelaide, as well as in the south half of Lobo. Sandy loam or loam and sand were reported in Walsingham, Houghton, Townsend, and Windham in Norfolk, in Burford and Oakland in Oxford, and in Yarmouth in Middlesex. Finally, mixtures of sand, loam, and clay were noted in Woodhouse and Charlotteville in Norfolk, in Southwold in Middlesex, and in Blenheim in Oxford county.

Despite the general enthusiasm for the soil and topography, there were some reservations about certain areas. Several townships, London, Ekfrid, and Dunwich, for example, contained large bogs. In 1817 the inhabitants of Windham admitted the existence of a 1,000 acre swamp in their township, although they allowed that it might, in time, become the best section of it.[103] In 1837, however, the township was still described as 'partly swampy.'[104] The Reverend William Proudfoot noted in 1834 the presence of water-soaked land about Catfish Creek in Yarmouth.[105]

In certain areas the soil was considered too light or too dry for good farming. In 1834, James Marr Brydone stated that the soil of the southern part of Lobo was sandy and unsuited to agriculture.[106] Proudfoot, discussing Aldborough, noted that the soil was 'sandy and very light, the surface is very much cut up with deep ravines.' In Bayham he observed the existence of sandy ridges, which ran along Talbot Street into Houghton and spread throughout Middleton, and wrote that the soil here was 'without controversy the very worst I have seen in America.'[107] In 1837 an anonymous diarist recorded that the land in Charlotteville near the lake 'is very rough in many places, and of an inferior quality'[108] and in the late 1830s Hugh Murray found that much of Norfolk county, particularly its interior, had a 'sandy and barren aspect.'[109]

Of particular concern to some were the oak 'plains' or 'openings,' level areas containing scattered oak trees, found around London and Long Point, in the south of Yarmouth, and in Brantford, Oakland, and Dumfries townships. Patrick Shirreff deemed the openings in south Yarmouth of the poorest sand,[110] while Brydone thought those in the western part of Brantford township consisted of inferior land.[111] These latter plains quite appalled another traveller, Alfred Domett, who recorded that, as he journeyed from Brantford in the early thirties, 'wide plains covered with small oaks stretched on either side, whole forests of these scorched and burnt-up trees with their brick-red withered leaves, unvaried by a speck of green or any fresh foliage, followed one another, their parched and thirsty appearance exciting an oppressive feeling of hopelessness lifelessness and drought such as one may be supposed to experience travelling the desert sands of Africa.'[112]

The farming techniques used to cultivate fall wheat, the main crop of the west, on the western peninsula's oak openings often distressed travellers accustomed to the refined agricultural practices of England. Hugh Murray noted that the sandy soil of these plains would yield but 'one or two crops of tolerably good wheat' before being 'quite exhausted.'[113] When this happened, the land was left fallow for several years, in effect bearing a crop only every other year. Proudfoot remarked that 'a worse mode of farming could hardly be thought of.'[114] Others, however, marvelled that the oak plains constituted 'a second edition of Illinois. No chopping, just break the ground & sow.'[115] William Dunlop, a resident of Huron county and an official of the Canada Company, observed that, even though the soil about Long Point degenerated 'into something very little superior to the sand of the sea-beach,' those living in the area felt favoured because they had little or no clearing to do. He added that local farmers could fertilize their crops with gypsum,[116] presumably taken from the gypsum workings near Paris. Another advantage of the oak plains, particularly in the Long Point area, was that cattle, which were not generally kept in the province because of American competition, could readily be pastured.

Today, soil scientists have thoroughly classified and analysed the soils of the area. Scattered throughout it are several family members of the Dark Grey Gleysolic Great Soil Group. These soils are either clays or sandy loams, stone free, but all are poorly drained and hence are still of limited agricultural value. In the days of first settlement they would have been virtually useless as farm land. By far the greatest part of the area, though, has soils belonging to the Grey-Brown Podzolic Great Soil Group. The soil textures of this group range through clays, clay loams, loams, sandy loams, and silt loams, the surface drainage varying from imperfect to good. Except for southwest Dumfries, which is exceedingly stony, most are stone free.[117] In general, these soils are well suited to the variety of crops supported today and, when first stripped of their forest cover, these soils were relatively productive.[118] Hence, the early settlers were initially a favoured lot, possibly excepting those who settled on lands with soils of the Fox Series, in present-day Norfolk, Oxford, and Elgin (the southern part of old Middlesex county). Fox soils are now the principal tobacco soils of southwestern Ontario but their dryness made them unproductive before irrigation was introduced in conjunction with tobacco,[119] long after the pioneer period.

Whatever the agricultural liabilities of specific locales, the farms and farming communities of the west were generally considered to be prosperous. In 1837 one anonymous commentator noted that Dumfries township in Halton county was 'one of the best settled in the Upper Province ... This is a fine wheat country and land sells high.'[120] Another, merchant Adam Hope of St Thomas, approaching Brantford from the west, encountered excellent wheat lands with 'large Barns, fine Houses & fine Roads.'[121] Others had a similarly high regard for the more southern areas of Oxford county. As early as 1828 passing along the Governor's road in East Oxford, archdeacon John Strachan noticed 'a long succession of farms, in a high state of cultivation.'[122] Six years later, journeying from Oxford East to Oxford West, diarist George Leith found himself amidst 'a very old settled and comparatively wealthy country.'[123] The prosperity of Norwich impressed a number of visitors and the fact that Norwich supplied many men for the rebel 'army' in 1837 amazed several observers for, as Adam Hope recorded, 'the township of Norwich is perhaps one of the best settlements in Upper Canada; the country is thickly settled; well cleared; and you meet with better farms & better houses, gardens & barns in a shorter distance than you will do almost anywhere else that I know of.'[124] One loyalist who passed through the township in 1838, A.W. Light of North Oxford, recorded: 'a finer country I never saw, the ground that had been cropped for thirty years, without any manure during all this time bore as fine crops as any I have ever seen in England. The country appeared like that around York or Canterbury, and many of the roads were excellent; the whole country was strewed with most substantial and picturesque farm houses, beautiful orchards, &c, and plenty appeared to abound.'[125]

In 1837 an unidentified tourist travelling from Burford in Oxford county through Norfolk to Long Point observed that the land of the area was good 'and the farmers appear to be very comfortable.'[126] The following year a Baptist preacher, 'Brother' Tapscott, travelling through Townsend, Windham, and Woodhouse found that 'the country here is fine and rich beyond description, and the settlers wealthy.'[127] Further west in the southern townships of Middlesex county the situation was similar; here Samuel Picken reported that the farms of Bayham, Malahide, Southwold, and Yarmouth were productive and developing rapidly.[128] The Methodist preacher Samuel Rose described Bayham and its adjacent area as 'a beautiful country and a fruitful one.'[129] The Reverend William Proudfoot noted in going from St Thomas to Malahide some of the best cleared land he had yet encountered. 'The fields in general,' he wrote, 'have not a stump in them; the houses are good and remarkably tasteful, some of them even elegant, barns seemed good, in general large.'[130] In 1834 Brydone recorded that the settlers of Southwold and Westminster townships had well cleared farms and were 'enjoying superior comforts.'[131]

Universal prosperity did not, of course, obtain throughout the townships. In Aldborough Proudfoot saw what he supposed to be inferior crops, adding that the 'housing and barns are ill made or carelessly kept.' The population, he thought, were poor and 'all had the appearance of highland filth.' He also noticed areas of Malahide which lacked the evident wealth of other areas of that township and of Yarmouth.[132]

To supplement their incomes farmers often engaged in the lumber trade. Although the farm labourers were employed only part-time or seasonally, others were involved in lumbering all year. Among the latter were some of the raftsmen and cutters as well as those who financed the trade by purchasing land and building sawmills and by selling the wood products.

In the 1830s lumbering had not yet reached the heights it was later to attain in Norfolk, a county blessed with 'the finest and largest white pine of which there is record' in North America,[133] but sawmills were being established in those areas of Windham, Houghton, and Middleton just opened to the settler. Bayham township, however, profited most from the lumber and timber trade, not only because it had excellent timber of its own but also because the courses of Big Otter Creek and its tributaries in Dereham, Middleton, and Norwich ensured that the products of these townships would be exported through Port Burwell in Bayham. By 1833 twenty-nine sawmills had sprung up along the banks of Big Otter Creek and its branches.[134] These, in turn, helped spawn a small, but locally important, shipbuilding industry at Port Burwell.

Farming and lumbering were the characteristic occupations of the west, though there was some commercial fishing on Lake Erie and one industrial enterprise, the Long Point iron works, on its shore. Large deposits of iron ore were found in Middleton, Charlotteville, and Windham in Norfolk county. The local farmers went into the swamps in the winter, dug up the ore, and took it to the Long Point Furnace at Normandale in Charlotteville. The Furnace, established in 1818, had a satellite forge at Port Dover, another in or near Simcoe, and employed in all some 400 people.[135] Houghton, Norwich, Dereham, and other townships of the London district were also reported to contain supplies of bog ore. By 1837 the Dereham Forge was in operation in the southeast corner of Dereham township but its employees were few and its prospects limited.

There were few true industrial workers in the area. Even many of those engaged at the Long Point iron works were farmers earning a little extra money. A variety of different craftsmen worked in the towns of the region. One traveller, Anna Jameson, found that they were numerous in the rapidly expanding centre of London,[136] but they were also scattered through the rural villages. Thus the distinction between urban and rural occupations was not always firm for even merchants were often engaged in farming. Those whose livelihoods did not depend directly on agriculture none the less understood that their prosperity depended on the fortunes of the farmer, a realization which militated against the development of classes and of class consciousness. To be sure, recent arrivals from Britain often had very definite perceptions about the way in which society in the new world would be ordered and, in some instances, in Adelaide and Woodstock, for example, those of them who foresaw for themselves a favoured place in the colony affected an air of refined English gentility. Pretensions to breeding or even claims to landed wealth, however, did not notably impress the province's North Americans; if they were prepared to recognize the existence of an upper class in the province, they were doubtless most likely to view the province's various officials as its representatives. Thus, although the little coterie of government officers in London might insist upon, and sometimes receive respect, the 'nobs,' if they were thought of at all, were held to live in the distant provincial capital.

The lack of class consciousness was also a product of the fact that there were so few towns and consequently little opportunity for the various strata of modern urban society to develop. In 1836 only an estimated 44,000 of the province's 370,000 inhabitants were urban dwellers.[137] In the thirty-five townships there were only six centres of consequence: Brantford, St Thomas, Simcoe, Paris, Galt, and London. None was very large.

Brantford's population in 1837 was estimated at from 1,200 to 2,000 persons. Perched above the Grand River, the little town boasted a newspaper, an agricultural society, a post-office, several churches, a large chair factory, and various other manufacturing establishments and mills. London, with 1,090 inhabitants in 1837, was a relatively new centre with stumps still dotting some of its streets. Anna Jameson credited it with a number of schools, seven inns, and a variety of grocery stores which were in reality taverns.[138] London, the district town since the mid-twenties, housed not only most of the district's officials but also a new Gothic-style court house of which many Londoners were inordinately proud but which some considered overdone[139] and others 'of execrable workmanship.'[140] St Thomas' population was calculated at 700 to 1,000 people. The village had by 1837 a woollens factory, a bank, the usual taverns, and two hotels, both reputedly good.[141] Paris, with a population of 800, possessed a mill for manufacturing gypsum, a number of stores, a wagon shop, a tannery, a distillery, a woollen mill, two blacksmith shops, and at least one tavern.[142] Galt had several large mills and factories, various schools and taverns, and a population of 500.[143] In 1837 the town of Simcoe with the nearby villages of Wellington and Colborne apparently housed 700 persons in 175 homes. The three little centres contained ten stores, two breweries, four distilleries, three sawmills, two grist mills, and one iron-producing furnace.[144]

In addition to these 'major' towns, scattered through the area were a number of small villages, each of which had from 50 to 300 inhabitants. In Brantford township were Mount Pleasant and Springfield, in Dumfries were St George, Jedburgh, and Nithvale. In Oxford county were Burford and Bishopsgate in Burford township, Scotland and Oakland (Malcolm's Mills) in Oakland township, Embro in Zorra, Dereham Forge in Dereham, Woodstock in Blandford, Ingersoll and Beachville in West Oxford, and Otterville and Sodom in Norwich. Middlesex contained Delaware village in Delaware township, Wardsville in Mosa, Adelaide and Katesville in Adelaide township, Pond's Mill in Westminster, Five Stakes and Selborne in Southwold, Port Stanley, New Sarum, and Jamestown in Yarmouth, Aylmer and Temperanceville in Malahide, and Vienna, Port Burwell, and Richmond in Bayham. Finally, Norfolk boasted Port Rowan in Walsingham, Colborne in Windham, Vittoria (the former district town) in Charlotteville, Port Dover in Woodhouse, and Waterford in Townsend.

The inhabitants of these towns and of the surrounding countryside all felt their distance from the larger centres of population. Although the farmers closest to Lake Erie could ship their produce to the outside world, even they were handicapped by the lack of nearby markets.[145] By 1837 stage-coach service was available at St Thomas, London, Ingersoll, Woodstock, Brantford, and, presumably, at intermediary points.[146] Unfortunately, the roads were often in atrocious condition. Although the Talbot road, running from Fort Erie to the Detroit River and northward from Southwold to the Western road near London, was considered to be good, the other highways were, like the rest in the province, 'more properly speaking mud canals' than roads.[147] Even the major roads were sometimes nearly impassable. In 1837 one traveller who later attained political prominence, John Sandfield Macdonald, noted that those between London and Hamilton – the Governor's road and the Hamilton and Brantford road – were the worst he had ever encountered.[148] Local roads, of course, often dependent on the fulfilment of settlement duties for their opening and on statute labour for their maintenance, were in even worse condition. Thomas Green, an Anglican missionary travelling in Nissouri in 1837, complained that 'in many places I could not well distinguish' the road 'from other parts of the wood, as it was not what we call *chopped out.*'[149] One settler, diarist George Leith, remarked that, striking north from London for Goderich, he encountered 'the most abominable road.'[150] and an itinerant minister, James Skinner of the United Secession Church, felt that anyone who had not seen the roads about Yarmouth and Southwold could 'scarcely form a proper conception' of them.[151]

It is not surprising that there was a good deal of enthusiasm for railroads by the mid-thirties. In 1834 a charter was granted to a company to build a railroad from Burlington Bay to London. Three years later this organization, now under the name of the Great Western Railroad Company and under obligation to build a line all the way to the Detroit River, received a loan of £200,000 from the legislature. Yet the actual building of this railroad lay some fifteen years in the future. In 1837 the inhabitants of the London area still had to import and export their goods via Kettle Creek and Port Stanley on Lake Erie,[152] while farmers from as far west as Middlesex continued to ship their produce by the Governor's road to Brantford and on to Hamilton.[153]

The populations of the several townships thus shared the experience of geographic isolation from the heart of the province around Lake Ontario. In addition, the residents of the area faced many of the same economic difficulties and were conscious that their world was essentially agrarian and rural. Conditions common to all could have produced in the west a stable, contented society, but the continuing influx of immigrants produced tensions based in part on the fact that after the War of 1812 the newer settlers were primarily from Great Britain, while the older ones were primarily North American in origin. Moreover, national issues were often heightened by sectarian religious conflicts. Thus national and sectarian differences produced division and dislike, the more so as disputes involving religion and origin were inevitably affected by the turbulent political issues of the day.

3
Political Discontents

Early in the province's history, political factions were at odds. At first, such groups revolved around personalities but, as Upper Canada's population increased, so did its political sophistication. By the early 1830s a conservative-reform dichotomy had emerged, based largely on constitutional issues. The provincial constitution ensured that the management and direction of Upper Canada would be controlled by the British government through a coterie of appointed officials, who would be hampered only slightly by democratic institutions.

The essentially oligarchic nature of the provincial administration, dominated both by a governor chosen by the Colonial Office and by appointed executive and legislative councils, was reflected in the machinery of local government. The province was divided into districts, each having its appointed clerk, who handled a multitude of duties, and its appointed sheriff, who maintained the law and drew up jury lists from which the members of the Grand Jury were selected. The latter power was an important one, for the Grand Jury acted as a court of inquiry, delving into the operations of local officials, making recommendations on a variety of subjects, and sometimes commenting on purely political matters.

The most important district functionaries were undoubtedly the justices of the peace, who superintended various township officials, acted as law officers, and, as commissioners of the Court of Requests, judged cases involving small debts. Meeting in the Court of Quarter Sessions, they controlled the district's finances, choosing the district treasurer and exercising a wide range of other powers as well. They were selected by the lieutenant-governor, usually on the advice of his councillors.

Ordinary people were involved in the administration of local government only at the township level. Every year the taxpaying householders of a township or of adjacent townships met to elect a number of officers. Some of the positions involved were regarded as important and conveyed a degree of status and distinction on those holding them. For the most part, however, the duties of the various officials, such as overseeing statute labour on the roads, assessing and collecting taxes, supervising the control of domestic animals in the locality, were onerous and unrewarding.

The organization of the government, both provincial and local, ensured that groups of functionaries would share certain assumptions and characteristics, for the lieutenant-governor and his subordinates customarily dispensed patronage in a narrow and exclusive way. As has been noted, the officials at the capital came to be designated as the 'Family Compact.' Local compacts could similarly be identified and existed at an early date in Norfolk and Middlesex.[1] By the early thirties, however, a group of officials whose influence transcended county boundaries came to dominate the affairs of the entire district.

One of this group was John Baptist Askin, who had been born in 1788 at Detroit when it was still in British hands. His father was John Askin II of the prominent fur-trading family. His mother, whose identity is unknown, was either an Indian or a white captive. In 1810 John Baptist went with his father to the Wisconsin region to trade. The two were there when the War of 1812 broke out and both helped capture the fur trade post of Michilimackinac for the British in July 1812. Later that summer the son led two to three hundred Indians south to aid Major-General Isaac Brock in his campaign against Detroit, but they arrived too late. He did see action, however, the following January at the battle of Frenchtown, where he served as an Indian interpreter.

Towards the end of the war he married Eliza Van Allen of Haldimand county and for a time had a position with the army's commissariat, relinquishing it in 1819 when he moved to the capital of the London district, Vittoria in Norfolk county. That year, despite his lack of formal legal training, he was appointed the district clerk of the peace and the next year, clerk of the district court. By 1820 he had thus acquired two of the most important offices he was to hold.

In 1826 the fledgling village of London became the district capital, but it was not until 1832 that Askin moved there. He lived just outside London, in comparative splendour on a large estate,[2] and busied himself with his many official duties and with acquiring extensive properties, particularly in the nearby town.³ Perhaps some of those duties (he was the local government land agent) helped him amass his holdings. Certainly, the sizable fees attendant upon his several offices did. In fact, by the mid-thirties his income had become so large that it was a source of concern to the district's Reformers[4] and to at least one other local official, Mahlon Burwell, registrar of Middlesex and member of the provincial assembly.[5]

Askin was well paid for his services and performed them conscientiously. He also accepted a wide range of financially unrewarding positions including a seat on the district board of education, a majorate in the militia, the presidency of the Middlesex agricultural society, and the supervision of a local road. Also, he helped found the first London mechanic's institute.[6] All of this suggests that Askin had a sense of civic responsibility though politically he was prone to vivid imaginings, fearing the mob and the threat it might represent to property.[7]

His service in the War of 1812, his militia commission, his property, his offices, and his sense of civic obligation assured his 'welcome in the best houses in London,'[8] though he was probably not a diverting guest being both officious and humourless.[9]

Other members of the London district Compact included Mahlon Burwell of Southwold, Thomas Talbot of Dunwich, John Bostwick of Port Stanley, George C. Salmon of Simcoe, and John Harris and James Hamilton of London. Like Askin, all had one or more government appointments and all were members of the Church of England. Each had also actively demonstrated his willingness to take up arms in defence of the empire – either by having helped defend the province in the War of 1812, or by having served in the regular British forces, or by holding a militia commission, or, indeed, by any combination of the above.

James Hamilton, Askin's cousin, had been born in Upper Canada. Talbot was Irish, Harris and Salmon were English, but these three had by 1837 all been resident in the province for at least twenty years. By then all except Hamilton, who was 45, were past 50. Burwell and Bostwick, also in their fifties, were both of American birth. Burwell claimed that his was a United Empire Loyalist family and Bostwick had come to the province in 1797 as a young man. The careers of both suggest that Americans who had been in the province for many years, who had demonstrated their willingness to defend the colony, and who were members of the Church of England could achieve power and influence.

In Upper Canada those settlers of conservative political bent who sought to maintain the constitution of the colony, and who, therefore, took little objection to the existence of the various circles of élite officials, had their greatest strength in the towns and in the old Loyalist settlements in the eastern sections of the province.[10] The Tories, however, were far from being a negligible force in the west. In this area there were natives and American-born residents who counted themselves Tories, but it would appear that by the 1830s the British-born settler was in the majority in the conservative coalition. Certainly, 'the better class' of British immigrant inclined to the conservative side of politics. As one London district resident, Mrs M.A. Seabrooke of Caradoc, wrote, 'all Respectables from the Old Country are High Tories.'[11] The half-pay officers were particularly noted for their 'loyal' political views. Even the ordinary colonists from Britain leaned towards conservatism for, as Patrick Shirreff observed, immigrants from Great Britain who acquired a few acres of their own 'seem to consider themselves part of the aristocracy and speak with horror of the people and liberality.'[12] Moreover, as Edward Marsh, a minister of the Niagara Presbyterian Church at Brantford noted, those from Britain who were attracted by democracy and republicanism settled in the United States, not in Upper Canada.[13]

The province's Reformers had emerged as an identifiable group by the early 1830s and their main criticism was of the colony's constitution. They analysed the various institutions of government and demanded, especially their more radical members, that a greater extension of democracy be given the province. The lack of popular participation in state affairs and the economic backwardness of Upper Canada were often contrasted with the 'popular sovereignty' and prosperity seen in the neighbouring republic. In 1834, for example, a resident of West Oxford, Pelham C. Teeple, travelled in the United States. At one lake port he observed 'sawmills, saltworks, canal and lake boats, all in full operation,' and thought this 'a pretty sample of Yankee freedom.'[14]

The Reformers' tendency to equate democracy and prosperity, to decry the existence of various monopolies, such as the British-run Canada Company, and to denounce the privileged position of the Church of England helped win them the support of the majority of Upper Canada's non-Loyalist Americans and native Upper Canadians of 'Yankee' parentage. The Scots in the colony are also said to have been partial to the Reform cause.[15] In the west the Scottish settlers of Dumfries in Halton county and of Aldborough and Dunwich in Middlesex supported the Reformers. In the rest of the London district, however, it would seem that in the early thirties those Scots who had recently settled evinced little or no interest in any politicians, while the Highland Scots of Zorra were active Tory partisans.

51 Political Discontents

The precise political affiliations of the various national groups in each township are not always easy to document because the few newspapers of the region, particularly the Tory ones, have largely disappeared. Yet the Tory and Reform support in and about St Thomas and London and the political skirmishes that developed can be charted with some degree of success, thanks to the survival of some papers issued in those centres and also some relevant correspondence, the London officials having frequently written to York (or Toronto, as it became known in 1834) detailing local political developments.

I

The Reform politicians of Middlesex first established their own journal, the St Thomas *Liberal*, in the late summer of 1832. Originally financed by forty-eight individuals, by November it had over 600 subscribers.[16] Its opponents charged that its readers were all American settlers and that its principles were entirely republican.[17] The Middlesex Reformers designated themselves 'Liberals,' a term borrowed from English politics which denoted an advanced reformer, and a term which, its Upper Canadian adopters doubtless hoped, would muffle the cry of disaffection.

In December 1832, the York Reformers created a political union based on unions developed in England by those seeking an extension of democracy by securing a wider franchise for elections to the House of Commons. The British unions had been very successful and the Reformers at York hoped that their supporters in the province would be inspired not only to arrange themselves in similar organizations but also to begin an effective campaign for change in the Upper Canadian government. On 17 January, a political union was formed at St Thomas. Allegedly, some 400 persons joined and subscribed to its limited reform programme which called for the abolition of primogeniture and entail, the amendment of the jury law, and the appropriation of the Clergy Reserve revenues for educational purposes.[18] Of the nine individuals selected to form a union committee, five were from the south of Yarmouth, one from Malahide, one from Bayham, and one from St Thomas. The residence of the ninth is unknown. At the close of the meeting the Reformers were attacked by a number of Tories, most of whom were apparently Orangemen from Port Talbot whose activities certainly had Colonel Talbot's blessing.[19] The colonel had already appeared in public the previous April to damn the Radicals, curse the burgeoning temperance societies, and praise the existing constitution. In any event, the St Thomas political union and those elsewhere in the province were short-lived as political passions cooled and as attention turned to the prosaic work of furthering the economic development of the province.

One politician who stood apart from the political union movement and concerned himself very much with developmental projects was Charles Duncombe of Oxford. Duncombe was an American, born in Connecticut in 1792, the first of five children. While he was still quite young, his family moved to neighbouring New York state. Charles, who had been educated by his mother, taught school and then became a student at the College of One Hundred and One Members of the Medical Society of the City of New York. In 1813 he married Nancy Howes. Family tradition is that her father, a wealthy farmer of German extraction, disapproved of him, feeling that that man was best who laboured with his hands. Possibly a forbidding father-in-law was one of the factors helping persuade the young doctor to leave New York. In any case, he travelled in 1819 to Upper Canada's western region, which was then a logical extension of the American frontier, easily accessible to Americans via the Niagara peninsula and providing ready access to Michigan Territory. In that year the region was still American in character and this likely influenced his decision to stay. He settled first in Delaware township, near present-day London, then returned to New York for his wife and three young daughters and for his brother, David, and his sister, Huldah, as well.[20]

In October 1819 the doctor was licensed to practise medicine in the colony.[21] Not long after he moved some fifteen miles south to St Thomas, where he developed a large practice. In 1824 he opened the Talbot Dispensatory, in association with that aspiring politician and unlicensed physician, Dr John Rolph of Norfolk county. The Dispensatory, intended to provide medical instruction to students and free medical advice to the general public, soon closed, however, though so quickly that it has been suggested that it may have been established merely to earn the goodwill of its patron, Thomas Talbot, patriarch of the Erie shore, and to win Rolph election to the assembly.[22] Duncombe had students to instruct, however: his brothers David and Elijah, the latter having arrived in St Thomas in 1822. They concluded their studies at Fairfield Academy in Herkimer, New York, and then became licensed practitioners in Upper Canada.[23]

In 1828 Duncombe and his immediate family moved some forty-five miles to the east of St Thomas, to what was to become Bishopsgate on the Burford-Brantford town line. He had been acquiring property throughout the west, much of it in Oxford county, and had built up large interests in his new locale. In the ensuing years he enlarged his holdings, acquiring

UEL rights, purchasing lands from individuals and from the government, and obtaining claims to former Indian lands along the Grand River. All told, he amassed several thousand acres. Some he sold at a profit, including 200 acres to a married daughter, Eliza Tufford,[24] some he presumably intended holding until its value had increased, and the rest he evidently intended working and managing. He was, after all, 'a good practical farmer.'[25] So large had his properties become by 1834 and so great his interest in them that he resolved to retire from medicine and devote much of his time to their superintendence.[26] He probably never fully carried out his resolve, however, merely reducing rather than abandoning his medical activities. He surrendered neither his commission as the regimental surgeon of the second Middlesex militia issued in 1825, nor his seat on the provincial medical board awarded in 1832. Further, in August 1834, the same month he announced his determination to retire, he accepted a position on the St Thomas Medical Board of Health.[27]

Duncombe's various medical appointments testify to his ability as a doctor. They also demonstrate his eagerness for office (he unsuccessfully sought the registrarship of Oxford county in 1834)[28] and suggest his associations and friendships with those capable of helping him secure appointments, such notables as Thomas Talbot, Sheriff A.A. Rapelje of the London district, and Assistant Adjutant-General of Militia James Fitzgibbon of Toronto. The latter he knew particularly well, for they were fellow Masons and had toured the province in the 1820s organizing the provincial Grand Lodge. Duncombe himself had become a Master Mason as early as 1820.[29]

Not surprisingly, Duncombe, with his profession, large properties, and influential circle of friends and acquaintances, found political favour. By 1830 a naturalized British citizen, he stood for election as one of Oxford's two representatives to the assembly and was successful, defeating both Tory and Radical Reform candidates.[30] Once elected, self-interest may have dictated that he generally support the Tories in boosting the fees of officials.[31] Also, economic interests, his own and those of his constituents, led him to back various developmental projects. Indeed, he was instrumental in securing the building of three bridges across the Grand River, and he became a commissioner for two, at Brantford and Paris. He supported the incorporation of the London and Gore Railroad and was one of its charter members. Appointed a commissioner of the Welland Canal, he proved to be energetic, going to Cleveland to inspect a steam dredge, which he then persuaded the canal company to use.[32] Though he was generally at one with the Tories in championing developmental projects, he was capable of independent thought, concluding that the Welland Canal Company's ready access to public funds and its control of a vital provincial asset obliged the province to take over its work.[33]

Though Duncombe did not join the St Thomas political union in 1832, he did flirt with the Reformers in the assembly of 1830–4. He felt strongly that the colony needed an educated population and argued in the assembly that the provincial government was far too niggardly in its suport of public education. He advocated the diversion of Crown lands revenues to the common, or public, schools. He also sided with the advanced Reformers in championing measures designed to extend democracy and increase colonial autonomy.[34] Not all Reformers were happy with his record, however. In December 1832 the St Thomas *Liberal* chided him for missing the vote on Peter Perry's Jury Bill, which had been narrowly defeated. The editor, Asahel Lewis, observed that 'when any important question has engrossed the attention of the House, this member's seat is often vacant. This won't do, Doctor, no skulking – no dodging.'[35] Possibly, Lewis' annoyance was heightened by the knowledge that Duncombe was the Burford area agent for the rival Tory London *Sun*.[36]

Another Reform newspaper editor, William Lyon Mackenzie of the *Colonial Advocate*, also held a comparatively low opinion of the member for Oxford. In 1831 Mackenzie, then sitting for York, had been expelled from the assembly for libel. Duncombe argued that Mackenzie had indeed transgressed but that his offence was not sufficient to warrant his expulsion. Mackenzie could not accept this reasoning and attacked Duncombe as a 'false reformer,' putting him on his blacklist of candidates for the 1834 elections. This helped ensure the doctor of the opposition of the Oxford Radicals in that contest.[37] In the campaign he tried to stake out his claim as a moderate Reformer, declaring that he was 'a warm advocate and a firm supporter of Reform, by every constitutional means, but as firmly and decidedly opposed to revolution and revolutionary principles.'[38]

The Reformers enjoyed considerable success in the 1834 elections, capturing control of the assembly. In the west Halton elected two Reformers, James Durand and Caleb Hopkins, as did Wentworth with Harmannus Smith and Jacob Rymal. Middlesex elected Reformers Elias Moore and Thomas Parke and Oxford, Reformer Robert Alway and Charles Duncombe. Norfolk, however, chose a Conservative, Francis Leigh Walsh, but also elected David Duncombe, whose politics were very close to those of his elder brother.

Charles Duncombe took his seat in the new assembly knowing that both

Tories and Reformers claimed him as their own. He deemed himself a moderate Reformer, one answerable to his conscience rather than to party discipline. Soon, however, he earned the wrath or so he thought, of Lieutenant-Governor Colborne by seconding the nomination of the Reform candidate for Speaker, M.S. Bidwell, who was elected. He further alienated powerful Tory interests by chairing the committee voiding the election of Attorney-General Jameson in Leeds county and by presiding over yet another committee which pointedly drew attention to the money Solicitor-General Hagerman still owed the province from his days as collector of customs in Kingston.[39]

If the Tories were unhappy with Duncombe, so were certain Reform elements. In January 1834 he publicly condemned the well-known letter sent to Mackenzie by Joseph Hume, a leading British Radical, bemoaning Britain's 'baneful domination' over Upper Canada.[40] Perhaps this helped prompt one assemblyman to write an anonymous letter to the *Liberal* and persuade John Kent, who had taken over the editorship of the paper in December 1833 after the death of Asahel Lewis, to print it. The writer argued that both Charles and his brother David, since voting for Bidwell as Speaker, 'have been in general ... on the tory side. Where Charles goes, David, like a true brother, follows. They stick like brothers on all questions. They are in the enviable situation of Mahomet in his coffin, hanging betwixt and between.'[41] Over the next twelve months Duncombe's political position became increasingly clear as he unequivocally aligned himself with the Reformers. Publicly he was to argue in January 1836 that 'times are materially altered, and our laws and institutions require a corresponding change.'[42] Privately, he was far more vehement, confiding to his brother Elijah that he wished the Tories of British North America might 'dig their own graves ... and fall into the pit they have digged.'[43]

The reasons for Duncombe's shift can only be surmised. He may have felt under attack by powerful Tory interests, a feeling reinforced by the fact that in November 1835 the executive council had refused to grant him a patent for property he had acquired which had originally belonged to one Benajah Mallory. The council had been willing to convey the patent to him until Colborne informed its members that Mallory, an attainted traitor from the War of 1812, should have had his lands confiscated. Though Duncombe was bitter at the council's decision,[44] his switch from moderation to incipient Radicalism may well have been prompted less by narrowly personal motives than by his conviction that the province's existing constitution could be used all too effectively to deny people their proper voice in public affairs.

In 1836 he opposed the lieutenant-governor's attempt to extend his influence over the provincial medical board by having those on it sit at his pleasure.[45] Earlier that year, unhappy with the existing masonic organization's close ties with Britain and the general lassitude of the provincial body, he had helped establish a breakaway Grand Lodge at London. Though that lodge was short-lived, he had the fleeting pleasure of being its Grand Master.[46]

Duncombe's increasing disposition to view the Tories with hostility, to resist what he saw as the extension of autocratic authority, and to cast about for new arrangements, whether in political or social affairs, was all the more important for his assuming a prominent role in the assembly. He chaired most committees investigating financial matters, and was one of three commissioners appointed by the assembly in 1835 to delve into a range of social issues. He did most of the commissioners' work, travelling extensively through the United States, collecting information and ideas, and writing the three reports they presented to the assembly in February 1836.

In those documents Duncombe demonstrated his advanced position on several issues. In one he urged the establishment of a provincial lunatic asylum to care for the insane, hitherto confined in the province's jails. In a second he revealed a conviction, shared by a growing number of penologists, that criminals could be reclaimed, their characters reformed. He, like others, was prepared to stress the environmental causes of crime, particularly with juveniles. His third report, on education, outlined his twin beliefs that the province needed an educated electorate and its economy an educated population. These tenets underlay his proposals to make education more accessible to the general public by increasing the funding of the common schools and to offer in those schools a more practical and less classical curriculum.[47]

The three reports bore little fruit. Although many of Duncombe's recommendations for a revamped prison régime were immediately implemented at the penitentiary recently established in Kingston,[48] his main suggestion, albeit implicit rather than explicit, that the penitentiary adopt the Philadelphia rather than the existing Auburn system, was overlooked. (Both systems were designed to reform the criminal and both operated on the rule of silence, but the former stipulated unrelieved solitary confinement for the prisoners.) Duncombe had equally little success with his proposal for an insane asylum; one would not appear in the province for another decade. His educational reforms, although embodied in a bill presented to the assembly and passed by it, were rejected by the legislative council. One authority, J.H. Aitchison, has argued that the bill deserved its fate, since it was 'impracticable and poorly drafted.'[49]

By 1836 Duncombe was not the only Reformer disenchanted with the state of things. Indeed by then the divisions between the two groups, between moderate and radical Reformers, had clearly widened. In general, the former favoured a rather limited programme of reform, while the latter conducted a broad attack on the existing constitution and advocated the adoption of elective institutions. The Radicals, of course, were particularly open to charges of disloyalty and a variety of other sins. A Church of Scotland minister, P.C. Campbell of Elizabethtown, insisted that they were 'all infidels or Methodists & chiefly Yankees.'[50]

In the assembly the leader of the Radicals was William Lyon Mackenzie, the splenetic Toronto newspaper editor. Increasingly, he inclined towards democratic and republican principles as the fierce political warfare of the province eroded his affection for Britain and her institutions. He secured the establishment and the chairmanship of a grievance committee and used that position to pry and probe into every evil which beset the colony. The intemperate report he produced alarmed the British government and helped persuade it to relieve the province's lieutenant-governor, Sir John Colborne, of his post.

On 25 January 1836, Sir Francis Bond Head arrived in the province. A posturing, vainglorious individual devoid of political experience and common sense, forty-three-year-old Head proved to be the wrong man in the wrong place at the wrong time for he was to collide violently with the demand for responsible government, a demand first advanced by various Reformers in the months prior to his arrival.

The theory of responsible government, as enunciated by its two leading advocates, Dr W.W. Baldwin and his son, Robert, both of Toronto, insisted that the members of the executive council hold office at the pleasure of the assembly. It is doubtful if many of those who supported it as the remedy for the province's political ills clearly understood its true nature, however. A writer to the St Thomas *Liberal* of 18 February 1836, for example, declared that the so-called Radicals, of whom he was evidently one, sought the establishment of a responsible legislature, advocating a change in one of the two bodies of the legislature, that is, in the legislative, rather than in the executive, council.

Shortly after his arrival in the province, Head, hoping to conciliate the Reformers, brought Robert Baldwin and Dr John Rolph, Duncombe's old associate, into his executive council. Baldwin quickly became disillusioned at the lack of consultation between the lieutenant-governor and the council and on 4 March was able to persuade all the councillors to present a memorandum to Head which insisted that he confer with the executive council on all items of business and stated that he was bound to accept his councillors' advice on certain issues. Head correctly denied the legality of these claims, adding that those who sought to introduce responsible government simply coveted the power and patronage of the Crown.[51] The six executive councillors refused to withdraw their memorandum as Head insisted they should. On 14 March he therefore instituted a completely new council composed entirely of Tory members.

The Reform majority in the assembly established a select committee to report on the crisis. In April the committee issued its report, incorrectly asserting that responsible government was a feature of the constitution and advising the assembly to stop supplies. On 15 April the assembly adopted the report and implemented its recommendation. Head retaliated by refusing to grant contingencies, by withholding his assent to those money bills already passed, and by proroguing and then dissolving the legislature.

The issue was joined between Reformer and Tory, with the King's representative, Head, and thus 'loyalty,' firmly on the side of the latter. In no area of the province was the contest fiercer than in the London district. Here the struggle was conducted by a variety of agencies, the most prominent of which was the press. The local Reform paper, the *Liberal*, had changed editors again early in 1836. John Kent had stepped down, to be replaced by thirty-nine-year-old John Talbot, the son of Richard Talbot, who had led the first group of settlers, all Irish, into London township in 1818. The *Liberal* was now owned, in large part at least, by Bela Shaw, an American-born merchant of St Thomas. Under Talbot and Shaw the paper appealed to British precedent but also contemplated separation from Great Britain.[52]

Prior to the election of 1836, the *Liberal* doubtless bombarded its readers with appeals to support the Reformers but the press was not the only weapon used by the Reform politicians. Occasional glimpses can be caught of their activities at the local or township level: petitions, perhaps devised in Toronto, circulating in Charlotteville and Bayham, a meeting held in St Thomas.[53] In several localities the Reformers had used the Local Government Act of 1835 to build up a patronage system which could be used at election time. This Act had created for each township three new commissioners, who were allotted the former powers of the justices of the peace over the various township officers and who were given some of the justices' judicial duties. In some townships Reform members of the legislature had tried to see that their adherents were elected to township offices in January 1836. In 1838 a British settler, John Burn, complained that in Dereham and Norwich 'every situation has been in the hands of the Americans' and that under 'the new Township Officers Act, irresponsible Commissioners,' who discriminated against British residents in the allocation of work and contracts, 'were chosen by the people.'[54] In view of the fact that Reformers had previously used township meetings and township officials to further their ends, it seems likely that they persuaded their elected comrades to campaign actively for them.

The Liberals also attempted to secure the support of the various churches by capitalizing on the furore created by Colborne's endowing the Church of England with forty-four rectories in 1836. In the election the Reformers were probably supported, tacitly if not openly, by the Episcopal Methodist Church and by the congregations of the Niagara Presbytery, which advocated two causes with which the Reformers were identified – voluntaryism and temperance. The Reformers could also expect strong backing from other voluntaryist groups, or from those sympathetic to voluntaryism such as the United Secession Church, the Universalists, the Christians, the Quakers, and the Congregationalists.

While the Reformers could thus count on the support of a number of small religious sects whose adherents were concentrated in a few localities, the Tories found that the largest denominations rallied to them. The Church of England, of course, provided enthusiastic support. The Anglican minister at London, for example, campaigned for the Tories throughout London township.[55] Although the Church of Scotland did not, as it felt it ought to do, share in the division of the Clergy Reserve revenues, it did receive considerable financial aid from the provincial government and was therefore firmly opposed to the voluntaryist cause. In the London district the two resident Kirk ministers, the Reverend Alexander Ross of Aldborough and the Reverend Donald McKenzie of Zorra, travelled among the Scots of the region preaching Tory doctrine.[56] Similarly, the Roman Catholic Church, which enjoyed its share of government monies, threw its weight behind the Tories with Bishop Macdonell, for instance, publicly damning the Reform cause.[57] After the election of 1836, it was noted that in areas where Catholics were not numerous – the counties of Norfolk, Oxford, and Middlesex and the ridings of York – the 'republicans' were victorious.[58]

The British Wesleyans inclined their former Episcopal brethren, who had united with them in 1833, in a conservative direction, a task made easier by the cessation of political comment by the *Christian Guardian*, the official organ of the Methodist union, and by William Lyon Mackenzie's impolitic attack on the parties to the Methodist alliance in his grievance report. Although the establishment of the rectories annoyed many Wesleyans, particularly those who favoured voluntaryism, several of the itinerant preachers proselytized on behalf of the Tories. Moreover, the editor of the *Guardian* and the majority of those attending the Wesleyan conference of June 1836 clearly aligned themselves with Head and his cause.[59]

The churches may have found it difficult to remain aloof because Head clearly implied that it was the duty of every right-thinking man and every sound organization to vote for or to support the Tories. Suggesting that the Reformers were conspiring with forces outside the province, he apparently convinced 'a great portion of the people ... that they were called upon to decide the question of separation by their votes,' and won for the Tories, so Lord Durham later claimed, the backing of most of the British electors in the province.[60] After the election, John Rolph was to complain that Head had appealed to the United Empire Loyalists and to the Englishmen, Irishmen, and Scotchmen, but 'forgot the CANADIANS! ... The emigrants were thus significantly marshalled against our hospitable natives!'[61]

In addition to his appeal to loyalty, Head suggested that the assembly's action in stopping supplies was detrimental to the economy of the province. This charge was particularly potent as the commercial depression of 1836 had begun to effect Upper Canada. The depression, world-wide in scope, began with the overexpansion of capital works in Great Britain and the United States and was followed by an international contraction in credit. In Upper Canada ready cash was scarce at the best of times and transactions were often carried on by barter. With the depression, creditors demanded their money and specie began to flow from the province. In July 1836, Francis Evans, the rector of Woodhouse, noted that 'the whole country is in a state of *bankruptcy*, and there are many respectable people who are unable to meet the smallest pecuniary demand.'[62] Although the hard times were by no means the fault of the Reformers, who had constituted the majority of the late assembly's members, they could not escape public censure for their economic policies.

It may be that in the west real differences existed between Tories and their more moderate brethren, the Conservatives, but because of the lack

61 Political Discontents

of extant documentary evidence fine distinctions cannot be made with much accuracy and, in this study, the two terms, Tory and Conservative, are used interchangeably. By May 1836, buoyed by the Reform disabilities, all Tories were active. In that month the British Constitutional Society, dedicated to preserving the province's link with Great Britain, was reconstituted. Attempts were made to form branch societies in the London district and in May a meeting of loyal persons from London, St Thomas, the south of Yarmouth, Dunwich, and possibly from other areas was held at St Thomas. That same month, loyal addresses were sent to Head from Bayham and Woodstock.[63] Despite their efforts, however, the prospects for the Tories in the London district elections were not bright, James Ingersoll, the Conservative candidate in Oxford county, admitting that he was 'by no means Sanguine of Success.'[64]

It was, however, within the power of the government to influence the western elections which generally were held in early July. Steps were taken to ensure that settlers favourable to the Tory cause who did not have patents for their property acquired them, thereby becoming eligible to vote in the forthcoming contest. On 6 June the London district clerk, J.B. Askin, wrote to Head's private secretary, John Joseph, declaring it a shame that the army pensioners and old soldiers of Adelaide township, who were loyal to a man, would be unable to vote because, though most had performed their settlement duties, they had not received their patents.[65] On 21 June the news was relayed to London that Askin's memorandum had been conveyed to Toronto and that 'Mr. Spragge has several deeds ready for London and will have *all* in very good time.'[66] This quotation doubtless referred to the patents for Adelaide, because after the election the *Liberal* complained that around eighty old Adelaide soldiers had been given their patents prior to the election along with instructions on how to vote.[67] In fact, of the 151 patents issued in the London and Gore districts prior to the election, fifty-four were for lots in Adelaide township.[68]

On 11 June, Mahlon Burwell, the Tory candidate for the town of London's seat, wrote John Joseph a confidential letter enclosing the names of nine individuals who would vote for him if they received their patents. All, he said, had performed their settlement duties. If the patents were sent immediately to Askin, there would be no doubt, he wrote, of his election.[69] All nine individuals involved duly secured their patents. While eight of the documents were officially listed as having been issued from 16 June to 21 June, one, John O'Brien's or O'Beirne's, was falsely dated 21 May.[70]

62 The Rising in Western Upper Canada

On 29 June 1836, John Young of Hamilton wrote the commissioner of Crown Lands, Peter Robinson, that he owned two lots in Brantford and was desperately eager to receive the patents for them in order to vote in the Wentworth elections where the 'constitutional,' or Tory, candidates, MacNab and Aikman, were engaged in a close fight with their Reform opponents.[71] Young received the relevant document for at least one of his lots in time to vote. The official return, moreover, dated the issuance of his patent at 17 June – almost two weeks prior to his request that the patent be sent him![72] These cases indicate that there was indeed fraud in connection with the enfranchisement of individuals in the election of 1836. Although many who received their patents prior to polling day had doubtless taken steps on their own to secure them, it is obvious that in an unknown number of cases Tory officials skirted the letter of the law and violated the supposed disinterested workings of the Crown Lands Office to obtain patents for Tory voters.

Other measures were taken to ensure that the results of the election were favourable to the Tories. When the polls opened in Middlesex and Oxford in early July, Reformers complained of being turned away by returning officers for not being able to produce certificates that they had taken the necessary oath of allegiance.[73] Violence was used as well. One observer, a Reformer, claimed that at the poll in London the magistrates allowed an Orange mob, 'headed by a negro,' to beat and drive Liberals from the polls, and to threaten the Reform candidates.[74] After the election, Thomas Talbot admitted that in Middlesex 'the Rebels are too numerous and their barefaced audacity astonished me,' but he was pleased that 'my Boys with Twigs kept the scoundrels in order.'[75] Violence was also reported in Wentworth and Haldimand. Lord Durham later decided that Tory mobs had been able to affect the outcome of more than one election.[76]

Violence and corrupt electoral practices doubtless played some part in the sweeping Tory victory at the polls. The 'constitutionalists' returned forty-four members, five from the study area. Mahlon Burwell won election in the town of London, as did Absalom Shade and William Chisholm in Halton, and Michael Aikman and Allan N. MacNab in Wentworth. There were to be only sixteen Reformers in the new assembly, but no less than six were from the London district. Charles Duncombe and Robert Alway were victorious in Oxford, Thomas Parke and Elias Moore in Middlesex, and John Rolph and David Duncombe in Norfolk. The Liberals had won the Norfolk and Oxford seats in particularly decisive fashion.[77]

63 Political Discontents

11

The results of the election astounded many Reformers. Leading personalities such as M.S. Bidwell, Peter Perry, Samuel Lount, Robert Baldwin, and W.L. Mackenzie had all been defeated. Some Reformers were outraged. Charles Duncombe was one, despite his brother David's victory in Norfolk and his own triumph in Oxford. Duncombe, whose return had been aided by the fact that Mackenzie, impressed by his political re-orientation in the assembly of 1834-6, had decided to support his re-election, was quite convinced that electoral corruption and fraud had largely determined the outcome of the provincial contest. He was appointed on 11 July by the executive committee of the Constitutional Reform Society, which had been organized in June, to travel to England to protest election irregularities.[78] In Britain that summer Duncombe presented a petition to the House of Commons that levelled general charges about the conduct of the election and referred to some specific abuses which allegedly had occurred.[79] Head had already beseeched the colonial secretary, Lord Glenelg, not to see Duncombe, 'an American, and a rank Republican.'[80] Consequently, Glenelg would not confer with the doctor, though he was prepared to receive missives from him. Duncombe was furious and wrote to Glenelg that he was unaware that the colonial secretary had ever turned any Upper Canadian Tories away from his door.[81] He also told Robert Baldwin, who was in England at the time, 'I wish the people of Upper Canada could see exactly how these Whigs manage matters, they would soon see that if ever they have good government in Canada they must look among themselves for the means of producing it.'[82]

If Duncombe was upset at the reception Glenelg gave his public pleas, he must have been equally chagrined at that given his private requests. He had sent Glenelg a petition protesting the executive council's decision not to grant him a patent for the land he had acquired from Benajah Mallory. Duncombe assured Glenelg that Absalom Shade of Galt had purchased land from Mallory and had received patents for it but that Duncombe had been treated differently because he had angered former Lieutenant-Governor Colborne 'by his independent vote & conduct in the H. of Assembly' and had also offended Attorney-General Jameson and Solicitor-General Hagerman. Hagerman had threatened to pay Duncombe back – 'a threat which it appears was not forgotten.'[83]

Glenelg refused to comment on the accusations that political animosities had conspired to rob Duncombe of his patent but allowed that, if the doctor were correct in asserting that others' property rights had been confirmed in the same circumstances and that the Upper Canadian authorities had permitted him to occupy and improve the land before refusing the patent for it, then his case should be upheld. Consequently, the petition was to be referred back to Upper Canada, in order to obtain verification, if possible, of these assertions.[84] Duncombe must have been somewhat vexed at the thought that the provincial government, which he had so thoroughly castigated, was to investigate the justice of his claims!

In Upper Canada the new Tory-dominated assembly began considering Duncombe's grievances, establishing a committee to investigate the charges in his election petition. The committee, which first met on 25 November, originally consisted of four Tories and two Reformers. In December its composition was altered to six Tories and three Reformers. On 7 January 1837 the committee's report appeared. It denounced the petition to the British House of Commons and denied the validity of the specific charges made.[85] Duncombe did not reply to the report, nor could he have done so successfully, because the documentation he needed to sustain his allegations was buried in the correspondence of various government officers. Another reason for Duncombe's apparent lack of interest in challenging the findings of the committee may well have been that he was sunk in grief for, on returning to the province, he had been greeted with the news of the death of his only son, fourteen-year-old Charles, who had been thrown from a horse. Moreover, a fire had devastated his property.[86] In any case, the committee's findings constituted an important Tory triumph, although Rolph insisted that the three Reformers on the committee had been prevented from introducing evidence of electoral fraud and had consented neither to the report's drafting nor to its adoption.[87]

Reformers in the west of Upper Canada, upset at the treatment Duncombe and his cause had received in England and in the province, were also alarmed at the vendetta carried on after the election against those Reformers who held government offices. Head's dismissal of W.W. Baldwin as a judge because of his political activities and his refusal to elevate a prominent Reformer to a judgeship and reappoint another Reform justice, despite Colonial Office instructions to do so, were matters of notoriety. Less well known was the purging of a wide range of minor officials.

During the excitement of the election campaign, forty-year-old John Burwell, who was a postmaster, justice of the peace, collector of customs, commissioner of the Court of Requests, and a brother of Mahlon Burwell, informed Head's secretary, John Joseph, that Bela Shaw, the postmaster at St Thomas, had published a flyer during the campaign supporting the Reformers. Burwell demanded his removal, and some time later reported that John Scatcherd, a justice of the peace from Nissouri, had in the *Liberal* termed the King a 'Public Calumniator.' Both Shaw and Scatcherd lost their posts, as did Shaw's successor as postmaster, after Burwell had challenged his loyalty as well.[88]

Through the closing months of 1836 and on into 1837 Reformers added grievance to grievance. The new assembly declared that, contrary to custom, it need not be dissolved when Britain's enfeebled monarch died. The British Parliament consented to the governor-general taking funds from the Lower Canadian assembly that it had refused to grant. This represented a serious threat to the assembly which, controlled by a largely French-speaking block of self-styled Reformers, had battled an entrenched and largely English Tory oligarchy.

In 1837 political discontent was exacerbated by economic hardship. Aside from the continuing trade depression, the 1836 harvest in Upper Canada had been poor for the potato crop had largely failed and the wheat harvest had not been successful. Wheat merchant Adam Hope of St Thomas claimed that the yield of wheat in 1836 in Oxford county 'was more deficient than perhaps [in] any other part of the Province.'[89] The Reverend William Proudfoot of London recorded that the crop of 1836 had been so bad and the winter of 1836-7 so severe that many farmers, lacking fodder to feed their cows, had lost much of their livestock.[90] More cattle died in the Gore district from foot-rot.[91]

Most serious was the hardship suffered by the human population. In 1837 the St Thomas *Liberal* declared that in 1836 the Middlesex farmers, seduced by high prices, had sold more of their wheat than they should so that in 1837 they were forced to buy corn and flour at extremely high prices. Many of the poorer families, the paper claimed, 'are reduced to starvation.'[92] Adam Hope noted that in Zorra, 'where a great many Highland Scotch are settled, & but recently settled the scarcity of provisions, especially breadstuffs is very great.'[93] In the late summer of 1837 a Woodhouse farmer, William Wood, lamented that the price of a barrel of flour was 'very very dear.' He did not regret his extravagance, however, thankful that 'we have bread once more and good it is to a hungry soul filled with nothing the last ten days but potatoes and cucumbers with a little milk as a treat.'[94] As food prices increased, in some instances by four and five times,[95] demands began to be heard that the province reduce the pressure on prices by restricting the export of foodstuffs.[96]

The crisis in food production coincided with the depths of the commercial depression. Money became exceedingly scarce. Reportedly, 'men that are worth thousands cannot loan a dollar.'[97] At London Proudfoot observed that poverty had fallen upon thousands.[98] The contraction of the province's money supply threatened to become even more serious when the provincial banks began to agitate for the right to suspend specie payments, a right exercised by banks elsewhere in North America. Banks resorted to suspension in order to prevent a run on their reserves by depositors fearful of losing their money and by those distrustful of paper currency.

A special session of the provincial legislature, sitting from 19 June to 11 July, learned that provincial banks might indeed suspend specie payments, provided they received the assent of the governor-in-council, a difficult feat. None the less, the demand for relief on the part of the banks, which was supported by most merchants, created a suspicion that those very institutions which had helped produce the commercial crisis now sought to escape the consequences of their own actions by sacrificing the interests of their depositors.

Economic distress combined with the political discontent in Reform ranks produced a combustible situation. Recent European history illustrated as much. In eighteenth-century England and France outbreaks of rioting had notably coincided with poor harvests.[99] An agricultural crisis had gripped France in the years prior to the Revolution. In Regency England 'disturbances seemed to occur ... only when and where there were, in addition to particular causes of industrial or political discontent, evidence of sudden, sharp, unrelieved distress.'[100] In the early 1830s in England rural unemployment and economic dislocation had produced the Swing riots, a series of incendiary disturbances involving rural workers and agricultural village labourers. Also, the initial phase of England's Chartist activity in the spring of 1837 had occurred after the onslaught of hard times.[101] Historical antecedents, of course, demonstrate equally that economic difficulties need not cause unrest and that countries might even escape the coincidence of depression and political or social discontent without turmoil. None the less, the unfortunate conjunction might have suggested to the perceptive that tumultuous times might well lie ahead in Upper Canada.

III

The immediate instigator of insurrection in Upper Canada was the little Scot, William Lyon Mackenzie, who on 4 July 1836 had established in Toronto the *Constitution*, a paper which was intemperate above all others.

67 Political Discontents

In the summer of 1837 Mackenzie predicted the imminence of revolt in Lower Canada.[102] Obviously inspired by the success of the political union movement which had helped secure a widening of the British franchise in the Reform Bill of 1832, he proposed a new reform organization for Upper Canada consisting of a series of political unions arranged pyramid-fashion on local or township unions containing no more than twelve people. He observed that such an establishment 'could be easily transferred without change of its structure to military purposes,' though he assured his readers that this was purely coincidental.[103]

On 28 July, a group of Home district Reformers met at Doel's brewery in Toronto and, systematically cataloguing their grievances and noting that the Reformers in Upper Canada should unite with those in Lower Canada, called for the adoption of Mackenzie's political union scheme, adding that a convention of Reform delegates should assemble at Toronto to consider the political and economic state of the province.[104] In the west the *Liberal* applauded the cry for political unions, telling the Reformers – perhaps with Duncombe's trip to England of the previous year in mind – that 'neither the Lord Glenelg nor the Imperial Parliament will listen to your complaints.'[105]

The Liberals in the west appear to have suffered no diminution in strength from the previous summer. A Burford township resident claimed that the township elections of January 1837 had gone uniformly in favour of the Reformers,[106] and indeed known Liberals had been elected to the important post of township clerk in the London district townships of Delaware, Dorchester, Lobo, Mosa, Westminster, Yarmouth, Townsend, Oakland, Norwich, and possibly others, while known Reformers had occupied township offices in Oakland and Nissouri.[107] In July 1837 Proudfoot noted that 'the Liberal party is becoming more confident, and the Tories more quiet than they have been for some time back.'[108]

To a great extent the organization of the agitation that was to occur in the west was carried out by Liberals prominent in their own localities but not in the province as a whole. Such a person was thirty-six-year-old Eliakim Malcolm of Oakland, a leading member of the Malcolm clan. Eliakim's father, Finlay, was a Scot, born in 1750 who had been brought to America as a boy. When still a young man he became a shipowner in Maine but left the United States during the American Revolution for what was to become New Brunswick. In 1795, accompanied by his wife, Tryphena, and eleven children, he came to Oakland township in Upper Canada's western peninsula, where he had received a Loyalist grant.[108] In 1805 he (or possibly his third son and namesake, twenty-six-year-old

Finlay) was accused along with Benajah Mallory of compiling fraudulent assessment rolls.[109] Both men were found not guilty[109] but the incident may indicate an association between Malcolm and Mallory, a known dissident who turned traitor in the War of 1812. The Malcolms were staunchly loyal during that conflict, however, and several members of the family suffered considerable property damage from marauding American forces. After the war, Finlay Malcolm and his sons Finlay and John entered claims upon the provincial government for losses. These were not settled until 1833, when the Malcolms received, as did other claimants, only 25 per cent of the sums asked.[110] Perhaps the long controversy over the war claims and its unsatisfactory conclusion helped incline members of the family to the Reform side of politics.

Politically, the best-known member of the Malcolm clan prior to the rebellion was young Finlay who in 1828 was elected a member of the assembly for Oxford county. He did not run in 1830 but was a candidate in 1834 when he was backed by the Radical reformers.[111] He was unsuccessful; both Duncombe and Robert Alway topped him at the polls. Finlay's brother, Eliakim, born in Upper Canada in 1801, was another prominent Malcolm. Though he was very young during the War of 1812, he fought in it or so he later claimed.[112] In 1822 he married and, like most of his brothers, stayed in Oakland where he raised his children. Eliakim became a prominent figure in his township, where he purchased almost 1,000 acres of property, thereby contributing to his reputation for being 'extremely acquisitive.'[113] His profession as a surveyor increased his prominence. In 1821 he had been appointed a deputy provincial land surveyor and in 1828 he participated in a resurvey of much of nearby Norwich township, his findings helping to pit neighbour against neighbour in a long and extraordinarily acrimonious dispute which earned him the censure of his colleague, John Arthur Tidey of Norwich, who later examined his work for the government.[114] None the less, he was appointed one of the two surveyors of highways for Oxford county in 1834.

In 1831 Mahlon Burwell reported to the lieutenant-governor that Eliakim was 'quite superior in every way to his brother who was a member of the Assembly.' He was, Burwell thought, a 'rather clever person for his opportunities,' and, despite being 'rather *radical* in his politics,' would make a good magistrate.[115] Two years later he became a justice of the peace, to the concern of J.B. Askin, who deemed his appointment 'injudicious.' Askin later reported that Eliakim had 'behaved tolerably well' until the summer of 1836 when he had 'supported the Election of

69 Political Discontents

Duncombe and Alway and Identified himself with that party,' even going so far as to address a public meeting at which he had heaped scorn upon the lieutenant-governor's head.[116] So active had he been for the Reformers that, after the election, the *Constitution* erroneously reported that he had been relieved of his post.[117]

Malcolm soon became involved in the Reform agitation begun by Mackenzie. Ironically, in the late summer of 1837 he found himself, on behalf of the Liberals, in Norwich, the very township whose inhabitants he had done so much to divide. His task now was to unite them in support of Mackenzie's political union scheme, a job made easier by the almost uniform radical political inclinations of the politically involved of that township. On 2 September he addressed an enthusiastic throng in Sodom. He was there to help organize a political union and he spoke 'at considerable length – tracing and exposing the growing corruptions of colonial misgovernment down from period to period.' Those at the meeting endorsed the declaration of the Reformers gathered at Doel's brewery, chose a 'vigilance committee' of fifteen men, and selected two delegates to the projected provincial convention of Reformers. One of those delegates and the man elected president of the political union was surveyor John Tidey.[118]

Malcolm was not active at the next Liberal assembly, held some distance from Norwich at Sparta, 'a small Yankee village'[119] in the south of Yarmouth. Some 250 people attended that gathering. Significantly, both meetings were held in the midst of the London district's two Quaker communities. The resolutions of the Sparta meeting have survived, for they were reprinted in the *Constitution*, and are one of the four extant sets of resolves adopted by area meetings. Those who assembled at Sparta on 9 September embraced certain principles that were to be reiterated at later gatherings. They pronounced themselves in favour of a responsible executive council and emphasized the importance of an impartial governor. As well, they proclaimed the futility of seeking a redress of grievances from Great Britain and the necessity of the Liberals' allying themselves with the oppressed Lower Canadians. They challenged Head's ability to govern, warmly approved the declaration of the Toronto Reformers, and named three delegates to the impending convention at Toronto.

They did pass a number of resolutions which were atypical. Later resolves proclaimed their loyalty to the British connection, but their first incorporated that section of the American Declaration of Independence which asserted the right of the people to abolish despotic governments.

Another declared their intent not to let anyone impede their right of free discussion. This took on particular significance in the light of a resolution proposed by David Anderson, an Irish tavernkeeper from the village of Selborne. Anderson declared that, as Orangemen were encouraged by the authorities to assault Reformers, 'to preserve peace, and defend Her Majesty's subjects from assassination, it is absolutely necessary to form armed associations, and determinedly oppose force by force, whenever our people are attacked in the peaceful exercise of their undoubted rights and privileges.'[120] Anderson's 'armed associations' were not established but he and various young men of south Yarmouth made a flag emblazoned with the word LIBERTY which they flew at the Sparta meeting, evidently alarming the secretary of the meeting, John Talbot. His paper, the *Liberal*, suggested that American flags not be flown at Canadian gatherings and that Reformers 'leave such childish gew gaws as Orange ribbons, lillies, flags and garters to those who need them.'[121]

The Lake Erie Tories were not disposed to allow the local Liberals to mobilize without demonstrating their own strength. A further Reform gathering was scheduled for 23 September at the village of Richmond on the Talbot road in Bayham. John Talbot had reputedly advised those attending the meeting 'to take with them loaded rifles.' The Reformers assembled, including, it was said, sixty armed men from the south of Yarmouth, only to find that they were outnumbered by 'constitutionalists,' who succeeded in organizing their own meeting. The Tories, led by John Burwell, vociferously proclaimed their loyalty and the necessity of maintaining the British connection. They decried agitation and rebellion and declared themselves ready to defend the province 'against the insidious attempts of the seditious and disaffected to promote a Rebellion in this happy land.'[122]

Some of the Tories quickly had their resolve put to the test. After their meeting, the constitutionalists retired to an inn to which the Reformers, having held their own proceedings, also came. A general *mêlée* ensued. From an upstairs window of the tavern, magistrate Doyle McKenny, a forty-year-old Malahide resident, read the riot act. He and his 'sidekick Metcalf' (presumably Henry Medcalf, a fifty-nine-year-old Irish miller) were unceremoniously 'taken by the necks and waistbands and thrown, head foremost, down stairs.' At this, the battle grew fiercer. Twice, the *Liberal* reported, the Reformers beat back Tory assaults and, after the final thrashing, the victors 'marched up and down with their flag flying, and then left the village in triumph.'[123] Despite the victory of the Reformers, in Toronto William Lyon Mackenzie observed that 'the tories

71 Political Discontents

appear to be rather stronger in the London District than previous accounts had given us cause to expect.'[124]

The Tories in other parts of the London district were no more quiescent. One constitutional stronghold was the township of London where the majority of settlers were Church of England Irishmen renowned for their Conservative views. On 12 July, for example, the *Liberal* reported that Orangemen from 'the uncivilized concessions of the township of London' had marched with flags and weapons to the Episcopal church in London 'to hear a homily from a "chaplain" of the gang,' the Reverend Mr Flood of Caradoc. The *Liberal* had expressed surprise that eventually the Orangemen had gone home 'without killing or maiming any body'![125] Clearly, the London Tories would not stay away from the great Reform meeting scheduled for the neighbouring township of Westminster in early October. Thus John Grieve, a thirty-year-old Scots Lowland farmer and a member of Proudfoot's Presbyterian congregation, in giving John Talbot notice of the assembly, added that it would 'be well to advertise that as some evil-disposed persons having endeavoured to organize a mob to disturb the proceedings on the day of the meeting it is desirable that those who attend will come *prepared* to maintain the peace. We learn on good authority that a riot is intended.'[126]

Before the Westminster meeting, however, the local Reformers organized their own gathering on the second concession of that township, possibly on 5 October, to form a political union and choose provincial delegates.[127] On 6 October the Middlesex Liberal meeting was scheduled but before it could take place the field where the Reformers were to assemble was taken over by the Conservatives from London. The *London Gazette*, one of two Tory papers in the area (the other being the *Brantford Sentinel*), stated that those Tories mustered numbered 400.[128] They consisted of only '150 squalid Orangemen and "NEGROES!"' retorted the *Liberal*.[129] (The negroes came from Wilberforce, a small colony of Ohio blacks north of London.) Intimidating those Reformers already gathered, the Tories proposed and passed a number of resolutions including a declaration that the Lower Canadian malcontents had displayed an anti-commercial, agricultural disposition by refusing to improve the Saint Lawrence and by taxing both British immigrants and the timber and produce from Upper Canada. Such practices, the meeting affirmed, had harmed the upper province's commercial and agricultural interests. A series of resolutions decried the agitation raised in the London district, pronounced the loyalists' determination to resist rebellion, and declared that, should those who were spreading sedition and seducing others from their allegiance 'incur our vengeance, their day of mercy we must consider past.' Those present demanded that the provincial executive arrest William Lyon Mackenzie for treason and sedition. Among those they praised for loyalty was 'that truly constitutional personage,' the Catholic bishop, Alexander Macdonell.[130] The meeting concluded, according to the *Gazette*, with the disarming of 'a few disaffected Yankee scamps,'[131] although the *Liberal* later insisted that the Tories' proceedings had rapidly terminated on the approach of the main body of Reformers.

Liberals poured into the grounds from the Middlesex townships of London, Delaware, Dorchester, Lobo, Westminster, and Yarmouth, and from a few of the Oxford townships. The *Liberal* claimed that the gathering of 900 to 1,000 persons represented the largest crowd ever drawn together in the London district, adding that: 'It is true there were none of the Squirearchy there, none of the Office-holders, none of the half-pay half-witted Aristocrats, but the cultivators and OWNERS of the land were there, the Workingmen were there – the people and intelligence of the country were there.'[132]

Once assembled, the Reformers, many of whom were armed, proceeded to the customary resolutions, some of which were similar to those adopted in Sparta on 9 September. Their expression of dissatisfaction with an irresponsible government, their declaration that petitions to Britain were futile, their sympathy for the Lower Canadian Reformers, and their naming of delegates for Westminster and Lobo all had Spartan counterparts. In addition, they decried the act prolonging the life of the assembly and the existence of a Tory mob in the Home district. More seriously, they expressed discontent with the colonial system which, they said, enriched Britain while saddling Upper Canada with a ruthless and corrupt government. Their prime concern, however, was the economy. No fewer than four of their fourteen resolutions voiced grave anxiety over the depressed economic life of the province and attributed it to the lack of good government.[133] Thus to these Reformers, most of whom were farmers, the depression was of vital concern even though the 1837 crop had improved over that of the previous year. The improvement had not been sufficient, however, for, as Proudfoot noted, the 1837 harvest 'will do no more than support the farmers' families, at least in this district.'[134] They would have little left, he observed, to pay their debts with the merchants.

The Westminster meeting, which ended with 'a *fue* [sic] *de joie*,' fired from no less than five hundred guns and pistols,[135] represented the high point of Reform agitation and organization reached that fall in the

73 Political Discontents

London district. Gatherings were yet to come, but they were all to be purely local, none approaching the great Middlesex one in size or enthusiasm. That assembly clearly alarmed the local Tories because on 13 October twenty-three prominent individuals, most from London but some from Bayham, Malahide, and Caradoc, addressed an open letter to James Hamilton, the district sheriff, asking him to call a public meeting to adopt measures to prevent the further gathering of 'great numbers of misguided individuals' bearing 'fire arms and other dangerous weapons.'[136]

That meeting occurred in London on 21 October. The *Liberal* later disputed the Tory claim that 150 people were present, gloating that not even the 'Niggers' of Wilberforce had attended.[137] The important officials of the district were out in force, however, and passed six resolutions deprecating the armed and seditious meetings being conducted. They condemned the tumultuous Radicals of south Yarmouth and its area and declared that the government must suppress the province's incipient rebels.[138]

Head had received a request from Colborne, the lieutenant-general commanding the forces in the Canadas, to send as many men as possible from the Twenty-Fourth regiment to the aid of the constituted authorities in Lower Canada. The lieutenant-governor had assured Colborne he would dispatch all the troops required. Later, he would, in fact, dismiss the Toronto garrison and ask the lieutenant-general to remove all British regulars from the province in order to give the inhabitants of Upper Canada an opportunity to prove the strength of their allegiance to the empire. Doubtless his confidence in the residents of the province led him to assure those attending the London meeting of his intention to uphold the laws of the colony. He was certain 'that for the suppression of sedition and insubordination he will not call in vain upon the vigilance of the Magistracy and the loyalty of the people.'[139]

The Reformers and Tories of the London area settled down to a war of words. On 21 October the *London Gazette* warned the armed 'banditti' of the south of Yarmouth, who were, the paper said, 'ruffians ... composed mostly of young men having no property in the country,' that their days were numbered if they persisted 'in their nefarious work.' The *Liberal* was by now in the vanguard of agitation perhaps in part because its owner, Bela Shaw, had been chosen a delegate by the political union formed at Sparta on 9 September.

Few issues of the paper are extant for 1837 but a copy of the 2 November issue has survived. It was full of items calculated to heat inflamed tempers. Referring obliquely to an act allowing the district justices to establish much-needed houses of industry, it declared that the assembly had legislated into existence a poor-law system which could be used to incarcerate Reformers as paupers. Head had spies everywhere, it continued, adding that some local magistrates were considering prosecuting *Liberal* subscribers under the summary punishments act. The journal, which devoted copious space to the doings of Reformers in both Canadas, reported an admittedly unauthenticated rumour that the Lower Canadians intended to burn Montreal and Quebec and added that Robert Gourlay was apparently going to lead an invasion into Upper Canada from Ohio. Conciliation must be quick or Canada would be forever lost to England.

Despite the combined efforts of Conservative and Reform journals, passions subsided in the weeks succeeding the Tories' meeting of 21 October. J.B. Askin, the district clerk, however, took it upon himself to investigate the loyalty of two postmasters with whom he was not acquainted, including the one at Norwich, 'a regular nest of Radicals.' He also kept an eye on certain individuals who 'are looking out for the favor of the people at the present crisis of affairs, who would like to be considered as very faithful and loyal subjects to the Government.'[140]

Although Askin may have been active, Charles Latimer, a prominent young English Reformer who operated a store in London, observed on 5 November that 'nothing has transpired hereabouts worthy of notice. The Tories ... seem to have left off the [sic] flogging the Radicals.'[141] The Reformers were also quiet. Even though they published the news that delegates had been chosen for the impending provincial convention from the Middlesex townships of Yarmouth, Westminster, Lobo, Delaware, London, and Dorchester,[142] they had not held any meetings to organize political unions in the last three townships.

In the latter part of October the Reform impetus swung from Middlesex to Oxford where the efforts of local politicians like Eliakim Malcolm were joined by those of Charles Duncombe. After returning from England in November 1836, Duncombe had appeared in the assembly on 2 December but for the remainder of the session, which lasted until 4 March, his attendance was at best irregular. Certainly, his brother, David, attended far more often than he.[143] Charles was evidently lethargic and depressed and was relatively inactive in the mobilization of the Reformers in the few months after the declaration at Doel's brewery. A report of 4 September stated that he had been in London for a few days to plan a forthcoming gathering of the radical faction, possibly the one at

75 Political Discontents

Westminster.[144] Despite this, he never appeared at any of the Middlesex meetings and, when he finally did rouse himself in the fall, he confined his efforts to Oxford county. In late October he wrote to Robert Davis of Nissouri, author of *The Canadian Farmer's Travels*, to tell him of an impending gathering and to indulge in some political reflections. The refusal of the colonial secretary to see him in 1836 still rankled and he noted 'that it is high time for the reformers to be up and doing,' as the 'doors of the colonial office are closed against reformers' and the province was labouring 'under the dynasty of a foreign governor and an Orange oligarchy' and suffering deeply for it. In view of the fact that he had years ago condemned Mackenzie's publication of Hume's 'baneful domination' letter, it is significant that Duncombe now insisted 'that while this baneful denomination [sic] continues, we have not the slightest chance for prosperity, and that if we will be governed we must govern ourselves,' because the sole interest of the province's oppressors was 'the plunder they can amass and carry away with them.' He observed that 'a Nation can never rebel,' inasmuch as 'those only are rebels who resist the will of the people, from them, the people emanates all legitimate Constitutional Government.' Rather melodramatically, he announced that 'the time has come when we are to decide whether we will be bondsmen or slaves.'[145]

On 2 November, a meeting was held in Oakland township attended by some two to three hundred people from as far away as Bayham in Middlesex and doubtless involving Reformers of the nearby Norfolk townships and adjacent Burford and Brantford. Duncombe addressed the gathering with 'eloquence and spirit' and Eliakim Malcolm spoke at 'considerable length' and enumerated the Liberals' grievances.[146] One observer, Cyrus Moore of Burford, alleged that 'Malcolm was particularly violent in his language and said he was determined to support Papineau and McKenzie [sic].'[147]

The meeting adopted nine resolutions, most of which were similar to those passed at Sparta and Westminster. The Oakland concourse did, however, sound one new and rather ominous note. The legislative assembly had been elected by corrupt means. This, together with the fact that it had unconstitutionally prolonged its life on the death of the King, robbed it of any validity. Those Reformers at the meeting would thus not consider any laws passed by it as binding.[148] For the first time, then, a direct denial was made of a constituted provincial authority, a denial coupled with the threat of widespread civil disobedience.

The increasing Reform agitation evidently unnerved some Oxford county settlers. American Indians had moved into the backwoods of

Zorra, gathering, some feared, to organize plundering expeditions. As it turned out, their intentions were peaceful but, as Philip Graham, a North Oxford magistrate, explained, 'It will not be surprising that the sudden appearance of such strangers should, in these particular times, create some anxiety and various surmises among the loyal subjects of Her Majesty, which the few rebels would not be backward in encouraging.'[149]

If the discovery that the Indians were peaceful calmed the frayed nerves of the 'loyal subjects,' the 16 November meeting of the Reformers at West Oxford doubtless helped to unsettle them again. This assembly was intended to encompass the Reformers of the three Oxfords, and of Dereham, Zorra, and Nissouri townships. Elisha Hall, an Upper Canadian-born mill owner, wrote to the *Liberal* advising of the gathering and wondered if the province's inhabitants should not look 'for some constitution more natural to the free soil of America, and the free spirit of Britons, than Head's despotism, the family compact, and Orange ascendancy.'[150] Duncombe was at this meeting, and spoke for two hours to a crowd estimated by the Tories at 150 to 250 people and by the Reformers at 250 to 300 persons.

The resolutions adopted by the West Oxford assembly were similar to those agreed upon at Sparta on 9 September, at Middlesex on 6 October, and at Oakland on 2 November. There was, however, an oft-repeated threat of physical violence. Those there claimed that Head intended disarming the provincial militia, for he 'has entered into some base and treasonable alliance with the king of Hanover and other European tyrants.' They enjoined the province's inhabitants not to allow themselves to be denuded of weapons, and proclaimed the right of the oppressed Lower Canadians 'at whatever risk' to resist tyranny. If the London Tories harmed any Reform leader, those assembled declared they would consider the provincial administration of laws inadequate and retaliate with 'a just and terrible judgement.' The Oakland meeting had spoken of ignoring provincial laws; the Oxford gathering countenanced violence. Clearly, the resolutions of the two Oxford county meetings held in November were far less moderate than those adopted by the Middlesex meeting a month earlier.

The West Oxford gathering was also notable for its mention of some specific grievances ignored by the other three meetings: the operation of the trade acts involving American goods, the sale of lands to the Canada Company, the granting of large blocks of land to private individuals, and the administration of the Clergy Reserves.[151] Some of these grievances may have been cited in an attempt to win the support of the Highland

77 Political Discontents

Scots of Zorra who bordered the property of the Canada Company, were perhaps affected by its alleged despotism, and, as members of the Church of Scotland, were not disposed to side with the government on the Clergy Reserves issue. The Kirk's claim for a division of the Clergy Reserves revenues had been rejected by government officers in the assembly, and the church's congregations had organized a mission to Great Britain to present their case there. If the issues of land granting and Clergy Reserves were raised by the Oxford Reformers to win the support of the Zorra Highlanders, they were to be disappointed for the Scots had previously scheduled a loyal meeting to be held at Embro on the termination of the Radicals' gathering in West Oxford.[152]

The Highland Scots of Lobo township in Middlesex, who were Baptists and Secessionist Presbyterians and reputed by the *Liberal* to be 'staunch Reformers,'[153] proved little more amenable to the persuasions of the Radicals than their Zorra brethren. Their township was the scene of a Reform meeting on 16 November. The *London Gazette* jubilantly reported that scarcely ten men were present, besides those from Westminster and three or four from the town of London. 'The Scotch of Lobo are not revolutionists,' the paper declared, because they had not attended the meeting in any great numbers,[154] although the secretary of the gathering, Hugh Carmichael, was a Scot. One Reformer who had been there, when asked if the Highlanders had turned out, angrily replied, 'No, God damn them they know nothing; it takes a year to learn them anything.'[155]

The tempo of agitation in Middlesex had clearly decreased, although on 17 November thirty-two people, including Duncombe's brother, Elijah, organized a political union in St Thomas. Among the officers chosen were Bela Shaw and John Talbot.[156] The last political union organized in the London district prior to the rebellion was in the township of Delaware, whose Reformers purportedly had already selected their delegates.[157] On 2 December, some twenty people, most from Delaware with a few from the adjacent townships of Caradoc and Westminster, met. Alvaro Ladd, a local merchant, spoke and allegedly suggested that those present form an agreement not to pay taxes,[158] though Ladd himself later recalled he had merely proposed that those joining the political union 'use all lawful means to reduce the revenues of the Government in every manner that laid in their power.'[159] Reportedly, he advised those in attendance to prepare themselves for defence.[160]

Gideon Tiffany, a sixty-year-old American-born farmer and long-term resident of Delaware, also addressed the meeting, counselling his hearers to pursue a course of civil disobedience by not paying the taxes imposed by the provincial government. He also proposed that the province, to avoid the horrors of revolution, should secure a 'peaceable separation' from the mother country.[161] Apparently, a resolution in favour of severing colonial ties passed without opposition. The meeting established the 'Delaware Reform Association or Branch Political Union,' securing the membership of ten or fifteen people. Late-comers could join by signing the constitution posted in Ladd's store.[162] Delegates were not named to the provincial convention, presumably because Ladd and Tiffany had already been publicly designated as Delaware's representatives.

IV

As the rebellion approached, the west was generally quiet. Most historians of the period believe that the Reformers held about 200 meetings in the province in the late summer and fall of 1837.[163] If that is correct (which is doubtful), then certainly the Liberals of the western peninsula were inactive, particularly in the month or so prior to the outbreak of the rebellion and in comparison to the Reformers elsewhere in Upper Canada. In Middlesex county in November and early December the local Reformers organized only three gatherings, all poorly attended. The Middlesex gathering of 6 October remained the high point. In early and mid-November the Oxford county Liberals conducted two relatively strident meetings but then ceased their activity. David Duncombe and his fellow Norfolk Reformers met not at all.

To the north of Middlesex and Oxford counties, in the Huron Tract, there was some Reform activity, promoted largely by one man, Anthony Van Egmond. He organized a meeting of dissatisfied settlers on 10 November but it was concerned primarily with the grievances harboured against the reputedly overbearing and rapacious Canada Company and not with the traditional complaints of the province's Reformers. Those present resolved to send two delegates to Mackenzie's proposed convention.

To the east, the Gore district was relatively quiescent. Throughout 1837 Reformers there had been on the retreat in and about Hamilton. In February the Reform paper, the *Hamilton Free Press*, had closed, at least temporarily, leaving the *Hamilton Express* alone. Despite the assertion on 6 November of John G. Parker, a wealthy American-born merchant, that throughout the Gore district political unions were formed and ready to 'ACT *at an hour's notice*,'[164] a political union was not established at

79 Political Discontents

Hamilton until 24 November. Evidently only twenty people attended its organizational meeting.[165] Towards the end of November Reformers did meet at Wellington Square (present-day Burlington) to form a rifle company and apparently create a political union as well.[166] Their Guelph counterparts, however, failed to found their projected union.

The Niagara district, like the Gore district, was also relatively quiet. The editor of the *St. Catharines Journal* was not alarmed by whatever agitation existed in his region,[167] an agitation that was largely confined to the Short Hills area south of the town, and even there a political union was not organized until early December.[168]

The impetus for rebellion clearly came from the Home district and from Mackenzie in particular. Mackenzie had been in contact with the Lower Canadian Reformers, who were rapidly moving in the direction of an armed confrontation with the provincial authorities. In early November he set off up Yonge Street in Toronto to canvass the unions of the area about the wisdom of revolt. Although the extent to which he consulted others in Toronto and its vicinity about the practicality of insurrection has given rise to heated debate, there is little room for doubt that he did not confer with the leading Reform politicians of the London district on the subject of rebellion; all that fall he had had remarkably little contact with them. Indeed, on 18 October, Mackenzie denied that he had drafted the resolutions for the meetings held in the London district, adding that he did 'not recollect writing a line in politics to any person in that district for months past.'[169] His memory appears to have been accurate. In Middlesex county John Talbot and a group of politicians about St Thomas and London were primarily responsible for organizing the Reform agitation. The only correspondence extant between Mackenzie and any of these individuals is a relatively innocuous letter from John Talbot to Mackenzie of 21 November.[170] Talbot evidently wrote to his fellow editor in his capacity as secretary of the newly formed St Thomas political union.

Eliakim Malcolm and Charles Duncombe were the principals in the mobilization of the Oxford and northern Norfolk county Reformers, though Sir John Colborne assumed that this honour belonged to Duncombe's fellow assemblyman, Robert Alway.[171] Mackenzie had remarkably little contact with Malcolm and Duncombe that autumn and no correspondence has survived. In fact, Duncombe and Mackenzie, who were to be the two chief leaders of insurrection in the province, were not particularly close either before or after the rebellion. In 1838 and 1839 Duncombe sent only a few formal letters to Mackenzie and Mackenzie evidently regarded the doctor with suspicion.[172] The lack of communication and warmth between them in these years was in accord with their previous personal relations, however.

Though Mackenzie had apparently been thinking of revolt for some time, he and his co-conspirators in Toronto seem not to have determined until late November to raise an insurrection. Duncombe, in fact, later concluded that Mackenzie had not made the decision until a week or so prior to the actual outbreak.[173] Mackenzie recalled afterwards that, revolt once settled upon, in only one instance had notice of the intended rebellion been sent 'beyond the limits of the County of York.'[174] The notice apparently was not sent to Duncombe, however. In 1838 he complained bitterly that, though he had seen Mackenzie in November 1837 at Niagara during the editor's trial for libel over charges he had made concerning the operation of the Welland Canal, Mackenzie had not then given him 'the least hint' of his intention to raise a rebellion,[175] and presumably had not done so thereafter. In 1838, moreover, William H. Draper, the province's solicitor-general who examined the outbreak of revolt in Toronto and in the west, reluctantly declared that 'little has appeared to establish any previous concert or general agreement to co-operate' between the rebels of the two areas.[176]

On 24 November, one day after rebellion had erupted in Lower Canada, Mackenzie once again rode up Yonge Street, this time to gather insurgents. Presumably, he and his cohorts, including Norfolk's member of the assembly, John Rolph, who lived in Toronto, intended to secure control of Toronto and organize a provincial convention. Mackenzie's paper on 15 November published the draft of a new provincial constitution predicated upon the province's gaining independence from Great Britain and incorporating many elective features of those state government constitutions to the south. On 29 November, Mackenzie's journal avowed that the task of creating revolution in the province was 'a bible duty.'

Clearly, rebellion in Upper Canada was imminent. In the Home district radicalism was strong and members of political unions had met and drilled under the guise of conducting turkey shoots. There was no such training in the London district, a hopeful sign that the Reformers there would exercise restraint. Such was the opinion of J.B. Askin who on 12 November doubted that the Radicals of the district would move beyond mere agitation. His belief was founded in part on the assumption that the Liberals lacked leadership. He was 'happy to say few very few men of property and none of character' had attended the Reformers' meetings.[177]

81 Political Discontents

Despite the apparent tranquillity of the London district after the great Middlesex gathering, there were ominous portents. The young men of the south of Yarmouth and the surrounding locality had demonstrated an alarming willingness to carry arms to their meetings. Though they had not been assembled in a group since Middlesex, their obvious spirit of rebelliousness had helped produce a breakdown of law and order along the lakefront of Yarmouth where 'a young ruffian defied the Law Officers at the point of his rifle for weeks together.'[178] In Oxford county, in the south alone – in Norwich, in Oakland, and in West Oxford – three political unions existed. Moreover, the resolves adopted in November at Oakland and West Oxford demonstrated an inclination towards extremism. None the less, there was no reason to think that, at the end of November, rebellion would spontaneously ignite in the London district. The tinder was there. The spark was not.

4
The Revolt

At the provincial capital William Lyon Mackenzie and a small group of Reformers decided to raise an insurrection and, on 24 November, Mackenzie struck north from Toronto to gather about him his Radical supporters. It was a bold stroke he and his co-conspirators had taken and time was of the essence: Toronto, denuded of troops, might well be captured if the Tories were given no opportunity to mobilize those loyal to the existing régime.

Mackenzie himself had prodded the government into action. The provincial administration had previously decided to ignore the armed meetings taking place in the province but the province's executive councillors could not ignore the 29 November issue of Mackenzie's *Constitution*. Its content was '*highly seditious* if not treasonable.'[1] At a meeting on 2 December, the executive council decided that Mackenzie must be arrested and belated precautions taken. Two militia regiments were to be mustered, and the colonels of militia were asked to summon their men to tell them that various persons had gathered in both the London and the Home districts to drill. Those in authority were 'to discountenance' this drilling and 'to discover and make known those who promote and take part' in such activities.[2]

Dr John Rolph, one of the rebel chieftains, learned of the executive council meeting on the very day it was held and quickly deduced the nature of its discussion. He obviously felt that Mackenzie's personal safety and freedom, and perhaps his own, were now endangered. The rebels, he decided, must move quickly. It has been a matter of sharp and often vindictive controversy whether or not Rolph literally ordered Mackenzie to muster the insurgents at Toronto on 4 December, three days earlier than planned, or whether he merely suggested the change in date. It is

83 The Revolt

certain, however, that Rolph did send a message to Mackenzie, that two of Mackenzie's lieutenants, Lount and Anderson, received it before it reached 'Little Mac,' that in consequence they decided to move their men to the outskirts of the capital on 4 December, and that this rescheduling of events severely jeopardized the revolt's already slim chances of success. On 3 December Mackenzie learned of the premature movement of Lount and Anderson's men. Furious, he spurred his way southward, arriving at Montgomery's Tavern a few hours before Lount and Anderson but still too late to reverse the march of events.

The rebellion, whatever its initial prospects, had little chance of success. Its haphazard, ill-planned nature ensured that. R.B. Sullivan, the province's commissioner of Crown lands, noted later: 'Had the rebel leaders taken time to organize a really dangerous plan of insurrection there can be no doubt that it would have been discovered and the leaders would have been arrested and punished but the fact was that little was discovered because there was little to discover. The state of affairs in Lower Canada and the vigilance of this Government hurried McKenzie [*sic*] and his adherents into a premature rising.'[3]

The revolt was short-lived as well as premature. The fourth of December had almost passed before the citizens of Toronto learned of the danger to the capital. Head and the various government officers readied the defences of the city and sent out dispatch-riders summoning aid. A foray led by Mackenzie south towards the capital on 5 December ended with rebel troops running in one direction and the members of a small defensive guard in the other. On 6 December volunteers poured in upon the city.

Thirty-nine-year-old Allan MacNab of Hamilton was one of those volunteers. Tory assemblyman, Speaker of the House, merchant, hotel keeper, steamship line operator, land speculator *par excellence*, and would-be railroad entrepreneur, MacNab was a prominent man and one who cherished his and his family's military exploits. His father had been a lieutenant with John Graves Simcoe's Queen's Rangers and, during the War of 1812, young MacNab himself had fought with the Forty-Ninth Foot. At the end of the war he had reluctantly left the military but had found peacetime existence humdrum. Accordingly, he had misspent a number of years before settling down in Hamilton to a busy legal and commercial career. He had maintained his military connections by serving as an officer in the militia, rising to the rank of lieutenant-colonel. When news came to him on 5 December of the rebellion, he felt duty-bound and even eager to respond, especially because he and

Mackenzie were old enemies. MacNab had been elected to the assembly in 1830 as a Tory and had played a vital role in Mackenzie's five expulsions from the House in 1831-2.

MacNab quickly gathered sixty-five men and steamed off across the lake to Toronto. There he found the citizens frightened, the authorities confused. Head was delighted to see him and anxious to give him command of the loyalist forces, evidently feeling that he had more energy and enterprise than the senior officer on the spot, Acting Adjutant General of Militia Colonel James Fitzgibbon. The latter protested mightily. Consequently, on the seventh, he became the titular, MacNab the actual leader of the 1,200 or so loyalists marched north to meet Mackenzie's far smaller force. A few shots and a short skirmish at Montgomery's Tavern saw the rebels disperse and MacNab and his men triumphant. Mackenzie's revolt was over but for many a rebel the suffering had only begun. MacNab, however, not only had sent an old enemy scurrying off once more, but also had helped save from the rebel chieftain's grasp many leading members of the Family Compact, the very people who had systematically obstructed a number of MacNab's commercial schemes and opposed his political ambitions.[4] He was now in the enviable position of having demonstrated his worth to them and of having placed them in his debt.

I

News of the outbreak at Toronto had spread rapidly along the province's main highways and waterways. When MacNab had received word of the rebellion on 5 December he had not only resolved to lead a contingent of men to the beleaguered capital but also to alert the west. He had immediately dispatched a messenger along the Ancaster road to Brantford some twenty-five miles distant. That evening, Colonel James Racey of Brantford had before him the intelligence from Toronto and orders to muster the local militia.[5] By 7 December, news of the revolt reached London[6] and radiated from there and from other centres along the secondary roads into the remote townships.

Almost everywhere the first reports of the rebellion were confused. Initial accounts in St Catharines had the rebels in possession of the bank and the person of the lieutenant-governor, 'facts' soon contradicted.[7] In London there were a variety of rumours.[8] Initially, however, the version of events throughout the province had Toronto taken and the rebels victorious.

85 The Revolt

Tidings of the supposedly successful revolt at Toronto were carried into the Burford-Oakland area by a youthful Reformer, George Washington Case of Hamilton. He also conveyed the alarming report that the sheriff intended jailing Charles Duncombe and one of the Malcolms,[9] doubtless Eliakim, presumably because the active roles the two had taken in the Reform agitation fostered suspicions that they were involved in the rebellion. Case may also have brought word of the arrest on 5 December of John G. Parker of Hamilton. Several of Parker's letters which showed how severely his loyalty had been compromised had come to the attention of the local authorities who, on hearing that insurrection had broken out in Toronto, had had no hesitation in jailing the unfortunate merchant, believing that he was an important link in a chain of conspirators. If Case did, in fact, bring the news of Parker's detention, it would have added credibility to his assertion that Duncombe and Malcolm were also to be imprisoned.

Evidently, Duncombe was convinced of the truth of the rumour that he was to be arrested. On 11 December, when he received word that no warrant existed for his apprehension, he decided he 'dare not' take the risk that such assurances were authentic.[10] To save himself and possibly some Reform associates, he decided to emulate Mackenzie by raising the standard of revolt. His resolve to act was doubtless strengthened by his belief that Mackenzie's men had triumphed at Toronto, that Lower Canada's rebels had been successful, and that a bold stroke could relieve the province of its Tory yoke.

The Home district revolt had been scheduled originally for 7 December. It is clear that Duncombe had no prior knowledge of the intention to rebel on that date and that he was not acting in concert with Mackenzie because he mobilized the Radicals of his area only on 6 December, shortly after he learned of the Toronto outbreak. On the sixth, he must have conferred with Eliakim Malcolm of nearby Oakland in Oxford county about the seriousness of the situation and the steps which they were obliged to take. That day Duncombe sent letters to some of the more prominent Reformers of the nearby townships. One of those to whom he wrote was Solomon Lossing, a Norwich justice of the peace and a lapsed Quaker, informing him of the Toronto rebellion and suggesting that a public meeting be held in Norwich. Some three hours after the arrival of his letter, Duncombe and several other men entered the Norwich village of Sodom, where people had already mustered. Here, Duncombe spread the report that warrants were out for the arrest of the province's leading Reformers. At least three individuals were told that their personal freedom and safety were in imminent danger.[11] The report appears to have been generally accepted.

On 7 December Duncombe held a meeting at Sodom during which he reportedly stated that writs had been issued against all the leading men of the Liberal party and that he himself had been forced to flee to Norwich for safety. Those in power, he said, would not allow complaints or petitions to reach the young queen. Adding that people throughout the province were rising against the tyrants in the colony, he advised those assembled to take up arms.[12] His appeal was successful and a group of men was organized, ostensibly for 'the defence' of Norwich.[13]

On Saturday, 9 December, or possibly on Friday, 8 December, a second meeting was convened. The majority of the 200 to 300 people attending were inhabitants of Norwich, although a few came from East and West Oxford and, possibly, from Dereham. They heard Duncombe, one of their members of the provincial assembly, describe the attempt of the Toronto authorities to arrest William Lyon Mackenzie in order 'to put him to death without a trial.' They heard, too, of the rising of the Toronto populace to free their tribune. Duncombe added that a 'Mr. Park' had been thrown into the Hamilton jail, and he forecast 'that all the reformers would be kidnapped and suffer without any trial, unless the people rose and opposed the Government.' Pointing out that Head had publicly declared he would not grant Upper Canada the British Constitution, Duncombe insisted that English precedent conferred upon the people the right to rise in 'a formidable body' to secure desired laws and changes. Upper Canada needed, he reasoned, an elected council 'and a Cheap and responsible Government.' Mackenzie, Eliakim Malcolm, and himself had conferred, he added, and had decided 'to raise as many men as they could.' In this way, they would be able 'to demand what they wanted, and it should be granted.'[14] Some eighty people were thus persuaded to enlist in the cause of rebellion and to begin drilling. After the meeting, these incipient rebels did not hesitate, sure as they were of their strength, to resort to threats in order to persuade people to take up arms.[15]

The assembly adjourned and a vigilance committee was established in the township comprising the officers chosen by those enlisted and several prominent township Reformers and presided over by Duncombe himself.[16] On the eve of the departure of the Norwich 'soldiers' for Oakland, a 'Home Department' of the committee was organized, 'the duties whereof seemed to be to remain behind in order to collect Stragglers and send on any Volunteers that might come in from surrounding settlements.'[17] The department's members actively collected arms within the township even after the departure of the rebels and harassed the local Tories as well.[18]

On 12 December, after a deputation from Eliakim Malcolm and his brothers apparently brought word to Duncombe of the state of preparations in their area, the Norwich rebels mustered to march to Oakland. The lowest contemporary figure quoted for the number of those enrolled was 100,[19] but the most common, and perhaps most reliable, estimate was that 200 men had assembled.[20] John Treffry, an English settler of pacifist principles who had resisted the arguments of the rebels as he was to resist those of the loyalist troops, observed the departure of Duncombe's men. He had heard with some disquiet the reports spread by Duncombe, including the rumours that Mackenzie had virtually captured Toronto and that the Lower Canadians had taken Quebec City and were preparing to defend their province against expected British attacks. Treffry reported that Duncombe addressed his troops before they set off and suggested that, as they might have to call on the United States for aid, they hoist the liberty flag, and lower the one emblazoned 'British constitution and the rights of the people.' Treffry was obviously opposed to the mustering of Duncombe's men, reporting that, as they left, 'the foolish deluded people ... went on crying the British Constitution and the rights of the people, but all the rebels knew the cheat.'[21]

Duncombe led the Norwich men to Oakland township, for it was here that the local rebels were to gather, Oakland being a radical stronghold close to the town of Brantford – the obvious objective of initial rebel military action. On 6 or 7 December, when news of Mackenzie's bold stroke at Toronto had first arrived, people began to gather in Oakland township in response to rumours that 'the most cruel and oppressive measures' were to be taken against the province's Reformers in retaliation for the rebellion in the Home district. It was also said that the Grand River Indians intended launching 'a barbarous attack' upon the residents of the neighbouring area. Further, the defensive measures advocated by the leaders of disaffection were 'impudently' declared to have been 'approved of by their Sovereign and her Ministers at Home.'[22]

Eliakim Malcolm and William McGuire, a local school-teacher, were the most active promoters of the rebel cause in Oakland. They quickly identified themselves as insurgents and asserted that they were cooperating with Mackenzie at Toronto.[23] In reality, however, they had no connection with Mackenzie and, like Duncombe with whom they were in contact, were doubtless frightened by the report that prominent Reformers were being arrested, and were encouraged to revolt by the news of apparent rebel successes in the Home district and in Lower Canada.

Both Malcolm and McGuire addressed a meeting at Scotland village in Oakland on 7 December. Some fifty to one hundred people were present from the townships of Oakland, Burford, Windham, and Townsend. Edwin Guillet has claimed that at this meeting a committee was formed to co-operate with Mackenzie's provisional government,[24] but no mention of such a committee can be found in the documents of the day. Nevertheless, Malcolm and McGuire did call for volunteers to march to the support of the supposedly triumphant Mackenzie at Toronto and were rewarded with the declaration of fifty-two individuals that they would 'bear arms in the cause of Reform.'[25] That same day, rebels were seen drilling in Scotland, and Eliakim Malcolm was heard to say that the Oakland men were going to Hamilton to free Parker,[26] whose incarceration had become a tangible symbol of the evil intents of Tory officialdom. His name became a rebel rallying cry.

Preparations in Oakland and its vicinity were quickly pushed ahead. On the ninth there was drilling in Scotland involving from 50 to 120 people. Armed guards were given to Eliakim Malcolm and to several of his brothers who were involved in the revolt,[27] evidently to prevent their arrest and imprisonment by officials sent from Brantford. Persons of questionable political affiliation were harassed. Duncan McDermid, a resident of Mount Pleasant in Brantford township, recalled that William McGuire had had him locked up for four hours and that he was only 'librated under a promise extorted from him, that he should go home and not bear arms against' the rebels.[28] Similarly, John Book of Scotland was detained by order of Eliakim Malcolm, and 'charged to remain at home until Brantford was taken.'[29] A Brantford township tavernkeeper, Henry Merwin, was kept captive by those assembled and released only after his neighbour, William Lyons, a known Radical sympathizer, swore that 'he knew Merwin to be a reformer for some length of time.'[30] Job Tripp, a clerk in Abraham Cook's store in Mount Pleasant, was arrested by the rebels because his loyalties were suspect.[31] Tripp, however, later redeemed his character in the insurgents' eyes by helping them secure powder from his employer's premises. The rebels also contemplated seizing the Long Point mail lest knowledge of their assembling be spread throughout the countryside. Though a group of insurgents under William McGuire was evidently embodied to accomplish the task,[32] it never actually carried out the project.

On 12 December, Eliakim Malcolm and his thirty-eight-year-old brother James led an armed party of some eighty men into the village of Waterford in the township of Townsend where they held a meeting, chaired by James L. Green, a local merchant who professed to fear that a warrant was out for his arrest.[33] Malcolm spoke, assuring his audience that

Mackenzie had Toronto under siege and that the Lower Canadian rebels had been victorious: the entire country was 'in the possession of their party.' Malcolm promised reserve lots to those who enlisted in the rebel cause and pointed out that those who signed a paper circulated among the audience 'should remain in the quiet possession of their property & c.'[34] Presumably, those who did not sign the document, likely a recruiting circular, were not to be so fortunate. After the meeting, the Malcolms led their followers back to Oakland, taking with them arms they had requisitioned in Waterford.[35] By the twelfth, Eliakim and his confederates had raised some 200 men in and about Oakland.[36]

The Malcolms of the Burford-Oakland region did not restrict their recruiting activities to their own particular area. The second son of Finlay Malcolm the elder, sixty-year-old Daniel, had moved from Oakland township to the tenth concession of Bayham. His thirty-eight-year-old son, also named Finlay, occupied a nearby farm. Radicalism had seemingly influenced the entire Malcolm family; at least one Tory acquaintance, Cyrus Moore of Burford, thought them 'all bad enough.'[37] About 7 December, James Malcolm of Oakland wrote to his nephew Finlay of Bayham informing him of Mackenzie's victory at Toronto and urging him to bring men to Oakland where others would muster before marching to free innocent men in the Hamilton jail. He suggested that the province's Reformers were in a position to stage a bloodless coup.[38] James' letter may have been responsible for introducing into Bayham and southern Dereham both the report of 7 December that Lower Canada was in a state of general revolt[39] and the rumour of 8 December that 'George G. Parker [sic] of Hamilton was in Gaol at Hamilton that he was to have a mock trial and then to be hung.'[40] If these rumours had preceded the arrival of his letter, they could only have heightened its impact.

His uncle's call-to-arms stirred Finlay Malcolm to activity. He travelled to Yarmouth to alert the Radicals there to the news and to the need for action. He probably took with him his uncle's letter, as it appeared in the hands of Reformers in both Yarmouth and Southwold.[41] In Bayham he mustered the local Liberals, passing on the message that three Reform leaders had been jailed at Hamilton and that 'all of them below' wished the Bayham men to meet them at Oakland in order to go to Hamilton to free the prisoners.[42] A 'union paper,' intended to get those singing 'to stand together,' was circulated through the northern concessions of Bayham.[43] On 10 December, some twenty-five or thirty men left the township from Richmond,[44] and marched north-east to Dereham Forge. Here, on the eleventh, Malcolm addressed the assembled inhabitants, assuring them that if they turned out, 'they would have things go in their own way without much difficulty.'[45] 'Seven or eight hands' from George Tillson's foundry at the Forge joined the little group.[46]

The Radicals of south Yarmouth had won a good deal of notoriety in the fall of 1837 for their armed attendance at various Reform meetings and were obviously considered by many to be potential rebels. Supposedly, on 6 December Mackenzie dispatched two men bearing messages for Duncombe. These emissaries never reached him despite assertions to the contrary[47] and may, in fact, have never been sent. A Home district Radical, however, did arrive on 9 December in the south of Yarmouth to preach rebellion. He was Martin Switzer, a fifty-nine-year-old Streetsville resident and an acquaintance of Mackenzie's. Although he may not have been sent by Mackenzie, some individuals made the logical assumption that he had.[48] In any event, Switzer was in Yarmouth, drawn there by the known radicalism of the area and by his acquaintance with Elias Moore, a Quaker resident who had been elected as a member of the assembly for Middlesex in 1834 and 1836 and chosen on 9 September 1837 as a delegate of the Sparta political union to the projected Toronto convention.

Duncombe was also aware of the suport that might be mustered in that Quaker township and dispatched Elias Snider, a forty-one-year-old Norwich farmer, to Sparta with a copy of a letter from him 'To our Reform friends in Middlesex.' This document was allegedly signed by about a dozen leading Reformers, including Thomas Parke and Robert Alway, members of the assembly, and by both the *Liberal*'s owner, Bela Shaw, and its editor, John Talbot. The signatories purportedly pledged 'ourselves our lives our properties and sacred honors in the Cause of Reform.' Duncombe's letter declared that the time had come for all Reformers to take up arms. Snider emphasized that appeal by asserting that Mackenzie had 2,000 rebels at Toronto and that Duncombe had raised two Norwich companies of eighty men each.[49]

Both Switzer and Snider attended a small gathering at Sparta on 9 December. Switzer addressed those assembled, telling them that Mackenzie had taken Toronto. If the Reformers of Upper Canada gathered in arms, he added, they could now remedy their grievances without shedding any blood. At the conclusion of the meeting, approximately twenty-five men volunteered to enrol in the rebel 'army.' Four were elected officers.[50]

On Monday, 11 December, a second meeting was held at Sparta to organize the expedition to Oakland. Once again Switzer spoke of the glorious opportunity that lay before the rebels. Apparently, he did not claim that Toronto had fallen but he did state that Mackenzie was within four miles of the city with 5,000 followers. If the Yarmouth men followed him to the capital, he said, fighting would doubtless not be required of them, as the city would be taken long before they arrived. For their exertions, however, they would be well rewarded. Accordingly, those marching to Oakland were enrolled and arrangements were made to set off the following morning.[51]

A few of those who did assemble on 12 December had been at a meeting the night before in the Baptist schoolhouse in the neighbouring township of Malahide. There, Ebenezer Wilcox, an American-born farmer active in the temperance movement who had been conferring with those mustered in Bayham by Finlay Malcolm, reportedly advised the sixty or so people gathered to arm themselves. A political union, described as essential for protecting the lives and property of its members in case of attack from the Tories, was formed with many of those present joining it. A further gathering was planned for Thursday, 14 December, at which time a captain and various officers of the 'defence' force were to be appointed. Those attending were advised to come armed. Enoch Moore, an elderly farmer and a brother of Elias Moore of Yarmouth, was selected to act as captain until Thursday, and was given authority to summon the members of the union should danger threaten.[52]

On the twelfth approximately fifty rebels assembled at Sparta. Some were from Malahide and Southwold, but the majority were residents of the south of Yarmouth and were later described as being a group of 'political fanatics, chiefly young men.'[53] George Lawton, a fifty-one-year old English Quaker who had been selected a provincial delegate by the Sparta meeting of 9 September, and Walter Chase, an Upper-Canadian-born commission merchant of Port Stanley, bolstered the rebels' spirits by informing them that they would be met at Hamilton by reinforcements bringing artillery under the command of Dr John Rolph. Rolph had fled Toronto on 6 December, when the loyalists were rallying that city, and had made his way to Buffalo. Although Chase had very recently been in Buffalo, he evidently had not seen Rolph there; his information about Rolph's activities came from a letter sent from Toronto.[54] It would seem, however, that rebel sympathizers in Buffalo had given Chase assurances of aid that may have led to the claim made at Oakland that the rebels had received one hundred kegs of powder from Uncle Sam.[55] Buoyed by promises of support and the prospect of an easy campaign, the Yarmouth rebels, under tavernkeeper David Anderson, set off in high spirits, some on foot, some riding the two baggage wagons acquired. As elsewhere, those departing left behind persons responsible for mustering further supplies and money to aid the cause.[56]

While Duncombe, Switzer, and the Malcolms had all helped induce the men of south Yarmouth to rebel, Duncombe took upon himself the responsibility of arousing not only Norwich but the other Oxford county townships as well. As early as 6 December, one of his circular letters was passed through Brantford township, which was close to his home, and on through West Oxford.[57] On 9 December, the Hagle family of the north of Dereham received the letter, which called upon them to gather at Oakland and join the forces there, in order 'to show their strength' and to secure the release of a number of persons held in the Gore district jail.[58] On 11 December, Robert Alway, who had also been sent one of Duncombe's letters, met with the Hagles and others in Dereham, and apparently gave a brief résumé of the 'facts' as they were known: Mackenzie had attacked Toronto and Duncombe was raising a force at Oakland. Reportedly, Alway, affirming the numerical superiority of the rebels and the probability of a bloodless coup, advised those assembled to join Duncombe's force.[59] If Alway did give such advice, it was his sole contribution to the rebel cause. He, unlike Duncombe, was not prepared to shoulder arms.

In West Oxford a meeting was scheduled for the Harris Street Baptist Church on 12 December. Attendance at the gathering was urged by one Thomas Putnam, probably a member of the locally prominent Putnams of Dorchester. He spread the report that Toronto was surrounded, that 700 sympathizers had massed at Lewiston ready to cross into the province, and that rebels would be joining Duncombe from Oxford county and from Westminster township. The force gathered under Duncombe would set fire to Brantford town, he added, noting as well that rebel activity would also flare up in and about the village of London.[60] The meeting at Harris Street, however, was a disappointment. Despite the fact that Duncombe's appeal had circulated in Westminster, and that an agent for him had been recruiting in the adjacent township of Dorchester,[61] aid was not forthcoming from either. Local rebels may also have been disheartened by an accident suffered by one of their leaders, Elisha Hall. Hall, an Ingersoll mill owner, had initially been contemptuous of Mackenzie's rebellion, terming it a 'premature squall.'[62] But his attitude had changed, doubtless at Duncombe's prompting, and he was reputedly the selected leader of the rebels of the West Oxford area. Unfortunately, on the morning of 11 December, while journeying to confer with

Duncombe, he had fallen from his horse, hurt his back, and been kicked in the head. He was incapacitated. This had 'struck dismay among those who looked to him as a leader.'[63] Thus, despite the fact that in mid-November the West Oxford region had seemed to be a hotbed of radicalism, only some ten to twenty men left the Harris Street meeting prepared to follow Pelham C. Teeple, the twenty-eight-year-old son of a noted United Empire Loyalist settler, to Oakland.[64]

The rebels were able to attract some support in the townships of Blenheim and Dumfries, which had not been touched to any notable degree by the agitation in the fall. On 12 December, approximately twenty people gathered together in a schoolhouse located nearly on the mid-point of the Blenheim-Dumfries town line. The meeting was apparently summoned to secure volunteers for Duncombe's forces,[65] and speeches were made urging the audience to enlist in the rebel cause. A company of men was formed and instructed to scour the neighbourhood for arms and ammunition. The supplies collected were to be sent to Oakland. At the end of the meeting, then, various individuals visited nearby houses 'often taking such arms and ammunition as they could find.'[66]

On the day of the meeting, Horatio Hills, a farmer's son in his mid-twenties, led nine Blenheim and Dumfries men to Oakland to join the rebel ranks.[67] Hills was extremely zealous in the cause, searching for arms on his way, informing individuals as he went that, if they did not turn out, they would be pressed into service by 'a party sent from Oakland,'[68] and returning to Dumfries to obtain more men and secure the area for the rebels. He was not particularly scrupulous about the methods he used. John Winegarden of Dumfries, a 'husbandman,' found himself taken from his house by Hills and others and prodded southward for ten or twelve miles at the point of Hills' dirk. Poor Winegarden, 'slightly wounded,' was then released at the urging of several of Hills' companions.[69] That same day, James Grigg, who worked for a Galt brewer, met Hills' group, and was ordered to join it. He refused and struggled when two of Hills' men at their leader's orders tried to seize him. Thereupon, 'Hills drew a dagger, & repeatedly wounded [Grigg] ... to the effusion of his Blood.' Like Winegarden, however, Grigg was released and Hills explained to him 'that he had taken him for a spy, & had orders to prevent any person from going to Galt.'[70]

On 13 December, when Sir Francis Bond Head deliberately misled Lord Glenelg by writing to him that, as far as he knew, there were no longer any assembled groups of insurgents in the province,[71] the western rebels had all gathered in the villages of Oakland (Malcolm's Mills) and

Scotland in Oakland township, and were billeted upon the local population.[72] Contemporary documents provide twenty-eight references to the size of Duncombe's 'army.' The lowest estimate was that only 200 had gathered at Oakland; the highest, that 1,600 had assembled. Eight different sources recorded that the rebels had numbered 400, while three more that they consisted of 400 to 500 persons. The latter estimate seems reasonably accurate: some four hundred rebels were thought to have been collected from the Norwich and Oakland areas, over fifty men marched from Yarmouth, and smaller groups left from Dereham and West Oxford, and from Blenheim and Dumfries townships. Among those mustered there were many 'Captains and Colonels ... *but few* Privats.'[73]

The rebel turn-out must have been somewhat disappointing as predictions of a crushing rebel victory, implying massive support for the insurgents' cause, had been freely made. Thus Samuel Marlatt, a Dumfries farmer, disconsolately stated that he had been led to believe that, on reaching Oakland he would find 1,600 men in arms, a number that would swell by 400 or more when Reform contingents came in from some of the farthest townships.[74]

11

As we have seen, the provincial administration knew of the armed meetings taking place in the London district in the fall of 1837 and when revolt broke out in the Home district, government officials looked for a similar rising in the west. As early as 6 or 7 December rumours circulated in Toronto of a rebellion in the western part of the province. On 7 December, while preparations for Duncombe's uprising were yet barely underway, the *St Catharines Journal* mentioned a report that 'a large body of insurgents' had collected in the London district 'and threaten to march down upon Hamilton and Toronto.' That same day Colonel MacNab was directed to proceed immediately to the London district, taking with him some 500 volunteers drawn from the provincial militia, who were to receive pay and allowances for thirty days.[75]

In the west, MacNab was to have the aid of the militiamen of the area as well. Generally, in Upper Canada each county contained several militia regiments, each consisting of all the able-bodied resident males of given townships who were between the ages of sixteen and sixty and who were British subjects by birth or by naturalization. The authorities thus had a ready-made military organization to deal with the rebels. MacNab, of course, had already been in touch with militia officers in and around

95 The Revolt

Brantford, having ordered them out on 5 December in response to the news of the Toronto revolt. On 7 December, the men of the First regiment of the Gore militia began assembling in Brantford and learned of the rebel activity in the area to the west and south-west. Thomas Wallace, a young English merchant of the village of Sodom, who later recalled that preparations for the Duncombe rebellion in Norwich had been quite open, had sent word to Brantford of the activities within the township.[76] On 8 December, Colonel James Racey of Brantford wrote to Colonel Coffin, the adjutant general of militia, to assure him that he would keep him informed of the movements of the people west of Brantford.[77]

By 10 December, MacNab in Hamilton had definite knowledge about the efforts of Charles Duncombe and his allies to raise revolt. On that day, Charles Strange Perley, a thirty-six-year-old Burford farmer and a native of New Brunswick, spoke to Colonel Robert Land of the Hamilton garrison and to three local justices of the peace, telling them that Duncombe had mustered from 100 to 200 men in Norwich and that Eliakim Malcolm had collected an additional sixty at Scotland.[78] On that day as well, Land received a letter declaring that the insurgents intended to rescue Parker from the Hamilton jail.[79] MacNab had all the information he needed to move against the rebels. Volunteers were plentiful, for the local militia had already been mustered in response to earlier unconfirmed reports received in the first week of December that Hamilton was to be attacked.[80] In a few days Allan MacNab would be ready to march against the unsuspecting men gathered under Duncombe and the Malcolms.

It took a few days longer for those along the Lake Erie shore to learn of events in Norwich and Oakland, events in their own area being of prime concern. The first loyalist stirrings in Bayham and Malahide were on 9 December, when Doyle McKenny, the Malahide justice of the peace, wrote 'in great haste' to John Burwell at Port Burwell to warn him that the Bayham Radicals were rising in revolt and were attempting to inflame their Yarmouth brethren.[81] Burwell, who claimed to have warned the lieutenant-governor that a rebellion would occur in his area the moment the signal was given in Lower Canada or in Toronto, immediately conveyed the news to John Joseph, Head's secretary, and recommended that the local militia be summoned into service immediately. Burwell himself was ready to offer his services in defence of Her Majesty's provincial government.[82]

By 11 December, McKenny and Captain Henry Medcalf of Bayham had raised some twenty men from the townships of Bayham and

Malahide. They did not know, however, what actions to take in the best interest of the queen. McKenny wrote to a fellow justice of the peace, Edward Ermatinger of St Thomas, of their dilemma. 'The Boys are manifesting every manly feeling,' he wrote, and 'we have united as one man to march to any part we may [be] told and to give every assistance to [the] Lieutenant-Governor or any lawful authority and to defend our Lawful Sovereign with our lives and property.' He went on, nevertheless, to lament their lack of 'orders [and] armes.' For his own part, McKenny felt that the little loyalist group should pursue the Bayham rebels, who had just lately left for Oakland.[83] That same day, he and seven other men resolved to march at 12:00 M. the following day either to Simcoe or to Hamilton to join the government's supporters presumably gathered there.[84] McKenny and his comrades did not depart, however, for on that day the Yarmouth insurgents, led by David Anderson, entered the townships of Malahide and Bayham.

On the evening of the twelfth, Anderson's party passed from Malahide into Bayham via the Talbot road. Two loyalists rushed to guard the bridge at Big Otter Creek to prevent the Yarmouth party from crossing it. They arrived too late, however, as did fifteen others who went to ambush the rebels at a ravine.[85] That evening at Port Burwell, Captain John Burwell mustered the seven officers and forty-one privates of his militia company who had volunteered for service. He intended intercepting Anderson's party on Talbot Street.[86] The following morning, Captain Henry Medcalf enrolled a second company of militia volunteers which included Doyle McKenny, three other officers, and twenty-eight privates.[87] This force presumably included those individuals who had gathered about McKenny and Medcalf on the eleventh. Neither Burwell's nor Medcalf's company, however, came into contact with the Yarmouth men. The latter set off for Oakland early on the morning of the thirteenth, having been informed of Burwell's anticipated attack upon them by two Bayham men who joined their force, and having learned from two Yarmouth residents that the loyalists of St Thomas and area would soon be in hot pursuit.[88]

Not long after the Yarmouth party had been on the road, two of the rebels, Lyman Davis of Malahide and twenty-four-year-old Benjamin Page of Yarmouth, determined to secure horses for themselves. Both had been drinking. From one house Page took a saddle and bridle. At Jeremiah Wilson's, near Little Otter Creek, each stole a horse, though not before Page had been shot in the arm.[89] The two spurred their way back to the rebel column, to be greeted with derisive laughter from those who 'had got Horses.'[90] They also encountered David Anderson's disapproval and he 'desired them to take the horses back.' Accordingly, the two were left behind to carry out their commander's wishes and, indeed, never rejoined their comrades.[91] The rebels arrived in Oakland on the thirteenth, swelling the number there but bringing as well the disconcerting news of the movements of the loyalists to the west.

Word of the Tories' awakening had previously reached the ears of those gathered in Oakland township. On 10 December George Alexander Clark, a merchant of Brantford, went to Scotland in an attempt either to confer with the rebels or to persuade them to disperse. He reported back to Brantford, it was said, that those Eliakim Malcolm had gathered at Oakland (Duncombe had not yet arrived with the Norwich men) would 'lay down their arms if Parker was let out of prison, and they have a free pardon granted them.'[92]

On 13 December, the Reverend Francis Evans, Church of England rector of Woodhouse, fell into the insurgents' hands. On 11 December, on receipt of a report that eighty armed rebels had gathered north of Waterford, the militia had mustered at Simcoe,[93] and the following afternoon Evans and eight other men had left Woodhouse for Brantford with a message for the authorities there that on 13 December the Simcoe volunteers would march to Round Plains, a few miles north-west of Waterford, to await couriers from Brantford. If none were received, the Woodhouse force would retire to Simcoe.[94] After Evans and his comrades had delivered this message, the rector went on to the rebels' camp to plead with them to take advantage of the lieutenant-governor's Proclamation of 7 December.[95] Directed at the Home district insurgents, this document declared that, except for five leading figures of the uprising who were specifically proscribed, all those who had taken up arms who now returned 'to their duty to their Sovereign,' who obeyed the laws, and who lived 'henceforth as good and faithful Subjects' would find 'the Government of their Queen as indulgent as it is just.'[96] For his troubles, Evans was detained by the rebels.

That evening, however, a rider brought the insurgents a shattering piece of news: MacNab was in Brantford![97] The colonel had left Hamilton on 12 December with some 300 volunteers,[98] and the following evening had marched into Brantford. It seems likely that the rebel leaders, after an unsuccessful attempt to contact Mackenzie on or possibly before the thirteenth,[99] had also received news of the suppression of the Home district uprising. Authentic news of the dispersal of Mackenzie's band had reached both Ingersoll and London, via the Western road, on 9

December.[100] The report soon filtered down the side roads, and by the twelfth the news, or rumour as some believed it to be, had reached Waterford from Simcoe.[101] The catastrophes of Mackenzie's defeat and MacNab's arrival evidently determined the rebel leaders to flee.[102]

The leaders of the rebels at Oakland had discussed the possibility of an assault upon Simcoe, a project favoured by Eliakim Malcolm, and in preparation for an attack upon Brantford had stationed guards on the roads about the rebel camp and had travellers stopped. Once they had taken Brantford, they apparently intended to push on to Hamilton.[103] These brave plans they now abandoned as they gathered their men. (At this juncture most of the insurgents were at Scotland.) Confusion reigned. The first word given the bewildered rebels was that they were going to intercept a force from Simcoe. They were marched for a distance from their encampment, then made to retrace their steps, and, upon returning to Oakland township, were dismissed. Yet, within an hour of being disbanded, they were mustered again. The officers now summoned those who had baggage wagons, telling at least some of the drivers that they were preparing for a final march towards Simcoe.[104] Other members of the little force, however, were led to believe that they were retreating to Norwich township, as they were about to be attacked by cannon. In Norwich, they understood, they could evade their enemy, 'as Cannon could not git there.'[105] The insurgent force, with twelve wagons in train, set off for the Quaker township. Desertions from the ranks began. In the early hours of Thursday, 14 December, the bedraggled and weary remainder of Duncombe's army entered Sodom. By morning, most of the rebels, including the officers, had melted away. Others slumbered in improvised sleeping-quarters, while the commander himself prepared to leave.

It is not clear if Duncombe spoke formally to his men before he himself departed. He did, however, advise a number of rebels, albeit privately, to return to their homes. He told Finlay Malcolm of Bayham, for example, that it would be best for those remaining 'to go home and be as still as possible about it.'[106] He comforted another with the assurance that the assembling of the insurgents would, in fact, be termed a meeting, not a revolt, because no property had been destroyed, no lives taken. Only the leaders of the rebels would be prosecuted, he said. Hence he himself 'was much frightened,' fearing 'that if he was taken he should be executed.' In the early morning of 14 December, therefore, he galloped off on horseback, heading for Michigan,[107] leaving his army and his family behind him. He may have found consolation in the fact that, although his

99 The Revolt

son-in-law John Tufford had become embroiled in his armed movement, his brothers Elijah of St Thomas and David of Norfolk had kept clear of it. They were not to suffer, as many others were, for joining him in arms.

III

While the Duncombe rebels had been marching to Norwich, Colonel MacNab and his men had been en route to Oakland township. MacNab later recorded that he had learned at 9:00 P.M. on Wednesday, 13 December, that Duncombe and some 400 followers were at Scotland preparing to retreat to Norwich. He immediately sent dispatches to Simcoe, Woodstock, and London requesting volunteers to meet him. With his 300 men, bolstered by 150 recruits from the Brantford area and 100 Indians from the Six Nations Reserve, he set out at 1:00 A.M. Later that morning the loyalists bore down on Scotland from three different directions – the Indians from the rear and the others from the two roads into the village.[108] As the force drew near, the cavalry forged ahead and swept into the settlement, encountering shots from a number of sentries Duncombe had left behind. One of the officers' horses was hit, but otherwise the few shots discharged were without effect. The riflemen, after offering this token resistance, fled. Reportedly, 'the INDIANS were let slip in pursuit & three of the unfortunate men were shot down & scalped.'[109] This later account, or versions thereof, gained wide circulation. A correspondent for the *Rochester Democrat*, present at the scene, recorded that:

the Indians were sent out at Scotland, against the unresisting radicals, like bloodhounds to hunt them from the forests – murdering and scalping unarmed men ... two men were found in the same wood through which I passed, with withes about their necks, hanging to small saplings, which had evidently been bent down for the purpose and sprung into the air. This circumstance I related to a retired navy officer who was amongst them, and who spoke exultingly of the event, and boasted that he had offered one of the chiefs a dollar a piece for the scalp of every damned rebel.[110]

Perhaps the Indians, who had daubed their faces with war paint, did play the part of savage warriors at Scotland, shooting, hanging, or scalping some of Duncombe's followers. Nevertheless, none of the rebels, their relatives, or friends ever mentioned such an event in the flood of petitions they sent to the government after the revolt. One might reasonably expect the families, comrades, or neighbours of slaughtered rebels to have protested that slaughter to the government, or to have asked for punishment for those responsible for such deeds, or to have requested aid for bereaved wives and children; none did. Indeed, Lieutenant-Governor Head praised the Indians' conduct as 'humane and steady,'[111] an assertion that the province's Reformers let pass unchallenged. Some doubt is certainly cast then on the report that rebels died at Indian hands at Oakland.

After occupying Scotland, the loyalist forces discovered Charles Duncombe's and Eliakim Malcolm's papers in a field. They were mostly of a trivial nature, however, and of little aid to MacNab and his men in identifying the local insurgents. They soon had considerable help in that task though, as volunteers came pouring in from all sides, so MacNab said, to the number of 1,000 or more. The first to arrive were from Simcoe. On 13 December, 200 men from the Woodhouse area had marched out of Simcoe only to return again. Presumably, they had gone to Round Plains and had returned home when they failed to encounter couriers or reinforcements from Brantford. On the fourteenth, aware of MacNab's presence, they mustered anew, 160 strong, and marched to meet the colonel.[112]

One hundred and sixty-seven Yarmouth volunteers arrived that afternoon at Scotland, where so lately the rebel flag emblazoned with 'The People's Rights' had flown.[113] The Yarmouth men had been raised by John Askin, clerk of the peace for the London district, who had been stirred to action by events in London. On 8 December thirty Reformers, on learning of Mackenzie's supposedly successful rising, had gathered in the bar-room at Flannagan's Tavern. Worried lest the local Tories assail them in retaliation for Mackenzie's outrage, they formed a defensive association.[114] Three days later Askin received information that London was to be attacked that night. This report appeared to be substantiated by a confused account that came to him that same evening of the decisions taken earlier at Flannagan's. He immediately set about alerting the loyal population to its 'danger' and mustered 200 men who rallied to the courthouse to defend against an attack that never came. The next day, Askin, having received orders from the province's attorney-general to arrest John Talbot and seize his papers, set off for St Thomas. On 13 December he discovered that Colonel Bostwick of Port Stanley had obtained word from Colonel Salmon of Woodhouse that an armed band had assembled at Scotland and intended to fall upon Simcoe. Askin also learned that a group of insurgents had left Yarmouth to join the Oakland rebels. He requested and received Colonel Bostwick's permission to raise a body of loyalist volunteers. Three hours later, Askin's recruits were levied and on their way to Oakland. They covered the sixty miles to the rebel camp in twenty-three hours, arriving at 12:00 M. on Thursday, 14 December, shortly after MacNab's men and those from Simcoe had entered the Oakland encampment.[115]

On that day, the loyalist volunteers at Scotland observed a deputation of three individuals enter the village. They had come from Norwich to ask MacNab on what conditions those who had taken up arms might be forgiven by the government. It is not clear what reply the colonel made. He later insisted that he had refused to consider various pleas for pardon 'until the leaders are delivered into my hands.'[116] Solomon Lossing, a member of the delegation, however, recalled that MacNab had promised that, if the rebels would surrender, he would do all he could to ensure that the authorities took no action against them.[117] The next day, 15 December, the colonel, by now aware of the dispersal of the insurgents in Norwich, led his force out of Oakland on the road to Sodom.

It has often been said that MacNab's men marched through the countryside spreading terror and destruction in their wake, particularly in Norwich.[118] The correspondent of the *Rochester Democrat*, a consistent, persistent, and widely circulated source of misinformation, half-truths, and hyperbole, wrote that the part of the country over which MacNab's volunteers had travelled, 'bears the marks of the ravages of war ... The blight of the destroying angel is visible wherever you go.'[119] Many of the stories circulated then and now of the vindictive nature of MacNab's occupation of Norwich stem from the fact that his troops were quartered on the local population. No choice was given the householder and where lodgings were not willingly offered they were secured by 'a dozen rifles & the "Queen's Name", with a threat that remuneration was optional.'[120] Injustices and injuries there were, of course, but they were minor. Dark feelings were both engendered and exacerbated by the necessarily haphazard nature of the commissariat arrangements. Chits were given for services and supplies which were to be honoured by the district treasurer. Bureaucratic confusion contrived to rob many of just payment, however, and various claims recognized to be legitimate were not redeemed for years.

As MacNab's men moved into Norwich from the east, other government supporters took up positions in the north between Norwich and the Governor's road. They were to scour the locality for rebels and intercept those in flight from the Quaker township. The loyalist body here consisted of men from Woodstock and Ingersoll. News of the activities of Duncombe and his associates had been conveyed to Woodstock and its vicinity on 10 December. On 11 December, Philip Graham, justice of the peace of North Oxford, was reported ready to lead the Highlanders of Zorra against the rebels and great energy was said to prevail among the loyalists of Woodstock. Those of Ingersoll and its locality, however, were reputedly immobilized by fear.[121] On 14 December, the forces gathered at Woodstock received orders to advance on Norwich in conjunction with MacNab's volunteers. At 5:00 P.M. sixty Woodstock area men, commanded by P.B. de Blaquiere, set off for a rendezvous on the following day with fifty recruits raised from the Ingersoll region by Captain Rothwell. It was this combined force, then, that on 15 December was intercepting those fleeing northwestward from Sodom.[122]

At Sodom on Saturday, 16 December, 103 inhabitants of the Norwich area, confessed rebels all, presented a petition to Colonel MacNab, now in occupation. They admitted they had had no grievances against the government but had simply been led astray by 'wicked & designing leaders.' They asked MacNab to intercede with the lieutenant-governor to secure forgiveness for them. Should they be pardoned, they promised to live peaceful lives and to do their utmost to secure the capture of those men who had deluded them so.[123] While the petition was being presented, MacNab arrested Solomon Lossing, justice of the peace, mill owner, lapsed Quaker, and a member of the Norwich deputation. Lossing was accused of aiding the rebels with advice and provisions. His detention, the colonel thought, had 'a very salutary effect.'[124] MacNab then spoke to the 200 or so persons assembled. The petitioners had, he said, put themselves in a terrible position because, by 'their wicked and unnatural conduct they had forfeited their lives & properties.'[125] Nevertheless, he would allow the majority there to return to their homes on the condition that they would surrender themselves if the lieutenant-governor did not concur in this grant of clemency.[126] Despite this qualification, those released evidently felt that they would not be troubled further.[127] MacNab, however, did have some of the purported leaders of the revolt and some of its more zealous participants detained for transportation to London jail.

In dealing with the insurgents, both surrendered and captured, the colonel had to make immediate decisions and hope that those in higher authority would agree with them. The Proclamation of 7 December had implied that a policy of leniency was to apply to all but the principal rebels. Although it is by no means clear that the Proclamation was intended to extend to the Duncombe insurrectionists, MacNab obviously let himself

103 The Revolt

be guided by its general tenets. A further order of 10 December from the lieutenant-governor had forbidden any militia officer of any rank from liberating prisoners captured either as rebels or as persons suspected of having engaged in treasonable practices. In every instance, such captives were to be held until their cases were thoroughly examined.[128] A Proclamation of 14 December, however, had decreed that only 'notorious offenders' should be arrested by the militia, acting under the direction of the local magistrates.[129] Thus MacNab's decision of 16 December to free all but the most forward of the assembled Norwich rebels coincided with official policy. Head, therefore, agreed in essence with the colonel's decision, informing him through his secretary that all 103 of the Norwich rebels should have been let go except the perpetrators of violence against 'the persons or property of their fellow subjects.' Those released were to be bonded to appear at the next Court of Oyer and Terminer and General Gaol Delivery at London to answer any complaints that might be lodged against them.[130]

MacNab's force remained in Sodom until 19 December. Returns were forwarded from the detachments scattered through the area of arms and ammunition taken from captives, of prisoners' papers, of their depositions, and of the charges to be pressed against them. On the eighteenth, the colonel reported that his force had taken nearly 500 prisoners and between 100 and 200 rifles.[131]

Rebels had gathered at Scotland from fourteen townships of the counties of Oxford, Norfolk, and Middlesex, as well as from the townships of Dumfries and Brantford, and the work of pacification was carried on throughout those areas. In Dumfries Absalom Shade had organized a volunteer company at Galt, but reportedly had advised the government not to call out the militiamen of his township because they could not be trusted. Dumfries' militia was not mustered, but a company was ordered from Fergus to Galt, where it remained for ten days guarding the bridge across the Grand. Aided by some Dumfries men, it also arrested several Duncombe rebels in the interior of the township.[132] In Woodhouse various parties searched the countryside for those who had shouldered arms, taking some sixty-six prisoners, who were then lodged in Simcoe jail.[133] The Cayuga militia meanwhile sealed off the escape route to the east.

On 18 December, the St Thomas volunteers led by Askin left Norwich and MacNab's men behind them to begin a systematic sweep of the disaffected Lake Erie townships to the south-west. They 'marched through Dereham, scouring the country.' By the time the volunteers reached the Otter Creek in Bayham, they had in their possession '20 to 30 prisoners of no note.'[134] One of the loyalists, Adam Hope, a St Thomas wheat merchant and political moderate, recorded:

Our official men were anxious to shew the fruits of their mission by dragging these poor deluded people from their homes to immure them in a jail for no purpose whatever. The whole prisoners taken by McNab's [sic] people with few exceptions were discharged with a suitable reprimand. I spoke to the authorities on behalf of the men our party had taken but without effect. To tell the truth *catching* these mistaken & misguided men did not suit my ideas at all. The most of these prisoners surrendered voluntarily & after their deposition was taken it could have been transmitted to the Governor and he could have granted them pardon or not as he might have deemed proper. I got disgusted with the parade which was made of the prisoners before they reached London.[135]

On 19 December, the force under Askin marched along Talbot Street, through Malahide, turning southward in Yarmouth to Sparta where Anderson's force had collected, that 'small village noted as a rendesvous [sic] or assemblage of Rebels.'[136] On 12 December young Philo Bennett of London, a former Ryanite preacher, had arrived in the village with a copy of Head's Proclamation of 7 December promising pardon to those rebels who surrendered. This, read to an assembled crowd (though not by Bennett), created much 'agitation and violence' among those gathered; they tore up the Proclamation, and swore that 'they would tear the Governor to pieces in the same way, if he were there.'[137] Voicing general defiance of the government, they expressed confidence in the ultimate victory of the rebels. On the nineteenth, however, when Askin's men marched through the settlement, the settlers offered no resistance.

On 20 December the volunteers were back in St Thomas with thirty-eight prisoners who were transferred to London jail on 22 December. In reviewing the progress of those under his command through the countryside, Askin concluded that only in Norwich and the south of Yarmouth was disloyalty rife. Elsewhere, he thought, people were loyal and willing to serve the government.[138] Such was certainly the case in and about St Thomas where the local rebels and Radicals had already been rounded up by Sheriff James Hamilton who, on 14 December, had led a body of militiamen from nearby London into Yarmouth. This force remained for a week or so. Hamilton had also sent men to instruct the settlers of the townships around London to prepare for possible attack by Duncombe's men. The loyalists had come out in

105 The Revolt

strength and volunteers had flocked into London from as far away as the Huron Tract.[139]

Not everyone was eager to take up arms on behalf of the government, of course. Robert Davis of Nissouri tried to mobilize his neighbours to resist the militia's attempt to requisition arms.[140] In the end, he had to flee to Michigan. Less dramatically, other Reformers in the area gathered together to discuss what action to take. Some seventy-five met in Dorchester township on 14 December to form 'a mutual safety association.'[141] The Liberals of Delaware, who had learned on 15 December of Duncombe's defeat, were fearful lest a victorious and vengeful government loose the Munceys and Delaware Indians of the nearby reserve upon them and met to organize the members of the Delaware Political Union for defensive purposes and to request the Indians to remain quiet should trouble occur.[142]

The several meetings the fearful Reformers hastily convened could be, and were, construed by unfriendly observers as traitorous and treasonable; yet, outside of that band of townships stretching from Oakland to Southwold, the London district witnessed little activity in the first half of December directly connected with the Duncombe rising. Outside the arc of rebel townships, only in Mosa in western Middlesex did Duncombe's cause evidently have much appeal. There, on 15 December, Alexander Roberts, a local farmer, persuaded some seventeen militiamen to desert the ranks and join the band he had collected and march to St Thomas to join the Duncombe rebels. In all, Roberts assembled some forty to fifty men. They were addressed by one John White who urged them to adopt the rebels' cause and told them that support would soon be coming from the United States. These would-be traitors decided to try to secure arms and ammunition from the republic and to gather should any attempts be made to arrest any of their number. Within a few days, however, they knew of the dispersal of Duncombe's force. On learning that a party of militiamen was out, the principals promptly fled to the United States.[143] Treason in arms in the London district was thus at an end.

On 19 December Colonel MacNab led his force out of Norwich to complete the job of pacification. Despite Head's letter to him of 18 December bearing warning of further plans for rebellion in the London district, he had little left to do there.[144] He had announced his intention to establish volunteer corps of 100 to 150 men each in London, Brantford, Woodstock, and Simcoe, reduced the strength of his own troops, and made a hurried march to London.

MacNab's sojourn in the west had been successful but he and his troops had failed in one respect, however: the apprehension of the leading rebels. In 1838, John Wilson, a lawyer for some of the jailed insurgents, complained that 'nearly all the principal leaders have made their escape, and most of the persons convicted, stand in the second, third or fourth degree of culpability.'[145] A number of Malcolms and a variety of minor notables were apprehended but the main participants all avoided capture, as Mahlon Burwell had feared they would.[146] Eliakim Malcolm, Charles Duncombe, David Anderson, Martin Switzer, and Pelham Teeple all reached American soil. Rewards were offered for various prominent personalities implicated in the rebellion, leading the *St Catharines Journal* to remark on 21 December that 'traitors' were 'the only marketable cash article we have among us.' Five days earlier prices had been put on the heads of six Duncombe insurgents: £500 for Duncombe, £250 each for Eliakim and Finlay Malcolm and Robert Alway, £100 for David Anderson and Joshua Doan,[147] a young Yarmouth rebel and the son of a prominent settler. Of the six individuals named, only Finlay Malcolm and Robert Alway were to be taken. The rest escaped, as did most other leading figures of the Duncombe rising – some to remain to harass the Upper Canadian government another day, some to settle in the United States permanently and never return, some to glory thereafter in their roles as rebels, and some, perhaps, to rue the revolt and the parts they had played in it.

It must have been bitter for the rebels to reflect that Duncombe's rebellion had been defeated before it had begun. Solicitor-General Draper may have correctly assessed the situation when he remarked that, 'although the number of actual insurgents' in the London and Gore districts was 'limited, had any success attended' their movements, 'there is but too much reason to believe their numbers would have received great additions, particularly in the London District.' To some extent, however, Draper contradicted himself by declaring, with particular reference to the Duncombe rebellion, 'that the insurrection was the act of a few reckless desperadoes, not at all approved or intended by the great body of the reform party.'[148] Indeed, it would have made little difference whether or not the London district Reformers had risen up en masse for, in truth, the western rebellion had already been defeated the moment Mackenzie's men fled north up Yonge Street on 7 December. All the hurried planning, all the frantic recruiting, were in vain. Defeat and despair were the twin legacies left by Duncombe and his lieutenants to their supporters in the revolt.

5
Repercussions

After the Duncombe rebellion had been suppressed, the furor in the west abated little, if at all. The Tories were provoked by the revelation that, as news of insurrection in Upper Canada had spread, Reformers in many parts of the province had met, not to offer their services to the Crown, but to debate what actions they should take and to decide on which side of the contest, if any, they should throw their weight. Rage grew into fury as absconding rebels and their 'Yankee' sympathizers began, almost immediately after the scattering of the Upper Canadian insurgents, to launch raids upon the province in vain efforts to instigate a popular insurrection. All through the winter of 1837 and the early spring of 1838, the west found its peace shattered by attacks and rumours of attacks from the American shore, by the continuing apprehension of those implicated in the western rising, and by the arrest of those not resident in the rebel townships who were none the less suspected of having engaged in treasonable activities. Events culminated in the treason trials of March and April in London and Hamilton, trials which, some hoped, would demonstrate to those who sought the overthrow of the government that the lot of convicted traitors was indeed a hard one.

I

In December 1837 rebellion had broken out in the London district counties of Middlesex, Oxford, and Norfolk. Not all of the townships of these counties had produced men for the rebel ranks yet in many, especially in Middlesex, in the weeks following the revolt people were apprehended for various activities, real or alleged. The arrests increased ill feelings and many Reform-minded people thought that a second

Spanish Inquisition had begun. Treason had indeed broken out in the west, the magistrates there did have to investigate the actions of many settlers but, on balance, those investigations were conducted with a reasonable degree of impartiality. In large part, allegations of a 'reign of terror' gained widespread acceptance because the justices had to deal with many people whose actions had been suspicious although they had not been directly involved in the Duncombe rising.

The events in Mosa, the meetings in Delaware, Dorchester, and London were all of obvious concern to the officials of the London district, and arrests were made in each of these locales. To deal with those sent to the London jail accused of disloyalty, the district clerk, John Askin, acting on instructions from Lieutenant-Governor Head,[1] established a board of magistrates on 21 December. This body, which was to secure depositions and to decide on the immediate fate of the prisoners, originally consisted of Askin and four magistrates, but its membership was eventually expanded to include three other justices of the peace. The brunt of the commission's work fell most noticeably on magistrates Laurence Laurason of London and Harry Cook of Caradoc who attended respectively thirty-one and twenty-two of its thirty-two sittings.

Almost immediately, the magistrates began their examinations of those taken in the area. In all, they dealt with forty-eight people accused of a variety of supposedly treasonable activities essentially unconnected with the Duncombe rising. (They also examined a further thirteen taken for reasons unknown.) Some of the forty-eight could justly complain of official harassment; for example, two Mormon ministers, Jeremiah Willey and Michael Yeomans, were accused of spreading 'seditious doctrine,' along with their religious beliefs.[2] These two were merely brought to London, questioned, and released, however. Most of the others examined had been dangerously indiscreet or had talked too freely. Others had attended meetings in London, Delaware, Dorchester, and elsewhere that were particularly compromising.

The magistrates recognized that in disposing of these sixty-one cases they were not invariably dealing with determined rebels. Consequently, they were anxious to free 'all we can on bail calling the least offensive, & most penitent for that purpose.'[3] Five were examined and quickly freed; thirty-four more were granted bail after having been imprisoned from periods varying from a few days to a month; and a further thirteen were bound over after spending just over a month behind bars. Eight others were refused bail. The records do not reveal the fate of one man. In sum, the magistrates at London treated the large number of prisoners who appeared before them and who were unconnected with the Duncombe

109 Repercussions

rebellion with a reasonable degree of leniency and dispatch. There were, of course, exceptions to this general pattern and these should not be overlooked.

Just as men were jailed to the west of the rebel area for offences unconnected with the events in Oakland, men were also cast into jail to the east in Hamilton. As Solicitor-General W.H. Draper later noted, 'the few individuals in and about Hamilton who were implicated in the rebellion were almost one and all connected with the rising at Toronto, and not with any attempts at insurrection elsewhere.'[4] One man, Jonathan Bishop, was detained on suspicion of attempting to contact the Duncombe rebels,[5] but that remains unproven.

Shortly after the rebellion, twelve people, for reasons that can be documented, were jailed or taken at Hamilton. A thirteenth man, Robert Armstrong of Guelph, was detained for accumulating a suspiciously large amount of powder and shot.[6] Also jailed at Hamilton towards the end of December were three men from the Scots-dominated township of Eramosa in Gore who had on 7 or 8 December attended a meeting called to discuss the report that Toronto had fallen to Mackenzie.[7] (A meeting in neighbouring Nassagaweya, another Scots township, had already voted to aid Mackenzie.)[8] Besides the Eramosa men and the others, a further thirteen men were jailed or detained at Hamilton for unknown reasons. All told then, twenty-nine people were taken from Hamilton and its environs.

Of the twenty-nine men, the militia guard detained five and then quickly released them. A magistrate examined and then immediately freed another. Eleven found themselves in jail for periods ranging from a day to a month, while three were there for a month or more. No less than seven were never granted bail. (The precise disposition of the remaining two is uncertain.)

Unlike London, where a board of magistrates sat to deal with the 'state prisoners,' individual militia officers and magistrates at Hamilton dealt with the accused. The failure to establish an examining board did not occasion comment in official circles, either at the local or the provincial level, but it did bode ill for those, Duncombe rebels and others, sent to the Hamilton jail from the west. Few arrangements existed for processing their individual cases.

II

While the weeks that followed the Duncombe rebellion saw arrests of people in and about the towns of Hamilton and London on a number of charges essentially unconnected with the western rising, the various government officers in the London and Gore district townships directly affected by the revolt continued to search out those suspected of having been involved in the Duncombe rising. The process of catching and jailing those implicated in the western insurrection lasted some time. One of the Yarmouth disaffected, Duncan Wilson, later recalled that in December 1837 'report from the veriest villain was sufficient for the imprisonment of an honest man, if he was known to be favourable to the cause of Reform.'[9] The situation was not quite that black, however. Some magistrates at least did not simply commit accused men to prison, but instead bound them over to appear at the next Court of Oyer and Terminer and General Gaol Delivery, should charges be preferred against them. The amount of bail required varied from township to township, but was customarily set at £100, £200, or £250, although Bela Shaw, who owned the presses of the *Liberal* and was therefore almost automatically suspected of having helped inspire the western rebellion, was obliged to post £1,000.[10] Evidently those bound over, like their counterparts freed by the London magistrates, had to put up the full extent of the money themselves and then secure two sureties, each of whom had to provide a further 50 per cent of a like sum. Those bailed were enjoined 'to keep the peace and be of good behaviour' for a specified period.

In the rebel townships were twenty-eight individuals who, the available evidence strongly suggests, had taken up arms under Duncombe and Eliakim Malcolm but who were bound over and not thereafter proceeded against, although three might simply have escaped further legal action because they had fled the province after being bound over. Fifteen other rebels were examined, and were not obliged to give bail.[11] Seven people who had provided the insurgents with aid were bailed and then freed, while four others in the same category were merely questioned and promptly liberated.[12]

A further seventeen were bound over for reasons now unknown though it would appear from circumstantial evidence that most or all were suspected of having been in some way embroiled in the Oakland uprising. (See appendix 6.) For example, twelve were released on bail in Norwich on 17 December along with five known rebels.[13] The justices of the area affected by the revolt also dealt in December and January with five settlers who were charged with offences not immediately connected with the Duncombe insurrection: with helping Toronto rebels to escape, with urging Reformers to rise up in arms again, with importing weapons into the Niagara district, and with making seditious statements. Three were granted bail, the other two were jailed. (See appendix 7.)

In the townships directly involved in the uprising the magistrates bailed a further seventeen accused of having been in arms or of having aided the insurgents. In some instances the evidence now available is contradictory; in most cases it is limited to the deposition of but one witness. The justices jailed an additional twenty-three men in the same category, while a Grand Jury indicted for treason one other suspect who had absconded. (See appendix 8.) Doubtless some of those forty-one people were treated unjustly. For example, David Curtis, a fifty-one-year-old West Oxford tavernkeeper who had been the host at the Reform meeting of 16 November, had been arrested and jailed on suspicion 'of having been in arms,'[14] though when finally examined the magistrates could find 'no evidence against him.'[15] Several may have been suspected merely because they lived near Oakland, and some were apprehended because they were known to have attended the various rebel meetings. In fact, at least fourteen of the forty-one had been at the gatherings in the fall and in December, while a further ten (including six who had also attended the meetings) had been politically active prior to the fall of 1837. In many instances, then, it is possible to see why these men incurred suspicion and to understand that those who acted against them were not motivated by mere malice or unreasoning prejudice.

In December 1837 those men suspected of being implicated in the rebellion were imprisoned in the London, Hamilton, or Simcoe jails. At Simcoe those who were not bailed were confined in the cells of the town's partially completed jail. A later report stated that in December several men had met at Waterford in Townsend to discuss the possibility of freeing those imprisoned.[16] Two inmates, however, did not require aid to win their freedom. William Herrington, a young tailor from Richmond in Bayham, 'one of the Damndest scoundrels in the Rebel party,'[17] and David Sturgis, a merchant from Vienna in the same township who was accused of being one of Duncombe's men, broke out of Simcoe jail together by jumping out of a window.[18] They fled westward to Detroit.[19]

Shortly after, the rest of the Simcoe prisoners were transferred to the London jail where they found a good number of others confined. Within a month or so of the rebellion, sixty-eight of those identified in this study as being insurgents had been imprisoned at London,[20] as had twelve who had aided the rebel cause,[21] and thirteen suspected by the officials of being either insurrectionists or their abettors, but against whom there is not sufficient evidence to consider the suspicion verified. Of course various settlers from in and about London were also lodged there on a number of other charges.

The London jail was not designed for the comfort of its inmates, consisting as it did 'of subterranean cells' under the court-house 'where darkness and dampness reigned supreme.'[22] Even in January 1837, when the jail harboured relatively few prisoners, the Grand Jury discovered the cells to be 'in a very unclean State with filth and Vermin' and the inmates complaining that they lacked food, water, fuel, and bedding. In the summer of 1837 the same body decided that the prison badly needed ventilation.[23] In the fall of the year the newly appointed sheriff, James Hamilton, reported that the jail was extremely overcrowded.[24] After the rebellion he found it necessary to lodge various captives in the court-house. Even so, one inmate complained in the winter of 1838 that the prisoners at London lived in such close quarters and amid such confusion that the 'continual bableing' which resounded therein resembled nothing so much as 'the shouts and peals of a thundering Bedlam.'[25]

The examining magistrates at London, perhaps mindful of the conditions in the jail, pursued as liberal a bail policy towards those implicated in the rebellion as towards those imprisoned on other charges. The same basic formula was used, although the amount of money required appears to have been slightly less, on the whole, for the rebels, who were commonly bound over for £200, occasionally for £100, and, in the more serious cases, for £400 or £500.

All those bailed at London were required to appear at the next Court of Oyer and Terminer and General Gaol Delivery if they were indicted by the Grand Jury. They were also 'to keep the peace and to be of good behaviour.' Those bound over after 5 January were made to swear 'not to leave this Province till their trial.'[26]

The magistrates in December and January allowed bail to thirty-eight of the sixty-eight individuals identified here as rebels.[27] Sixteen were later indicted by the Grand Jury and recommitted and three others fled the province. Twelve people were in jail who had aided the insurgents. Six were also bound over, although one was later imprisoned again for trial.[28] Of the thirteen prisoners who were accused either of having shouldered weapons or of having aided those who did – but against whom insufficient evidence has been found to consider them guilty – eleven were bailed.[29] In addition to those bound over, three prisoners were granted bail but were unable to raise it and were kept in the cells.[30]

The majority of those implicated or suspected of being involved in the Duncombe revolt who did receive bail were released within a month of their initial confinement at London, although three men languished in jail for almost two months before being bound over.[31] One of them, David Curtis, the West Oxford tavernkeeper, was released only because of his age and poor health.³² The justices had been particularly willing to allow bail to those prepared to become Crown witnesses. Ten men who agreed to testify against their fellow prisoners thus achieved their freedom.³³

In some instances suitable candidates were not bound over. The most notable case was that of John Riley of Yarmouth, a youth of just fourteen or fifteen who was prepared to be a Crown witness. He fully admitted his involvement in the rebellion, although he did insist that he had marched only a part of the way to Oakland with David Anderson's body of recruits.³⁴ Nevertheless, he was kept in the cells. Similarly, young Charles Travers, the son of a West Oxford merchant, claimed to have been led astray by Pelham Teeple; he pled in vain to be bound over.³⁵

Undeniably, some who were refused bail should have been granted it, but there were prisoners whose attachment to their cause and hostility to those examining them was so great that it is little wonder bail was denied them. Uriah Emmons, a twenty-two-year-old labourer from Norwich, admitted having taken up arms but flatly refused to pledge to be loyal to the queen in order to secure bail.³⁶ Another labourer, twenty-two-year-old Amos S. Bradshaw of Yarmouth, an American, told the magistrates he would rather be shot than fight for England.³⁷ Charles Scrivener of Yarmouth was also belligerent, freely admitting that he had marched armed to Oakland, adding that he 'is still a Reformer and does not regret going to Oakland; says that if the party had been attacked he would have fired and fought – He would have done anything his Commander had told him.'³⁸ Scrivener's case is unusual because, although he was committed to the cells after this outburst, no mention is ever made of him again on any prisoner list or in any official correspondence that has come to light. His fate is entirely unknown. The mists of history, and possibly of the London jail, have enveloped him.

Not all of those implicated in the Duncombe rebellion and jailed ended up in the London prison. Fifty-one others were lodged in December and January in the Hamilton jail. Thirty-four of them had taken up arms, nine had aided the rebel cause, and the remaining eight men were accused of having been involved in the revolt but the evidence of their guilt is unreliable.

Most of the Hamilton prisoners received far worse treatment than their counterparts in London. The cells at Hamilton were also underground and were wet and damp.³⁹ Here, too, overcrowding was a problem, particularly because the prisoners from the west shared space with suspected traitors from around Hamilton as well as with the other inmates. A doctor touring the prison on 29 December reported that captives lacking money to buy provisions received only bread and water. None the less, he found the inmates to be on the whole 'in a tolerably good state of health.' Those held because of the revolt, whom he felt should be separated from the others as much as possible, evidently had not been allowed out of their cells for any purpose; the doctor recommended that parties of four or five be permitted to exercise in the hall and that 'the prisoners be allowed to have access to the yard for the calls of nature, as nothing vitiates the air so much as having any collection of filth in confined apartments.' He further suggested that several people be appointed to aid the jailer in keeping the cells clean.[40] It is not known to what extent his recommendations were implemented but from 7 January on meat was provided those who had been arrested because of the rebellion,[41] and in March the Grand Jury reported that those still in jail testified they had been treated 'in the most humane, attentive and indulgent manner.'[42]

At Hamilton a board of magistrates had not been empanelled to question the state prisoners. Most of those apprehended from that city and its vicinity, however, had been taken before individual justices of the peace to make their statements. Such was not the case with the captives from the west, the assumption apparently having been made that those sent eastward by MacNab and his officers had previously been questioned. Only occasionally at London was a prisoner jailed who was never examined; at Hamilton, however, of the fifty-one accused traitors from the west, only six appear to have been interrogated – all on their arrival on 17 or 18 December.[43] Thus Stephen Smith, an American from Norwich, complained that he was never examined at all prior to his trial,[44] and Henry P. Goff, a Windham schoolteacher, insisted that he had been jailed for four months without being questioned 'or even a shadow of accusation' being made against him.[45] As there was no board of examining justices at Hamilton, few of the prisoners implicated in the revolt received bail there. In fact, only four did and two of them promptly fled the province.[46]

III

In December and January there were further challenges to the security of the province, at each end of the western peninsula, when patriots (Canadian refugees and their American sympathizers, who were sworn to rescue the province from its supposed subjection to a reign of tyranny) invaded Upper Canada. These attacks created great consternation in the

115 Repercussions

area affected by the western insurrection, fears being expressed that landings would be made along the Erie shore to coincide with uprisings of the disaffected people still living in the region. Thus the loyalists of the London district spent the winter of 1837–8 in a state of considerable apprehension, and kept a close, careful watch on those suspected of treasonable inclinations. Such an atmosphere did not augur well for the fortunes of the area's Radicals and Reformers, associated in the minds of many people with the rebellion.

The first patriot threat occurred along the Niagara frontier. After the dispersal of his force at Toronto, Mackenzie arrived in Buffalo, a city of 20,000 inhabitants, on 11 December. Here, he found support and attacked and seized Upper-Canadian-owned Navy Island in the Niagara River opposite the village of Chippawa. On 13 December from his occupied stronghold, he issued a proclamation urging the residents of the province to join his cause, declaring that he had formed a provisional government which included Charles Duncombe among its members.[47]

Although Mackenzie's initial occupying force numbered only a few dozen men, the threat posed was a real one, as the population along the American frontier was turbulent and might well have been persuaded to join the venture. The prospect was doubly disturbing for the provincial administration because the British Regulars normally in the upper province had been sent to the lower to suppress the revolt there. If the colony were to be defended from an American onslaught, it would have to be by the militia; thus the militiamen of the Niagara district were immediately gathered to defend the border. Colonel Allan MacNab, who had put Duncombe and his men to flight, was to command operations around Chippawa. After returning from the west, he left Hamilton on Christmas Day for the frontier, taking with him well over 1,000 men, including, Askin reported, 'a lot of our boys from London.'[48]

At Navy Island a stalemate quickly developed. The militia could not evict Mackenzie's men, who in turn could not cross into the province proper. The patriots were being supplied by a small steamer, the *Caroline*, from Buffalo. On the night of 28 December, acting on MacNab's orders, a little band set out led by Andrew Drew, a Woodstock man and retired captain of the Royal Navy. They found the vessel at its wharf on the American shore. The Upper Canadians drove off those on board, killing one of them, and set the ship adrift. It grounded above the falls. Many Upper Canadians applauded the assault on the *Caroline*, and within a few days hawkers on the British side of the Niagara River were selling snuff boxes allegedly made from sections of the ship rescued from below the

116 The Rising in Western Upper Canada

falls.[49] Patriotic fury, however, seized an outraged American populace. The patriots' cause suddenly grew in popularity, and by 6 January a mixed force of 450 Canadians and Americans, primarily the latter,[50] were on Navy Island. The enthusiasm displayed, however, was temporary and after a few weeks Mackenzie's band melted away. The patriot threat was not over, however.

Duncombe had fled to Detroit, and by late December reports were filtering back to the London district that he was organizing the Canadian refugees there for an invasion of the province. John Talbot and David Anderson were also reputed to be mustering men for an attack.[51] The rumours about Duncombe and Anderson were probably true, but Talbot evidently tried to avoid contact with the patriots.[52]

The possibility that a hostile force would attempt a landing along the Upper Canadian shore opposite Detroit was taken seriously in the province because there were a number of 'Yankees' only too anxious to participate in such a venture. Moreover, the loyalists about Windsor, Sandwich, and Amherstburg distrusted the numerous French Canadians in their area. In addition, the militia of the Western district was 'in a comparatively unorganized state.'[53] Towards the end of December the militiamen who could be mustered from the area and others from the western sections of Middlesex county in the London district were out along the Detroit River.

In the meantime, the patriots opposite Windsor had organized the 'Army of the North-West,' begun laying plans for an invasion, and had stolen some 400 rifles from the Detroit jail. On 8 January, a patriot force, after being warned by a reluctant Governor Mason of Michigan either to leave the United States or to disband, cast off from the American shore in a small fleet, heading for the island of Bois Blanc in the Detroit River. The force apparently comprised some 700 men.[54]

Bois Blanc was in British waters about one-third of a mile from the town of Amherstburg and Fort Malden, 'a wretched little useless fort.'[55] On the Upper Canadian side the loyal militiamen waited, some 350 strong. One of the patriots' ships, the *Anne*, came under heavy fire and eventually ran aground. Those shooting from the shore waded out and captured her and took some thirty prisoners. Although most of those taken were American citizens,[56] their ranks included David Anderson (who died of his wounds) and Walter Chase, both from the Port Stanley area. Robert Davis of Nissouri was also captured. He, too, had been wounded and died that summer from his injuries, 'an intelligent & brave but a most desperate rebel, and he died one to the last.'[57] Duncombe himself was not aboard the *Anne*. In fact, he was nowhere to be seen, though he was certainly rumoured later to have been involved in the raid.[58] If he was, he witnessed another venture against the Upper Canadian government end unsuccessfully as Governor Mason had the remaining would-be invaders evacuated from their refuge on Sugar Island and returned to the American shore.

For the time being the menace in the west was at an end. British Regulars released from duty in Lower Canada had come back into the upper province, beginning in December when Colborne started returning the Twenty-Fourth and Thirty-Second regiments. Some were sent first to the Niagara peninsula; then in mid-January six companies of the two regiments were dispatched to the western frontier, with four field pieces.[59] In January, men of the Eighty-Third also began arriving in the colony.[60] In addition, American officials began to pay some attention to the maintenance of the American neutrality laws. Washington deployed troops along the borders; those it sent to Detroit arrived towards the end of January.[61] Federal authorities had already arrested Mackenzie for his part in the Navy Island affair, and now those of Michigan apprehended several participants in the Bois Blanc raid.

While threats to Upper Canada's western peninsula were materializing along both the Niagara and the Detroit frontiers, the militiamen of the London district were out in force to secure the rebel townships and, if necessary, to repulse patriot raids. Late in December, Askin calculated that some 3,600 men from the counties of Huron and Middlesex had either taken up arms already or were prepared to do so. Five hundred Norfolk militiamen were embodied, he said, adding that in Oxford county 500 Scots Highlanders and 200 settlers from around Woodstock had been mustered. He predicted that the loyalists of the Burford area would mass 200 strong.[62] In fact, a rare return demonstrates that in January the county of Oxford secured just over one-third of its 2,589 effective rank and file militiamen for duty. Apparently only volunteers were enrolled. The rebel townships of Burford, Blenheim, and Oakland produced approximately the same proportion of recruits as did the county as a whole, but Norwich yielded only 62 of its 423 militiamen for service. Zorra, on the contrary, had 354 of a possible 554 volunteers in arms.[63]

Militia detachments were serving at points throughout the area directly affected by the Duncombe rising. A company of forty to fifty men was maintained at Brantford. At various times, militiamen were stationed at Port Stanley, Port Burwell, and Port Dover along the lakeshore. Inland, troops were placed at Simcoe, at Waterford, and in Oakland township.[64] Doubtless, companies were also quartered elsewhere, for example, in Norwich.

The defeat of the insurgents and the posting of militiamen through the entire region appeared to mean that Radicalism and, by association, Reform, were crushed. As early as 24 December, Adam Hope wrote: 'Never was a party more completely prostrated than that known under the name of "the Reform party" in this Province. A general election tomorrow would terminate in the return of not one solitary opponent of the Government ... The Tories have unfortunately neither sense nor moderation to profit by their victory. Greedy & intolerant they will disgust numbers of people and compel them to leave the Province.' Hope, however, foresaw the possibility 'of a party of "juste milieu" reformers arising.' None the less, he refused Bela Shaw's offer to him ' and to a *half Whig* Magistrate' of 'the use of the Press types office &c' of the *Liberal* 'if we would start a Paper on our own views.'[65] The *Liberal* was, in fact, succeeded briefly by the *Table of Events*, a newspaper of which little is known and whose demise marked the final end of John Talbot's journal.

The Reformers and Radicals of the west were unquestionably on the defensive. In the township elections of January 1838 in the London district, most Reform township clerks were replaced.[66] Moreover, although many Liberals had previously sat on the London district's Grand and Petit juries, very few appeared on the jury lists of the winter of 1838. Not until the fall did their names begin to reappear in appreciable numbers.[67]

In the winter of 1838 Reformers and Radicals found themselves harassed by a series of petty measures. Some historians, indeed, have likened the abuses that occurred to the excesses of the French Revolution. Fred Landon, for example, deprecated the establishment in the west of 'a veritable reign of terror.'[68] There were Tory outrages, to be sure. A few of the captured insurgents charged that, after their arrests, loyalists had sacked their homes, and Eliakim Malcolm's family lamented the loss of five books, including a two-volume history of the French Revolution by a scholar named Kelly and greatly enhanced in value because it contained sixty-two plates.[69] An unsuccessful attempt apparently was made to fire James Malcolm's house,[70] and an army officer passing through Burford recorded that 'one of the farms by the wayside was pointed out to us as having belonged to the rebel Duncombe. His house had been burned down and his family resided [in?] a miserable looking cottage.'[71] Perhaps the fire that destroyed Duncombe's house had been that of 1836 and had not been set by angry loyalists. Still, the conclusion that some government supporters behaved badly after the revolt is supported by the report from the vicinity of Caradoc in January that the Adelaide militiamen were pressing provisions, teams, and women for themselves 'in a most wonton manner.'[72]

In 1838 Lord Durham had harsh words for some of the magistrates who had subjected 'the whole body of reformers' to 'harassing procedures.'[73] No justice in the province had acted more disgracefully than had John Burwell of Bayham. He had rallied the loyalists of his area in December and that winter he allegedly refused to levy charges against local Tories who were physically abusing local Reformers. He was accused not only of inciting some of his cohorts to set upon the Liberals but also of assaulting one of his political foes himself. In his capacity as postmaster he evidently withheld mail from the region's Reformers.[74] Burwell's conduct went unchecked temporarily but an investigation was ordered by the government after word of his misdeeds reached Toronto, and after it was learned there that he had violated both the morality of the day and the dignity of his magisterial office. Evidence revealed that his neighbours knew him to live with 'a woman of Notorious bad and loose character,'[75] and many objected to his custom of bellowing in public the most obscence oaths.[76] Commissioner of Crown Lands, Robert Baldwin Sullivan, declared, 'I don't wonder there are rebels where such Magistrates are permitted.'[77] It was not until 1839, however, that Bayham was freed from Burwell.[78]

Other magistrates were said to have hounded the Reformers continually throughout the winter. For example, Elijah Leonard of St Thomas, an American who owned a foundry, later recalled that he had been arrested four times on 'trivial charges.'[79] He may have been examined on several occasions but he was almost certainly neither arrested nor jailed. Stories such as his, however, have fed the myth of a 'reign of terror.'

The belief that extreme repression blighted the lives of the Reformers seems to stem in part from the fact that arrests, examinations, and incarcerations continued after the suppression of the insurrection. In late January or early February, five individuals, two of whom had been rebels, two of whom had aided the insurgents and one who had been accused of doing so, were finally apprehended and bound over or jailed.[80] In addition, Joseph Bowes of Bayham, a forty-year-old 'Yankee' who had been at Oakland and had been captured and released by MacNab, was imprisoned for foolishly declaring while drunk that he intended to take up arms in an attempt to secure a republican government for the province. He wished, he said, to see the American flag flying over Upper Canada.[81]

In London in late January and in February seven men were jailed and one bound over for allegedly treasonable activities. Two men in Brantford, one in Nissouri township, and one in Bayham township were taken up on treason charges and then bailed. These twelve individuals were drawn from a wide area, suggesting that, although some may have been apprehended unjustly, no systematic legal persecution of the Reformers occurred in any one locality in the winter of 1838.

The acts of the assembly and legislative council are sometimes used to support the thesis that the Tories were extraordinarily severe. That winter the two bodies passed a series of relatively harsh laws of limited duration. Some received the lieutenant-governor's assent on 12 January, others on 6 March. Several were designed to deal with those filling the province's jails. One piece of legislation, 'an Act to authorize the apprehending and detention of persons suspected of High Treason, misprision of Treason, and Treasonable practices,' declared that those imprisoned for offences committed after 1 December 1837 on charges of treason, treasonable practices, or on misprision of treason, that is the withholding of information about treasonable acts, could be held without bail. Judges were not to bind over those charged with the above offences without an order from the lieutenant-governor. The act also deprived the accused traitors of their right of habeas corpus, decreeing that the writs thereof were not to be returnable for thirty days after being allowed.[82] A further law (1 Victoria C. 10) provided that anyone charged with treason could, before being arraigned in court, petition the lieutenant-governor admitting guilt and asking for pardon, whereupon the governor-in-council might grant the request on whatever terms deemed suitable.[83]

A third act forbade people from meeting and drilling 'without any lawful authority for so doing;' under this legislation justices were authorized to seize weapons held 'for any purpose dangerous to the public peace.'[84] Another act dealt with those taken in the Navy Island operations and with the captives from the border raids who had joined with those in the province who were in arms on or after 12 January 1838. Under this statute foreigners, and their cohorts who were British subjects, were to be tried either by a court martial or by the Court of Oyer and Terminer and General Gaol Delivery.[85]

In some ways the most extraordinary piece of legislation was a statute which granted loyalists immunity from prosecution for actions taken to suppress the rebellion. Any legal proceedings against them were to 'be discharged and void.' Those accused were to 'be freed, acquitted, discharged and indemnified,' and, if involved in court cases, awarded 'double costs.'[86] Clearly, this legislation, providing blanket protection to all who claimed they had acted to subdue the rebels, was open to abuse and abuses doubtless occurred. None the less, the members of the assembly did feel it necessary to give encouragement as well as succour to a loyalist population which felt itself besieged by enemies from within and without the province. That these laws were unusual cannot be denied, but the times were extraordinary and must be recognized as such by those who insist on the unparalleled severity of the Tory reaction.

The members of the assembly also unseated several of their number who were absconding traitors, including Dr Charles Duncombe of Oxford and Dr John Rolph of Norfolk. The MPPs, however, allowed Robert Alway and Elias Moore, who were accused of treason and lodged in jail, to retain their places. There exists no information about the elections held in the west for the two vacant seats there but an address to the voters of Oxford by Roger Rollo Hunter, a Scot, is extant in which he declared he would be a 'Reformer' wherever necessary. He expressed his conviction, though, that the province's laws and government were 'the best that have yet been discovered.'[87] Hunter took his place in the legislature on 4 March, Rolph's replacement, William Salmon of Simcoe having taken his on 27 February.[88] Both men were probably Tories, for no 'loyal' outcries were raised against their elections.

Within the assembly, little opposition existed either to the unseating of members or to the extraordinary laws passed. What opposition there was was usually headed by Thomas Parke, the Liberal member for Middlesex, occasionally joined by Charles Duncombe's brother, David. However, David's attendance at the session, which lasted from 28 December to 6 March, was not entirely regular, and his voting record was not completely satisfactory, at least from Parke's point of view. On 9 January, for example, David voted with seven others for an amendment proposed by Parke which would have blunted the act granting loyalists blanket immunity for actions taken to suppress the revolt;[89] on 20 January, however, he voted for the expulsion from the assembly of his fellow-MPP from Norfolk, John Rolph. Only Parke and one other member, Malloch, opposed that expulsion. (That same day Charles Duncombe was expelled without a recorded division.)[90] David Duncombe thus did little to strengthen the weak opposition forces within the assembly although time and circumstances (including the fact that he was the brother of a known traitor) did, of course, severely limit his freedom of action.

122 The Rising in Western Upper Canada

In large part, the opposition in the assembly was weak because the patriot threat seemed to demand that everyone support the measures advanced to curb rebellion and prevent invasion. For a time, the measures either taken or contemplated by the government and its officers against the patriots and the rebels appeared to have been effective. Rebellion in the province had been put down and the frontiers pacified. On 30 January most of the militia in the province then on duty were dismissed, although 1,950 volunteers were enrolled for further service until 1 July.[91] The reduction of the militia could be justified because the rebels had been subdued and the numbers of British Regulars in the province had increased.

By mid-February Colonel John Maitland, who for a time had been in command on the Niagara frontier, was charged with keeping the London and Western districts secure. He had five companies of the Thirty-Second regiment, one of the Twenty-Fourth, and two of the Eighty-Third, as well as a detachment of artillery. London had become his headquarters, beginning the long association between the military and that town which proved so important to its growth and character. Leaving most of his men in London, Maitland himself led three companies off to Amherstburg in mid-February to bolster the defences of the Western district,[92] which, unknown to him, the patriots were planning to invade at several points.

Some 100 miles from Amherstburg lay Cleveland, a city of 5,000 to 6,000 people and a hotbed of patriot activity from the start. In January Eliakim Malcolm's arrival had been reported by an enthusiastic *Cleveland Herald*.[93] No firm evidence exists that Malcolm was involved at this juncture with the patriots, but he had written William Lyon Mackenzie on 29 December from Buffalo that he and a group of young men, evidently dedicated to overthrowing the Upper Canadian government, were going to strike off for Detroit.[94] Moreover, his appearance in Ohio roughly coincided with the conclusion of an agreement among a group of men at Conneaut to invade Pelee Island in British waters in Lake Erie. The invasion was to be carried out in conjunction with a series of attacks along the Detroit frontier. In February Charles Duncombe himself issued three proclamations promising land and money to all the residents of Upper Canada willing to enrol in the patriot cause.[95]

On 23 February, Duncombe participated in an abortive raid which saw a force of 152 men land at Fighting Island in the Detroit River a short distance from Sandwich. On the twenty-fifth, Maitland's men from the Thirty-Second and Eighty-Third regiments forced the invaders back to the American shore where they were dispersed by American troops.

123 Repercussions

Other threatened incursions into Upper Canadian territory along the Niagara frontier and around Kingston failed to materialize.

A major attack, however, was that at Pelee Island. On 26 February, a force variously estimated at from 400 to 1,000 or more men (virtually all Americans)[96] crossed on the ice from the Ohio shore to the island. On 2 March, Maitland arrived from Amherstburg with four companies of the Thirty-Second regiment, two of the Eighty-Third, some Essex militiamen, and twenty-two men of the St Thomas cavalry, and drove the patriots back to American soil. Reportedly, eleven patriots were killed, forty-five wounded, and eleven taken prisoner. Twenty-eight of Maitland's force were wounded, and two were killed, including a member of the St Thomas troop. Three others later died from their wounds.[97]

The Pelee Island raid awakened the fears of the west. After mid-December, the rebel area and its environs had been relatively quiet although in January it had been reported that treasonable meetings were still being held in Norwich and near Scotland and that a troop of militia was being dispatched to sweep the region for arms.[98] In February it was rumoured that the rebels were making cannon at Dereham Forge.[99] Nothing further came of these reports, and the loyal residents of the counties of Oxford, Norfolk, and Middlesex took some comfort from Colonel Maitland's post at London. The raid on Pelee, however, showed how vulnerable the settlers along the Erie shore were to American attack, particularly once the navigation season opened. Andrew Connors, a rebel freed on bail, swore before justice Doyle McKenny of Malahide that the traitors imprisoned at London had instructed their associates to tell the magistrates that all of the insurgents' weapons had been captured, for 'all the Guns of their party would be wanted next Spring when the Americans would come over to upper Canada and help them fight the Toreys and Liberate the prisoner[s].'[100]

On 12 March, Colonel John Bostwick of Port Stanley wrote with six other magistrates to Lieutenant-Governor Head requesting that British Regulars be stationed there. They explained that the village was just a few hour's sailing time from Cleveland and added that 'many of the Rebels being intimately acquainted with this part of the Country, and some of them having left behind them their family and valuable properties, leaves us little reason to doubt that attempts will be made to enter Canada at this point.'[101]

That same day, John Burwell pointed out to the authorities that there were thirteen ships in Port Burwell's harbour. He insisted that the patriots were fitting out an expedition at Cleveland, intending to seize the vessels and march inland from Bayham upon either Hamilton or London.[102] In his capacity as collector of customs Burwell requested the governor's permission to detain two ships then at anchor in the port because their masters, he felt, were inclined to favour the rebel cause. Consent was refused.[103] On 16 March John's brother, Mahlon, wrote urging the government to commandeer the schooners in the harbour and use them as gunboats in order to forestall a patriot landing which he thought might command support from the traitors of the townships of Norwich, Dereham, and Oakland. The matter was urgent, he said, as the navigation season would shortly open.[104] But his proposal was not viewed with any more favour than was John's

On 17 March, George C. Salmon of Simcoe recorded that he was daily importuned by people living along the lakeshore to urge the government to establish troops along the front before the ice was out, because those rebels who had fled the region had threatened to return to plunder the area as soon as the navigation season had begun. He added that many families were preparing to move into the interior and were particularly resentful at being obliged to do so when so many troops were maintained at London which was well inland.[105] From Vittoria came a plea from Colonel A.A. Rapelje for artillery for Charlotteville's lakefront to prevent any rebel landing there. He pointedly reminded the government that the Malcolm settlement was only fifteen miles from the Erie shore.[106] On 19 March, a Port Dover resident, Benjamin Meade, noted unhappily that the ice had gone out the preceding day and that the local inhabitants 'now hourly expect' the patriots to land, 'to rob, plunder and burn.' He suggested that the area's Radicals were threatening to set fire to their enemies' homes even before the anticipated invasion occurred.[107] But the government, beseiged with cries of alarm from every quarter, could do little to calm the fears or meet the many requests for troops.

IV

It was against a general background of alarm in the west that the 'state trials,' which were to be held in both the London and Gore districts, began in Hamilton. The prisoners arrested on various charges of treason, all punishable by death, were to be tried by the Court of Oyer and Terminer and General Gaol Delivery. Commissions for this court were issued whenever cases involving capital felonies arose in the districts for such cases could not be tried by the courts of quarter sessions. Sittings of the Court of Oyer and Terminer were popularly referred to as the 'assizes.'

125 Repercussions

At Hamilton the Grand Jury began on 8 March. It freed twenty-four individuals when it failed to find bills of treason against them. Those liberated included eight men who definitely appeared to have been rebels, two who had provided the insurgents with aid, and five who had been accused either of having taken up arms or of having helped those who did, but against whom not enough information is available.[108] One of the rebels, Alonzo Foster of Oakland, years later asked for £17.5.0 indemnification for his three months' imprisonment.[109] He was less ambitious but as unsuccessful as Joseph Smith, who asked for £200 for the same reason.[110] Those liberated also included five persons arrested for reasons unknown and four taken for activities near Hamilton.[111] The jury returned true bills on charges of treason against fifty-one people, including seven who had absconded to the United States.[112]

Not all of those indicted were to face trial, however. The provincial assembly had enacted a statute (1 Victoria C. 10) which allowed state prisoners to petition for mercy, as Chief Justice John Beverley Robinson explained in a memorandum prepared for internal government consumption, because there had been 300 to 400 people in jail in Upper Canada on treason charges. If all were to be tried, the trials would drag on into the summer, 'occasioning a vast inconvenience and expense in guarding them, continuing in great measure the uneasy state of excitement produced by the insurrection, and subjecting to the danger of disease and death, and the certainty of much suffering, many unhappy persons whom the Government would doubtless consent to pardon, and, in some cases on very favourable terms.'[113] Yet, only fourteen of those indicted at Hamilton managed to avoid being tried by petitioning before they were arraigned.[114] They included two settlers from Nassagaweya who had been prepared to march to Toronto in December to aid Mackenzie, nine men identified here as having been among those who rallied at Oakland in December 1837, and three persons known to have aided the insurgent cause.[115] John Tufford, who had been at Oakland with his father-in-law, Charles Duncombe, later claimed that he had wished to petition but had been told his case was of such an aggravated character that he could not be allowed to do so.[116]

Solicitor-General Draper, arriving in Hamilton to act as Crown prosecutor, found that everything was 'in confusion and utterly unprepared for me.'[117] He enlisted the support of Allan MacNab in preparing the cases, and quickly concluded that 'many prisoners have been confined here on charges, so indifferently supported by evidence as to make it appear a hardship that they have not been much sooner released.'[118] The fact that he freed Abraham Vanduzen, against whom a bill of indictment had not been found by the Grand Jury, demonstrates that at least some of those not indicted had been kept imprisoned until Draper's arrival. As well, the solicitor-general, or possibly some other authority, ignored the bills against John Malcolm, identified here as a rebel (who years later vainly sought £25 reimbursement from the government),[119] Michael Showers, who had provided the insurgents with aid, and Robert Alway, who was accused of persuading men to take up arms.[120] Obviously, opinion was that there was insufficient evidence to justify their prosecutions and probably all three were bailed.

On 26 March, the treason trials opened. The presiding justice was James Buchanan Macaulay, 'a sound lawyer and a fair and impartial judge,'[121] who sat with three associate justices. The first trial was on 27 March, and involved seven Eramosa men indicted for treason for their parts in the meeting of 8 December. (Legally, the testimony of at least two independent witnesses that the accused was guilty was necessary to secure a conviction on a charge of treason.) The proceedings lasted all day, but the jury took only a few minutes to decide that all should be released.[122]

In the succeeding week nineteen other prisoners were tried for treason. At this relatively late date, Draper ordered seventeen-year-old Norman Malcolm (who reputedly had threatened those arresting his father) freed despite his indictment because no evidence was forthcoming against him.[123] Willard Sherman, accused of hoarding weapons in preparation for the revolt, was found not guilty, as Draper expected.[124] John Hammill, said to have been at the rebel camp and to have advised the insurgents to march on Brantford, was placed on the stand. His trial records have not been found and, although other documents examined revealed only one witness willing to testify against him, he was found guilty and condemned to death. But he was assured that the executive council would be advised not to enforce the sentence.[125]

Three men defined here as having aided the insurrectionists were also brought before the bar. One was Solomon Lossing, the lapsed Quaker and Norwich magistrate. Although the jury heard a welter of contradictory evidence, it took only five minutes to find him not guilty.[126] Judge Macaulay thought that the testimony given could have supported either verdict,[127] but Allan MacNab, who had had Lossing arrested before an assembled throng at Sodom in December, insisted that the prisoner had been freed only because one or two material witnesses could not be procured.[128] (In 1845 the Lossing estate unsuccessfully sought £158.5.0 for the expenses Solomon had incurred during his imprisonment and trial.[129]) Both Nathan Town and Stephen Smith of Norwich, who like Lossing had provided aid for the insurgents, were tried, found guilty, and sentenced to death, though Town was recommended to mercy.[130]

Fourteen people identified here as having taken up arms in the Duncombe rising also appeared in court. Seven – William Lyons, Finlay Malcolm of Oakland, Oliver Smith, John L. Uline, Adam Yeigh, George Rouse, and Samuel Marlatt – were acquitted. Draper commented that against Lyons 'there was strong but not conclusive evidence.' He felt that the case against the former member of the assembly, Finlay Malcolm, had been a good one, but he was 'convinced the Jury were activated by motives of conscience and sound discretion in his acquittal.' He was, however, somewhat surprised at the freeing of Oliver Smith of Bayham, against whom he thought the Crown had amassed considerable evidence. He was particularly taken aback at the verdicts in the cases of Yeigh, Uline, Rouse, and Marlatt, attributing them to the fact that the prisoners had secured the most favourable juries possible by extensive use of their right to challenge jurors. Draper, who had evidently not yet raised objections to any juror, determined to do so in the future.[131]

Seven other men previously named as rebels – John Tufford, Charles P. Walrath, Elias Snider, Peter Malcolm, Horatio Hills, Ephraim Cook, and William Webb – were pronounced guilty of treason. It is not certain if the judges condemned Snider to death but Webb, Hills, Walrath, Cook, Tufford, and Malcolm were all to be taken to the scaffold on 20 April. The executive council would be requested not to enforce Webb's sentence, however, and the verdicts against Cook and Snider were 'qualified.'[132]

The Gore district trials closed on 4 April 1838. In all, twenty-six prisoners had been tried, sixteen of whom had been judged not guilty. The remainder had been found guilty of treason and apparently sentenced to death. The chances were remote that the sentence of death would actually be carried out. On 31 March, the new lieutenant-governor, Sir George Arthur, who had replaced Sir Francis Bond Head a week earlier, had informed the executive council that Lord Glenelg was anxious to avoid hangings.[133] On 3 April, the council had decided to implement the death sentence as seldom as possible.[134]

In Toronto on 13 April, two of the convicted principals in the Home district uprising, Samuel Lount and Peter Matthews, were executed, despite the fact that the government had been deluged with petitions, 4,420 for Lount and 354 for Matthews, requesting that they be spared. Their deaths were evidently considered enough, however, for on 14 April Arthur informed the colonial secretary that he thought that there would be no further hangings and that henceforth 'the worst and most dangerous traitors' would be transported.[135]

The executions scheduled at Hamilton for 20 April were thus not carried out, though it is not known when the condemned men were told that their sentences were to be respited. In any event, the public did not know of the reprieves. On 18 April, rumours that the patriots were going to attempt to free the inmates led to the placing of extra guards about the jail.[136] On the nineteenth, Colonel Robert Land, in response to reports that armed men were moving on Hamilton from the Oakland area, sent out cavalry patrols to watch for the approach of expected patriot bands.[137] That night one man was arrested in Hamilton on suspicion of being involved in a plot to free the prisoners.[138] Nothing further happened, but one of the men captured that summer in a raid on the province, Linus Miller, insisted that he and others from the United States had been partner to a conspiracy in April to rescue those confined in the Hamilton jail. The plan, however, had been thwarted at the last moment.[139]

Meanwhile, on 9 April, the Grand Jury at London began its deliberations. On 10 April, the executive council directed that the local authorities take no action against those freed on bail unless their cases were aggravated ones.[140] Evidently, the magistrates at London had not been much hampered by the statute limiting the rights to bail of accused traitors, for they had bound over no fewer than ninety-five. Nineteen of them, sixteen who had taken up arms,[141] Duncan Wilson who had aided the Yarmouth rebels, and Alvaro Ladd and Moore Stephens, both of whom had been implicated in the 'Delaware conspiracy,' had subsequently been recommitted, probably before the order of 10 April. Wilson was later released once again when no bill of indictment was found against him. Ladd and Stephens, and one of the rebels, Robert Cook, were indicted and later tried, while the other fifteen were indicted but petitioned under the act 1 Victoria C. 10.

A further fourteen men, who had been in the London jail for two months or more, were not indicted by the Grand Jury. Three of them have been described here as rebels and two as having aided the insurrectionists. Three of the others were accused of having been in arms or having furthered the insurgents' cause, but insufficient evidence has been found to consider them guilty. Five had been arrested on charges arising from events which had occurred in the London district not directly connected with the Duncombe rebellion. The last of the fourteen prisoners had been confined to the cells for a reason still unknown.[142]

The London Grand Jury found eighty-one bills of indictment.

Included were bills against twenty-four men who had fled the province. Before the trials began and before the execution at Toronto of Lount and Matthews, twenty-six inmates of the London jail had petitioned under 1 Victoria C. 10. Twenty-five have been identified as rebels in this study;[143] the twenty-sixth, Nathaniel Deo, had participated in the Dorchester meeting of 14 December. After the hangings at Toronto, a further thirteen prisoners petitioned. All had been with Duncombe at Oakland.[144] One, Isaac Moore of Yarmouth, was obliged to stand trial, presumably because his case was considered an aggravated one, members of his family having been prominent in the insurrectionary movement along the lakefront. A further four petitioned at dates now unknown.[145] In all, forty-two people petitioned from London, yet the official return listed only thirty-eight names.[146] Two of those omitted, John Riley and Mire Wethy, and possibly a third, Abraham Sackrider, were overlooked because they were Crown witnesses held in prison. The intention appears to have been to release them only after they had testified. The name of the fourth man, George Hill, was omitted erroneously. None of the four was indicted.

After the Hamilton trials, MacNab and Draper had proceeded to London to prepare the Crown's cases there. On 24 April, before the court opened in that town, the solicitor-general wrote to Arthur's secretary asserting that he felt that 'an example of some severity is in my opinion necessary in this district as well for the subduing [of] the spirit which even yet exists in some quarters, particularly in Norwich and the south part of Yarmouth.' He had heard, he confided, that some Crown witnesses had been leaving the country, and felt that 'they have been got out of the way by the friends of those who are indicted.'[147] Draper's suspicion is borne out by the declaration of the two men who had stood bail for young Sobiske Brown of Malahide, who had been in Anderson's party and who had been arrested and then bailed as a Crown witness, that Brown 'was frightened or bribed to leave the Country.' By fleeing, Brown had forfeited his bond. The Crown moved to estreat his recognizance but the executive council, responding to the petition of his two sureties, asked the attorney-general to stay proceedings. The council noted that Brown had never been indicted.[148] Legally, that was immaterial because Brown, like others bailed, had promised to appear at the assizes to answer whatever charges he might face. Many others who were bound over and who were not indicted also ignored this condition of their bonds. Draper thus authorized the estreating of their recognizances which, of course, led to complaints from the aggrieved, whether principals or sureties, that he had treated them unjustly. If those concerned appeared and paid the court clerk his legal fees, Draper subsequently allowed the actions involved to be withdrawn.[149] On balance, then, in these cases the government acted with considerable generosity. Such generosity could not be extended to three others cases, however: those of Lyman Davis, John Massacre, and John Van Arnam. These men had been involved in the Duncombe rising, had been captured, bailed, indicted, and had, like Brown, fled the province.

On 30 April, the preliminaries over, the treason trials opened at London with Justice Henry Sherwood presiding. MacNab was again to have assisted Draper, the Crown prosecutor, but he fell ill before the trials began and was unable to appear. (Ironically, Draper himself had fallen ill during the Grand Jury's deliberations at Hamilton, and MacNab had handled the Crown's affairs on his own then.)[150] The London trials were to involve nineteen prisoners. During the proceedings this number was reduced, however. Cases were dropped against two St Thomas residents, Descom Simons, identified here as having furthered the insurgent cause, and Anson Gould, who was accused of having done so but on evidence that this study has found to be insufficient. Charles Tilden, who had attempted to raise recruits in Dorchester and Westminster for Duncombe, was considered too ill to be placed on the stand and was released on bail. Elias Moore, M.P.P., who had encouraged the people of the south of Yarmouth to rebel, was indicted on misprision of treason, but his trial was postponed because an important witness had absconded.[151] Moore had been freed on £500 bail on 19 February[152] and, like Tilden, was never jailed again.

Fifteen people faced trial, three of them (William Hale, Charles Latimer, and William Putnam) for their parts in the meeting at Flannagan's Tavern in London on 8 December. They were accused of attempting to raise a revolt in London and of trying to secure aid for Mackenzie.[153] The three were acquitted, and the verdicts bore out the sensible conclusion that the London Reformers had not been plotting rebellion.

Gideon Tiffany, Alvaro Ladd, Moore Stephens, and John Stephens were all tried for their parts in the so-called 'Delaware conspiracy,' involving alleged attempts to spread disaffection among the Indians. All but Ladd were judged not guilty. Even Judge Sherwood was surprised at the verdict against Ladd, however, and reserved his case for further consideration.[154]

The court tried five prisoners who had aided the Duncombe rebels.

Three (John D. Brown, Enoch Moore, and Ebenezer Wilcox) were from Malahide, and two (Harvey Bryant and John Moore) were from neighbouring Yarmouth, forming a rather select geographical circle. Brown was acquitted but the other four were found guilty. Sherwood reserved Wilcox's case, however, because the testimony of two independent witnesses was necessary to secure a conviction and Wilcox had been judged guilty on the basis of the testimony of one witness and on a confession he had made before examining magistrates. Sherwood simply did not know if this evidence warranted a conviction.[155] But Harvey Bryant and the two Moore brothers were condemned to death. In passing sentence, Sherwood commented that he had no reasonable doubt that all were guilty.[156] Although Draper felt that there should be at least one execution in the London district, he advised the government that none of these three men could be condemned as their cases were no worse than those of others elsewhere who had not been put to death.[157]

Only three men who had actually been at Scotland with Duncombe were tried: Isaac Moore of Yarmouth, Robert Cook of Bayham, and David Hagerman of Norwich. Isaac Moore, whose petition under 1 Victoria C. 10 had been refused consideration, was acquitted, the Crown producing virtually no evidence against him.[158] Hagerman, too, was freed, much to Draper's surprise as he felt that ample proof had been presented of his guilt.[159] Cook was convicted, but Sherwood reserved his case for further consideration because the evidence against him was identical with that against Ebenezer Wilcox.[160]

When the trials closed at London in May, six people had thus been found guilty of high treason, three of whom were under sentence of death. The editor of the *London Gazette* on 19 May remarked that mercy pled 'for lenity to the unfortunate beings, many of whom have no other fault than a fanatic desire to kill those who are contented to live in peace.' Had the rebels been victorious, he assured his readers, they would have shown no compassion to their enemies. The insurgents were, in fact, still unrepentant. Therefore, he concluded, in apparent reference to the condemned London prisoners, the traitors 'must be removed from the possibility of ever again attempting to drench the land with the blood of unoffending citizens.' None the less the editor was not prepared to urge the government to carry out the projected executions and, indeed, the lieutenant-governor stayed them on 20 May.[161]

To judge by the way in which they disposed of the captured rebels' cases, the authorities had not engaged in a bloody witchhunt. Some injustices had doubtless been perpetrated but no one had been sent to

132 The Rising in Western Upper Canada

the scaffold. Indeed, in the entire province only Lount and Matthews had been put to death for their parts in the uprising. Certainly the loyalists of Upper Canada had good reason for feeling that their government had acted with comparative leniency towards those captured for treason. It is interesting to note that in England the 'Swing Riots' of the early 1830s had witnessed violent outbreaks of agrarian unrest as the desperate populations of numerous rural communities resorted to intimidation and violence to stop the introduction of machinery by their employers, the large farmers. Eventually, over 1,900 of those participating were tried. Nineteen were executed, 644 imprisoned, and no less than 481 sent to the penal colonies.[162] Although the analogy between the Swing riots and the Upper Canadian rebellion is far from precise, the two movements were roughly contemporaneous and the treatment received by most of those who had joined either Charles Duncombe or William Lyon Mackenzie was far more lenient than that allotted in England.

After the assizes at London, Draper concluded that

The flight of many important witnesses for the Crown in the interval between the service of the list containing their names and the trials, the violent though anonymous threats used against other witnesses of great importance: the absconding of many who had been bailed and against whom no prosecutions were instituted and even of some in whose favour verdicts of acquittal had been rendered, compel the admission that disaffection has spread in the London District more widely than from the actual numbers of insurgents might have been imagined.[163]

Disaffected spirits or 'secret well wishers to the revolutionary cause' as Draper called them still lurked in the west and he expected that they would soon renew their agitation 'in the hopes of producing at a future period a more favourable result to their efforts for the establishment of republican institutions.' He also contended that most of the potential traitors were natives of the United States. In fact, because a sizable number of individuals to the south (some of whom had been former residents of the province) were determined to liberate Upper Canada from its supposed thraldom, there was an obvious danger that hostile forces within and without the colony would attempt a new, co-ordinated uprising. The prospects for a peaceful summer and fall were not propitious.

6
Consequences

The assizes of the spring of 1838 had left a number of prisoners scheduled for a variety of punishments and the animosities between the disaffected and the loyalists were further inflamed as the ultimate disposition of the prisoners became a matter of public debate. The difficulties faced by the government in securing certain Crown witnesses and the hostility with which the proceedings of the assizes had been regarded in some quarters had demonstrated that the Liberal, Radical, or disaffected spirit of the west had not been broken. The prospect that residents of treasonable disposition might unite with marauding bands of patriots seemed distinctly possible and later appeared to many to be a reality. Thus initial distrust of the Liberal segments of the community often turned into hatred as the long controversy over the political future of the province entered its final, and in some ways most critical, phase.

I

Through the late spring of 1838 there was a continuing fear that the Lake Erie townships would be subject to patriot invasions. Although Mahlon Burwell, who had predicted earlier that a raid would be conducted on Port Burwell, was convinced by 21 April that the danger had subsided and that militia forces were not then required 'in any part of the District,'[1] other inhabitants of the area were still uneasy. For example, when Stephen Fuller, a Port Dover resident who was to become a government spy, learned that the local militia guard of twenty men was to be discharged, he wrote to R.B. Sullivan, the commissioner of Crown lands. He asserted that one of the town's residents who had joined Mackenzie on Navy Island (presumably Moses Chapman Nickerson, a Mormon and a partner in the Port Dover harbour development company) intended to lead a patriot onslaught against the community. The situation was particularly critical because a 'nest' of traitors in the village would willingly aid the invaders. One of them who had repeatedly been refused a tavern licence because of his disloyal conduct had begun an inn in the town 'in open defiance of the law,' daily collecting about him a band of 'regular rebel ruffians.' Thus Fuller thought that the militiamen should not be dismissed and should, in fact, be bolstered by 'a company of regulars' or of 'trusty blacks.'[2] The same day that his letter was sent to Toronto, a man was reportedly arrested at Simcoe for writing to a rebel who had fled to Detroit that the region was virtually undefended and that the militiamen on duty 'were in a state of mutiny in consequence of not having their pay.'[3]

On 24 April a ship grounded on Long Point. Colonel George C. Salmon of Simcoe, who had been informed that forces from the south were to land at various points on the Erie shore on 25 April, ordered out a troop of cavalry and 200 members of the First and Second Norfolk regiments. Assuring the government that the disaffected of the locality were 'very numerous' and 'as violent as ever,' he asked that regular troops be sent to the area.[4]

On 26 April, six men were sent by boat to investigate the vessel off Long Point. They found the ship to be the steamer *Bunker Hill* out from Buffalo on its way to Cleveland. It had been driven aground during a snow-storm. The captain, who had ordered the ship's colours lowered to half-mast, had already sent a boat back to Buffalo for help. On 30 April a second steamer arrived and took on the *Bunker Hill*'s 150 passengers, its 18 horses, and the rest of its cargo. The stricken vessel got off under its own power on 5 May.[5]

Meanwhile, Lieutenant-Governor Arthur had ordered a militia detachment stationed at Brantford to Port Dover to report on the situation at Long Point. The men found that at every tavern where they halted on the march the settlers were 'extremely insolent and abusive.' Moreover, the residents were at every crossroads to taunt them. At Simcoe and at Port Dover they encountered rebellious spirits, and the commanding officer, Major T.W. Magrath, was assured that 'there were 100 men between Scotland, Oakland & there ready to turn out' with the patriots.[6] The local magistrates, 'evidently *afraid* of *those fellows*,' had been inactive. For their part, the militiamen on duty at Port Dover were ill-prepared and demoralized. Magrath did what he could to remedy the situation by establishing a line of communication from the village to Brantford, placing men in various centres between the two points and also at Simcoe, where there was already a detachment of Regulars from the Thirty-Second regiment.

On the return to Brantford, the troops found 'the people much more Insolent and abusive than before.'[7] One of the detachment riding on ahead was attacked by four men, and was released only through the intervention of a passer-by. The incident reinforced Magrath's conclusion that, if the patriots did invade the area, they would 'have plenty of fellows from this part of the country with them'; for they would be joined by many, who would perhaps enlist only for the sake of burning 'the property of those who are obnoxious to them.'[8]

In Brantford threats were made that any of Magrath's troopers venturing out on their own would be hanged. This did not deter Magrath from riding out alone to find and warn those who had assaulted the trooper to leave the country. He concluded that the individuals most forward in harassing him and his men had been 'fellows of no property in this country & strangers.'[9] Later in May, Magrath and his lieutenant were hanged in effigy and in Simcoe an American settler was reportedly jailed for encouraging men of the Thirty-Second to desert.[10] Reports of disaffection and of intended invasion led to the government decision in May to station two gunboats at Port Stanley and Port Dover.[11]

Trouble was anticipated in the rebel area partly because Charles Duncombe was active among the patriots across the border. He was a founding member of the Candian Refugee Relief Association established in Lockport, New York, on 29 March.[12] On 28 May, his brother Elijah of St Thomas observed that the Tory newspapers had reported that Duncombe was at Lockport with 800 to 1,200 men. Thus, Elijah noted, the local Tories expected 'another Skirmish in a few weeks.'[13] For his part, he was distressed. He himself had not been involved in the rebellion but had been forced by the officials to keep one Rufus Turkey for a month to see if Charles was hiding in his house. He had also been forced to billet 160 militiamen (and was to be obliged to wait seven years for only partial payment).[14] Moreover, there were still three companies of militiamen in the village who had not, Elijah thought, 'conducted themselves very well.' Gloom was in the air, increased by emigration to the United States, the depression of property values, and sickness. Elijah concluded professionally that 'there has been more death in this Part of the Country than there was for 5 years Past but Principally old People and Children –. The Scarlet fever and Canker Rash has been the Principal cause – some severe colds from Military Exposure.'[15] Over this scene hung the threat of further troubles.

On 30 May, the Upper-Canadian-owned steamboat, the *Sir Robert Peel*, was attacked and burnt in the Thousand Islands by a band of Americans. Alarm increased all along the frontier, particularly in some of the lakefront communities which had lost their militia guards. On 3 June, John Burwell of Port Burwell informed Arthur's secretary, John Joseph, that 'we are in constant fears in this quarter of some marauding excursion.'[16] A few days later, he added that many people formerly of the area had enrolled in the patriot cause who had 'personal as well as local feeling of revenge to gratify.'[17] On 6 June, Edward Ermatinger, a magistrate and a merchant of St Thomas, confided to the government his belief that the disaffected in Upper Canada and their sympathizers in the United States planned a co-ordinated uprising and invasion. He was convinced that 'a constant communication is kept up by means of itinerants between the pirates in the United States and persons' in Yarmouth and expressed great concern over the defenceless state of Port Stanley.[18]

Further inland in the rebel area others were apprehensive. Warner Worthington, a black, later claimed that on 4 June, militia muster day, 'a few Americans got together' in Burford and cursed 'the old country people saying that it would not be long now when they would let them see that Canada was not their country.'[19] Strangers from the United States had passed through the township and the local rebels would go out 'under pretence of shooting game in the woods when the real object is to practise firing at a mark.' The names of those who had fled Burford appeared on a letter circulating in the township which also listed their properties and conveyed the promise, or threat, that they would return soon.[20] The wife of one Burford settler indicated that the loyalists found it necessary to carry arms with them.[21]

In early June, Moses Johnson, a Blenheim militia captain, informed John Joseph that he had discovered that the Radicals were planning to arise in every township and dispose of their political enemies. Consequently, he had put his men on the alert.[22] William Brearly, colonel of the First Oxford regiment, reported on 9 June that the disaffected held meetings in Norwich nightly and that those involved were in contact with American agents, some of whom were then in the township 'spreading alarm and creating mistrust & apprehension.' The residents of Norwich who supported the government were threatened 'to an extent never before experienced.'[23]

Later in June, Colonel Holcroft of the Fifth Oxford regiment noted that treasonable sentiment was prevalent in Oxford and that 'the pardoned rebels are the most forward and audacious' of the disaffected spirits.[24] The local justices had been unable to secure information about the activities of the traitors in the region who were 'under oath of secrecy & are assembling in various places at night & passing through the Townships with spies & scouts in communication with the different bands.' Holcroft felt that the authorities could place little confidence in the militiamen of Oxford county, adding that nine out of ten of those they could trust were British-born. He ardently hoped that some regular troops would 'scour these rebellious Townships, Norwich, Dereham, parts of East & West Oxford, Burford & Nissouri.'

The outbreak came, however, not in the rebel area but to the east in the Short Hills region of the Niagara district. In New York state, the head of the Canadian Refugee Relief Association, Dr A.K. Mackenzie of Hamilton, had been busy securing men for a raid on the province. Reportedly, Duncombe, a member of the association, had also been busy enrolling volunteers.[25] Young 'Colonel' George Washington Case of Hamilton, who had been with Duncombe at Oakland, and a fellow patriot, 'Colonel' James Morreau of Pennsylvania, tried to muster a force from the American shore against the Niagara district, but could persuade only a few men to follow them.[26]

Case gave up for the moment, but on 11 June Morreau led a group of twenty-nine men into the province. The raiders made their way into the Short Hills region back of St Catharines, an area which had, like Yarmouth and Norwich, a large Quaker population. On 15 June, four or five others from the United States joined the force. Among the invaders, many of whom were young Upper Canadians, were two men who had taken up arms under Duncombe and had then fled across the line: Garrett Van Camp of Burford and Jacob Beamer of Oakland. Dr Duncan Wilson of Yarmouth, who had furthered the rebel cause and had consequently been held in London jail for much of the winter, was also with Morreau.

On the night of 20 June, the marauders, joined by a number of local inhabitants, marched upon the village of St Johns, which was the base for a troop of fourteen Queen's Lancers, militia cavalrymen sent into the Short Hills in mid-June under Lieutenant James Magrath to collect information about rebel activities reported there. The patriots had earlier determined to attack the Lancers to capture their arms and to defy the provincial government. By this time, the raiders numbered forty to seventy men. They fell upon the inn housing the troopers and eventually drove them out by setting fire to it. They took the Lancers captive, made them march about a mile into the woods, and then freed them, minus their horses and weapons. Morreau and his comrades returned to their camp but, finding that the militia of the area had been quickly alerted, dispersed in an effort to escape.

Governor Arthur promptly ordered the Six Nations warriors mustered because he understood that those in arms in the Short Hills hoped to enlist their support. The Indians and the Norfolk militia were to seal off the escape routes to the west. The Iroquois braves were placed under William Johnson Kerr, a prominent local figure of mixed Scottish and Indian blood. Before leading them down the Grand River, Kerr sent 100 warriors through Oakland township and past the villages of Mount Pleasant and Paris in order to give the 'disaffected in these neighbourhoods the supposition that I was thereabouts with the whole Indian force, as my movements were closely watched in Brantford.'[27]

When he did set off down the Grand, Kerr had 150 braves with him and by the time he reached the lower end of the reserve his force had doubled. 'I found it impossible to restrain' the Indians 'or keep them back,' he reported. He marched his men eastward through the Short Hills to St Johns but failed to capture one rebel although Kerr claimed they flushed a number of fugitives from the woods who were promptly apprehended.

Some of the raiders escaped, including Dr Duncan Wilson, who slipped through the cordon and made his way into Burford. The local authorities in the London district had been quickly informed of the Short Hills affair and that 'our old friend Dr. Wilson has been conspicuous among' the raiders.[28] Wilson continued into Norwich where his brother, David, who had sided with the rebels in December, and his father, Justus, lived. Here he was captured. Two bailiffs, Cyrus Sumner and Philo Bennett, both of London, were charged with the task of conveying him to the district jail.

Nineteen men resolved to free the doctor and lay in wait for him and his captors along the Oxford-Burford road some six miles from Woodstock. As Wilson and his guards drew near, twelve of the would-be liberators lost heart and fled.[29] Those remaining opened fire on the little procession, killing Bennett's horse as well as the one drawing the wagon carrying the prisoner. Sumner's mount was hit, but not badly enough to stop 'Crazy Cy' from spurring his way to safety. Bennett was captured and his pistols taken from him and given to Wilson. The doctor and his rescuers struck off for Norwich, while Bennett, who had been released, fled to Woodstock to raise the alarm.[30]

Wilson left his liberators and fled south-westward towards Yarmouth. He kept to the woods by day, and took to the fields at night, for a band of twenty-seven men with dogs was quickly on his heels. On the night of 29 June he arrived at Richard McKenny's house in Malahide. McKenny had gone to the United States, probably looking for work, but his wife Eliza had stayed behind and she was shocked to see 'the pale and withered form of the once robust and healthy young Doctor; his eyes were sink in their sockets; their fire and intelegence were gone, his cloths were dirty and torn and his whole appearance was sufficiently wretched to have excited pity in the heart of [a] stoick.'[31] Wilson had not eluded his pursuers and he was taken at McKenny's by a group of men who conveyed him straight to London, where they were confronted by 'a pack of still fiercer bloodhounds,' who called them 'cowardly disaffected rascals for not shooting him the minet they saw him.'[32]

II

Wilson's release had widespread repercussions for it confirmed the fears of the Oxford loyalists that treason was rampant in the county. Robert Riddell, a Woodstock magistrate, informed Arthur that many of the residents of Burford, Blenheim, Nissouri, and the three Oxfords and all those of Norwich, Oakland, and Dereham 'are either wholly disaffected, or so indifferent to the cause of the Government, as to remain inert in its support.' In these townships the justices of the peace were in danger when performing their duties; there rebellious persons 'openly and unhesitatingly proclaim the immediate' overthrow of the existing régime. In Oxford only the inhabitants of Zorra and Blandford were well disposed towards the government.[33]

On 28 June, A.W. Light of North Oxford, the English-born colonel of the Second Oxford regiment, relayed the information to the adjutant general that insurgents (presumably Wilson's rescuers) were in arms in Norwich and Dereham. Meanwhile, militiamen from the surrounding area, some 400 in all, were making their way into Norwich;[34] some eighty Indians were in the company of Colonel George Washington Whitehead of Burford and his men.[35] On their arrival, the militiamen and the warriors scoured the woods for hidden traitors.

Those suspected of being implicated in Wilson's rescue were examined at Sodom and, on 30 June, two of the militia colonels reportedly discovered from an individual named Hill that 'the rebels in Norwich and Dereham had received a reinforcement of Americans, rifles, and ammunition, by a Schooner which had landed at or near Long Point.'[36] The insurrectionists numbered, so Hill thought, almost 800. P.B. de Blaquiere, lieutenant colonel of the Third Oxford regiment, which was drawn from Zorra, proposed to march all the available men under his command to Norwich.[37] Colonel Light, who had already sent troops there, now took an additional fifty volunteers to the Quaker township, 'determined to attack the rebels wherever to be found.'[38] The militia, however, tramped through Norwich and Oakland without discovering any clue to the whereabouts of the rebels.

The alarm did not abate, however. The magistrates and militia officers in Sodom made a further 'discovery' that several Americans had visited Norwich and other London district townships 'for the purpose of establishing a Lodge or secret society (the oaths, passwords, signs and rules were cogitated at Lockport).'[39] A branch of the organization had reputedly been created in Norwich of 150 men. That group, along with those in Yarmouth, Westminster, Oakland, Blenheim and Dumfries, a part of Burford, in fact with all the disaffected townships in the province, planned to arise on the night of 3 July to 'disarm the Volunteers, kidnap the magistrates, Militia officers, and principal loyalists, and put to death all who resisted them – establish a government of their own – all in connection with influential Americans.'[40] Colonel Whitehead of Burford was quite convinced that the Norwich men planned 'a general rising' on the third, 'having for their object a general plunder of the Loyal Inhabitants and massacre if found to be necessary.'[41] It was, John Burn of Dereham thought, a 'diabolical project.'[42]

The existence of new patriot organizations increased the fears of Burn, Whitehead, and others. In June 1838 patriots had established in Michigan 'The Secret Order of the Sons of Liberty' whose members sought to establish a series of secret societies in Upper Canada preparatory to launching a great invasion of the province on 4 July.[43] The Sons, however, were quickly absorbed by another patriot organization, the Hunters, which had begun in the spring. The Hunters had grown quickly in part because they modelled their mysteries and rituals on those of another secret society, the highly successful Masons. By the summer of 1838 the Hunters were an important force in a number of American border towns and cities, particularly Rochester, Cleveland, and Lockport (hence the significance of the report that the secret society established in Norwich had been conceived at Lockport).[44]

Whatever the plans of the Hunters and the Sons of Liberty, neither group was active in Norwich on the night of 3 July. That night came and went without incident perhaps, the loyalists felt, because of their preparations. In any event, one can understand the alarm for rumours had long circulated that the disaffected were in touch with the patriots across the line, and the Short Hills raid and Wilson's release increased the uneasiness. It is possible as well that the examining magistrates had discovered the existence of a Hunter's Lodge in Norwich. The disaffected were fond of broadcasting that such a society existed, though their claims may have been as unfounded as their assertions that an uprising was imminent.

One Norwich resident, W.S. Moore, an American who had settled in the township in 1835, later recalled that:

The rebels got into the way of telling me their secrets all of which afterwards proved to be a pack of lies. One of their secrets was that there were thousands from the United States lying back in the woods, ready to help them and that it was well understood, through their secret meetings, there would be a general uprising on the fourth of July and those camped out in the woods would come out and assist them. I heard all this on the second of July and I made up my mind at once that I would leave the country.[45]

On 4 July, detachments of the Second Oxford regiment prepared to return to their homes in obedience to orders from Colonel Maitland of London. Colonel Light, however, sent twenty members of the regiment to Sodom to bolster the twenty-five men guarding the prisoners there. Though he and many of those under his command went back to their families, Light was far from convinced that Norwich had been subdued. He reported to Colonel Richard Bullock, the adjutant general, that in the militia searches in and about Norwich 'the male inhabitants were generally absent ... and I learn that they are all embodied in the woods, with arms and purposely keep out of the way to avoid being made prisoners.' He wrote that 'their names are well known, and a proscription or outlawry can be the only means of reaching them, that unless they deliver themselves up by a certain day, to be examined touching their delinquency, their estates shall be confiscated, or sold to the highest bidder ... They are all Yankees or descendants of Yankees, who have bought estates from settlers and the country can never be at peace till all these be extirpated root and branch.'[46] In Blenheim and Burford also, he added, sixty to seventy men had fled to the neighbouring republic, 'leaving their estates to join the rebels – and these still left behind mob the loyal men who turn out to endeavour to intimidate them from doing their duty.'

Leading spirits of the Duncombe rebellion were rumoured to be in the

Norwich area stirring up trouble. In July Stephen Fuller, a merchant who lived near Port Dover and who was investigating the Long Point area for the government, before proceeding on a spying mission to the United States, reported that he had discovered that '*Eli Malcolm* has been for a fortnight past very busy in the vicinity of *Norwich* and *Oaklands* [sic] ... Malcolm is a *bad one*.[47] Fuller was in touch with an absconding traitor, John Massacre of Townsend, who had returned to the region and was in hiding. Fuller felt that the Townsend farmer, who 'has the most unlimited confidence placed in him by "*Duncombe*," McLeod and other leaders on the opposite shore,' could provide him with vital information in return for the promise of a pardon. Fuller also hoped that he would be able to give him some clue about Malcolm's hiding place. Although Malcolm was certainly not found in Oakland or Norwich that summer, Massacre did receive his pardon early in 1839.[48]

In July several companies of militia continued on duty in Norwich and its surrounding townships. Colonel Holcroft reported from Ingersoll on 6 July that he had embodied all the men he could trust of the Fifth Oxford regiment, which was drawn from the three Oxfords and Nissouri. They amounted to no more than sixty settlers who were '*incessantly* employed in searching the woods night & day for rebels who have fled their houses & are concealed in secret hiding places throughout the Oxfords & Dorchester.'[49] He was, Holcroft lamented, surrounded by traitors, and had few '*good men*' at his disposal. He and two other magistrates were kept busy examining all the suspects brought before them.

The militiamen of Norwich were also turned out and kept on duty, but the loyalists could persuade only seventy-five of a possible 500 to 600 eligible inhabitants to carry arms. 'The rest upon any call fly to the woods or plead their exemption as being aliens.'[50] Norwich and Dereham, from which the First Oxford regiment was drawn, produced only 100 men for duty. The colonel of the regiment, William Brearley, an Englishman who had settled in Norwich in the early thirties, recorded that when the militia were summoned 'the Cheshires [Chasseurs] or Hunters as they call themselves I verily believe outnumbered the Militia.'[51]

The militia's conduct was not exemplary. Doubtless, some of the troops were overenthusiastic, others were frightened, and still others were perhaps drunk. Thomas Wallace, a Sodom merchant, alone supplied the militia with forty-seven gallons of whiskey and the Indians with four-and-a-half gallons.[52] The amount of alcohol consumed may well explain how a sentry on duty in Dereham wounded an ox 'in mistake supposing it to be rebels approaching'[45] or how Russel Babbit of East Oxford, while on his

143 Consequences

farm, was knocked to the ground and had a bayonet thrust through his hat and into his ear by a militiaman.[54]

One resident, Joseph Throckmorton, later recalled that Norwich had been 'a continued scene of riot and confusion,' for the loyalists had searched it night and day. One of the most zealous rebel-hunters, he said, had been Joseph Lancaster, a former officer in Duncombe's army. He declared that 'many of her Majesty's loyal subjects have left this place for fear of the bayonet, of the mob or of being sent to prison by their persecutors.'[55] John Treffry, the English pacifist who had refused to enrol with either the rebels or loyalists in December, complained in August that the militia had taken guns from the populace indiscriminately and that 'the improper method resorted to in searching ... has been extremely harrising [sic].'[56] He thought that the militia need not have been called out because an active magistrate and a few special constables could have kept Norwich peaceful.

Treffry's opinion was seconded by another settler who denied that 'Norwich is one mass of corruption and disaffection ... as Norwich Contains a large majority of as Loyal Inhabitants as can be found in the province.'[57] He protested to Arthur that the militiamen had imposed shamefully on the farmers, particularly the Quakers, adding that they had scrutinized those attending the Friends' meetings and had requisitioned the wagons of women and young children, forcing them to walk home. He also charged that militiamen, forty to fifty or sixty at a time, had burst into farm houses, and had 'caused the inmates of the house to provide food for them until their family stores were all exhausted.' Other people had had goods taken, and had received no receipts for them. Arthur's correspondent deliberately remained anonymous because, as he told the lieutenant-governor, 'any man who will at present venture to expose any of the unjust proceedings openly would be branded as a rebel and confined in Gaol untill the assizes.'

It must be noted that, by and large, most of the militia's transgressions were petty, if annoying. For example, the majority of complaints about ill-usage at the hands of militiamen involved the procedures used in requisitioning goods and services. Arthur did order a civilian inquiry into the militia's conduct, but his secretary, John Macaulay, pointedly reminded one Thomas Maitland (Colonel John Maitland?), who was evidently responsible for implementing it, that: 'many of the allegations are of a grave character, and such if they should prove to be well founded, as would naturally cause much murmuring and discontent among the Inhabitants. His Excellency therefore would be gratified to learn that upon a full and impartial investigation, this failed to be substantiated.'[58] Not surprisingly, when the London district magistrates presented their report, they completely exonerated the militiamen of committing any serious offences in Norwich and its surrounding area, although they did note the possibility that people had not been compensated for those supplies which had been urgently required.[59]

Admittedly, it is difficult to gauge the extent to which the militiamen and the magistrates gathered in Norwich in June and July did persecute the population of that township. Many of the records have been lost and it is not known how many residents were haled before the magistrates or were jailed on one charge or another. This study has identified only fourteen people who were arrested in Norwich that summer (see appendix 9) although doubtless others were detained. Five men – Enoch D. Doxie, Enos and Job Scott, John Dennis, and Isaac L. Smith – were jailed for allegedly being involved in the release of Dr Wilson. Smith was freed after a week but Doxie and Dennis were held for an undetermined period of time – probably a month or more. Dennis had taken up arms under Duncombe in December, but had escaped official notice, while that same month Doxie had been accused of being a rebel on what appears rather uncertain evidence and had been jailed for a few weeks before being freed. The two Scotts, who do not seem to have been involved in the Duncombe rebellion, were tried in the fall of 1838 for the theft of Constable Bennett's pistols and sentenced to three years' imprisonment.

Daniel Hatcock of Norwich was detained in Sodom for a week while the militia searched for his guns.[60] Andrew Wilson was also imprisoned at Sodom for a few days and then released when nothing could be found against him.[61] James Wood of East Oxford, who had been a rebel captain in December, was sent to London, charged with being involved either in Dr Wilson's release or in the alleged projected uprising.[62] He was jailed until September, when he was bound over.

Six men – Calvin Austin, Horace Lossing, John Fish, Jesse Matthews, and Benjamin and William Hillaker – were taken for 'treasonable practices.' Benjamin and William Hillaker, father and son, were incarcerated at London for knowing a password by which they would be preserved from harm should an invasion or insurrection occur.[63] They were freed on some undetermined date, probably in the fall. Horace Lossing, the young son of Solomon, the Norwich magistrate tried and freed at Hamilton in the spring for having aided the rebels, was originally jailed at Sodom to ensure that his father would surrender a rifle to the authorities there. Solomon, who was still a magistrate, duly brought the

145 Consequences

weapon in, and Horace was released, only to be re-arrested as the authorities claimed that, when in jail, he had been inducted into the Hunter's Lodge.[64]

Calvin Austin, John Fish, and Jesse Matthews all appear to have been implicated in the alleged plans for an uprising on 3 July. Austin, who had taken up arms under Duncombe in December and been bound over, was sent to the Hamilton jail and discharged on bail in mid-August. Fish, Matthews, and Lossing were lodged initially in the Gore district prison as well but were not released for some time. The precise dates are not known but Matthews, who was freed in February 1839, was reportedly the last of the prisoners detained from the affair of the previous summer.[65]

The 'second Norwich revolt,' as the events of June and July came to be called, had dire consequences for some like Matthews and his fellow prisoners. For most the repercussions were less dramatic, though still significant. Many loyalists in the area were confirmed in their conviction that they were threatened on all sides by rebel neighbours made doubly dangerous by the active support of American sympathizers. On the other hand, many non-Tory inhabitants in and around Norwich were more firmly convinced that the local loyalists would use any pretext to harry them. In sum, the second Norwich rising hardened the lines of division.

III

The actions of the magistrates and militiamen in and about Norwich in the summer of 1838 are understood more readily when the hysteria throughout all of the western peninsula is considered. On 25 June, William Gardiner of Mosa, who had been implicated in the attempt to muster rebels in Mosa in December, swore before a justice of the peace that a fellow settler, Christopher Lang, had asked him 'to join the Patriots – an American army.'[66] Lang reportedly had said that on 4 July 1,000 men from the United States were going to attack Canada at seventeen different places. He claimed to have been sworn in as a captain in the force by an American officer, and stated further that the invaders intended 'to murder every Person in Canada who opposed them.' The patriots had allegedly received the co-operation of the American government, and had smuggled weapons into the province 'to be given to the friends of the Rebels, so as they might be ready to join the army on its arrival.'

Gardiner's report might never have gained credence had events not conspired to give it the ring of authenticity. Rumours of patriot raids abounded along the St Clair border and on 27 June a store near the frontier was robbed.[67] The following day a band of nine 'Hunters' encountered some loyalists in a house in Dawn township and a fight ensued. One of the patriots, William Putnam, who had been tried at London in the spring for his part in Flannagan's meeting of 8 December, shot and killed one of the militiamen, a Captain Kerry.[68]

Accounts of these events, all greatly embellished, and of assorted raids, all imagined, spread quickly and appeared to substantiate Gardiner's deposition. The further away from the frontier, the more fanciful the rumours. In Delaware, J.B. Clench, the local Indian superintendent, was sure that a crisis was fast approaching and was convinced that the local population could not be trusted. On 27 June he wrote to the head of the Indian Department, S.P. Jarvis, that he had often been told that the rebels intended to hang him at his own door and then murder the Indians. 'Give us Arms & ammunition,' he begged, 'that we may die like Men!'[69] Reports of a patriot advance from the west reached nearby London. The invaders, it was thought, planned to be in that town on 4 July. To increase the panic, it was learned on good authority that, on 29 June, 1,400 rebels were within forty miles of the town.[70]

Colonel Maitland, commanding the Thirty-Second regiment and in charge of the defences of the Western and London districts, made representations to Arthur who agreed to rush two companies of the Thirty-Fourth regiment to him, as well as to provide warriors of the Six Nations.[71] From London Maitland had sent out two scouts, one down the Western road towards Mosa and Chatham and the other to Port Sarnia and the St Clair frontier. The former, Lieutenant Grogan, sent back particularly alarming and alarmist reports.[72]

By 1 July people were flocking into London from the surrounding area, panic-stricken. Colonel Maitland had authorized the embodiment of fifty militiamen at Port Stanley and a further sixty to eighty at Port Burwell to defend those places from attack. The fifty members of the St Thomas cavalry were also mustered as were 150 Muncey Warriors, who were to guard the western approaches to London. The regular troops were put on the alert and the bridge across the Thames barricaded.[73] Fears were probably heightened by the arrival in London on 1 July of the Chatham magistrates escorting some sixty prisoners.[74] On the previous day, it had been reported in Chatham that William Gardiner had infiltrated the rebel ranks and that he had learned there was to be a general uprising on 3 July. He had apparently related his information to the Chatham justices of the peace and had given the names 'of some forty rank rebels' who lived along the Thames. The magistrates had immediately set about arresting those named, and it was these men they delivered in London on 1 July.[75]

On 3 July, a settler swore that he had been captured on the town line of Malahide and Dorchester by a party of 400 to 500 men who had tried to induct him into a secret society and who had told him of plans for an uprising on the fourth.[76] Although Colonel Maitland felt the informant had overstated the case, he none the less ordered a 'vigorous search' for the alleged abductors.[77] They were not found. By this time, the residents of London and its vicinity appear to have realized that the danger facing them had been grossly exaggerated, so that, when members of the Thirty-Fourth regiment arrived in London on the evening of 3 July, they found it tranquil. So wild had been the rumours in circulation that earlier that day these soldiers had heard 'that a party of insurgents had brought a fort a mile long from the States and located it on the Canadian territory!'[78]

July the fourth came and went without incident in and about London and in Upper Canada at large. Though attacks had been expected in the Home, Gore, and Niagara districts, as well as in the London and Western districts, fear had perhaps been greatest in the west. The loyalists of the area were positive that only their preparations had averted disaster. At least two historians of the patriot movement, Orrin Edward Tiffany and Oscar Kinchen, are convinced that the Sons of Liberty in the United States had planned a great invasion of the west of Upper Canada for the fourth of July, an invasion which was aborted only when the indiscreet and unauthorized activities of some of their members had alerted the Upper Canadian authorities to the danger facing the province. Kinchen suggests, in addition, that at Cleveland Charles Duncombe had been engaged in laying plans for a separate raid on the province on the fourth.[79]

During the crisis, Captain Kerry's life was not the only one that had been taken. The Indians summoned out by Maitland had scoured the London area for insurgents. In Westminster a band of warriors had spied one Nathan Allan sitting 'in a suspicious posture.' Allan was hailed and told to present himself to the Indians. He stood up, approached them in an 'oblique direction,' and then made a dash for some nearby woods.[80] The Indians fired and Allan fell. He died the next day, after 'wallowing in his blood,' a fugitive from the west declared, 'for 18 hours.'[81] Oddly enough, his death occasioned virtually no comment, either officially or among the province's Radicals and Reformers, possibly because he was a notorious horse thief.

After the scare was over, the disposition of the prisoners lodged in the jail remained to be settled. Men had been placed in the cells even after the panic subsided and the *London Gazette* noted that those of them who had promised to lay down their lives for liberty were 'in a fair way of proving to the world, that ... they cannot be fairly accused of *perjury*.'[82] The government sent Solicitor-General Draper to London to help the local magistrates with the examinations and to advise which prisoners should be committed, bailed, or discharged. Arthur impressed upon Draper that no persons should be kept in jail against whom the evidence was 'not of such a nature as to render their being brought to trial necessary and proper, and their Conviction morally certain.'[83]

The records of the period are sketchy in the extreme but it is certain that three men from Mosa were imprisoned at London from 5 July to 13 July. They were released by the end of the month. Warrants were issued for the arrest of five other Mosa settlers but were never served. Eleven individuals from Camden or Howard townships in the Western district were incarcerated in the two weeks from 30 June to 13 July, and were freed in the period 20 July to 27 July on bail. In addition, a further twenty-one men were jailed, all of whom were committed in the weeks from 1 to 14 July and all but four released by 26 July. Probably, the seventeen men freed were from the area west of London as the *London Gazette* shortly declared that all of those confined from the Western district had been liberated.[84] By the time that these individuals had returned to their homes, the great scare was over, and the west was relatively calm.

IV

Meanwhile the administration at Toronto was obliged to consider the fates of the various state prisoners. The matter had become pressing as conditions in the London jail were far from ideal; in May it was reported that a great number of inmates were sick, some with typhoid fever. To accommodate them a temporary hospital had been built.[85] The unhealthy atmosphere of the prison had already claimed one victim. Young Joseph Moore, a Yarmouth rebel and the son of John Moore, who had also been committed, had been bailed in January but died soon after.[86] John Grieve, a Westminster settler, had been released on 10 April suffering from 'jail fever' and died on 1 June at the age of thirty-one, leaving a young family.[87]

After the assizes of March and April, considerable numbers were still locked in the cells at Hamilton and London on charges connected with the rebellion. Six men had been tried and found guilty of treason at London, and ten at Hamilton. Forty-two prisoners in London had petitioned for pardon under 1 Victoria C. 10, as had fifteen from the Gore jail, one of whom, John G. Parker, had been transferred to Toronto.

In May the executive council decided to pursue a liberal policy towards many of those confined at Toronto, and adopted a similar attitude towards most of the petitioners from the west. On 6 June, eleven of the fourteen petitioners at Hamilton were freed. Two of those discharged, Duncan McPhederain and Robert Laing, were from Nassagaweya. Three others who had assisted the Duncombe insurgents were also released, as were six rebels.[88] Each man set at liberty was bound over on posting a bond of £200 and upon securing two sureties, both of whom were obliged to put up £100. From 1 to 19 June, no less than twenty-four rebels were freed from the London jail.[89] The *London Gazette* noted that all had been bound over for a period of three years, adding that 'we are afraid there has been rather too much mercy extended to them; but time and a fair trial will show.'[90] One of those released, however, young William Watts, did not have much of an opportunity to demonstrate anything for he succumbed to jail fever.[91]

Those petitioners not discharged in June were faced with a variety of sentences. Seven men who had taken up arms in the west of the province were to be banished for life. Six of them were Americans, but the other, Uriah Emmons, had been born in Norwich. Edward Carman of Yarmouth, originally slated for fourteen years' servitude in the penal colony of Van Diemen's Land (Tasmania), was to be jailed in the penitentiary at Kingston for three years and then banished for ever.[92] A similar fate was scheduled for Nathaniel Deo, who had been active on 12 to 14 December in Dorchester and Yarmouth. Nine rebels who had been prominent in rallying the insurgents – Philip Henry, Joseph Hart, James Bell, John Arthur Tidey, John Kelly, Horatio Fowler, Charles Chapin, William Thompson, and Finlay Malcolm of Bayham – were to be transported to Van Diemen's Land for fourteen years, though the executive council relented in Kelly's case and freed him in July. Both Walter Chase and John G. Parker, then in jail at Toronto, were also to be sent to the penal colony for fourteen years. One rebel captain from Norwich, Paul Bedford, was to be transported for life. The fates of two other petitioners, Jonathan Steele and Luther Hoskins, both of whom had taken up arms, appear still to have been under consideration in June.[93]

Six of those who had petitioned and who were not released openly lamented that they had ever been persuaded to throw themselves on Arthur's mercy.[94] Nat Deo complained that he had petitioned only because he had thought that under the terms of 1 Victoria C. 10 Arthur would grant him 'an unconditional discharge.' He had not realized, he insisted, that a petition 'was tantamount to an acknowlegement of guilt,' and declared that he was, as he had always been, innocent of the charges against him.[95] Indeed, it is evident that there was among the London prisoners a misunderstanding about the nature of the provincial statute allowing them to ask the governor for clemency. Many had petitioned Arthur praying for a complete pardon. Draper had been instructed to tell those doing so that they could request only a 'merciful reconsideration' of their cases.[96]

The London and Gore district jails also held those men tried at the spring assizes and found guilty of treason. Three of the London prisoners – the rebel Robert Cook, Ebenezer Wilcox, who had aided the insurgents, and Alvaro Ladd, who had been involved in the so-called Delaware conspiracy – had had their cases set aside for judicial review. It had been decided by the executive council that three individuals who had not taken up arms but had helped instigate the rebellion – John Moore, his brother Enoch, and Harvey Bryant – were to be transported for life, though the sentences of the last two were then revised to fourteen years of penal servitude. This sentence was also given five of the ten convicted traitors at Hamilton: John Tufford, Charles Walrath, Peter Malcolm, and Horatio Hills, all Duncombe rebels, and Nathan Town, who had actively promoted rebellion in Norwich. Five other men in the Gore jail had been found guilty of treason: Elias Snider, Ephraim Cook, and William Webb, all of whom had taken up arms, Stephen Smith, who had helped promote the cause of insurrection, and John Hammill, who was said to have given the rebels counsel but against whom insufficient evidence has been found. In Smith's case at least, the councillors decreed that he should be imprisoned for three years at the provincial penitentiary and then banished from the province.[97]

The opening of the Short Hills trials in Niagara on 18 July temporarily diverted public attention from the disposition of those arrested the previous winter. On 21 July, James Morreau was tried and found guilty of high treason. Nine days later, after the trials had been recessed, he was taken to the scaffold. His executioner, Sheriff Alexander Hamilton of the Niagara district, had arranged as 'an act of kindness' that he would plunge eighteen feet before being snapped to his death. He was not, as might have been expected, decapitated, and did, an onlooker thought, die instantly.[98]

The remaining trials dragged on intermittently until 18 August. Dr Duncan Wilson was conveyed to Niagara to take his place on the stand but he escaped prosecution because two of the Crown witnesses, who were later demonstrated to be perjurers, failed to identify him as the Dr Wilson who had accompanied the raiders into Upper Canada.[99] Wilson, nevertheless, was called upon to testify, for he had admitted being in the Short Hills at the time of the outbreak. Although the *Niagara Reporter* stated that he 'seemed much inclined to speechify' and decided that 'his evidence was totally unworthy of credit,'[100] on 2 August he was, in fact, very reluctant to be examined, lest 'he might implicate himself.'[101] In any case, he was taken back to London to be tried there on a charge of receiving stolen property – Philo Bennett's pistols which had been taken from the constable during Wilson's rescue in June. The doctor had been given the weapons by Job and Enos Scott. Wilson was found guilty but the judge reserved the case for the justices at Toronto because the Crown prosecutor had not introduced evidence to prove that the Scotts had indeed been convicted of stealing the guns in the first instance.[102] Later that fall, Wilson was discharged for good.

Not all of the Short Hills' raiders were as fortunate as Wilson; when the trials ended on 18 August, twenty death sentences had been pronounced. Both Garrett Van Camp and Jacob Beamer, who had been with Duncombe's force the previous December, had been sentenced to hang. Eventually, however, all of the death sentences, save Morreau's, were remitted. Three of the prisoners were sent to the penitentiary, and it was decided that the rest, including Beamer and Van Camp, should be transported.

The rather harsh policy adopted towards those found guilty at Niagara, in an attempt to dissuade the patriots from continuing their attacks upon the province, was of indirect benefit to those still in jail. The executive councillors felt the example of the convicted raiders would be sufficient to deter the disaffected from taking up arms and that they need not make examples of the other state prisoners.[103] On 13 August, eight of those jailed for their parts in the Duncombe rebellion were ordered released and banished from the province. The eight included the seven petitioners mentioned earlier and Ephraim Cook, an American doctor who had been judged guilty of treason. That same day, the council decided that three more petitioners who had taken up arms under Duncombe – Charles Chapin, William Thompson, and Jonathan Steele – were to be freed, as were three men who had been convicted of treason – John Moore, John Hammill, and William Webb.[104] All appear to have been discharged within a relatively short period of time and doubtless had been required to post bail.

The council further recommended on 30 August that another fourteen prisoners from the west be freed and bound over to keep the peace for three years. This released seven convicted traitors – Alvaro Ladd, Harvey Bryant, Robert Cook, John Tufford, Elias Snider, Stephen Smith, and Nathan Town – and seven petitioners – Nat Deo, who had been scheduled for three years' imprisonment, and six Duncombe rebels.[105] They were not all released until the fall, however, and one, the rebel John Tidey, not until 13 November.[106] All seem to have been required to advance £200 bail and to secure two sureties each willing to post £100.

On 28 September, Martin Switzer, who had returned to his farm in the Home district, been arrested, and then had petitioned, was freed on bail. Early in October, two convicted traitors from London, Ebenezer Wilcox and Enoch Moore, were also discharged after being bound over. From Woodhouse the Anglican rector, Francis Evans, urged the liberation of Peter Malcolm of Oakland. Although at the spring assizes he had lauded Malcolm's efforts to protect him from harm when he had been detained by the rebels,[107] Evans had testified against Malcolm at Hamilton. On 2 October, he had been scheduled to preach in the Congregationalist church at Burford, to which Peter and several of the Malcolms belonged, but the minister, the Reverend Mr Nall, refused to let him use the building. Reportedly, a mob including the recently liberated John Tufford occupied the church to ensure that Evans did not gain admittance.[108]

On 18 October, Evans informed Macaulay, Arthur's secretary, that, because he had testified against both Malcolm and Charles P. Walrath of Windham in the spring and because both were still in prison, 'a vague kind of impression lies in the minds of their friends that I am the cause of the greater measure of severity dealt to them.' Averring that the situation could only harm the church, he asked that Walrath and Malcolm be pardoned.[109] In response to representations made to him about the state of the prisoner's health, Arthur ordered Malcolm freed on £500 bail and on his securing two sureties, each of whom was to post £250. Malcolm was then bound over for three years.[110]

Walrath was evidently not to be released. He was 'a bold good looking young man'[111] who had drilled the rebels at Scotland, and he did not need the governor's fiat to secure his freedom. He had been lodged in the Home district jail. On the night of 6 November, he cut through the iron bars of his cell, dropped onto a shed below, and was gone,[112] becoming the second Duncombe rebel to secure 'leg bail.' In August, Walter Chase, who had been confined at Kingston, had broken out of the penitentiary with John G. Parker and eight other men. Though Parker had been recaptured, Chase had succeeded in eluding his pursuers.[113] In November another Duncombe insurgent, Horatio Hills, also escaped, but by dying in the Toronto jail from a severe chest infection.[114]

In the fall, while the government was pondering the fate of the various prisoners, it was faced with the problem presented by those men involved in treasonable activities who now wished to return to the province. Through an intermediary, Arthur informed Jacob Yeigh of Burford that any person who was 'sincerely anxious to assume those duties as a loyal subject from which he may have been in an evil hour seduced by the subtle leaders of the Insurrection' need not 'hesitate to cast himself upon the lenity and generous forebearance of the Government.'[115] Yeigh was also told that, if his case were no worse than it was represented to be, he could return home.

By the end of September, Lord Durham, who had arrived in British North America in June and who had been strenuously debating with the governor of Upper Canada his constitutional powers to dispose of the state prisoners, had decided with Arthur to declare a general amnesty. Proclamations were issued on 22 October calling on some sixty-one individuals who had been indicted and who had fled the province to surrender themselves by 1 February or suffer the full penalties imposed on those convicted of treason. Twenty-one were from the London district, six were from the Gore district, and five from the Niagara district.[116] Those concerned who were not listed or not in custody were pardoned.

The names of such leaders as Charles Duncombe, Eliakim Malcolm, James Malcolm, Pelham C. Teeple, Henry Fisher, and Elisha Hall appeared on the various proclamations. They were all liable, as was any convicted traitor, to have their property seized. In fact, various absconding traitors had already had some of their personal effects and belongings confiscated by the government. Norris Humphrey, a Bayham merchant who had marched to Scotland and then fled to the United States, had requested friends to forward the merchandise in his store to him, but magistrate Doyle McKenny had intervened and asked the government what he should do with the goods. He had been told that if there were solid evidence that Humphrey was indeed a rebel the sheriff should seize the wares.[117] Also, the government had refused to return Eliakim Malcolm's impounded papers and surveyor's equipment to his wife, Samantha, on the grounds that, as he had been indicted for treason and fled, his property had become forfeit to the Crown. Samantha Malcolm had been informed as well that her husband no longer had any legal claims on money owed him.[118]

Other property losses were not as serious. For example, some prisoners discharged from the London jail had discovered that they could not recover the rifles taken from them by Colonel Mahlon Burwell's men.[119] The weapons of suspected traitors could obviously be used by the loyal militia, but what became of other goods and belongings seized? A letter of August 1838 from John Macaulay to some Middlesex militiamen states that the property of attainted traitors belonged solely to the Crown. They were instructed that a horse which they had recovered from a fleeing rebel should be sold and the money collected sent to a fund then being raised for the relief of widows and orphans of soldiers killed in the rebellion.[120]

No estates were seized, and it was even decided that petitioners under 1 Victoria C. 10, who had been obliged to admit that they were guilty of treason, were not subject to the laws governing the properties of traitors.[121] Some men, John Askin, for example, had expected that the lands of various absconding and convicted traitors would be confiscated.[122] None were, however, though some rebels certainly had difficulties with officials over their estates. One was Charles Duncombe, whose brother Elijah had erroneously reported in May 1838 that all of Charles' property had been taken.[123] The executive council had not, in fact, confiscated his property but had tied it up. In 1839 it refused to recognize the sale of land Duncombe had made three years earlier to his son-in-law, John Tufford, on the grounds that it did not acknowledge the property transactions of convicted traitors.[124] Duncombe's holdings in Brantford township had already been sold, however, 'under an execution against goods and chattels.'[125] In 1839 the executive council argued that the properties of absconding traitors like Duncombe should be confiscated, as judgments were being secured against their lands by their friends, who then gave the proceeds to the fugitive rebels, who had been unable to enter the province to liquidate their holdings.[126]

V

One of the effects of the Duncombe rising was the conviction among the loyalists that danger still lurked. At various times in the fall, Dr John George Bridges, a resident of Bayham and then of Norwich, wrote Arthur's secretary to say that the disaffected, especially in Norwich and Dereham, were 'at work again.' He reported that traitors regularly met at

155 Consequences

Dereham Forge at night and that those of Burford, Norwich, and Dereham continued to brag of the large numbers of men they could muster.[127] Seventy-one residents of the latter two townships complained that their townships were in the grip of 'a democratic faction' and that 'a very great majority' of the settlers were prepared to take up arms 'in the approaching crisis.'[128]

In the fall, a Brantford militia officer charged that his regimental area embraced 'a great proportion of disaffected Men, not to be trusted with arms.'[129] A party of Indians searching for game about Big Creek, which ran through Walsingham and Windham, claimed to have met a group of armed men in the woods. The latter were, it was assumed, 'Patriot Hunters.'[130] From Vittoria in Charlotteville came the lament that 'the disaffected in this vicinity are apparently very busy at the present time' holding secret meetings.[131] Indians were sent to scour a cedar swamp in the rear of Oxford county for arms supposedly hidden there by potential traitors.[132] Such reports and activities inspired Arthur to declare that 'Duncombe's Country should be narrowly watched & I hope the Magistrates are doing so.'[133]

Several times that fall militiamen were turned out in response to rumours that the patriots were to launch attacks; the 'Hunters' in the United States had not been checked and those in the Ohio area had been particularly active. In September they held a convention at Cleveland at which they had launched a provisional republican government of Upper Canada. Duncombe had addressed the convention at length, outlining a new banking system for the province and suggesting the creation of a 'Republican Bank' to finance the Patriots' activities. The gathering had apparently decided the date for a full-scale invasion of the colony.[134] The provincial authorities were expecting an attack on the province because in late October news had reached Simcoe and its vicinity that '*without doubt*' an assault (which never materialized) was to be made on Port Dover on the twenty-seventh.[135] Accordingly, 100 warriors of the Six Nations were sent by the commanders of the local militia to subdue Norwich and prevent its bursting forth in rebellion. (The officials involved were subsequently reprimanded by the adjutant general for calling out the Indians without authorization.)[136] Militiamen were mustered to defend Simcoe, Port Dover, and Port Ryerse. Relatively few settlers, however, volunteered for service and the commander of the British Regulars at Simcoe, Captain J.H. Evelegh, declared that he was surrounded by disaffected people, 'who I have not the slightest doubt, in case of a Landing would attack me.'[137]

The Norfolk militia officers were not the only ones to have difficulty in mustering their men. On 31 October, a militia general order authorized the enrolment of 9,978 militiamen throughout Upper Canada for six months' duty, because Arthur and Colborne feared that the patriots planned a great descent upon the province. In the west, detachments of 107 men were to be stationed along the lake at Ports Stanley, Talbot, Burwell, Rowan, and Dover. Similar bodies were to be placed at St Thomas, London, Vittoria, and Simcoe. Troops of cavalry were also to be positioned at St Thomas and Simcoe. One hundred and ten men were to be posted in Oakland, over 200 in Norwich, and more than 500 in Brantford.[138] In many cases, however, the western regiments could not fulfil their quotas of volunteers and drafting was necessary.

Many saw the reluctance of the militiamen to come forward as evidence of increased disaffection. There were, nevertheless, several reasons for it. For one thing, those called out on duty in the past had often been forced to wait unconscionable lengths of time for their pay. A report in November stated that those who had been on duty in Norwich the previous summer had not been remunerated and were now unwilling to 'put themselves out again.'[139] Moreover, some militiamen had been obliged to serve under such incapable or tyrannical officers as Colonel Craig of Caradoc, whose regiment had been stationed on the Detroit frontier in 1838. Craig was accused, among other things, of failing to requisition necessary mattresses and supplies for his men, obliging them to sleep on bare boards in their clothes, 'whereby they were overrun with vermin, and their health greatly injured.' He had also allegedly refused to dismiss them when instructed to do so, and had kept them on duty long past their designated period of service, 'rendering them totally destitute of either pay or provisions to carry them to their homes, upwards of one hundred miles.'[140]

Objections were lodged against officers on a variety of grounds. In the summer a public meeting held in Brantford to discuss militia appointments had declared that 'British Emigrants are British subjects in common with Canadians, and are not entitled to take the precedence of the old and respectable inhabitants of the Country in filling any offices in the gift of the Crown – and that the appointment of children and strangers to be officers of Militia is calculated to produce dissatisfaction and dissension in the Country.'[141] In December 1838 some seventy Mosa militiamen were to complain that they had not 'the least confidence' in the 'Bravery or Conduct' of their officers.[142] Particular individuals, such as the Reverend William Proudfoot, even suspected that certain militia officers

157 Consequences

were responsible for creating the various alarms that troubled the country in an attempt to secure commissions and pay for themselves. In November Proudfoot reported that he had 'heard to-day that one of the Officers had said that they (the officers) had found out a cure for all the excitements which so agitate the country, viz; to hang up half a score of Militia Officers.'[143]

There were other reasons why the militiamen were reluctant to turn out. Some, for example those about Zorra, resented the fact that the government had been slow to pay the claims of those who had earlier provided goods and services to the province's forces.[144] The militiamen of the Brantford area who belonged to the First Gore regiment were unwilling to volunteer for further service, in part because they had been mustered on every conceivable occasion, while the men of the Fourth Gore, the settlers of Dumfries township, had never been called out.[145] Other factors explaining the militiamen's reluctance to reenlist include their difficulties in providing for their families while on service, their conviction that drafting was to be instituted and that rich farmers would pay handsomely those available to take their places, and their feeling that the six months' term of service was too long.[146] Arthur, however, felt that the two major reasons for the lack of enthusiasm for militia service were that immigration had declined and consequently that the price of labour had been enhanced and that the loyalists were convinced that 'the lenity shown' the state prisoners constituted 'a punishment to them.'[147]

None the less, the militiamen turned out bravely enough when real danger threatened. On 10 November, the Hunters launched an attack near Prescott in the east of the province, an assault that ended a few days later with 150 of the invaders taken prisoner and 15 militiamen killed. On 4 December, a force variously estimated at 150 to 1,000 strong crossed the Detroit River and landed on the Windsor shore, surprising and killing four militiamen and burning the steamer *Thames*. Twenty-five of them were slain, including William Putnam of London, and four prisoners who were brought to Colonel John Prince, who had them shot. The colonel's action led one Tory in the east of the province to remark that 'that man is a Prince by nature as he is by name.'[148]

At least three Duncombe rebels had participated in the raid. George Washington Case avoided capture but Joshua Doan and Daniel Bedford were taken, as were seven other former residents of the London district. One of the prisoners was James Aitchison, a nephew of the Reverend William Proudfoot who petitioned Arthur to consider his case with mercy. The request was spurned, and Proudfoot himself, in a face to face meeting with the governor, was accused of being 'a disaffected person' and told that the government had 'papers' about him.[149] Two of the other captives had prominent relatives in the west, John Burwell Tyrell of Bayham being a nephew of Mahlon and John Burwell, and Amos Perley of Burford a cousin of Charles Strange Perley, who sat on the militia court martial judging his kinsman and the rest of the accused.

Forty-four patriots were tried, and all but one were found guilty. Sixteen were transported to Van Diemen's Land, twenty-one were eventually deported to the United States, and six were hanged, including Cornelius Cunningham of Beachville and Joshua Doan and Daniel Bedford. The bodies of the latter three were returned to their homes for burial despite Arthur's disapproval. He noted that 200 to 300 people had attended Bedford's funeral in Norwich, 'a pretty good proof of feeling in that part of the Country.'[150]

Official policy towards the captured patriots was clearly much more severe than that adopted towards the Duncombe rebels, who had been, after all, inhabitants of the province. A desire to punish those from the United States found in arms in the province and the Upper Canadian refugees allied with them, as well as the conviction that only harsh sentences would deter further raids upon the colony, helps explain the treatment afforded the various imprisoned patriots. The severity shown those in the cells at Kingston and London in the latter part of 1838 did in fact help end the invasions of Upper Canada.

In view of the previous attempts upon the province and the known disaffection of a sizable proportion of the west's population, it is not surprising that throughout 1839 fears continued to be expressed that the would-be traitors of the western peninsula, in league with their associates to the south, were planning a co-ordinated uprising and invasion. In that year the disloyal settlers of Norfolk county and of Mosa were reported meeting at night. Disaffected persons were said to be making nocturnal jaunts between Yarmouth and Norwich,[151] and Colonel Brearley complained in August that strangers were visiting those residents in Norwich whose loyalty was suspect, adding that the same things were occurring as 'took place before the last two outbreaks.'[152] From London came the news that suspicious individuals had purchased unusually large quantities of powder and that among the Scots to the south of London lived many 'doubtful if not decidedly disaffected persons.'[153] None the less, 1839 was a comparatively tranquil year in the west and the fears of the loyalists were not realized.

VI

The turmoil in the west from December 1837 through 1838 helped persuade many inhabitants to flee the area. Towards the end of January, 'about forty sleighs laden with the Families & fugitive Persons principally from the neighbourhood of Oxford' passed through Adelaide towards Michigan.[154] In March, Elijah Duncombe reported that nearly one-third of the province's inhabitants, including the leading Reformers and numerous 'moderate Tories,' had either emigrated or were intending to do so.[155] By April many people from Norfolk county had allegedly travelled south.[156] In May numbers of residents reputedly were deserting 'the neighbourhood of Oakland & Scotland' for the republic;[157] the same month a report came from London that 'great dissatisfaction and excitement prevails in the Country and many are daily leaving.'[158]

In the summer, the *Hamilton Express*, a Reform journal, reported that emigration was proceeding apace and that in sections of the London district 'there are not males enough left to gather in a tithe of the crops.'[159] From Dereham came the news that 'the sons of most of the Americans for miles are left & gone to the States.'[160] In November William Proudfoot observed that 'every person considers Military service a burden; most young persons are going off to the States.'[161] A few weeks later, he added that 'multitudes have gone to the U.S. having made immense sacrifices in property.'[162] Kirk cleric W.M. McKillican, travelling through Lobo and its surrounding townships, noted in December 1838 that 'in some families one, two & three have gone to the States,'[163] while a militia colonel, William Holcroft, reported from Oxford county that 'many active young men have left their homes dreading the Militia law.'[164]

It is easy to assume that those leaving the country fled before Tory persecution; one absconding Duncombe rebel, John Van Arnam, wrote to Arthur in 1838 'that thousands of the most respectable and most loyal of her Majesty's subjects, are now in exile; (driven from their farms, their shops, their professions, their families, and their homes by the lawless violence of an excited and unprincipled soldiery).'[165] None the less, some at least of those who moved south left because of the continuing commercial depression which had begun in 1836. In October 1836 a Brantford resident, William Daubigny, noted that several of his acquaintances had departed for Michigan,[166] and a year later Proudfoot observed many wagons travelling west on their way to the same state.[167] The recession continued throughout 1838 and deepened because of the turmoil in the province. In March Elijah Duncombe alleged that the selling price of property had dropped to 50 per cent from its level three years previously,[168] though this was doubtless because of the large number of homes and farms then on the market. Proudfoot reported in August that there had been for the past year 'a stagnation of all business.'[169] Elijah Woodman, a former lumberman from Bayham captured in the December raid on Windsor, stated that 'in and about Vienna, all business is stopped as most of the business men have moved to the States. The saw mills are doing nothing and our vessels at Port Burwell are nearly all sold, and gone to other ports, and some on to Lake Ontario.'[170] Cash continued to be scarce. Improved harvests were the only encouraging features of an otherwise bleak year in the economic life of the province.

Hard times, the feelings of alienation and persecution harboured by many Reformers, and the contemporary observations that many were fleeing the province have all convinced historians that the emigration from the province after the revolt assumed dramatic proportions. R.S. Longley noted the impossibility of determining the exact number who had left the province but he did feel safe in assuming that at least several thousand had.[171] E.C. Guillet suggested that the emigrants, in fact, totalled some 25,000 people[172] (approximately one-sixteenth of the entire population) and W.H. Graham, in his biography of William 'Tiger' Dunlop, accepted Guillet's assertion.[173] Other authorities have been more circumspect in their estimates of the size of the migration, but none has doubted that it was of some magnitude.

The census statistics for Oxford, Norfolk, and Middlesex suggest, however, that the emigration may not have been as large as some historians have been prepared to believe. The population figures for the London district for 1838 are not available but those for 1839 are, and an examination reveals that the three counties of Middlesex, Oxford, and Norfolk registered slight *additions* in the numbers of their inhabitants in the years 1837–9. True, for all three the increases were less than those in 1834–7,[174] but in the earlier period immigrants from Great Britain had continued to flow into the region while in 1838 very few, if any, came. In the years 1837–9 eight townships in the study area, five rebel and three non-rebel ones,[175] suffered decreases in population, but the declines were limited, all of the townships, except for Norwich which lost 265 people, being reduced by less than 100. In comparison, six townships, three rebel and three non-rebel, had suffered declines in 1836–7.[176] These figures suggest not only that some historians have overestimated the size of the emigration after the revolt but also that many of those who did leave were young men without families. Had many of them been older men with wives and children, the census losses would have been more striking.

Even if the flight from the area was not as great as has been supposed, 1838 was a difficult year for the west. Beset by a variety of alarms, the inhabitants of the south-west had been kept in an almost continual state of excitement. Militiamen had been summoned on a number of occasions and the Liberals had often seen troops marching past their homes or had been mustered in the ranks themselves. So frequent had been the calls to arms in some areas that the inhabitants might well have thought that they were living in a garrison-state, and a strife-torn one at that, for issues both secular and sectarian continued to divide them.

One of the disputes had involved the ultimate disposition of those taken prisoner for their parts in the events of December 1837. At the end of 1838, some of those cases still remained in limbo. Edward Carman of Yarmouth, for example, had been sentenced to three years' hard labour, after which he was to be banished from the province. By the end of 1838, however, others whose cases were similar had already had their sentences remitted while he was still in prison. At some point, however, his sentence was reduced and he was never expelled from the province, for he was a resident of Port Stanley in 1842.[177] The cases of two other Duncombe rebels, Finlay Malcolm of Bayham and Paul Bedford of Norwich, were far more celebrated and contentious. Malcolm and Bedford were to be transported to Van Diemen's Land for fourteen years. Along with John G. Parker of Hamilton and seven other state prisoners, they arrived in England in December 1838. Prominent British Radicals immediately questioned the legality of their sentences. A long court dispute ensued and in July 1839 the decision was taken to free all ten men because, unless they were tried for treason in England, the British government had not the legal right to remove them from Great Britain and the administration of Van Diemen's Land lacked the authority to receive them.[178] All were freed on the stipulation that they were 'not to return to Canada, nor to appear within Fifty Miles of the Canadian frontier.'[179] In all likelihood Parker rejoined his family which had returned to its original home in the United States after his arrest. By 1851, however, both Paul Bedford and Finlay Malcolm had been reunited with their families in Upper Canada.[180]

In the summer of 1838, seven other Duncombe rebels had been banished from the colony for life. One of them, Dr Ephraim Cook of Norwich, had already returned home by January 1839. The authorities were evidently prepared to ignore him but he took steps to ensure that his property transactions were not affected by his attainture for high treason. He lived on in Norwich, a well-known figure who eventually became the representative of South Oxford in the legislature of the united Canadas for the years 1854–8.[181] No evidence exists that Walter Chase and Charles P. Walrath, who had broken out of provincial jails and were never recaptured, ever resettled in the province. In addition, eleven men, either implicated in the Duncombe uprising or accused of having been so, had fled the province after the rebellion but were not listed in Arthur's proclamation of 22 October which called upon those named to surrender themselves or suffer the penalties of convicted traitors. At least seven eventually returned to the colony.[182]

Of the twenty-seven residents of the London and Gore districts named in Arthur's edicts of October 1838, one, Joshua Doan, was executed in 1839. Another, sixty-year-old Peter DeLong, who had been active in organizing the rebels in Norwich in December 1837, had petitions forwarded to the government on his behalf, requesting that he be allowed to return to the province. One of them declared that he was 'an old and infirm man and very decriped [sic] in his limbs and quite in his dotage.'[183] One of the first settlers in Norwich township, he died in the United States before 1843, when the provincial government pardoned a number of those named in Arthur's proclamations. An official report of that year declared that the residences of twelve of the remaining twenty-five men proscribed in 1838 were unknown. At least one man had already returned to the province, however: Joel P. Doan, who had married the wife of his executed brother, Joshua, and who appears in the Yarmouth census of 1841–2 as an inhabitant of that township. John Massacre of Townsend had probably been pardoned in 1839. The report of 1843 stated that four traitors, Eliakim Malcolm, James Dennis, Henry Fisher of Bayham, and George Lawton of Yarmouth, had already been pardoned and had returned home. James Malcolm, who was to be pardoned, had also returned, and two others, M.M. Mills of Hamilton and M.C. Nickerson of Port Dover, had been pardoned, though had not yet returned. Two rebels, Pelham C. Teeple and Elisha Hall, both of West Oxford, were scheduled for pardon. Three more, George Alexander Clark of Brantford, George Washington Case of Hamilton, and Charles Duncombe, were said to be residing in the United States. The report provided no information on the last man, Lyman Davis of Malahide.[184]

Duncombe retained his association with the patriots for some time after 1838, although the pace of his activities certainly diminished. For some reason, William Lyon Mackenzie feared that Duncombe was in the

163 Consequences

employ of the American government and in January 1839 asked his son, James, who was in Lockport, as was Duncombe, what was his 'true character? Is he honest?'[185] James replied that Duncombe was unpopular in Canada but added, 'I think he is honest – most sincerely – the most so of the Refugees that I have seen in this quarter.'[186] In March 1839, Duncombe himself wrote to Mackenzie from Connecticut, his birthplace and where he evidently intended settling. He implied that he was financially embarrassed and that, as soon as he acquired some money, 'I shall devote my whole time to the good old cause to which I am pledged.'[187] And, indeed, in December that same year he was in Cincinnati trying to form a patriot society.[188]

In 1843 Duncombe petitioned the government for a pardon, saying that he had never sought the separation of Upper Canada from Great Britain and that he had raised the standard of revolt only to prevent his own arrest.[189] His plea was granted by the government which had been informed by its own officers that he was 'not known to have taken any part' in the patriots' activities.[190] Duncombe returned to Canada in June 1844 to attend to the disposition of some of his properties but, after a brief stay, went back to the United States.[191] He eventually settled in California where, like his comrade Eliakim Malcolm in Canada West, he became a respected and prominent figure in his local community, being elected to the state legislature as a Republican and dedicated to the abolition of slavery. Duncombe evidently missed his kinsmen who had remained in British North America for he complained in 1865 that 'I hear only occasionally from Canada. And seldom from my brothers and sisters.'[192] Still, in that same year he wrote to his brother Elijah that few men of his age 'have greater reason for sincere and heartfelt thankfulness,' as he had lived to see slavery abolished. 'I feel,' he added, 'that the ambition of my life has been accomplished and men are free, whenever they desire it.'[193] By 1865, then, his ambitions had been transferred to the American stage and had been realized by the successful fight against slavery. His dreams of freeing the people of Upper Canada from the yoke of the Tories were long dead. Ironically, when his own death came in October 1867, Canada West, once Upper Canada, had just become Ontario and was embarking on a long and prosperous life within the new Canadian Confederation.

7
Rebels and Loyalists

Duncombe died with the knowledge that his revolt had failed. Those he had rallied had been quickly put to flight by loyalists drawn both from the rebels' own neighbourhood and from the Hamilton area. The insurgents and their opponents had obviously been separated by their differing responses to his call to arms but it is not immediately clear if there were other points of difference between them. It might well be thought, nevertheless, that the members of the two groups were distinguishable from one another in a variety of ways: by nationality, by occupation, by religious affiliation, and by levels of prosperity, for example. To some extent the validity of such a theory can be tested by examining the areas where the rebels and loyalists lived. More concrete evidence that the backgrounds of the loyalists and rebels were substantially different can only be reached through an analysis of the characteristics of the individuals who rallied forth on either side in December 1837. Therefore, an investigation of the backgrounds of those who took up arms under Duncombe will be used as the basis for drawing some general conclusions about the traits of the insurgents. In addition, the rebel-loyalist dichotomy existing in the particular township of Bayham will be explored as fully as possible.

Contemporary sources generally indicate that from 400 to 500 men gathered under Duncombe at Oakland in December 1837. Unfortunately it is not possible to find out who they were by simply turning to the well-known prisoner list which ostensibly enumerates those detained in Upper Canada from 4 December 1837 until 12 November 1838 for 'INSURRECTION or TREASON.'[1] In the first place, most Duncombe rebels escaped arrest. In the second, the list has severe limitations. It includes many in the west and elsewhere who did not take up arms but were arrested merely on suspicion of having done so or of having been involved in activities related to the revolt. Moreover, it enumerates some who participated in the attempts to incite insurrection in the province in 1838. Finally, it does not include the names of all those who were imprisoned.

This study identifies 197 rebels[2] and 57 people who aided them by encouraging others to take up arms, by supplying weapons, ammunition, and advice to the insurgents, and by forming 'home guards.' (See appendices 1 and 2.) Identification has been made on the basis of confessions of guilt given before examining justices of the peace or made in petitions for clemency. Where no acknowledgment of treasonable activity was made, a subject, for the purposes of this study, was considered guilty if two independent witnesses testified that he was indeed one of the insurgents or one of their accomplices. To have accepted the word of only one observer would have led to the inclusion of many who were incorrectly identified or wrongly accused, perhaps through sheer maliciousness. Thus 75 men, accused by only one witness or by later historians on insufficient evidence, have been excluded from consideration. (See appendix 3.)

It may be objected that the testimony of two witnesses is insufficient evidence for concluding that a person was implicated in the uprising. Given the nature of the sources used and the frequent lacunae in documentation, however, it would be unrealistic to insist on more. In any event, only 13 of the 57 individuals judged guilty of aiding the rebels and 22 of the 197 men identified as insurgents were convicted solely on the basis of the evidence of only two people. Even in these instances, other circumstances often strongly suggested that the man in question was indeed guilty; if, for example, one of his accusers were a close relative or if he fled the province after the revolt. Fallacious evidence may, of course, have been sworn in some cases but it is, on the whole, unlikely to have happened more than a very few times.

I

One historian, R.S. Longley, suggested that Mackenzie's men were 'chiefly those who had not prospered economically.'[3] This may be true of the Home district rebels but certainly does not appear true of Duncombe's followers who have often been described as substantial yeomen. Of the 197 rebels and their 57 accomplices all but two[4] came from sixteen townships: Dumfries in Halton county, Brantford in Wentworth county, Blenheim, Burford, Oakland, East Oxford, West Oxford, Norwich, and

Dereham in Oxford county, Townsend, Windham, and Woodhouse in Norfolk county, and Bayham, Malahide, Yarmouth, and Southwold in Middlesex county. The homes of 109 of the 197 rebels and 43 of the 57 individuals known to have aided them are shown on map 6.

The townships in which the rebels lived were judged prosperous by contemporaries, an assessment borne out by the reflection that the longer settled a region was, the more likely it was to be heavily populated, to be cleared, farmed, and to have some amenities. Most of the areas from which the rebels were drawn were settled at an earlier date than were the northern sections of Middlesex and Oxford counties, which sent no men at all to Oakland. Contemporary evidence suggests that 60 to 70 per cent of the insurgents lived in townships opened to settlement prior to 1810. A further 15 to 20 per cent appear to have come from areas settled in the years from 1811 to 1820.

Townships with the largest number of residents were the ones most likely to have been settled earliest. In 1837 the rural sections of the sixteen rebel townships had a total population of 30,910 for an average of 1,919.4 persons per township, or 20.9 per square mile. The rural areas of the non-rebel townships of Norfolk, Oxford, and Middlesex counties which did not yield men for Duncombe's army contained only 19,530 inhabitants for an average of 1,085 persons per township, or only 10.8 per square mile.[5] These townships were not as heavily settled as the rebel ones because the tide of immigrants had not yet swept into them in full force, not because they could not support an equivalent population. As Table 2 illustrates, the numbers of inhabitants and the population density of the rural areas increased far more rapidly for the non-rebel than for the rebel townships between 1837 and 1871.

The conclusion that the insurgents came generally from the longest and most extensively settled, and perhaps most prosperous townships of their area is reinforced if the percentage of the acreage under cultivation in their townships is compared to the corresponding figure for the non-rebel townships in the counties of Oxford, Norfolk, and Middlesex.[6] Twenty-one per cent of the areas of the rebel townships were farmed, 4.7 per cent of the non-rebel. The median rebel township had over 15 per cent of its area farmed while the median non-rebel township had only 3 per cent. The highest proportion of acreage farmed in a non-rebel township was 15 per cent in Charlotteville, a percentage not even equal to that tilled in the median rebel township.

The rebels' prosperity depended not only on the economic health of their townships in normal times but also on the extent to which those

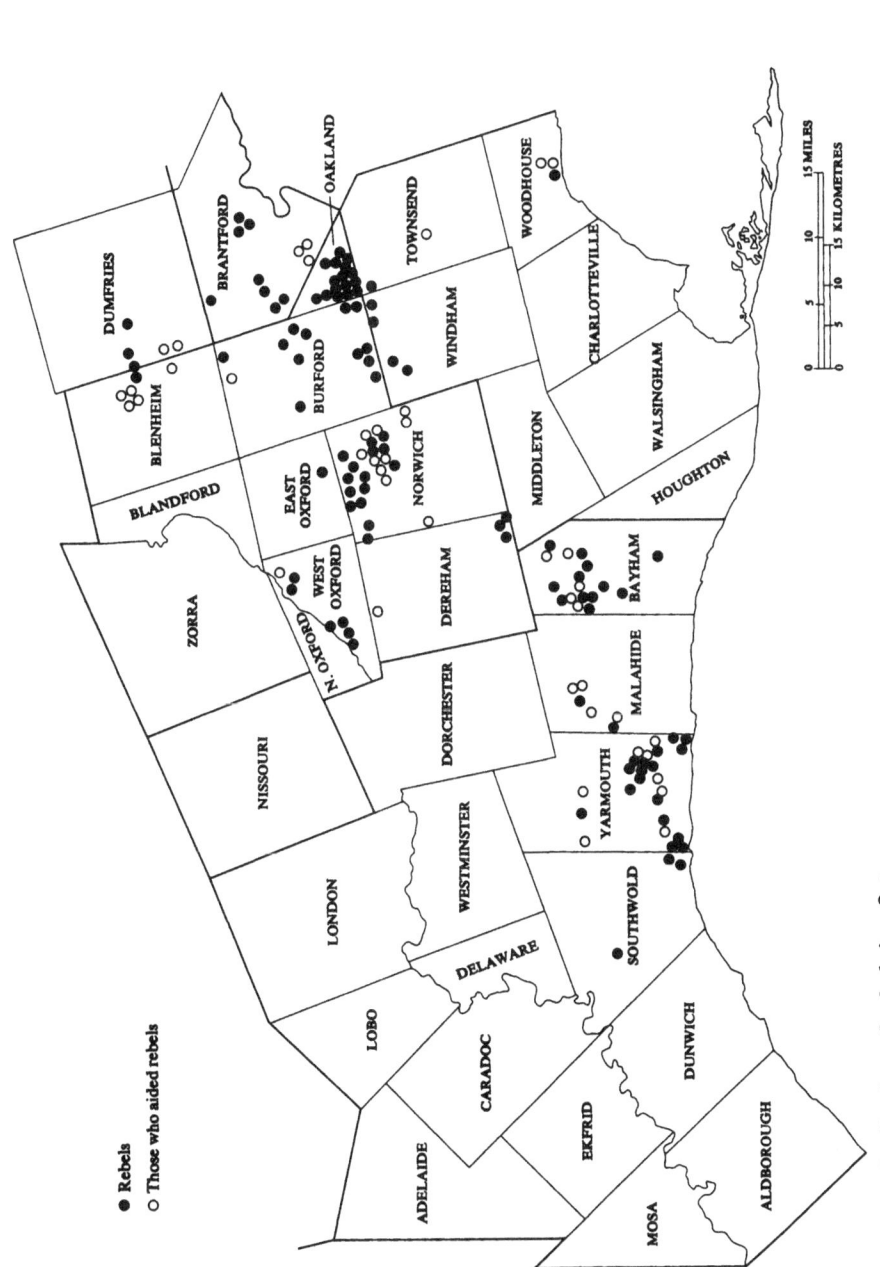

Map 6. Distribution of rebels in 1837

● Rebels
○ Those who aided rebels

TABLE 2
Population comparisons

	Rural areas of rebel townships		Rural areas of non-rebel townships	
	Population	Population per sq. mile	Population	Population per sq. mile
1837	30,910	20.9	19,530	10.8
1851	69,038	46.7	55,144	30.4
1871	82,696	55.9	85,625	47.2

townships were affected by the severe depression which had begun in 1836. One indicator, population growth, suggests that the rebel townships suffered no more than did the non-rebel townships. Of the townships examined, nine, four rebel and five non-rebel, maintained approximately the same rates of growth in the census year 1836–7 as they had in 1831–6. Nine others, again four rebel, five non-rebel, showed a greater increase in the former period. The town of London and sixteen townships, eight from each category, decreased in their rates of population growth in 1836–7 compared to the figures for the years 1831–6. In six of the townships, three rebel ones, Burford, Blenheim, and Norwich, and three non-rebel ones, Zorra, Adelaide, and Middleton, the numbers of residents declined from 1836 to 1837. Population trends suggest therefore that the rebel townships suffered to no greater extent from the depression than did the non-rebel ones.

It is difficult to determine if individual rebels were affected by the economic recession. The *Upper Canada Gazette* in 1838 contained notices of actions for the recovery of debts which involved twelve Duncombe rebels who had fled the province. The average owed was £111 pounds each, a large sum.[7] One merchant alone, however, Norris Humphrey of Bayham, accounted for £468. Also the largest debts had been contracted by those who might reasonably be expected to have credit extended them: two merchants, a mill owner, a land auctioneer, and two individuals involved in land speculations.

Contemporary statements concerning the prosperity of individual rebels are inconclusive. Five of Duncombe's men appear to have lived in relative poverty in 1837: one had a family dependent on him 'for subsistence,' another lived in 'indigent circumstances,' while the family of Finlay Malcolm of Bayham existed 'in very poor circumstances.' Two

169 Rebels and Loyalists

others were simply 'poor.'[8] It should be noted, however, that these descriptions were provided for the authorities *after* the rebellion and were designed to elicit sympathy. For instance, of two persons who claimed to be 'considerably indebted,'[9] one owned 'a good farm' and the other lived 'in good circumstances.'[10] One rebel was evidently 'a farmer in good circumstances,'[11] and five of the accomplices were described as enjoying a substantial degree of prosperity.[12] While any attempt to determine the precise economic circumstances of the rebels must be inconclusive, it is possible to estimate their general level of prosperity by examining contemporary statements about their employment and their property holdings, and by considering the relevant data assembled on the rebel sample.

II

This work attempts to examine the ages, nationalities, residences, occupations, religious affiliations, property holdings, marital status, and previous political activities of 197 rebels, 57 accomplices, and various other men. Unfortunately, it is not possible to secure all of this information on each man because existing documentation is incomplete. For example, the inquiry into property holdings, carried on through an examination of abstract indexes to the deeds, Crown lands papers, Upper Canada land petitions, township papers, contemporary maps, and so on, was hampered because no assessment rolls or directories exist for the area examined during the period of the rebellion.

Common names such as Smith, Brown, and Moore compound the problem. How does one determine which of the many James Moores of the Dereham vicinity who appear in the various records was the one who joined Duncombe? In some cases the difficulties are particularly exasperating. A Samuel Nevers of Blenheim township, a 'husbandman,' admitted that he had been with a group of men who had stopped and searched a wagon on the public highway, expecting to find guns for the Indians.[13] In May 1831 a Samuel Nevers had purchased lot 1 of concession 5 in Blenheim; in 1845 he sold it to his son, Samuel Nevers.[14] In the 1851-2 census, seventy-five-year-old Samuel Nevers and thirty-seven-year-old Samuel, both farmers, appear as residents of Blenheim. Was the Samuel Nevers who had stopped the wagon in 1837 the sixty-year-old land owning father or the twenty-two-year-old son for whom no property data before 1845 can be found? It was more likely to have been the latter but one cannot be sure; hence, as far as this study is concerned, the age and property holdings of Samuel Nevers must remain uncertain.

In addition, the rebel sample itself is not necessarily representative of all those who rallied to Duncombe. The insurgents named are not equally distributed throughout the geographical area of the rebellion. In part, at least, the zeal of various magistrates in jailing rebels meant that the insurgents from some townships were far more likely to find themselves imprisoned than were those from other jurisdictions. For instance, of approximately fifty men from Southwold, Yarmouth, and the western part of Malahide who marched to Oakland from the village of Sparta, thirty-six have been analysed. Some thirty men left Bayham and contiguous areas of eastern Malahide to join Duncombe's army of whom twenty-two have been identified. Thus the rebels from the lakefront townships of Middlesex county have mostly been identified, thanks largely to the eagerness of the militia and the diligence of the local magistrates who inquired deeply into the activities of the region's inhabitants during the revolt.

The same degree of success cannot be achieved in ferreting out the names of the rebels from other localities. Contemporary evidence suggests that anywhere from 100 to 200 men mustered from Norwich. Only thirty-five from that township, however, have been cited here. Similarly, the members of the Malcolm clan of Oakland and Burford townships secured perhaps 200 recruits from Oakland, Burford, Windham, Townsend, Woodhouse, and Brantford, only sixty-one of whom have been named. Perhaps as many as 100 more joined Duncombe's men from such other townships as Dereham, Blenheim, or Dumfries but only forty-two have been identified. Clearly, the rebels of Yarmouth, Malahide, Southwold, and Bayham are seriously over-represented in the sample and we can be much more certain of their characteristics than of those from elsewhere. (See Table 3.) Although the conclusions formulated below from the sample are thus necessarily tentative ones, they are supported by traditional kinds of evidence.

One good indication of the prosperity of the rebels is the extent of their property holdings. As noted earlier, it is impossible to collect complete data because the sources extant are either incomplete or uneven, differing from area to area and even from township to township. Moreover, private leasing agreements are usually untraceable and it is not therefore surprising that, for fifteen of the rebels identified as farmers, no precise information exists about their holdings. Despite these difficulties, evidence is available that 67 of the 197 insurrectionists listed, or 34.0 per

TABLE 3
Rebel identification

Place	Number identified	Probable number of rebels	Percentage identified
Lakeshore	58	80	72.5
Norwich	35	100 +	35.0 [max.]
Oakland and area	61	200	30.5
Elsewhere	42	100	42.0
Unknown	1	–	–

cent, held land either by renting property, by buying it on instalment, or by having legal title to it.[15] This makes it difficult to accept the proposition that the insurgents sought to acquire land for themselves, a proposition which in turn suggests that those assembled at Oakland were primarily landless persons representing an economically deprived sector of society.

The evidence that many of the insurgents were propertied farmers is supported by the remarks of different contemporary observers. Some were, of course, far from unbiased and wished to make the insurgents as attractive as possible. Edward Theller, for example, an American captured in January 1838 in a raid on the Western district near modern Windsor, later declared that, while being escorted through the London district to the Toronto jail, 'some of the richest and most eligible farms were pointed out to me as the property of rebels.'[16] Other sources confirm that many landed farmers were among the insurgents. For instance, John Treffry, a Norwich settler, asserted that by June 1838 many of the rebels had fled the country leaving behind 'fine farms.'[17] In the summer of 1838, Alexander Whalley Light of North Oxford pointed out that 'most, if not all,' of the disaffected of the Oxford area 'are Americans or descendants of Americans, who since the last was [sic] have bought property of Canadians, and some there are who rent the land or work for their daily bread.'[18] There are indications that insurgents elsewhere owned land. William Thompson and Charles Chapin of Oakland township, for example, swore that they and their neighbours had been told that if they refused to turn out with Duncombe's men 'their property would be confiscated.'[19] Obviously a percentage of the rebels in and about Oakland were land owners.

Occupations provide another indication of the economic circumstances of the Duncombe rebels. Unfortunately, the official list detailing

TABLE 4
Rebel occupations

Occupation	Number		Percentage of 140	Percentage of 197
Farmers	64		45.7	32.5
Labourers	27		19.3	13.7
Skilled workers or craftsmen	16			
Tavernkeepers	10			
Millers and tanners	9			
Professionals	6	49	35.0	24.9
Merchants	2			
Teachers	2			
Miscellaneous	4			
Total known	140		100.0	71.1
Total unknown	57		–	28.9
Total sample	197		–	100.0

the names and livelihoods of those imprisoned from 4 December 1837 to 12 November 1838 is of little help in determining the occupations of the western rebels. The return does not encompass all of the insurgents and, for the London district at least, its description of the employment of those jailed is woefully unreliable. Most of the captured Duncombe rebels were sent to London, and each man imprisoned there – even if indicated in other sources as a carpenter, tailor, merchant, tavernkeeper, labourer, doctor, miller, and land surveyor, or school-teacher – appeared on the schedule as a 'yeoman.'

Other sources, such as government reports, depositions, recognizances, and censuses, must therefore be used. Through them the livelihoods of 140 of the 197 insurgents have been found. The results are given in Table 4.

It might be tempting to conclude that all or most of the labourers were farm workers (recognizances and census returns simply list 'labourers' without differentiating the different kinds), but it must be remembered that even in agricultural areas there were numerous small craft and manufacturing establishments. In 1835 in Dumfries, for example, there were no less than 73 mills, distilleries, factories, blacksmith shops, and so on.[20] The millers and tanners included one man who worked for a miller in an unknown capacity. The craftsmen or skilled workers comprised blacksmiths, carpenters, well diggers, clothiers, tailors, cordwainers, and watchmakers. Included under miscellaneous were one commercial fisherman, one auctioneer, one gentleman's son, and one apprentice.

Thus, broadly speaking, there were three categories: farmers, labourers, and such various skilled workers as innkeepers, craftsmen, and professionals. In many instances the lines of distinction between various occupations tended to be blurred, however, because a man might well be engaged in more than one economic activity, millers and rural tavernkeepers farming, for example. None the less the facts clearly indicate that the traditional description of the insurgents as 'substantial yeomen' is much too narrow, although many may have been 'substantial' or at least reasonably prosperous. The phrase 'yeomen and mechanics' is not sufficiently precise either because it cannot comprehend all who were not farmers.

It is worth noting that several doctors were implicated in the uprising. No less than four, most notably, of course, Duncombe himself, took up arms in the rebel cause, a fact that may have caused an American editor to note that 'the rebellion seems to have enlisted all the Doctors in Canada.'[21] The Toronto *Patriot* commented on the extraordinary number of physicians both in the Home district and in the west who were embroiled in the revolt, but observed that 'all know how numerous have been the self-styled "doctors" implicated in the rebellion, but perhaps all do not know that they are almost one and all Yankee quacks.'[22]

It seems likely therefore that many of the Duncombe rebels were economically reasonably successful. It would be difficult to prove that those who had no property were those who escaped. Naturally, some were inclined to deprecate the social character both of Duncombe's followers and of the rebels at large. George Coventry, a Tory on the Niagara frontier at the outbreak of the rebellion in Upper Canada, referred to the province's insurgents as being 'principally confined to unlettered mechanics and farmers of no standing in society.'[23] His point appears to have been that there were very few, if any, 'gentlemen' among the insurrectionists. In direct contrast, however, Adam Hope, one of the St Thomas loyalists, was amazed 'at the number of people of *property* & respectability' implicated in the revolt throughout the province.[24]

If the rebels did not encompass the socially élite, they were, none the less, a well established group in the rural areas and their leaders, in some cases, had achieved the dignity of the magistracy. Contemporary observations suggest that the insurgents were relatively stable, well-settled people.

Evidence from censuses, prisoner lists, and one or two contemporary

TABLE 5
Ages of the rebels

Age range	Number
60–64	3
55–59	3
50–54	2
45–49	6
40–44	7
35–39	13
30–34	11
25–29	20
20–24	28
15–19	15
10–14	1
Total	109

NOTE: The median falls in the 25–29 range.

sources indicates that in general the rebels were mature individuals, the average age of 109 of the sample 197 being 30.2. (See Table 5.)

Of 128 of the 197 men in the sample, 84 were married. Many were, therefore, encumbered with responsibilities. As might be expected, however, little evidence is available on the ages and marital status of the rebels at large, though it might be noted that John Treffry of Norwich recorded in the summer of 1838 that many insurgents, who had large families and fine farms, had fled his township.[25]

The picture that emerges of the sample rebel population is that of a relatively stable, comparatively prosperous group of people. Evidence can be presented to suggest that other such men were caught up in 'revolutionary politics.' In appendix 2 57 men who aided the insurgents are identified and appendices 6, 7, and 8 list a further 63 taken in the rebel area by the authorities for unknown reasons, or for being implicated in the Duncombe rising on grounds which now seem uncertain, or for treasonable activities not directly connected with that rising. The low incidence of labourers, the high proportion of married men, the high average age, and the number of propertyholders, as shown in Table 6, suggest that they too were relatively well established.

No discussion of the political and economic characteristics of the rebels and their supporters would be complete without a recognition of the fact

175 Rebels and Loyalists

TABLE 6
Characteristics of accomplices and suspects

	Accomplices	Suspects
Farmers	23	11
Millers, craftsmen, professionals, etc.	18	15
Labourers	0	6
Married	36	24
Single	5	10
No. whose ages are known	31	27
Average age	41.0	34.7
Propertyholders	33	22
Total no. of subjects	57	63

that there was at least one distinct subgroup among them. On 18 December 1837, Mahlon Burwell of Southwold, militia colonel and member of the assembly for the town of London, informed the adjutant general that those gathered at Oakland had been a 'collection of vagrants.'[26] Burwell's impression, so different from those of many of his contemporaries, may have been influenced by his propensity to disparage the character of his political opponents and by the fact that those insurgents from his own immediate neighbourhood, Southwold, Yarmouth, and Malahide, do not appear to have fitted the traditional 'sturdy yeoman' decription of the rebels to the same extent as their counterparts from other areas.

Certainly, Martin Switzer from Streetsville, raising recruits near Sparta, made a special appeal to the 'young men' of Yarmouth and its vicinity to turn out,[27] and one rebel supporter, Charles Conrad of Yarmouth, indicated that the youths of the Jamestown area responded.[28] Moreover, Adam Hope noted that the fifty or sixty 'political fanatics' comprising the Yarmouth party were 'chiefly young men.'[29] Significantly, the data collected on the thirty-six people known to have been in this group suggest that they were notably younger than the rest of the sample population.[30] The average age of the 109 rebels whose ages are known was 30.2 years, but the average age of the 23 corresponding insurrectionists from Yarmouth, Malahide, and Southwold was 21.4 years. (See Table 7.)

As Table 8 shows, while 65.6 per cent of those insurrectionists whose marital states have been discovered were married, only ten Yarmouth

TABLE 7
Ages of Yarmouth and other rebels

Age range	Number of Yarmouth rebels	Number of other rebels
60–64	–	3
55–59	–	3
50–54	–	2
45–49	–	6
40–44	–	7
35–39	–	13
30–34	1	10
25–29	4	16
20–24	11	17
15–19	6	9
10–14	1	–
Total	23	86
Median	20–24	30–34

TABLE 8
Marital status of Yarmouth and other rebels

	Single	Married	Percentage single	Percentage married
Yarmouth	15	10	60.0	40.0
Others	29	74	28.2	71.8
Total	44	84	34.4	65.6

area rebels were, while fifteen were single. In keeping with their apparent youth, the Yarmouth, Malahide, and Southwold insurrectionists contained proportionately more labourers. Of the 140 men who mustered at Oakland whose occupations have been determined, only twenty-seven were labourers. Ten came from the Yarmouth region, an area which, as Table 9 shows, produced only sixteen insurgents engaged in other occupations.

One might suspect that, because the magistrates were especially diligent in scouring the lakefront townships for rebels and the insurgents there were younger and not as well established as the rebels from other

TABLE 9
Occupations of Yarmouth and other rebels

	Labourers	Non-labourers	Percentage labourers	Percentage non-labourers
Yarmouth	10	16	38.4	61.6
Others	17	97	14.9	85.1
Total	27	113	19.3	80.7

areas, in these other areas the young, single labourers escaped official attention. But contemporary observers noted the *exceptional* youth of those in the Yarmouth party. Further, the party from Yarmouth and its vicinity marched farther to Oakland than did any other group of rebels. Perhaps the natural reluctance of men to leave wives and families to make the long fifty-mile trek to Oakland from Sparta in the cold of a Canadian December accounts for the large percentage of youthful labourers among the rebels from this area. Certainly, the rebellion elicited the support of some fairly substantial members of the community who were prepared to aid the rebels but not to march to Oakland. Fourteen of the fifty-seven individuals identified as having helped the rebels came from Southwold, Yarmouth, and Malahide. The occupations of eleven are known: six were farmers, one a farmer's son, one a doctor, one an innkeeper, one a tailor, and one a millwright. None were labourers. Ten of the fourteen were married and two were single. The ages of seven are known and average 50.0. Thus Adam Hope had some reason for suspecting that, in the event of property confiscations, in Yarmouth alone they would 'perhaps reach $20,000. It is truly melancholy,' he added, 'to see the earnings of a life of honest industry swept away in a minute.'[31]

Moreover the data do not indicate that the authorities, as a matter of policy, customarily allowed young, landless labourers to escape. One hundred and sixty-five rebels who were captured are identified, thirty-two are named who were not. Occupations are known for 125 of the 165 men arrested and of them twenty-four, or 19.2 per cent, were labourers; occupations are known for fifteen of the thirty-two men not arrested of whom three, or 20 per cent, were labourers. The average age (from ninety-nine ages known) of the men arrested was 30.4; that of those not arrested (from ten known) was 28.4. The evidence thus demonstrates that there was no significant difference between the average ages or the number of labourers in the two groups.

178 The Rising in Western Upper Canada

To recapitulate, the Duncombe rebels may be divided roughly into three occupations: an agrarian 'proprietorial' group of farmers and farmer's sons; a more or less skilled 'middle class' of craftsmen, millers, professionals, and so on; and a 'lower class' of labourers and hired farm hands. Contemporary evidence suggests that the insurgents were not economically disadvantaged but were rather a reasonably mature, well-established body of men.

III

The nationality of the rebels was also a matter of concern to their contemporaries. The various national problems that had plagued the province ensured that the nationalities of the insurgents and, by implication, the loyalties of the various national groups would be closely scrutinized. As Table 10 shows, North Americans dominated the sample rebel population, Americans and Upper Canadians accounting for no less than 75.5 per cent of the sample for whom birthplaces could be identified.

As Table 11 shows, Americans and Upper Canadians were also preponderant among those who aided the rebels, as well as among those taken on suspicion of having committed a variety of treasonable offences, enumerated in this study in appendices 6, 7, and 8.

As Table 12 illustrates, many of the Americans had been in the province for considerable periods of time, long enough presumably to have become established and involved in the political process. Most had been in the colony for a number of years but a significant number had come in after the War of 1812, apparently undeterred by the government's efforts after that war to discourage American settlement. They may have brought with them some of the American hostility to colonial rule and colonial government.

Native Upper Canadians were another dominant group involved. Solid grounds exist for assuming that most of the Upper Canadians listed in Tables 10 and 11 were of American lineage. The origins of forty of the families of the seventy-four Upper Canadians there have been established and are categorized in Table 13. No less than thirty-eight of the forty families in Table 13 whose origins are known were descended from Americans who had moved into the colony from the United States either directly or through the Maritime colonies.

Various sources, such as settlers' letters, travellers' accounts, and local histories, taken together suggest that in 1837 most of the sixteen rebel townships were still dominated by American settlers and their Upper

179 Rebels and Loyalists

TABLE 10
Origins of the rebels

Place of origin	Number	Percentage of 135	Percentage of 197
United States	50	37.0	25.4
Upper Canada	52	38.5	26.4
'Canada'	2		
Nova Scotia	2	3.7	2.5
New Brunswick	1		
England	14	10.4	7.1
Ireland	14	10.4	7.1
Total known	135	100.0	68.5
Total unknown	62	–	31.5
Total sample	197	–	100.0

TABLE 11
Origins of accomplices and suspects (the latter in parentheses)

Place of origin	Number	Percentage of total known		Percentage of total sample	
United States	27 (17)	60.0	(45.9)	47.4	(27.0)
Upper Canada	11 (11)	24.4	(29.7)	19.3	(15.9)
New Brunswick	2 (–)	4.4	(–)	3.5	(–)
Nova Scotia	– (2)	–	(5.4)	–	(3.2)
Lower Canada	1 (–)	2.2	(–)	1.8	(–)
England	3 (4)	6.7	(10.8)	5.3	(6.3)
Ireland	1 (2)	2.2	(5.4)	1.8	(3.2)
France	– (1)	–	(2.7)	–	(1.6)
Total known	45 (37)	100.0	(100.0)	78.9	(58.7)
Total unknown	12 (26)	–	(–)	21.1	(41.3)
Total	57 (63)	–	(–)	100.0	(100.0)

Canadian children. (See map 3.) This was true in Brantford, Blenheim, Oakland, Burford, East and West Oxford, Dereham, Norwich, Windham, Townsend, and Woodhouse. In Bayham, Malahide, and Yarmouth, where several national groups had settled in strength the insurgents came from areas originally occupied by Americans. The same

TABLE 12
Lengths of residence of the American-born

Residency	Rebels	Accomplices	Suspects
45 +	–	1	–
40–44	4	1	1
35–39	3	1	–
30–34	–	1	–
25–29	5	6	1
20–24	3	3	–
15–19	7	4	4
10–14	2	3	2
5–9	2	1	1
0–4	7	2	1
Average	19.6	22.0	17.0
Median	15–19	20–24	15–19
Number known	33	23	10
Number unknown	17	4	7
Total	50	27	17

TABLE 13
Family origins of the Upper Canadians

Family origins	Rebels	Accomplices	Suspects
United States	27	6	5
Ireland	1	–	–
'Britain'	–	–	1
Total known	28	6	6
Total unknown	24	5	5
Total	52	11	11

was true in Dumfries where Lowland and Highland Scots formed the majority of settlers, and in Southwold where Highland Scots and Englishmen abounded.

Most critics of the 'Yankee' element of the province's population rarely distinguished between Americans and Upper Canadians or even admitted the validity of such distinctions. To be born in Upper Canada of parents from across the line was to be an American. Many were convinced that Americans and their progeny were behind the difficulties in Upper

Canada. For instance, the Montreal *Herald* declared that one need only look at those implicated in the Upper Canadian rebellion to see that 'in the *Hirams*, the *Elijahs* and innumerable other scriptural names, we have without further enquiry, sufficient evidence that *the disaffected of the country were principally* Americans or descendants of Americans.'[32] Closer to the Duncombe area, Alexander Light of North Oxford wrote that most, if not all, 'the disaffected are Americans or descendants of Americans.'[33] Light felt that further settlement in the province from the south should be severely restricted and suggested that in the future anyone who sold or rented property 'to any American or foreigner, without a special sanction of the executive power' be subject to 'a heavy fine and imprisonment.'[34] In 1838 John Burn, 'once a Tyne side Northumberland farmer' of Dereham, complained that the settlers in his township from the States had been quite rebellious through 1837, telling the English inhabitants that 'we should be drove out of the country' and saying that 'to be an Englishman was bad enough, but to be an English Torie was insufferable.' Burn continued to lament that both Dereham and Norwich, controlled as they were by township officers who came from the republic, 'have been more like American dependencies than being part of a British Colony.' He and others had found the Americans in the province to be 'crafty & deceitful,' 'possessed of unextinguishable hatred to British laws & institutions' and he felt that wholesale assisted immigration from Great Britain should be introduced to inundate them.[35]

Lord Durham, investigating conditions in the province in 1838, noted the 'disloyalty, or rather very lukewarm loyalty,' of that portion of the population of the western peninsula which had immigrated from the south.[36] Lieutenant-Governor Sir George Arthur had no hesitation in placing the blame for the revolt in Upper Canada squarely on the shoulders of the province's American settlers.[37] Further, a report prepared for him in 1839 declared that in 'the Talbot settlement ... Immigration from the United States was too freely encouraged, and the whole body of inhabitants of that class are found to be republican, and revolutionary in their sentiments and wishes.'[38]

Representatives of other nationalities were, of course, found in the rebel ranks. Fourteen Englishmen have been identified among Duncombe's forces, as well as three others who provided aid. These individuals were scattered through Dumfries, the Middlesex townships of Bayham, Malahide, Yarmouth, and Southwold, and the Oxford townships of Oakland, Brantford, Norwich, Dereham, and East and West Oxford. No one group of Englishmen provided men for the insurgent army. English immigrants did not generally settle together although there were sizable groups in some localities in the rebel area (the towns of Brantford, Paris, and Woodstock, for example, and the townships of Southwold, Malahide, Bayham, Norwich, and Dereham). All were steadfastly loyal as apparently they were throughout the province. Both Lord Durham[39] and T.R. Preston,[40] a traveller, observed that the British population, presumably meaning the Welsh, Irish, and Scots as well as the English, had quickly rallied to the government cause during the insurrection. An 'Old Country' resident of the Augmentation of Grenville, a community on the Lower Canadian side of the Ottawa River fifty-one miles east of Bytown, insisted that the British of both provinces had demonstrated their loyalty in the rebellions, although he admitted that a 'small number of rotten Sheep & most superlative rascals were of course found both in Upper & Lower Canada.'[41]

Evidently few, if any, Scots were among Duncombe's men. Within the immediate rebel area Brantford had a number of Scots, probably Lowlanders, for there was a large Lowland settlement in Dumfries, just to the north. Dumfries also contained Protestant Highlanders, as did Southwold and Yarmouth. Scots had also moved into West Oxford. Despite this, no persons known to be of Scottish birth were found either among the 197 men identified as having gathered at Oakland or among the fifty-seven who aided them, although the data on the rebels from Dumfries are admittedly weak. The origins of only four of the fourteen insurgents from this township are known. Three were Upper Canadians of non-Scots parentage and the fourth was an Englishman. The nationalities of two of the four Dumfries people who aided the rebels have been discovered: one was a New Brunswicker, the other an Upper Canadian. Although the names of two of the insurrectionists, John and Daniel Stewart, and one of their abettors, Franklyn Kenny, might suggest a Scottish background, it does appear that the rebels from Dumfries came from the west central part of the township and were to some extent removed from the older settled Highland and Lowland Scots communities in the eastern and northern sections.

Scots predominated in several non-rebel Oxford and Middlesex townships. Lowlanders were found in Westminster and London, Highlanders in Zorra, Nissouri, London, Lobo, Caradoc, Ekfrid, Mosa, Aldborough, Dunwich, and Westminster. Because of the haphazard nature of the revolt and its lack of planning, its leaders were unable to spread the news of the uprising to the Scottish townships and, indeed, would have had difficulty in communicating directly with the predominantly Gaelic-speaking Highlanders. These may well have been reasons why some of the Scots did not take part in the rebellion. Certainly, they did not march as a group under the insurgents' banners. P.B. de Blaquiere, a prominent Anglo-Irish immigrant who had arrived in the province in 1837 and been active in suppressing the revolt, noted that he had not been confident of the loyalty of the local Scots, disenchanted as they were with the government for refusing to yield to the claims of the Kirk. He was, however, relieved to discover that the Highlanders of Nissouri and Zorra had resisted various attempts to persuade them to join the rebels.[42] John Askin, clerk of the peace of the London district, observed that the Liberals had regarded the Scots of Lobo, Dunwich, Aldborough, and the north of Yarmouth as allies but were 'sadly ... disappointed,' for the Scottish settlers offered instead to enrol in the government's forces.[43]

Elsewhere in the province, the Scots were not immune to the contagion of revolt. Even before the Upper Canadian uprisings, there had been concern lest the Highlanders of Glengarry aid their Roman Catholic brethren in Lower Canada in rebellion.[44] This fear proved unfounded but some Scottish residents elsewhere in the province were disaffected. Some, in Halton county's Nassagaweya township which was populated primarily by Highlanders belonging to the Kirk, held meetings in Gaelic as soon as they received news of the rebel movements at Toronto. They then raised a small party to aid Mackenzie. The Highlanders of neighbouring Esquesing were accused of attending a gathering at which 'they openly avowed their intention of an appeal to arms.'[45] William Lyon Mackenzie was, of course, from Scotland, which may have been why some termed his uprising 'a Scotch Rebellion.'[46]

Attempts had been made to sow seeds of sedition among the Irish settlers before the insurrection. In November a letter from Oakland signed by 'Erin' had been published in Mackenzie's *Constitution*. It called on the Irish to forget their sectarian differences, arguing that the English had always capitalized upon Irish dissension to further their own ends. Hinting that there was '*something coming*,' the writer had urged his countrymen to rally about 'Liberal' principles[47] but they did not heed his urging to any appreciable extent. Sizable Irish communities existed in the towns of Brantford, Paris, and St Thomas and in the townships of Bayham, Norwich, and Burford. Yet only one Irishman from the town of Brantford, one from the township of Norwich, and two from the township of Oakland are known to have joined the insurgents. Ten of those who took up arms from Yarmouth, Malahide, and Southwold, however, were Irishmen. Possibly, the personal example and public prominence of the rebel captain, David Anderson, an Irish tavernkeeper in the hamlet of Suckertown in the south-east of Southwold, attracted at least some of his compatriots to the rebel cause.

Throughout the province the Irish appear to have been loyal. In early December in Hamilton there had been rival meetings to enlist Irish sympathy for the Radicals and Tories respectively. After the revolt, however, G.P. Bull, editor of the loyalist *Hamilton Gazette*, wrote with evident satisfaction to James Buchanan, the British consul in New York, to say that no rebels had been found among the 700 or so Irishmen at the head of the lake.[48] Reputedly, those Irishmen around Guelph and the surrounding townships had rushed to the aid of the government on the outbreak of the insurrection,[49] as had their compatriots in London township. In Toronto Anne Powell wrote that 'not a Man of the Green Isle has joined the Rebels, all are loyal.'[50] The Toronto *Mirror* agreed, noting that the Irish Roman Catholics in Upper Canada lacked the grievances impelling their countrymen in Ireland to disaffection.[51]

In summary, the data assembled on the national origins of the rebels do indeed suggest that the rebellion in the west was largely the work of American immigrants and native Upper Canadians although some inhabitants of other nationalities took up arms. A number of considerations indicate that such individuals were scattered throughout the rebel area (with the exception of the Irish from the Yarmouth region). It is tempting to speculate that the British-born generally had lived in the province for lengthy periods of time and may have adopted many of the attitudes of their distinctly North American neighbours. In fact, twenty-eight Britons were identified in the sample rebel population. The lengths of residence of twelve are known and average 12.5 years. For three people who aided the insurgents the average was 20.7 years and for three suspected of treasonable activities the average was 16.0 years.

IV

The religious affiliations of the Duncombe insurgents and their opponents were also of considerable interest to their contemporaries. The bitter strife among many of the religious groups in the west ensured that accusations would be made. Other individuals and organizations found it advantageous to insist that religious issues and allegiances had played no part whatsoever in the revolt. The *Canada Baptist Magazine and Missionary Register*, for instance, asserted that, if a few members of a particular

185 Rebels and Loyalists

denomination had been found among the rebel ranks, 'we should be unjust in ascribing disaffection to the whole body on that account, or in charging the instructions of the clergy with having a tendency to produce it ... The truth is, that religious or denominational party as such, had nothing to do with the late outbreak, it must rather be ascribed to the operation of certain pestiferous principles of which all parties ought to be ashamed.'[52] The same journal affirmed the existence of 'a wondrous alliance between Rebellion and Infidelity.'[53] And the Reverend Mr O'Neill, an Anglican cleric, insisted that a good number of the traitors lodged in the Hamilton jail after the revolt were disciples of the revolutionary rationalist Tom Paine.[54]

Various insurrectionists were not connected with any church. Table 14 outlines the religious affiliations of those in the rebel area as revealed by the first religious census, that of 1839.[55] Because of the time lag, its failure to represent Baptist strength adequately, and so on, that census does not fully reflect the religious profiles of 1837. It does, however, indicate that approximately one-quarter of the inhabitants of the region affected by the Duncombe rising had no particular religious affiliation.

Table 14 demonstrates that many in the rebel area had no ties with organized religion and also that certain religious groups, such as the Methodists, Presbyterians, Baptists, and the Church of England, claimed large numbers of adherents. Inevitably, the question arises if any of these groups were over- or under-represented among the Duncombe rebels or their sympathizers. Unfortunately, any inquiry into religious affiliations encounters several problems, not least that many church records of the day have not survived. Those that do exist are often skewed, for many people who did attend the services of a certain sect or group were not members and hence were of no interest to the church clerks although they often outnumbered regular members four and five to one. Thus, the religious records of the day are as disappointing as other collections. After the rebellion, magistrates examining accused traitors seldom took official note of religion. Consequently, the surviving depositions and various jail records, which often detail prisoners' nationalities, ages, and occupations, reveal nothing about religious affiliations. The first nominal census, that of 1841-2, has severe limitations as well. In the first place, much of it has been lost. Secondly, it was taken four or five years after the revolt and hence cannot provide reliable data about individual religious affiliations in 1837 as denominational and sectarian lines were crossed with some frequency. One cannot assume, for instance, that a man who was a Wesleyan Methodist in 1842 had been one in 1837. The religious data are

TABLE 14
Religious affiliations of the population of the rebel area, 1839

Affiliation	Number	Percentage of 24,741	Percentage of 36,098
Methodists	5,128	20.7	14.2
Wesleyan	2,718	11.0	7.5
Episcopal	1,589	6.4	4.4
Ryanites	821	3.3	2.3
Presbyterians	5,067	20.5	14.0
Church of Scotland	2,247	9.1	6.2
Other	2,820	11.4	7.8
Baptists	3,337	13.5	9.2
Closed Communion	2,050	8.3	5.7
Open Communion	954	3.9	2.6
Free Will	333	1.3	0.9
Church of England	2,780	11.2	7.7
Quakers	1,035	4.2	2.9
Roman Catholics	645	2.6	1.8
Congregationalists	180	0.7	0.5
Other sects	214	0.9	0.6
No affiliation	6,355	25.7	17.6
Total known	24,741	100.0	68.5
Total unknown	11,357	–	31.5
Total population	36,098	–	100.0

meagre indeed, so much so that the precise affiliation of Charles Duncombe himself is not known. His association with Freemasonry may have betokened an ardent Protestantism but does not suggest any particular denominational or sectarian loyalty. Contradictory evidence points to his having been either an Anglican[56] or a Methodist while his brother David was either a Methodist[57] or a Baptist.[58] Overall, then, the data are inadequate for quantitative study and must be buttressed by qualitative, intuitive evidence.

Table 15 presents the religious data collected on the 197 Duncombe rebels, the fifty-seven who aided them, and the sixty-three suspected by the authorities of being traitors.

Quakers form the largest group, twenty-seven in all, and, not surprisingly, were one of the two religious groups within the area most readily linked with the insurgents. They were particularly strong in Norwich and the south of Yarmouth and drew some support as well from Malahide

187 Rebels and Loyalists

TABLE 15
Religious affiliations

Affiliation	Rebels	Accomplices	Suspects
Quaker	12	10	5
'Quaker'	6	5	2
Hicksite Quaker	5	1	2
Conservative Quaker	1	4	1
Congregationalist	15	–	–
Baptist	9	2	3
'Baptist'	–	1	
Closed Communion Baptist	7	1	2
Open Communion Baptist	2	–	1
Methodist	5	1	1
'Methodist'	4	–	–
Episcopal Methodist	1	–	1
Wesleyan Methodist	–	1	–
Church of England	1	–	2
Interdenominational	–	1	–
No affiliation	2	–	–
Total known	44	14	11

and Bayham, although their numbers were not significant in any of the other rebel townships. The Anglican missionary Thomas Green noted that 'not a few' of the Norwich Friends were suspected of having joined Duncombe.[59]

No Quaker meeting supported the insurrection (or its armed suppression), for the Quakers were pacifists. On 13 December 1837 the Norwich women of the Hicksite Quakers and the men and women of the Conservative Quakers met as usual in separate meetings and did not refer to the revolt. They neither sanctioned nor condemned it. Further, in January 1838 the Conservative Quakers of Norwich recorded that only three of their members had participated in the 'war,'[60] that is, in the promotion or suppression of the revolt. How many Quaker 'hearers' became embroiled in the rebellion cannot be determined. Significantly, most of the Quakers identified in Table 14 were 'hearers' not members of their societies. None the less they were still Quakers.

No fully satisfactory explanation exists for the number of Quakers involved in the revolt. The general humanitarian impulse of Quakerism may have led some Friends to take up arms to redress perceived wrongs but that thrust should have been countered by the pacifism of the Quaker creed. Clearly, religious belief played no direct part in the Quaker insurgents' decision to side with Duncombe. Political grievances, a depressed economy, a misunderstanding about the actual balance between loyalists and rebels carried greater weight. Like most of their comrades, the Quakers acted from a variety of secular, rather than religious, motives. A number of prominent Quakers, however, notably Elias Moore of Yarmouth, a Middlesex MPP, urged rebellion. Other well-known Friends, among them Solomon Lossing, a Norwich magistrate, and Peter DeLong, an early Norwich settler and a large landholder, were deeply implicated in the revolt. Such Quakers, acting as individuals rather than as representatives of their religion, helped persuade many men, including other Friends, to join their cause. Thus, ties of community and kinship and political and economic grievances do more to explain Quaker participation in the rebellion than does the nature of the Quaker religion itself.

The Congregationalists were the other denomination whose members were frequently linked with the insurgents' cause. The census of 1839 and church records suggest that in 1837 the Congregationalists comprised significant segments of the populations of Oakland and Burford, and lesser portions of Paris, Brantford, and the township of Southwold. Of the forty-four insurrectionists whose religious affiliations have been determined, fifteen were Congregationalists. All came from the townships of Oakland and Burford: eight from the former, seven from the latter. Six were Malcolms and three were Kellys, an indication of the importance of family ties as well. No concrete evidence exists to suggest that members of the Brantford, Dumfries, or Southwold congregations were disloyal, although the last apparently was rent by dissension over the revolt.

Despite the fact that the parent Colonial Missionary Society in Great Britain asserted that no Congregational minister in Upper Canada, 'nor a single member of their churches,' nor any of their 'hearers,' was 'in the least degree' involved in the uprising,[61] the Congregationalists were widely suspected of being deeply implicated. John Roaf and Henry Wilkes, Congregational ministers at Toronto and Brantford respectively, explained that, 'our body being well known to entertain liberal opinions on all subjects relating to liberty, religion and education; when some in the Colonies who push these sentiments to dangerous and violent extremes, broke out into actual rebellion, odium, and suspicion fell on our friends as holding, though in a just and moderate form, the same general views with the insurgents.'[62] Although Roaf and Wilkes erred in maintaining the Congregationalists' total innocence, they do illustrate that at least some members of their church shared certain values and attitudes with the rebel leaders. All believed in voluntaryism, for instance. Further, the Congregationalists insisted upon the freedom of individual congregations to organize their own affairs, while Duncombe, Mackenzie, and others argued the necessity of political freedom.

The Baptists were even more significant than is suggested in Table 15. Contemporary evidence and the 1839 census indicate that they were in 1837 the largest single denomination in five of the rebel townships and the second or third largest body in five others.[63] Only in Dumfries and Yarmouth were they few in number although even here they had pockets of strength. The Open Communion Baptists maintained seven congregations in six Oxford, Middlesex, and Norfolk townships directly affected by the uprising, and they were the dominant Baptist denomination in three of them.[64] The Regular, or Closed Communion, Baptists had no less than twenty congregations scattered through thirteen of the sixteen rebel townships. Except for the townships of Burford, East Oxford, and Southwold, which were Open Communion strongholds, and Blenheim, where the two leading Baptist groups were apparently of equal strength, the Closed Communionists were probably dominant in the remaining insurgent townships. The Free Will Baptists were relatively inconsequential but did draw some support from the townships of Dereham, Southwold, and Burford.

Although they enjoyed a strong position in the area from which Duncombe raised his men, only seven Closed and two Open Communion Baptists are known to have mustered at Oakland. Of the two known Baptists who aided the rebels, one was a Regular Baptist, the second was of undetermined affiliation. These eleven disaffected Baptists (the authorities suspected three more of treason) came from throughout the region: four from Norwich, two from Malahide, and one from each of the townships of Bayham, Oakland, Southwold, and West Oxford. Another was from the Oxfords. The locations of the Baptist churches in the rebel townships do not correlate with the areas of rebel strength. The congregations of Blenheim, Oakland, Norwich, West Oxford, Malahide, Windham, northern Townsend, southern Yarmouth, and possibly of Brantford town and of Burford township would be considered within the rebel domain but those of Dumfries, Southwold, East Oxford, Bayham, southern Townsend, and of St Thomas would not.

After the uprising, the Baptists faced widespread accusations of disloyalty, sparked in part by the reluctance of many of the adherents of non-violence among them to serve in the militia and in part by the fact that some Baptists had certainly been among Duncombe's men. Most of the charges, however, appear to have been groundless. Thomas Green, an itinerant Anglican minister, observed that 'many *professed* Baptists' had been found in arms in the London district,[65] a remark which drew an angry retort from the *Canada Baptist Magazine and Missionary Register*, which said that it was unaware of any Baptist insurgents in the London district. If any existed, Green was assured, 'they are as widely recreant from our principles as from those of our Episcopal brethren.'[66] Noting that the Baptists' teachings were similar to those of the other Evangelical denominations and included the doctrine of the necessity of obedience to civil authorities, the *Magazine* asserted that 'Baptism as a profession of faith has surely no very peculiar tendency to make men rebels.'[67]

Despite the fact that only one member of the Yarmouth Regular Baptist Church, Andrew McLure of Southwold, marched to Oakland and that he was obliged to recant his desertion of pacifist tenets before his assembled brethren,[68] W.M. McKillican, a minister of the Kirk, later claimed that the Baptists of the Yarmouth area had met in the house of one Black and here had 'determined systematically to oppose the Government or stand neutral in 1837.'[69] An Anglican missionary, the Reverend Mr O'Neill, reported that the Baptist preacher at St George in south Dumfries had fled the district at the outbreak of the insurrection[70] but nothing in the records of the St George Church supports his accusation.[71]

Evidence exists that particular Baptists supported the loyalists. The Reverend Charles Carpenter claimed that both his colleague, the Reverend Mr Rees, the Regular Baptist minister of Brantford and the president of the Canadian Missionary Society, and 'the large and influential body' Rees represented had taken 'an active part' in the rebellion 'in favour of Her Majesty's Government.'[72] The Reverend Shook McConnell, the minister of the Regular Baptist Church of Bayham, was described by that ardent Anglican and Tory Mahlon Burwell as 'deficient in point of intelligence' but 'a very loyal man.'[73] All the Baptist churches condemned the insurrection and the Regular Baptist Church of Bayham excluded one of its members for, among other things, 'signing the political union with those opposed to the British Government.'[74] Both the Montreal-published *Canada Baptist Magazine and Missionary Register* and the Toronto *Baptist Missionary Magazine* roundly damned the rebels.[75]

In the rebel townships, the Baptists were probably outnumbered by the

191 Rebels and Loyalists

Methodists, whose activities are extremely difficult to pinpoint. An itinerant Catholic priest, Daniel Downie, noted that 'the fact is every private house is a church with the methodists & every man a preacher.'[76] Few of their records have survived for the area. The 1839 census and the sparse evidence available for the preceding years suggest that the Methodists were the foremost group in the rebel townships, constituting the largest single denomination in four,[77] and probably second or third largest in the remaining townships, except in Yarmouth where they were relatively inconsequential.

The Wesleyan Methodists, formed by the 1833 union of the Canada Methodists and the Wesleyan Church and the largest branch of Methodism in the province, appear to have been the primary Methodist group in ten of the townships directly involved in the rebellion.[78] In addition, they were strong in Malahide and equal in numbers to the Episcopal Methodists in Dumfries. The Episcopal Methodists, vehement opponents of the Wesleyans, were perhaps the foremost Methodist body in Blenheim and Norwich and important in the religious composition of three or four other rebel townships.[79] Another sect, the Canadian Wesleyans or Ryanites, was influential in four townships.[80] In the rebel townships of Blenheim, Bayham, and Malahide the three different Methodist sects seem to have enjoyed equal support.

Although the Methodists were the largest denomination in the area, only five of the forty-four insurrectionists whose religious affiliations are known were Methodists. One was an Episcopal Methodist; the precise sectarian loyalties of the other four are not known. Of the fourteen individuals who aided the rebels and whose religious ties have been ascertained, only one was a Methodist, an adherent of the Wesleyans. One 'suspect,' Norman Malcolm, accused of threatening the Tories who had arrested his rebel father, John, was, like his parent, an Episcopal Methodist. Of the seven Methodists identified here, three were from Norwich, two from Brantford township, and two from Oakland.

The Episcopal Methodists do not appear to have participated in the Duncombe uprising to any great degree but at least one of their ministers may have played a part in promoting it. Two Norwich rebels, one of whom was Abraham Sackrider, testified that a Methodist preacher named Bird who had spoken to the insurgents assembled at Sodom had 'preached politics as well as Gospel' and had 'encouraged them to go on as he thought they were doing well.'[81] He later recalled that Bird had indeed incited men to take up arms to fight for freedom. He 'never saw this Preacher before,' but 'heard that he had Preached at Sodom once or twice before.'[81] The truth of Sackrider's assertions remains clouded because the examining magistrates did not push the matter further. Still, it is worth noting that in 1837 the Episcopal Methodist preacher Francis Bird rode the Long Point circuit but was transferred to the Nelson circuit in 1838.[83]

Throughout the province, the Episcopals were accused of being involved in the revolt, particularly by members of the rival Wesleyan Methodists, Egerton Ryerson, for example, and the Wesleyan Conference president, William Harvard.[84] In the province as a whole, though not in the western peninsula, a good many Episcopals were jailed on charges of treason. In 1838 the conference of the Episcopal Methodist Church recorded that 'numerous are the instances in which those who seek our hurt have endeavoured to blast our character, and cause us to be deprived of personal liberty, by false accusations and unfounded rumours.'[85]

The Wesleyans themselves were not immune from accusation. The Roman Catholic archbishop, Alexander Macdonell, included them in his assertion that the Methodists and Presbyterians formed the majority of the rebels.[86] A British Presbyterian settler from Dereham, John Burn, insisted that 'several Americans in communion with the British Wesleyan's [sic] turned out and joined Duncombe.'[87] The annual conference of the Wesleyan Methodists in 1838, though praising the general loyalty of its members in the revolt, did find it necessary to regret publicly the treasonable activities of some of them.[88] In the London district at least, however, the Wesleyans as a body had supported the government in the insurrection. Even Thomas Green could find no quarrel with the loyalty of the Wesleyans, saying that, in so far as he could divine, all those Methodists connected with the British Wesleyans had rallied against the insurgents.[89]

A number of other denominations were active in the rebel townships: the Presbyterian elements that included the Church of Scotland, the United Synod, the United Secession Church, the Associate Reformed Church, and the United Associate Synod, also the Roman Catholics, the Christians, and the Mormons. No members of any of them are known to have been involved in the Oakland uprising. Despite the facts that several members of the United Secession congregation at London were jailed on suspicion of treason, as were members of the Reverend Robert Thornton's United Secession Pickering congregation,[90] and that various adherents of the Niagara Presbytery churches in and about Hamilton and the Niagara district were suspected (apparently with good reason) of being involved in treasonable activities,[91] the members of these churches within the rebel area do not seem to have compromised their loyalty or to have been accused of doing so.

One Mormon, Moses Chapman Nickerson of Woodhouse, joined the patriots and was indicted and attained as a traitor. According to one priest, five Roman Catholics took part in the Duncombe uprising or in associated activities.[92] Bishop Macdonell admitted that elsewhere 'a few vagabonds of our people,' notably about Lloydtown in the Home district,[93] were associated with the insurgents.[94] The loyalty of the Catholic and Mormon populations, however, was generally unquestioned, at least in the immediate aftermath of the rebellion.

The Church of England constituted one of the larger denominations in the rebel area but the 1839 census and contemporary evidence suggest that only in Yarmouth and Woodhouse were the Anglicans pre-eminent. In nine other townships they were perhaps the second or third largest group,[95] and evidently formed important minorities in the populations of Norwich and Townsend. Only in Dumfries were they relatively inconsequential. Of the forty-four insurgents and their fourteen accomplices whose religious affiliations have been discovered, only one, Ben Page of Yarmouth who marched to Oakland, was an Anglican. Two of those suspected by the authorities of helping inspire the revolt, however, John Talbot of the *Liberal* and Robert Alway, MPP, were Anglicans. Thomas Green, though, wrote that *'I know not of one member of the Church of England*, nor have I heard of any ... being detected in aiding or abetting this unnatural and unwarrantable outbreak' in the western peninsula.[96]

The settled Church of England congregations were on the periphery of the rebel area at Ingersoll, Beachville, in the northern section of East Oxford, at Galt, Brantford, Waterford, Port Stanley, St Thomas, and at various places in Woodhouse. The one exception was Bayham but the Anglican catechist there laboured in the southern parts of the township where none of Duncombe's men were evidently to be found. The 'interior' insurgent townships of Dereham, Burford, Norwich, Oakland, Windham, and Malahide had no established Anglican congregations. The Reverend Mr O'Neill observed that 'a comparatively inexpensive establishment of peaceful Missionaries of the Church, adequate to the wants of the Country would have altogether prevented' the revolt.[97] Throughout the province the Church of England ministers and their flocks demonstrated their loyalty to a unique degree during the turmoil of the revolt and afterwards may have been helped by a reputation for loyalty. Perhaps others joined convicted rebel John Tidey in his attempt to signify his new allegiance to the government by volunteering to become an Anglican.[98]

Several of the religious groups associated with the rebellion, however, suffered both from that association and from the emigration from the province in general. Most dramatic perhaps was the case of the Congregationalists. In 1838 a report of the parent British society stated that the Congregationalists' endeavours in Upper Canada had been injured by 'the prevalence of confusion, alarm and exasperated feelings' and that 'the brethren at Toronto, Hamilton, Westminster, Burford, and Kingston, appear to have been most exposed to the consequences of the conflict raging around them.'[99] The Toronto *Examiner*, referring to the Congregational minister who served London and Westminster, charged that 'the persecuting spirit of the high church magistracy ... could not allow him to exercise his sacred calling in peace.'[100] The church in Southwold was shattered by the events of 1837 and 1838, as the pastor and his flock were sorely divided.[101] In 1838 the minister at Brantford, David Lillie, left his charge when 'the unhappy rebellion occasioned uneasiness and discord among his people.'[102] Reverend Mr Nall remained in Oakland and Burford although 'this cause, and another in the same neighbourhood, have suffered most severely from our public calamities.'[103] The parent society recorded that, 'in consequence of the jealousies and distractions occasioned by the insurrection, many of his [Nall's] supporters have withdrawn into the United States.'[104]

Other religious groups suspected of providing supporters for the Duncombe rebels were adversely affected by the tumult following the revolt. In 1838 John Burn of Dereham, who reported that 'several Americans in communion with the British' Wesleyans had joined Duncombe's men in December 1837, also observed that others had left the province 'because they did not think it right for to take up arms in support of the Government, nor even, for natural born subjects to do so. They also did not like to hear the Queen prayed for.'[105] That same summer, the Wesleyan Methodist ministers of the Ancaster circuit protested 'that laboured efforts to create suspicion' in Arthur's mind about the loyalty of their followers 'should have been in the least degree attended with success.'[106] The records of the church of 1838 show a slight decrease in membership, though not as great as that which had occurred in 1837.[107] Oddly, the Episcopal Methodists registered a considerable increase in their members in 1838 and 1839,[108] even though in the latter year the president of the conference regretted 'the removal of many of our old and influential members' to the United States.[109]

Members of other denominations and sects, such as the Baptists and Quakers, were also suspected of being implicated in the western rising. Because their census records are incomplete, it is difficult to tell if their memberships declined after the rebellion. Probably, both groups suf-

195 Rebels and Loyalists

fered. The First Regular Baptist Church in Norwich, for example, held very few meetings in 1838, and was almost completely prostrated by the turmoil in the west.[110] In addition, as one Baptist reported, the Free Communion Baptist Church of Blenheim was 'greatly injured by the rebellion.'[111]

Some churches whose main endeavours in the west were outside the rebel area were also damaged greatly by the revolt. In December 1838 the Church of Scotland cleric, W.M. McKillican, made known his suspicion that the United Secession minister in London, William Proudfoot, and his Scotch Baptist counterpart in Lobo, Dugald Campbell, 'secretly cool & distract the minds of our Countrymen.'[112] Such suspicions, voiced from the earliest days of December 1837, harmed Proudfoot, his charge, and the United Secession congregations generally. In August 1838 Proudfoot glumly noted that, 'our Churches being all known to be voluntary, have been the object of particular dislike to the Tory party, and as that vile faction has gained for the present the ascendancy, they have in this district particularly done every thing in their power to hurt our cause – some members have left the Church on political grounds – and almost all occasional hearers have left.'[113] The minister of Union road in Southwold, James Skinner, recorded that the United Secession flocks were in decline and that a number of members had gone to the United States. His gloomy conclusion was that 'unless the present political discord shall speedily be diminished ... the Congregations will yet be more reduced and may eventually be broken down.'[114]

In January 1839 Lieutenant-Governor Arthur personally berated Skinner's colleague, Proudfoot, for alleged disloyalty, after a nephew of Proudfoot's had been jailed for being involved in the Windsor raid.[115] Although the Reverend Mr McKillican had associated Proudfoot and the United Secessionists with Dugald Campbell and the Scotch Baptists, Arthur was prepared to court the latter, possibly because they had not participated in the Duncombe rising and were clearly disenchanted with the drift of a number of church-state issues. He assured them through an intermediary that the government had no intention of elevating the Church of England to a position of dominance over them.[116] Despite Arthur's favourable treatment of Campbell and the Scotch Baptists, Proudfoot and the United Secession Presbyterians suffered only temporarily. By 1840 their congregations, including those of Proudfoot himself, were once more flourishing.[117] Other groups, however, were not as fortunate and suffered much more from the revolt and its aftermath.

One in particular, the Niagara Presbytery, had been in financial difficulty and thus weakened before the revolt. In 1837 the Presbytery had fifteen churches in the province and 807 members.[118] In December that year, although none of its members were involved in the western rising, some around Hamilton and elsewhere apparently were engaged in treason. Consequently, several Niagara Presbyterian clerics fled the province and, on 5 July 1838, a minister of the Presbytery at St Thomas, the Reverend J. Marr, recorded that as far as he knew he was the last minister of the organization left in the colony. Aside from the endeavours of the Church of England and the Church of Scotland, there was little evangelizing done in Upper Canada because 'many are afraid-to preach-and-indeed-some would-not-be-allowed-the privilege.'[119] He added that he himself had never been placed under restraint but that he was regarded with suspicion and had often been called a rebel. In September the parent society in the United States removed his name from its rolls, thereby abandoning its cause in Upper Canada.[120]

Other small sects not implicated in the Duncombe rising were also affected. In 1839 the Christians declared that they had 'suffered greatly in consequence of the late disturbances in this Province.'[121] In September 1838 a wagon train of Mormons reportedly fled Upper Canada.[122] The membership of the Universalists declined drastically.[123] The flight or decline of these American-based sects probably was satisfying to those loyalists who had insisted, without evidence, that American clerics and their English allies had been behind the rebellion. One such loyalist, an Anglican priest, was George Petrie, who asserted that the various American missionaries 'were paid as spies; and at the breaking out of the Rebellion it was distinctly proved, that all these Yankee teachers, and others of the same stamp, from England and elsewhere who had appeared ... were neither more or less than "Wolves in Sheep's clothing" – that they had been *purposely* sent, and were paid by the United States, in order to spy out the Land, and ripen the British settlers for Rebellion.'[124] Another Anglican, Alexander W. Light of North Oxford, argued that the various American sects should be hounded from the province, declaring that 'the Methodists, and Baptists, ranters, mucklatonians and American iterats [sic] who every season pervade and disturb the country parts with their revivals, wood preaching and folly, And those periodically visiting us from the United States to corrupt the morals of the people, and instill secret disaffection to the Government, should all be prohibited their nocturnal orgies, and put down with a strong hand with fine and imprisonment by act of Parliament.'[125] Clearly, as the months passed, the circle of those religious groups believed by such loyalists as Petrie and

197 Rebels and Loyalists

Light to be disloyal widened to include all those sects which were of American origin or whose teachings deviated markedly from the Church of England-Church of Scotland norm.

v

Questions inevitably arise about the precise points of difference between the rebels and the loyalists. Much time has been spent in identifying the 197 insurgents and in attempting to unearth and divine some of their salient characteristics. It is obviously impossible to secure data on the members of all the militia companies called out to combat the uprising. Even if it were possible, the inferences drawn would be questionable, for even the most somnolent loyalty could be awakened by the mustering of the regiment and the threat of military action against those refusing to heed the alarm. Ideally, an examination of the loyalists should isolate those who responded to the first call of duty, whether from a desire to suppress the rebellion and support the government, or from the hope of wreaking a measure of revenge upon their Radical neighbours, or from the prospect of military glory. No doubt a variety of reasons existed for both rebels and loyalists to bear arms.

In any event, the names are available of two groups of men from a specific geographic area who rallied *immediately* to the defence of the government. John Burwell, the justice of the peace in Port Burwell, submitted to the militia department a list of the forty-one members of the Second regiment of the Middlesex militia who enlisted under him 'on the night of the 12th Dec. 1837 and marched to intercept Anderson's Party of Rebels from the south of Yarmouth, on their route to join Dr Duncombe at Oakland, and afterwards advanced to Simcoe to join the Militia to attack them at Oakland – & then proceeded to Yarmouth with him to arrest and secure recreant Traitors.'[126] Captain Henry Medcalf of Bayham also sent a return to the office of forty men in the same regiment who rallied about him on the morning of 13 December to pursue the Yarmouth insurgents.[127] (One was Ira Cook, whose brother, Robert, had gone to Oakland to join Duncombe.) The majority were from Bayham and a few were from the surrounding area. These eighty-one men and the twenty-two Bayham rebels identified provide a good basis for a study of the loyalist-rebel dichotomy.[128]

Much of Bayham had been occupied in the second decade of the nineteenth century. The northern third and a section of the east-central portion of the township had been opened to settlement in the 1830s. The

Talbot road area and the northern part of Bayham had been settled predominantly by Americans, and Nova Scotians had moved into the township along the lake. English and Irish immigrants had followed them, locating near the small communities of Vienna and Port Burwell. By 1837, a considerable part of the township's population consisted of native-born Upper Canadians, largely the progeny of American and Nova Scotian stock. The main religious groups within the township were the Baptists, the Anglicans, and the Methodists. The first were primarily Regular Baptists, while the Methodists were divided fairly evenly into Wesleyans, Episcopals, and Ryanites, the Wesleyans being perhaps the largest of the three.

In 1837 the township contained 2,410 people, and had enjoyed a sizable and steady rate of population increase over the past nine years, a rate which had declined in the depression of 1836–7. The mainstay of the township's economy was farming, the chief drawback the distance from market. For the timber and lumber trade, however, there was a voracious market across the lake. Consequently, the local farmers often cut the timber on their own property and engaged in the trade on a part time or seasonal basis. Contemporaries enthused about the quality of the township's timber, John Burwell noting in 1836 the 'great quantities of the best white Pine timber,'[129] stands which an American entrepreneur, Luther Line, thought the finest he had seen in Canada.[130]

Bayham attracted its share of speculators. Some had schemes to buy lots in the township on instalment, strip them of their timber, and retire with the profits without paying more than the down payments.[131] In 1836 Isaac Titus, a Nova Scotian and one of Burwell's volunteers in 1837, complained to Peter Robinson, the commissioner of Crown lands, that 'a lot of Yancoes [sic]' had 'combined together to by [sic] up land and Anger British Subjects.' They were not above, he related, cutting timber on property they did not own.[132] It was not only the entrepreneurs who offended Bayham's citizens. In 1836 John Burwell and Isaac Draper, both justices of the peace, noted that the lumber trade attracted unsavoury people into the area in the form of raftsmen and 'the coarser characters of Labourers.'[133] In March 1838 Mahlon Burwell suggested that many of those from Bayham who had turned traitor had been engaged in timbering and lumbering as labourers.[134]

Bayham had only three small villages: Port Burwell at the mouth of Big Otter Creek, Vienna some two miles upstream, and Richmond, on the Talbot road at the western edge of the township. Both Vienna and Richmond were little more than hamlets, the latter containing in 1837 two tanneries, two hotels, and a general store.[135] The main centre of Bayham was undeniably Port Burwell, a town founded by Mahlon Burwell and presided over in his absence by his brother John, the chief spirit of the Tory 'Bayham Club.' In 1833 the village encompassed a church, a large warehouse, two stores, and twenty houses, with an additional twenty houses contracted to be built.

As the lumber trade grew, so did Port Burwell. In 1833 almost 1,500,000 feet of pine boards passed through the town's harbour on the way to the United States.[136] In 1834 the value of the port's exports, consisting mostly of lumber, spars, masts, and shingles, was estimated at £5,000.[137] In 1838 Mahlon Burwell stated that 4,000,000 feet of white pine boards and scantling had in recent years been exported annually, most of it to Cleveland.[138] The lumber trade gave rise to many sawmills along Otter Creek and its tributaries and, as well, inspired a ship-building industry at Port Burwell for vessels were required to transport the lumber to Cleveland and Buffalo.[139] None the less, it is doubtful if the population of Port Burwell in 1837 was much more than 200 persons.

It has been suggested that the loyalist cause in the revolt enlisted the support of Upper Canada's magistracy, bureaucrats, and merchants, the rebellion being an expression of the conflict between agrarianism and commercialism long waged in the political arena.[140] Such a division may have obtained in Bayham in December 1837. Map 7, showing the distribution within the township of those rebels and loyalists whose residences have been identified, demonstrates that the rebels and their sympathizers lived in the village of Richmond and the northern concessions. Few came from the south of the township: only one from the fourth concession and another from the village of Vienna. The loyalists, unlike the insurgents, were scattered throughout Bayham, and there was a notable concentration around Port Burwell.

The loyalists of Port Burwell may well have supported the government because they thought that it was economically progressive and concerned with fostering trade through the development of canals and roads. They may have judged that the Radical elements were agricultural and had been parsimonious with the public purse when in power. This may well have been the feeling throughout the province as well. It is more likely, however, that the inhabitants of Port Burwell and its area who mustered did so not because they recognized that the economic interests of the rebels were opposed to their own but because they were turned out by John Burwell himself.

Pointedly belligerent towards all waverers and potential traitors,

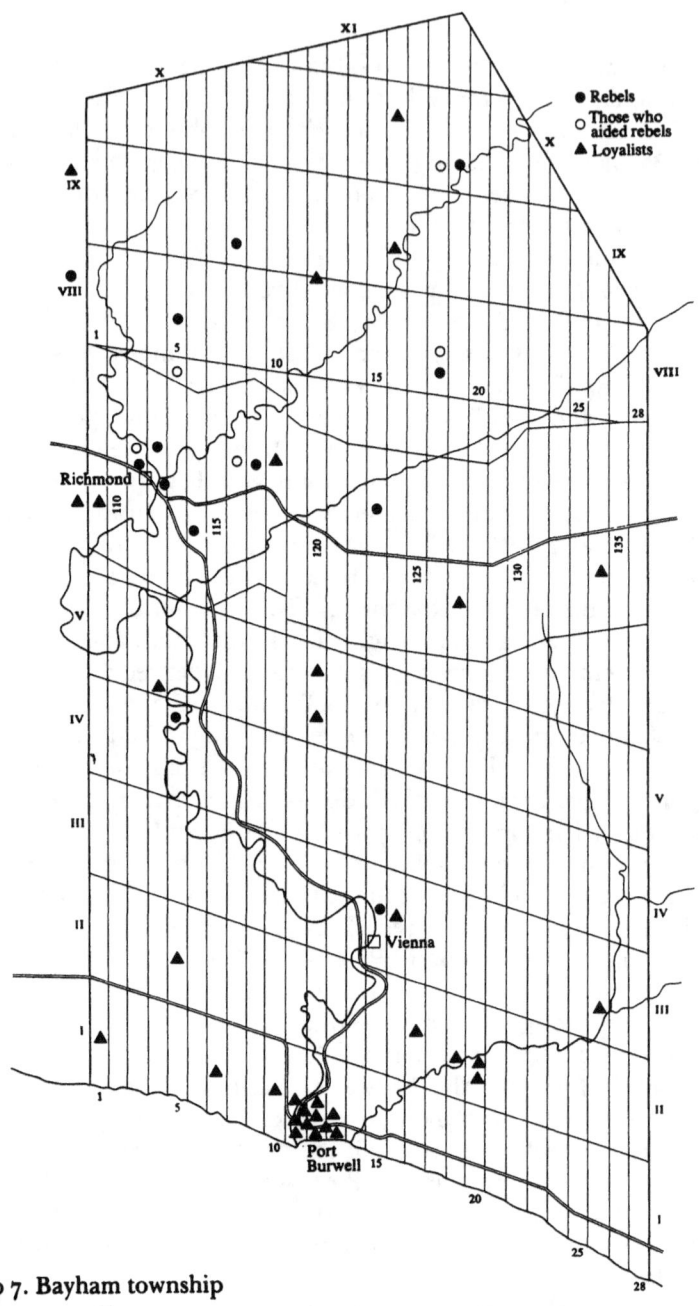

Map 7. Bayham township

Burwell rallied the forces of the port as did Isaac Draper, justice of the peace of Vienna, and Alexander Vance, a magistrate from the Lake road in Houghton. Captain Henry Medcalf of the fifth concession was greatly aided in his efforts to assemble his men by magistrate Doyle McKenny, who lived on the Talbot road in Malahide near Richmond. In the London district, at least, the justices of the peace typically lived in towns and villages. An active magistrate was a highly visible and often vocal reminder of the authority of the provincial government and of the necessity of maintaining it and demonstrating one's allegiance to it. If the towns were more loyal than the countryside in Upper Canada and if the residents of Port Burwell and Vienna were more loyal than the rest of the township, it may have been because the magistrates lived there.[141]

Little doubt exists that the bureaucrats and justices of the peace in Bayham supported the government; in fact, they formed one and the same group. John Burwell, for example, was coroner, collector of customs, and postmaster as well as magistrate. In 1837 eleven of the Bayham loyalists either were holding or had held in the past such appointments as district constable, postmaster, justice of the peace, and militia officer. Only one of the twenty-two Bayham rebels identified held a government post, a militia commission, yet before the autumn of 1837 the insurrectionists had evidently been as active politically as the loyalists. Three of the twenty-two insurgents are known to have been political activists as are seven of the eighty-one loyalists.[142]

No evidence can be summoned to show that the Bayham merchants clearly inclined to one side or the other; one merchant is known to have joined the rebels, another, the loyalists. In fact, as Table 16 demonstrates, there is no definite proof that obvious occupational distinctions of any sort existed between the two groups although the insurgents did include proportionately more farmers and their sons than did their loyalist counterparts.

By and large, the two groups studied were not markedly different. As Table 17 suggests, the loyalists may have mustered more younger men than the rebels, but the available data on marital status (see Table 18) does not indicate that there were more single men among the former than the latter.

The two groups deviated from each other in religious affiliation, however. Among the insurgents were one Baptist and another man of no particular religious persuasion. Among the loyalists, nineteen were members of the Church of England, four were 'Baptists,' and five were Regular Baptists. One might thus conclude that the Anglicans of the

TABLE 16
Loyalist and rebel occupations (the latter in parentheses)

Occupation	Number	Percentage of total known	Percentage of total sample
Agriculturalists	11 (11)	39.3 (61.1)	13.6 (50.0)
Labourers	2 (1)	7.1 (5.6)	2.5 (4.5)
Skilled workers and craftsmen	8 (2)		
Tavernkeepers	1 (2)		
Millers and tanners	1 (–)	53.6 (33.3)	18.5 (27.3)
Professionals	– (1)		
Merchants	1 (1)		
Miscellaneous	4 (–)		
Total known	28 (18)	100.0 (100.0)	34.6 (81.8)
Total unknown	53 (4)		65.4 (18.2)
Total	81 (22)		100.0 (100.0)

TABLE 17
Ages of loyalists and rebels

Age range	Number of loyalists	Number of rebels
60–64	–	–
55–59	1	1
50–54	2	–
45–49	3	1
40–44	2	2
35–39	6	3
30–34	5	3
25–29	4	2
20–24	11	2
15–19	6	1
10–14	–	–
Total known	40	15
Total unknown	41	7
Total	81	22
Median	25–29	30–34

TABLE 18
Marital status of loyalists and rebels

	Number single	Number married	Unknown	Percentage of known single	Percentage of known married
Loyalists	7	24	50	22.6	77.4
Rebels	2	13	7	13.3	86.7

TABLE 19
National origins of the loyalists and rebels (the latter in parentheses)

Place of origin	Number	Percentage of total known	Percentage of total sample
United States	1 (4)	2.0 (23.5)	1.2 (18.2)
Upper Canada	21 (6)	42.9 (35.3)	25.9 (27.3)
Maritime colonies	8 (2)	16.3 (11.8)	9.9 (9.1)
'Canada'	5 (–)	10.2 (–)	6.2 (–)
England	6 (4)	12.2 (23.5)	7.4 (18.2)
Ireland	6 (1)	12.2 (5.9)	7.4 (4.5)
'Britain'	2 (–)	4.1 (–)	2.5 (–)
Total known	49 (17)	100.0 (100.0)	60.5 (77.3)
Total unknown	32 (5)		39.5 (22.7)
Total sample	81 (22)		100.0 (100.0)

Bayham area and, to a lesser degree, the Baptists had been loyal during the rebellion. It must, however, be recorded that the religious allegiances of eight of the nineteen loyalist Anglicans (and two of the nine loyalist Baptists) were determined largely from a militia return prepared by Mahlon Burwell which itemized the religious characters of those volunteering for military service.[143] Burwell, being an ardent Anglican, might be suspected of portraying an unduly large proportion of militia volunteers as Anglicans to reflect credit on the Church of England.

The figures on the national origins of the rebels and loyalists are given in Table 19. Four of the seventeen rebels whose nationality is known had been born in the United States but only one of the corresponding loyalists,

Ephraim Cole Mitchell, had and he had lived in Upper Canada for forty-five years.[144]

The rebel orientation of Bayham's American inhabitants is underscored by the fact that most of the rebels identified, and those who aided them, came from sections of the township first settled by 'Yankees.' On the other hand, the loyalists were scattered throughout Bayham, though concentrations occurred in the southern section which was then occupied largely by settlers from the Atlantic colonies, England, and Ireland. Thus in Bayham, as in much of the rebel area, indications are that a significant national distinction helped divide loyalists from rebels.

Apart from their political characteristics, then, the rebels and loyalists were distinguished by their national profiles and religious affiliations, distinctions which may help explain why some men rallied to Duncombe's banner while some did not. Here, a discussion of various aspects of the insurgents' social characteristics such as their relative maturity and prosperity might be useful as well. In short, the foregoing examination of the rebels' characteristics can provide a basis for exploring further the causes of the Duncombe revolt and the purposes of the rebels.

8
Conclusion

On 3 November 1838 the Reverend A.N. Bethune, editor of the Anglican newspaper, *The Church*, sought to explain the rebellion in Upper Canada. Since the French Revolution, he argued, there had been unceasing conflict between anarchy and infidelity on the one hand and subordination and true religion on the other. There were 'unquiet spirits in every country,' and it would be 'strange if the moral convulsions of Europe, and the nearer agitations of the American republic should leave these infant Provinces unscathed.' His comments demonstrated the Tory conviction that in a world plagued by revolutionary ferment good citizenship and morality were to be found on the side of constituted authority.

Whatever the merits of his explanation of the causes of the rebellion, Bethune was correct in assuming that 'unquiet spirits' had been instrumental in producing it. Foremost of these was William Lyon Mackenzie, leader of the radical Reformers. Before the elections of 1836 he had been an influential but not necessarily the primary voice decrying the abuses of the existing régime. Though he himself was defeated in 1836, his own position among the Reformers was strengthened, for several leading moderates withdrew from politics in disgust after being defeated or, as they thought, cheated at the polls. Mackenzie and the Radicals subsequently moved to mobilize the rank and file, creating political unions and planning a great Reform convention in Toronto in December. Their cause was aided by the severe economic depression in the province which exacerbated existing grievances. In November 1837 Mackenzie organized his rebellion in Toronto. As we have seen, the first news reaching the west reported Mackenzie victorious, and Charles Duncombe and others raised a second insurrection, a hurriedly organized, ill-coordinated one whose immediate origin lay in the erroneous report from Toronto.

To muster men, Duncombe and his cohorts spread various stories, among them reports that the authorities intended rounding up leading local Radicals and turning the Six Nations warriors loose upon the rest. To John B. Askin the many 'false' representations made were 'most plausable' and 'insiduous'[1] and after the suppression of the revolt, both he and Allan MacNab[2] argued that such reports had led many astray. After the rebellion many captured rebels offered explanations for having joined Duncombe's force in group petitions begging for clemency. Sixty-eight provided such explanations individually in depositions sworn before examining magistrates. Only five of the latter said they had taken up arms because they had believed false information. If the story of Mackenzie's victory at Toronto is regarded as false information, however, it is reasonable to argue that all the rebels had been deceived, that none would have been in the ranks had they known the real situation. This may explain, in part, why the insurgents who petitioned the government after the rebellion for pardon or leniency characteristically argued that they had been seduced from their allegiance 'by wicked and designing' men.[3]

One report that was effective in persuading men to take up arms was that of the arrest and imprisonment of John G. Parker at Hamilton. Though embellished in successive retellings, the basis of the story was true and lent credibility to the rumour that the authorities intended jailing local Radicals. Fourteen of the sixty-eight rebels who individually explained why they had joined Duncombe declared that it was the report of Parker's confinement which had persuaded them. Most wished either to avoid Parker's fate or to free him from jail or both.

The promise of material rewards had apparently influenced the 103 rebels who petitioned MacNab en masse for clemency in December 1837 at Sodom. They had been led to revolt 'by Charles Duncombe, Eliakim Malcolm, and other wicked and designing leaders, who have induced us by promise of large grants of land and great pay for our services, to take up arms against Her Majesty's Government.'[4] Doyle McKenny, the Malahide justice of the peace, thought that James Malcolm's 'promise of 200 acres of land' had led '30 or 40' Bayham men to rebel.[5] Other Tories had no doubt that the rebels coveted their property. A Burford woman claimed that captured documents revealed that Duncombe's men had intended to 'murder every Tory's wife and child' and take over their farms.[6] One can imagine that some Tories in the immediate aftermath of the revolt might have believed this report but the rebels were neither as bloodthirsty nor as covetous as it suggests.

It is unlikely that the prospect of financial gain provided the primary

Conclusion

motivation for many rebels. Only two of those who individually gave their reasons for taking up arms (sixteen-year-old Augustus Chaple of Yarmouth and a recent newcomer to the province, George Conklin of Norwich) admitted having done so in the hope of receiving material reward.[7] Presumably, if others had similar hopes, they would have been too astute to admit them to examining magistrates. It is unlikely, however, that many rebels shared Chaple's and Conklin's hunger for personal gain. Most were better off than either, being neither as young as the one nor as recently arrived as the other.

In fact, most known to have mustered under Duncombe were relatively mature, well-settled, prosperous members of an agrarian community. This seems to have been true, documentary evidence suggests, of the Duncombe insurgents generally. In the regional society of the west neither clear economic nor social conditons distinguished loyalists from rebels. There is no basis for arguing that the rebels comprised a clearly disadvantaged sector of society and hence were driven to arms by economic despair or the prospect of plunder. Indeed, if the evidence of eleven apprehended Norwich insurgents who jointly petitioned for clemency is to be believed, they had joined Duncombe's men because they feared for their own property: 'most of us have been prevailed upon to take up arms against the country partly by threats used by the leading members of the rebel party, partly under the conviction that the Rebels were by far the most numerous part of the population, and that if we refused to fight for that party our lands and property would be confiscated.'[8]

Nine rebels testified in their depositions that threats against their persons rather than their property had led them to muster with Duncombe. A tenth, Abraham Sackrider of Norwich, swore that he had been dragooned, that his brother-in-law and Duncombe, after fruitlessly trying to persuade him to join their cause, 'took him to the Inn and gave him something to Drink and when Deponent was in liquor they got him into a Baggage Waggon and took him to Oakland' where he was kept under guard.[9]

Doubtless some men were tricked or forced into the rebel ranks but, generally, if a man really wished to avoid service with the insurgent troops he could do so. For example, John Treffry of Norwich, a pacifist, adamantly refused the order of a rebel sergeant to shoulder arms.[10] Duncombe himself was perfectly willing to leave the Tories alone, provided they swore not to combine against him or his men.[11]

The closely knit nature of much of western Upper Canada's agricultural society helps to explain the involvement of many men in the western rebellion. The Beamers of Oakland, Burford, and Townsend, the Kellys and Yeighs of Burford, the Bedfords, Dennises, Nicholls, Tuttles, and Thompsons of Norwich, the Cavanaughs and Doans of Yarmouth, the Moores of Yarmouth, Malahide, and Dereham, the Cooks of Bayham, the Hagles of Dereham, and the Spragues and Stewarts of Dumfries all sent two or more men from their families to the Oakland camp as, of course, did the Malcolms. One or two of these families, like the Cavanaughs, were British in origin, but most were American.

The rebels of British descent evidently fell into two broad categories. Some, particularly those from the south of Yarmouth and its area, were young men who were perhaps naturally inclined to rebel against constituted authority and only too anxious to seek a little diversion from the tedium of everyday life. Others generally appear to have lived in the province for a number of years and to have settled among North Americans. Perhaps influenced by their neighbours and the passing of time, they no longer felt the necessity of demonstrating loyalty to the existing government with its bonds to Britain. It is noteworthy that in the west those from Great Britain who had settled among their fellow-nationals, or who had emigrated to the colony in the 1830s when adult, were either neutral in the rebellion or active partisans for the government. They were not members of the rebel force.

The majority of rebels were either American-born or the offspring of American parents and may well have retained or adopted the deep American dislike of Britain and have been more willing to rebel, hoping to sever the provincial ties to Great Britain. Indeed, Charles Duncombe told Abraham Sackrider that 'he was going to take the country and make it independent.'[12] William McGuire, a school-teacher, and James and Eliakim Malcolm were reported to have said that the rebels would install in Upper Canada 'an independent Government, without any connection with the Queen or the Mother Country, Great Britain.'[13] Fifteen or twenty rebels apparently vowed, as they marched to join Duncombe, 'that they were determined to overthrow the British government ... asserting as their reason that the taxes had been raised and that the governor wanted to put tythes upon them as they did in the Old Country.'[14] Two other rebels, however, David Nicholls, whose family was probably American, and Preserved Thompson, who was an American, claimed that the Oakland revolt was raised merely to 'set up a constitutional' or 'Reform Government.'[15] Whether or not most rebels understood that the revolt was to establish an independent government or just to reform the one

Conclusion

they had, their American birth or parentage probably conditioned their response to the rebel call.

Some rebels claimed to be complete political innocents, however. Several told examining magistrates that they had played no part in politics before December 1837. A further eleven alleged that they had been unaware that their actions constituted rebellion. In 1838 barrister John Strachan of Hamilton, representing seven of them, insisted that they were 'obscure Peasants,' who were 'chiefly ignorant men, who had little knowledge of their duty as Subjects and thought little more of the insurrection into which they were seduced, than any common quarrel at a fair or Township Meeting. Few of them Know the nature of allegiance, and having no intention of actual rebellion were as much astonished at being accused of treason, the meaning of which they scarcely yet comprehend, as if they had been accused of Witchcraft.'[16]

Other rebels asserted that Duncombe and others had played on the insurgents' naïveté. Paul Bedford declared that Duncombe had suggested that the rebels in taking up arms were not, in effect, rebelling, for British precedent sanctioned an appeal to arms by an outraged and wronged populace.[17] Another insurgent, Malcolm Brown, stated that the rebel leaders told their men that they were 'loyal subjects, and determined to rely upon lawful and constitutional means to effect what they conceived to be necessary and reasonable reforms.'[18] Mahlon Burwell, however, firmly told his regiment: 'Every man of sane mind must have known that in quitting his peaceful home and joining the rebel vagrants with arms in his hands, and putting his loyal and peaceful neighbors in fear of being murdered, and their properties plundered, he was guilty of Treason.'[19]

Detailed lists of those attending the political meetings of the fall of 1837 are not available, but newspaper accounts, depositions, and so forth reveal that no less than eighty of the 197 rebels identified in this study had attended them. Also, twenty-four of the 197 are known to have been politically active prior to September 1837, voting in elections, signing partisan petitions, holding township offices, and so on. It is unlikely, therefore, that the leaders could have duped the majority of the rebels by pretending they were not engaging in rebellion. The leaders were instrumental in persuading men to turn out, however, by the force of their personalities and their positions in the area. In the essentially rural townships affected by the uprising, the local personalities were the ones most often admired and emulated. They were a living presence and example for those about them in a way that more widely known figures in Toronto could not be. Of the sixty-eight insurgents who gave their personal reasons for being involved in the revolt, two claimed to have been led astray by unnamed individuals, while no less than twenty-six identified specific people such as Charles Duncombe, Eliakim or Finlay Malcolm, whose arguments and example had induced them to take up arms.

In sum, the Duncombe rising would never have occurred had the rebels known the true state of affairs at Toronto. Those who answered the call to arms believing Mackenzie's revolt successful were certainly misled. Doubtless some men had their own reasons for turning out, a particular grievance against the government, for example, the loss by executive decree of a disputed lot to another claimant[20] or the confiscation of property for non-payment of taxes.[21] Others were driven by the desire for material gain, while others simply did not appreciate the significance of their actions. None the less most rebels turned out for similar reasons and purposes. Most were not members of the Church of England and so had not been exposed to its teachings about the necessity of loyalty to the Crown and the sanctity of the colonial tie. Most were North American in lineage as their local communities were in character. They were thus inclined to welcome change in a government which could be construed as British and colonial. In addition, significant numbers had been Reform partisans. Finally, when prominent men they knew as friends or relatives called them to arms, they responded.

Whatever the rebels expected to achieve for themselves and for Upper Canada, their hopes were disappointed. Their revolt was soon crushed by loyalist forces and they themselves put to flight. Subsequent events have led most historians to assert that the triumphant Tories then instituted a 'reign of terror.' The Tories did perpetrate some abuses, of course, particularly against the rebels who had been captured and confined in the Gore district jail at Hamilton. Most were not even examined on their arrival at the Gore jail, and no regular procedures were established to grant them bail. None the less, the great majority of those with whom the government dealt for their parts in the Duncombe rising were treated leniently, in the context of the times. Those times had witnessed the patriot raids upon the province, which had heightened the fears of the loyalists and contributed to the prevailing air of uncertainty and suspicion. That atmosphere helped to persuade some to leave the province and convinced others that Upper Canada's economic and political future was clouded indeed. Judging by its immediate repercussions, the Duncombe rebellion, like the Mackenzie revolt, produced more harm than good.

211 Conclusion

Apologists for the Canadian rebellions of 1837 have taken the longer view, arguing that the rebels hastened the advent of responsible government by forcing the Colonial Office to send out Lord Durham, who strongly advocated that principle, thereby transforming it into a great and forceful political cry. This view does not sufficiently weigh the fact that Durham's recommendation was ignored by British officials and responsible government was not achieved until 1848. Rather than hastening the advent of responsible government, it is as likely that the rebellions delayed it by discrediting and discouraging the Reformers, particularly those in Upper Canada. Indeed, in much of the province the Reformers took years to regain their strength.

In western Upper Canada, however, the Reformers and Radicals evidently suffered only temporary reversals by being identified with the revolt. In August 1839 the Reverend Mr Proudfoot noted that the Reformers were active once again and were determined to destroy the Family Compact.[22] That year Thomas Parke and George Hackstaff inaugurated a new Radical newspaper at London[23] and Elisha Hall, one of the leaders of the rebels in West Oxford in 1837, recorded that 'from what I can see the reformers are more noisey than ever in Norwich. I heard they taned the toris in stile, and in Oxford on the fourth of June they ware as dosile and harmless as she doves.'[24] Indeed, the Reformers in Norwich were so 'noisey' in 1839 that a belligerent Tory, John George Bridges, who had settled in the township in the wake of the rebellion, found it politic to flee it.[25] To the south-east of Norwich, in Norfolk, Charles Duncombe's brother, David, retained his influence among the Baptists, who were very 'numerous in that county, and nearly all reformers.'[26] His weight was deemed sufficient in 1840 to 'insure the election of any liberal candidate that he would support.'[27] Such evidence suggests that further detailed research is needed to judge the full effect of the Duncombe revolt on the Reformers of the west.

The long-term effects of the Duncombe rising on the political fortunes of the western Tories need further study as well. The generalization that most citizens of the town of London, which became an imperial garrison, were reinforced in any Tory inclinations is time-worn, and no historian has yet probed more deeply into the fate of the western Tories in the decade or so after the rebellion. The revolt did provide the Tories with a benchmark, however, in that for years to come a man would be asked what he had done during the rebellion. If he had not turned out against the rebels, he must have been disloyal then and, in all probability, was disloyal still. Such was the line of reasoning of an anonymous correspondent to Woodstock's *British American* who impugned Benjamin Van Norman's loyalty. Van Norman, a principal in the Long Point iron works, was not considered a loyal subject because he had taken 'no part in the valorous proceedings of certain parties in the London District during the famous years of 1836–37 [sic].'[28]

For such Tories the exploits they had performed in 1837–8 were indeed 'valorous;' they felt they had reaffirmed the allegiance of Upper Canada to Great Britain and saved the colony from republicanism. Peril emanated both from the American settlers of the west whose loyalties remained suspect for years (leading Sir John A. Macdonald to comment in 1856 that they helped form 'the most yeasty and unsafe of populations')[29] and from the Americans themselves, whose designs upon the colony had been revealed once more by the patriot raids. Like the Mackenzie revolt and its aftermath, the Duncombe rising and its repercussions led to a reaffirmation of that part of Tory tradition which insisted that America and Americans be watched with care for both were devious and predatory. This attitude has had an enduring history in Canada, and its reinforcement was one of the most significant results of the Duncombe rising and of the rebellion period generally.

APPENDICES

Introduction

Except for the loyalists, an attempt has been made to find out whether or not the men listed in these appendices were apprehended by the authorities. Some who were detained were questioned and freed, others examined and bound over, and still others sent to jail to be bailed, tried, or released after petitioning for mercy. The appendices also deal with the ages and national origins of those listed. For those born outside the province, their lengths of residency in Upper Canada are shown. In addition, the religious affiliations, occupations, residences, property holdings, marital status, and political activities of those registered are given. Regrettably, in numerous instances not all of the desired information proved to be available.

I

Although it is hoped that the appendices have been organized to be readily comprehensible, a number of points require explanation and several comments should be made about the methods adopted.

Names
Where more than one spelling of a name commonly occurred, the alternative spellings are given in parentheses.

Prison Records
In the appendices only the final dispositions of the prisoners are given. Court sentences or initial decisions of the executive council which were not implemented are not cited.

Often an entry such as the following appears in the appendices: 'bailed 8 Jan. 1838, recommitted, petitioned.' It would seem that in every instance, except that involving Dr Duncan Wilson (appendix 2, case 52), the prisoners were recommitted only after being indicted.

Two terms are employed to describe an inmate's release from jail: 'bailed' and 'freed.' The first is self-explanatory; the second indicates that no evidence exists that the prisoner was bound over on being liberated.

Nationality
The term 'Canadian' appears several times in the appendices and occurs because those described were so recorded in the census of 1841–2. Oddly enough, the census takers for some of the townships listed those born anywhere in British North America as 'Canadian.'

The designation 'British' is used occasionally and indicates that it is known that the subject was born in Great Britain but not whether in England, Scotland, Wales, or Ireland.

For those Upper Canadians and other British North Americans whose families are known to have entered British North America from either the United States or Great Britain, that information has been recorded. The subject's country of birth appears first, followed by his family's 'ancestral' nationality in parentheses.

Religious Affiliation
Before indicating that a man belonged to a particular denomination, contemporary evidence (which is very difficult to obtain) was required. For example, the fact that an individual was listed in the 1841–2 or 1851–2 census as a Methodist was not considered sufficient to prove that he was a Methodist in 1837 or 1838. It should not, however, be concluded that all of those denoted as having religious ties were members of good standing in the various denominations. If, for example, a man was expelled from fellowship in a Baptist congregation in 1834, it was assumed for the purposes of this study that he was still a Baptist in 1837. It is perhaps worth noting that the various sects expelled and readmitted people with some regularity.

A subject living at home with parents known to have belonged to a particular denomination was also considered to be of that denomination.

It has not always been possible to tell if a man was a Conservative or a Hicksite Quaker; thus the term 'Quaker' is used. Similarly, the designations 'Baptist' and 'Methodist' appear.

217 Introduction

Occupation
The term 'labourer' is not precise, for the individual involved might well have worked on a farm, or in a small manufacturing establishment, or in some other concern.

Occasionally, the term 'gentleman' is used, as the word was in contemporary use, although one might be hard pressed to say precisely what the economic circumstances of a 'gentleman' were.

Some men, particularly innkeepers and millers, often had more than one occupation. In this study the subjects are recorded as having but one livelihood, the activities that appear to have been secondary being ignored. For example, innkeepers or millers who were also farmers are listed as innkeepers or millers as that is how they were designated by their contemporaries.

Residence
The term 'Oakland' is used to denote Oakland township, not the village of Oakland.

Property Holdings
The evidence extant relating to the acquisition of land in the west is incomplete and unsatisfactory; thus, if a subject indicated that he owned a farm, but evidence could not be found of his holding property, he is listed as owning 'property (unknown amount).' This general rule, however, does not apply in the case of Martin Switzer of Streetsville (appendix 1, case 142) who stated that he owned a farm; a check of the relevant Home district records, which are much more complete than those for the west, did not substantiate this.

Marital Status
In a few instances subjects were found to be widowers with children. They are listed as married.

Political Activities
Two codes are used to describe political activities: 'politics 1' and 'politics 2.' The former indicates that a subject was involved in the Reform meetings of the late summer and fall of 1837 or in the gatherings just prior to the rebellion. The latter indicates that the subject had been active in politics prior to September 1837, voting in elections, holding township, district, or provincial offices, signing political petitions, and so on.

218 Appendices

The term 'no politics' indicates that a subject has sworn that he had never engaged in any political activities. Such assertions cannot, of course, always be trusted, and in instances where such claims conflicted with known facts the term was not used.

Literacy

Data on literacy have been collected by recording the names of those who wrote letters and those who affixed their signatures to documents or signed them by using marks. None of the material concerned has been incorporated into the study, however, and none of it appears in the appendices, because it is felt to be too unreliable. For example, using these criteria, 119 rebels were found to be literate and only 17 illiterate, undoubtedly not an accurate representation. The ability to sign one's name is clearly not a reliable test of literacy. For example, both Robert Laing and Duncan McPhederain of Nassagaweya allegedly signed a petition of 4 June 1838, yet described themselves as 'illiterate' (Petition of Robert Laing and Duncan McPhederain, 4 June 1838, PAC, RG5 A1, Upper Canada Sundries, 195/108404). Moreover, it was common practice for those unable to write to have someone else sign documents for them.

II

Ideally, references should be given for all information appearing in the appendices but, because the appendices deal with some 500 individuals, this is impracticable. Most of those listed would have required considerable footnoting. David Anderson, for example, the first individual listed in appendix 1, was a rebel leader from Southwold for whom a reward was issued in December 1837. If the facts about him were footnoted, his entry would read

> Anderson, David: taken at Windsor 8 Jan. 1838, and died of wounds.[1] Irish,[2] innkeeper,[3] Southwold,[4] property (unknown amount),[5] married,[6] politics 1.[7]

1 *Scotsman* (Toronto), 8 Feb. 1838.
2 St Thomas *Liberal, Constitution* (Toronto), 27 Sept. 1838.
3 Deposition of James Stewart, 24 Jan. 1838 UCS, 185/103427.
4 Inventory of Anderson's property, 7 June 1838, UWO, London District Surrogate Registry, no. 294.
5 Ibid. Anderson was said in the inventory to own a village lot and a house in Southwold

219 Introduction

as well as lot 14, concession 11, of Mariposa in the Newcastle district. A check of other sources, however, did not reveal any further information about his holdings, and it is not known if he owned all or part of the Mariposa lot. His holdings are listed, therefore, as 'property (unknown amount).'
6 Anderson's Estate, Bond of Administration, UWO, London District Surrogate Registry, no. 294.
7 See Deposition of Jonathan Steele, 20 Dec. 1837, RLDM, II.

APPENDIX 1

The Rebels

The first 165 men listed were examined, bailed, jailed, or indicted by the authorities; the last 32 were not taken for their parts in the Duncombe rising, though some were later jailed for subsequent activities. If the roles of the rebels in December 1837 were particularly noteworthy, they have been described briefly.

An asterisk indicates that the man marched with Anderson to Oakland.

1. Anderson, David: led Yarmouth men, taken at Windsor 8 Jan. 1838, died of wounds. Irish, innkeeper, Southwold, property (unknown amount), married, politics 1.
2. Anderson, William: bailed 23 Dec. 1837. Labourer, Woodhouse, politics 1.
3. Anderson, William A.: bailed 28 Dec. 1837. Bayham.
4. Arker (Archer), Thomas: jailed London 15 Dec. 1837, petitioned, bailed 19 June 1838. Age 18, English, Oxford, single.
5. Austin, Calvin: bailed 17 Dec. 1837, jailed 8 July 1838, in Norwich scare, bailed Sept. 1838. Age 38, American, at least 17 years in province, Methodist, watchmaker and gunsmith, Brantford town, unpatented town lot, married.
6. Beamer (Beemer, Bemer), Jacob R.: indicted, absconded, captured 28 July 1838 for his part in Short Hills raid, tried and convicted, transported for life. Age 29, Upper Canadian (American), innkeeper, Oakland, 300 patented acres, married, politics 1.
7. Beamer (Beemer, Bemer), Joseph: jailed Hamilton 16 Dec. 1837, not indicted, bailed 20 March 1838. Age 61, American, 39 years in province, Open Communion Baptist, innkeeper, Townsend, 250 patented acres, married, politics 1 and 2.
8. Bedford, Daniel: sergeant in a Norwich company, jailed London 18 Dec.

221 The Rebels

1837, petitioned, bailed 9 June 1838, hanged in 1839 as a Windsor raider. Age 27, Upper Canadian, innkeeper, Norwich, married, politics 1 and 2.

9 Bedford, Paul: captain in a Norwich company, jailed London Dec. 1837, petitioned, transported for 14 years, freed in England in 1839. Age 32, Upper Canadian, farmer, Norwich, married, politics 1 and 2.

10 Bell, James: appointed a captain at Oakland, jailed London Dec. 1837, petitioned, bailed Oct. 1838. Age 45, English, 20 years in province, farmer, Bayham, 100 unpatented acres, married, politics 1 and 2.

11 Berry, Matthew (Mathew): jailed London 18 Dec. 1837, bailed 6 Jan. 1838. Bayham.

12 Blake, George: jailed London 1 Jan. 1838, not indicted, freed 16 April 1838. Well-digger, Townsend, married.

13 Bowes (Bower, Boaz), Joseph: bailed 17 Dec. 1837, jailed London 2 Feb. 1838, petitioned, ordered freed and banished for life 13 Aug. 1838. Age 40, American, three years in province, farmer's son, Bayham, no property, married.

14 *Bradshaw, Amos: jailed London 28 Dec. 1837, petitioned, ordered freed and banished for life 13 Aug. 1838. Age 22, American, 1½ years in province, labourer, Yarmouth, no property, single, politics 1.

15 Brayman, John: examined 16 Dec. 1837 and freed. Mill worker, West Oxford, no property.

16 Brown, Malcolm: jailed 17 Dec. 1837 Hamilton, petitioned, bailed 6 June 1838. Age 34, Upper Canadian (American), farmer, Oakland, 100 unpatented acres, married, politics 1.

17 *Brown, Sobiske (Sobeisca, Sobeiske): jailed 20 Dec. 1837 London, bailed 5 Jan. 1838. Age 18, Upper Canadian (American), labourer, Malahide, no property, single, no political activity.

18 *Brunger (Bronger), Stephen: jailed 26 Dec. 1837 London, petitioned, ordered pardoned 21 May 1838. Age 24, English, three years in province, clothier, Southwold, no property, married.

19 *Carman (Carmon), Edward: jailed Dec. 1837 London, petitioned, to be jailed for three years then banished. Age 22, American, 11 years in province, Quaker, apprentice hatter, Yarmouth, no property, single, politics 1.

20 Case, George Washington: brought word to Oakland of Toronto rising, indicted and absconded. Age 17, gentleman (doctor's son), Hamilton, single, politics 1.

21 *Cavanaugh (Caviner, Cavanan), Dennis: jailed London 17 Dec. 1837, bailed 16 Jan. 1838, recommitted, petitioned, bailed 7 June 1838. Age 20, Irish, labourer, Yarmouth, no property, single.

Appendix 1

22 *Cavanaugh (Caviner, Cavanan), Robert: jailed London 16 Dec. 1837, bailed 14 Jan. 1838, recommitted, petitioned (bailed 7 June 1838?). Age 17, Irish, labourer, Yarmouth, no property, single, politics 1.

23 Chapin, Charles: jailed Hamilton 23 Dec. 1837, petitioned, bailed Aug. 1838 or Oct. 1838. Age 29, Upper Canadian (American), Congregationalist, farmer, Oakland, property (unknown amount), married.

24 Chapin, Lyman: jailed Hamilton 16 Dec. 1837, petitioned, bailed 6 June 1838. Age 24, Upper Canadian (American), farmer, Oakland, 100 patented acres, rented 100 acres, married, politics 1.

25 *Chaple (Chapel, Chappel), Augustus: jailed London Dec. 1837, bailed 9 Jan. 1838. Age 16, Yarmouth, no property, single, politics 1.

26 *Chase (Chace), Walter: tried to secure arms for the rebels, taken at Windsor 8 Jan. 1838, petitioned, escaped Aug. 1838. Upper Canadian (American), commission merchant, Southwold, three patented town lots, married, politics 1 and 2.

27 Cheeseman, William: jailed London 18 Dec. 1837, bailed 6 Jan. 1838, recommitted, petitioned, bailed 9 June 1838. Age 21, English, 18 years in province, farmer's son, Bayham, no property, single.

28 Childs (Childes), William: jailed London 21 Dec. 1837, not indicted, freed 18 April 1837. Norwich, single.

29 Christie, Charles: jailed London 17 Dec. 1837, bailed 18 Jan. 1838. American, Dereham, no property.

30 Church, David Clark (Clarke): bailed n.d. Dumfries, property (unknown amount), married, politics 1.

31 Coburn, Alden (Allan, Allen): examined 20 Dec. 1837 and freed. Open Communion Baptist, West Oxford, married.

32 *Coleman (Colman), James: jailed London 16 Dec. 1837, bailed 3 Jan. or 16 Jan. 1838, recommitted, petitioned, bailed 7 June 1838. Age 20, Irish, labourer, Yarmouth.

33 Congdon, Tracey (Tracy): jailed London 17 Dec. 1837, bailed 29 Dec. 1837. Age 29, American, farm labourer, Norwich, no property, politics 1.

34 Conklin, George: bailed 21 Dec. 1837. 1 year in province, Norwich.

35 Connors (Connor, Conners, Conner), Andrew: jailed London 20 Dec. 1837, bailed 5 Jan. 1838, recommitted, petitioned, bailed 12 June 1838. Age 21, Upper Canadian, farmer's son, Bayham.

36 Cook, Ephraim: active organizing rebels in Norwich, said to be surgeon of the 'army,' jailed Hamilton 23 Dec. 1837, bailed 28 Feb. 1838, recommitted, tried, found guilty, 17 Aug. 1838 freed and banished for life. Age 30, American, eight years in province, doctor, Norwich, 103 patented acres, married, politics 1.

The Rebels

37 Cook, Moses: jailed London 17 Dec. 1837, bailed 6 Jan. 1838, recommitted, petitioned, bailed 7 June 1838. Age 42, Upper Canadian (American), farmer, Bayham, 200 unpatented acres.

38 Cook, Robert: lieutenant in Bayham party, jailed London 20 Dec. 1837, bailed 16 Jan. 1838, recommitted, tried, found guilty, bailed 29 Sept. 1838. Age 39, Upper Canadian (American), 'no particular religion,' farmer, Bayham, 250 patented acres, married, politics 1.

39 Coon, Peter: jailed Hamilton 15 Dec. 1837, not indicted, freed 21 March 1838. Upper Canadian, blacksmith, Oakland.

40 *Coville (Coval, Colvil, Scovill), James: jailed at London 30 Dec. 1837, petitioned, ordered freed and banished for life 13 Aug. 1838. Age 21, American, 16 years in province, Quaker, farm labourer, Yarmouth, no property, single, politics 1.

41 Darrow, William: bailed 27 Dec. 1837. Age 30, American, blacksmith, Dereham, married.

42 *Davis, Lyman: stole horse on march to Oakland, jailed London 20 Dec. 1837, bailed 15 Jan. 1838, indicted, absconded, named in 22 Oct. 1838 Proclamation. Farmer, Malahide, politics 1.

43 Dennis, James: commanded a Norwich company, absconded, indicted, named in 22 Oct. 1838 Proclamation. Age 32, American, 17 years in province, Regular Baptist, farmer, Norwich, 100 patented acres, single, politics 1.

44 Denton, Losee (Loce): jailed London 20 Dec. 1837, bailed 6 Jan. 1838, recommitted, petitioned, bailed 9 June 1838. Age 25, Upper Canadian, Bayham, single.

45 *Doan, Joel P.: absconded, indicted, named in 22 Oct. 1838 Proclamation. American, 24 years in province (?), Hicksite Quaker, tanner, Yarmouth, 4½ patented acres, single, politics 1.

46 *Doan, Joshua G.: officer with Yarmouth rebels, absconded, indicted, named in 22 Oct. 1838 Proclamation, hanged in 1839 as a Windsor raider. Age 26, Upper Canadian (American), Hicksite Quaker, tanner, Yarmouth, married, politics 1.

47 Doty, Nelson: examined 20 Dec. 1837 and freed. Oxford.

48 Doxy (Doxsie), Samuel D.: bailed 27 Dec. 1837. Farmer, Norwich.

49 Dumon, John: examined 16 Dec. 1837 and freed. Dumfries, politics 1.

50 Duncombe, Charles: leader of the rising, absconded, indicted, named in 22 Oct. 1838 Proclamation. Age, 45, American, 19 years in province, doctor, Burford, 1,004 patented and 240 unpatented acres, married, politics 1 and 2.

51 Edison, Samuel: lieutenant with the Bayham rebels, absconded, indicted,

224 Appendix 1

named in 22 Oct. 1838 Proclamation. Age 33, Nova Scotian (American), 26 years in province, Regular Baptist, innkeeper, Bayham, married.

52 Elliott, Robert: jailed Hamilton 15 Dec. 1837, petitioned, bailed 6 (?) June 1838. English, Congregationalist, tanner, Oakland, married, politics 1.

53 Emigh, John: examined 16 Dec. 1837 and released. Regular Baptist, Norwich.

54 Emmons, Uriah: jailed London 21 Dec. 1837, petitioned, ordered freed and banished for life 13 Aug. 1838. Age 22, Upper Canadian, labourer, Norwich, single.

55 Fisher, Henry: active in organizing rebels in Bayham, absconded, indicted, named in 22 Oct. 1838 Proclamation. English, farmer, Bayham, 100 unpatented acres, married, politics 2.

56 Foster, Alonzo: jailed Hamilton 15 Dec. 1837, not indicted, freed 20 March 1838. Age 18, Upper Canadian, farm labourer, Oakland, no property, single.

57 Foster, Henry: examined 15 Dec. 1837 and freed. Farmer, Dumfries, 50 patented acres, married.

58 Fowler, Horatio: active in organizing rebels in Norwich, jailed London 19 Dec. 1837, petitioned, freed Oct. 1838. Age 43, American, 39 years in province, farmer, Burford, 195 patented acres, married.

59 *Franey (Freney, Traney), Robert: jailed London 17 Dec. 1837, bailed 16 Jan. 1838, recommitted, petitioned, bailed 7 June 1838. Age 21, Irish, labourer, Yarmouth, politics 1.

60 Hagerman (Hagaman, Heggerman), David: quartermaster of the 'army,' jailed London 18 Dec. 1837, tried, acquitted, released 30 April 1838. Age 40, American, at least 17 years in province, Methodist, carpenter, Norwich, 300 patented and 150 unpatented acres, married, politics 1 and 2.

61 Hagle (Hagel, Hogle), Luke: jailed London 17 Dec. 1837, bailed 30 Dec. 1837 or 13 Jan. 1838. Labourer, Dereham.

62 Hagle (Hagel, Hogle), Mark: jailed London 17 Dec. 1837, bailed 30 Dec. 1837. Labourer, Dereham, single.

63 Hall, Elisha: leader of rebels about West Oxford, injured self on way to Oakland, arrested 16 Dec. 1837, escaped 27 Dec., indicted, named in 22 Oct. 1838 Proclamation. Age 35, Upper Canadian, sawmill owner, West Oxford, 245 patented acres, married, politics 1 and 2.

64 Hart (Harts), Joseph: lieutenant with Norwich rebels, jailed London 18 Dec. 1837, petitioned, freed Oct. 1838. Age 40, American, 4 years in province, Norwich, married, politics 1.

65 *Hawes, Solomon: officer with Yarmouth rebels, absconded, indicted, named in 22 Oct. 1838 Proclamation. Yarmouth.

225 The Rebels

66 Hawkins, Joseph Douglas (Douglass): bailed 22 Dec. 1837. English, four years in province, teacher, Brantford township.
67 *Heaton, Levi: jailed London 16 Dec. 1837, bailed 12 Jan. 1838. American, 14 years in province, Hicksite Quaker, Yarmouth, politics 1.
68 Henry, Philip: officer at Oakland, jailed Hamilton 13 (?) Dec. 1837, petitioned, bailed Sept. 1838. Age 36, Upper Canadian, tanner and shoemaker, Oakland, married, politics 1.
69 Herrington, William: jailed Simcoe Dec. 1837, escaped, jailed Sandwich 10 July 1838. Age 25, tailor, Bayham, married.
70 Hill, George: bailed 28 Dec. 1837, arrested on way to Michigan, jailed London 3 Jan. 1838, petitioned, ordered freed and banished for life 13 Aug. 1838. Age 38, American, blacksmith, Bayham.
71 Hillaker (Heilaker, Hellaker, Hilliker), Egbert: jailed London 17 Dec. 1837, bailed 4 or 15 Jan. 1838. Age 25, American, Methodist, Norwich, property (unknown amount), married.
72 Hills, Horatio A.: tried to force various Dumfries residents to join rebels, jailed Hamilton 17 Dec. 1837, tried, found guilty, to be transported for 14 years, died 11 Nov. 1838 in Toronto jail. Age 24, American, two years in province, labourer, Dumfries, no property, single, politics 1.
73 Hoskins (Herskins), Henry: examined 16 Dec. 1837 and freed. Dumfries.
74 Hoskins, Luther: jailed London 21 Dec. 1837, bailed 26 Feb. 1838, recommmitted, petitioned, bailed Oct. 1838. Age 61, American, 43 years in province, innkeeper, West Oxford, 400 patented acres, married, politics 1 and 2.
75 *Howard, Asa: bailed 27 Dec. 1837. Age 27, Upper Canadian, carpenter, Yarmouth, 25 patented acres, single.
76 Humphrey (Humphries), Norris (Noris): jailed Simcoe Dec. 1837 and freed as no information then appeared against him, absconded, indicted, named in 22 Oct. 1838 Proclamation. Upper Canadian, merchant, Bayham, 1 patented acre, 1 patented lot and property (unknown amount), married, politics 2.
77 Hurd, Seth: bailed 22 Dec. 1837. Tailor, Brantford town, 1 patented town lot.
78 James, Joshua: bailed 23 Dec. 1837. Farmer, Oakland.
79 Johnson (Johnston), John: jailed Hamilton 16 Dec. 1837, not indicted, bailed (to appear at London assizes) 2 April 1838. Upper Canadian, cordwainer, Burford, leased 200 acres.
80 *Jolly (Joley), John James: jailed London 17 Dec. 1837, bailed 12 Jan. 1838. American, one year in province, 'no particular religion,' blacksmith, Yarmouth, married.
81 Kelly (Kelley), John: drilled rebels at Oakland, jailed London 17 Dec. 1837,

226 Appendix 1

petitioned, freed July (?) 1838. Age 49, Upper Canadian, Congregationalist, farmer, Burford, 200 patented acres, married, politics 1 and 2.

82 Kelly (Kelley), William Granville: bailed 23 Dec. 1837. Age 29, Upper Canadian, Congregationalist, farmer's son, Burford, no property, married, politics 1.

83 *Kipp (Kepp, Kip, Kiffe), Caleb: jailed London 17 Dec. 1837, bailed 11 Jan. 1838, recommitted, petitioned, ordered freed and banished for life 13 Aug. 1838. Age 28, American, 23 years in province, Hicksite Quaker, labourer, Yarmouth, married.

84 Ladon (Laden, Ladan, Landon), Peter: jailed Hamilton 16 Dec. 1837, not indicted, freed 15 March 1838. Irish, labourer, Oakland, no property, married, politics 1.

85 Lancaster, Joseph J.: ensign in rebel 'army,' jailed London 20 Dec. 1837, bailed 26 Dec. 1837 or 6 or 26 Jan. 1838. Age 24, Upper Canadian (American), Hicksite Quaker, farmer, Norwich, 80 patented acres, married, politics 1.

86 *Lawrence (Laurence), Charles: jailed London 19 Dec. 1837, petitioned, bailed 11 June 1838. Age 19, English, labourer, Yarmouth.

87 Leach (Leitch), Nelson: jailed London 20 Dec. 1837, bailed 17 Jan. 1838, recommitted, petitioned, freed June (?) 1838. Age 19, American, labourer, Bayham, no property.

88 Leavitt (Levet, Leavitte), George: bailed 26 Dec. 1837. Blacksmith, Dereham.

89 Lyons, William: jailed Hamilton 21 Dec. 1837, tried, acquitted, freed 30 March 1838. Upper Canadian, farmer, Brantford township, 190 unpatented acres and 1 unpatented town lot, married, politics 1.

90 Lypher (Sypher), Peter: examined 21 Dec. 1837 and freed. Age 21, American, Norwich, single.

91 McCarty (McCarthy), Cornelius: jailed London 16 Dec. 1837, bailed 14 Jan. 1838. Age 25, Irish, Norwich, no property.

92 *McLure (McClure), Andrew: jailed London Dec. 1837, bailed 1 Jan. 1838, recommitted, petitioned, bailed 6 June 1838. Age 25, Irish, two months in province, Regular Baptist, cordwainer, Southwold, ¼ acre patented, married, no politics.

93 *Malada (Milada, Milady, Melody), Patrick: jailed London 1 Jan. 1837, petitioned, bailed 7 June 1838. Age 18, Irish, labourer, Yarmouth, no property, single, politics 1.

94 Malcolm, Edy (Eddy): bailed 23 Dec. 1837, freed, jailed Hamilton 23 July 1838 (on suspicion of being involved in Short Hills raid?), freed 31 July 1838. Age 21, Upper Canadian (American), farmer's son, Oakland, single.

227 The Rebels

95 Malcolm, Eliakim: a leader of the rising, absconded, indicted, named in 22 Oct. 1838 Proclamation. Age 36, Upper Canadian (American), Congregationalist, deputy surveyor, Oakland, 330 patented and 600 unpatented acres, married, politics 1 and 2.
96 Malcolm, Finlay (Findlay, Finley): led Bayham rebels to Oakland, jailed London 21 Dec. 1837, petitioned, to be transported for 14 years, freed in England in 1839. Age 38, Upper Canadian (American), farmer, Bayham, 200 unpatented acres, married.
97 Malcolm, Finlay (Findlay, Finley): jailed Hamilton 23 Dec. 1837, tried, acquitted, freed 31 March 1838. Age 58, American, 42 years in province, Congregationalist, farmer, Oakland, 315 patented acres, married, politics 1 and 2.
98 Malcolm, Gustavus (Augustus): bailed 26 Dec. 1837. Age 17, Upper Canadian (American), Congregationalist, farmer's son, Burford, single.
99 Malcolm, Isaac Brock: jailed Hamilton 23 Dec. 1837, petitioned, bailed 6 June 1838. Age 25, Upper Canadian (American), Congregationalist, farmer, Oakland, married.
100 Malcolm, James: active organizing rebels about Oakland, absconded, indicted, named in 22 Oct. 1838 Proclamation. Age 37, Upper Canadian (American), farmer, Oakland, 176 patented acres, married, politics 1 and 2.
101 Malcolm, James (son): examined 16 Dec. 1837 and freed. Age 16, Upper Canadian (American), farmer's son, Oakland, no property, single.
102 Malcolm, John: jailed Hamilton 23 Dec. 1837, indicted, bill ignored, freed 10 March 1838. Age 61, American, 42 years in province, Episcopal Methodist, mill owner, Oakland, 820 patented acres, married.
103 Malcolm, Peter: drilled rebels at Scotland, jailed Hamilton 3 Jan. 1838, tried, convicted, ordered bailed 3 Nov. 1838. Age 41, Upper Canadian (American), Congregationalist, farmer, Burford, 99 patented acres, married, politics 1.
104 Malcolm, Shubal Downs: bailed 23 Dec. 1837. Age 23, Upper Canadian (American), Congregationalist, farmer's son, Oakland, no property.
105 Manns (Mans, Munns, Mann, Munn), Ezekiel: jailed London 21 Dec. 1837, petitioned, bailed 12 June 1838. Age 20, Upper Canadian, Norwich, politics 1.
106 Marlatt, Samuel: examined 16 Dec. 1837, jailed Hamilton 2 Jan. 1838, tried, acquitted, freed 31 March 1838. American, at least six years in province, farmer, Dumfries, 50 patented acres, married, politics 2.
107 Medcalf (Medcalfe, Metcalf), John: jailed London 18 Dec. 1837, bailed 6 Jan. 1838, recommitted, petitioned, freed in June (?) 1838. Age 30, Irish, 15 years in province, farmer, Malahide, 100 unpatented acres, married.

228 Appendix 1

108 Merwin (Murwin), Henry (Heny): bailed 19 March 1838. Upper Canadian, innkeeper, Brantford township, 37 patented and 108 unpatented acres, married.
109 Moore, Hugh W.: bailed 26 Dec. 1837. Canadian (American), Quaker, blacksmith, Dereham, 200 unpatented acres, married.
110 *Moore, Isaac: jailed London 17 Dec. 1837, bailed 11 Jan. 1838, recommitted, tried, acquitted, released 1 May 1838. American, 25 years in province, Quaker, Yarmouth, 100 patented acres, married, politics 1.
111 Moore, James: bailed 26 Dec. 1837. Dereham.
112 *Moore, Joseph: jailed London 20 Dec. 1837, bailed 9 Jan. 1838. Age 20, Upper Canadian (American), Conservative Quaker, farmer's son, Yarmouth, single, politics 1.
113 Moses, Leonard (Simon) B.: jailed London 17 Dec. 1837, bailed 4 or 26 Jan. 1838. Norwich, single.
114 *Neilly (Neily, Neely), Alexander: jailed London 19 Dec. 1837, petitioned, bailed 11 June 1838. Age 21, Irish, seven years in province, carpenter, Yarmouth, no property, politics 1.
115 Newton, Dudley: jailed Hamilton 17 Dec. 1837, not indicted, freed 15 March 1838. American.
116 Nicholls (Nichols), David: bailed 17 Dec. 1837. Regular Baptist, Norwich, politics 1.
117 Nicholls (Nichols), James: bailed 17 Dec. 1837. Age 21, Upper Canadian, Norwich, politics 1.
118 Nicholls (Nichols, Nicolls), John B.: jailed London 17 Dec. 1837, bailed 2 Jan. 1838. Labourer, Norwich, single.
119 Nicholls (Nichols), Shubal: bailed 17 Dec. 1837. Farmer, Norwich.
120 *Norton, Lewis (Louis), Adelbert: jailed Simcoe Dec. 1837, jailed London 30 Dec. 1837, petitioned, freed Aug. 1838, banished for life. Age 18, American, three years in province, worked on fishing boat, Yarmouth, no property, single, politics 1.
121 Oswald (Oswould, Oswold), James: jailed London 17 Dec. 1837, bailed 12 Jan. 1838. Congregationalist, farmer, Burford, 200 patented acres, politics 1.
122 *Page, Benjamin: stole horse on march to Oakland, jailed London 16 Dec. 1837, bailed 16 Jan. 1838, indicted, recommitted, petitioned, bailed 9 June 1838. Age 24, Upper Canadian (American), Anglican, tanner, Yarmouth, married.
123 Paulding (Pauling), Jesse: commissary with Bayham rebels, absconded, indicted, named in 22 Oct. 1838 Proclamation. Innkeeper, Bayham, 110 patented acres, married, politics 1.

229 The Rebels

124 Poole (Pool), Thomas (William): jailed London 17 Dec. 1837, bailed 12 Jan. 1838. Age 19, English, labourer, Dereham, single.
125 Pumroy, Milton: examined 21 Dec. 1837 and freed. Upper Canadian, Burford.
126 Ribble (Riball), George: jailed London 17 Dec. 1837, bailed 11 Jan. 1838. Bayham.
127 *Riley (Reily, Reilly), John: jailed London 30 Dec. 1837, petitioned, freed 9 May 1838. Age 14, Irish, Yarmouth, no property, single.
128 Roberts (Robids), George: examined 18 Dec. 1837, jailed Hamilton 3 Jan. 1838, petitioned, bailed 6 June 1838. Age 20, English, labourer, Oakland, no property, single.
129 Robinson, Benjamin: examined 20 Dec. 1837 and freed. Oxfords.
130 Rouse, George: jailed Hamilton 2 Jan. 1838, tried, acquitted, freed 31 March 1838. American, at least 25 years in province, farmer, Burford, 130 patented acres, married.
131 Sackrider, Abraham (Abram): jailed London 21 Dec. 1837, petitioned, freed June (?) 1838. Age 39, American, 26 years in province, farmer, Norwich, 100 patented acres, married.
132 Sage, Selah: examined 16 Dec. 1837 and freed. Farmer, Dumfries, politics 1.
133 Sands, Samuel: jailed London 21 Dec. 1837, petitioned, bailed 11 June 1838. Age 58, Nova Scotian, farmer, Bayham, property (unknown amount), married.
134 Sayr, Levi: examined 20 Dec. 1837 and freed. Oxfords.
135 *Scrivener, Charles: jailed London n.d., finally committed 26 Jan. 1838, fate unknown. Yarmouth.
136 Smith, Joseph: jailed Hamilton 15 Dec. 1837, not indicted, freed 21 March 1838. American, Congregationalist, Oakland, politics 1.
137 Smith, Oliver: active in organizing Bayham rebels, jailed Hamilton 23 Dec. 1837, tried, acquitted, freed 30 March 1838. American, doctor, Bayham, married, politics 1.
138 Snider (Snyder), Elias: sent by Duncombe to organize Yarmouth rebels, jailed Hamilton 23 Dec. 1837, tried, found guilty, bailed Sept. 1838. Age 41, American, 26 years in province, farmer, Norwich, 450 patented acres, married, politics 1 and 2.
139 Sprague, Alexander: examined 18 Dec. 1837 and freed. Age 22, American, farmer's son, Blenheim, no property, single, politics 1.
140 *Steele (Steel), Jonathan: treasurer of Sparta rebels, jailed London 20 Dec. 1837, bailed 15 Jan. 1838, recommitted, petitioned, ordered to be bailed 13 Aug. 1838. Age 31, Upper Canadian (American), Quaker, farmer, Yarmouth, 100 patented acres, married, politics 1.

230 Appendix 1

141 Storey (Story), William: jailed London 20 Dec. 1837, bailed 2 Jan. 1838. Age 32, English, 21 years in province, farmer, Bayham, 50 patented acres, married.
142 Switzer, Martin: active in organizing Yarmouth rebels, absconded, indicted, returned and arrested 15 July 1838, petitioned, bailed 28 Sept. 1838. Age 59, farmer, Toronto township, married, politics 1 and 2.
143 Teeple, Pelham (Pellum) C.: a leader of the West Oxford rebels, captured Dec. 1837, escaped, indicted, named in 22 Oct. 1838 Proclamation. Age 28, Upper Canadian (American), Regular Baptist, farmer's son, West Oxford, single, politics 1.
144 Thompson, Preserved: examined 17 Dec. 1837 and freed. Age 45, American, farmer, Norwich, 150 patented acres, married, politics 2.
145 Thompson, William: jailed Hamilton 21 Dec. 1837, petitioned, bailed 17 Aug. 1838. Age 36, Irish, 25 years in province, farmer, Oakland, property (unknown amount), married, politics 1.
146 Tidey (Tidy, Tydy), John Arthur: wrote messages for Duncombe, jailed London 7 Feb. 1838, petitioned, bailed 13 Nov. 1838. Age 38, English, at least nine years in province, Methodist, deputy surveyor, Norwich, property (unknown amount), married, politics 1 and 2.
147 Travers (Traverse), Charles: jailed London 16 Dec. 1837, freed 1 June 1838. Age 20, Upper Canadian (Irish), labourer, West Oxford, single, no politics.
148 Tufford, John: jailed Hamilton 15 Dec. 1837, tried, convicted, bailed Sept. 1838. Age 28, American, farmer, Brantford township, 200 unpatented acres, married, no politics.
149 Tuttle, Garrett (Garrat, Garratt, Garret): corporal in rebel 'army,' bailed 21 Dec. 1837. Four years in province, Norwich, 100 unpatented acres.
150 Tuttle, James: bailed 21 Dec. 1837. Four years in province, Norwich.
151 Uline, (Ulim), John Leonard: jailed Hamilton 15 Dec. 1837, tried, acquitted, freed 31 (?) March 1838. Upper Canadian, tanner, Brantford township, 50 unpatented acres.
152 Van Arnam (Vanarnam, Van Arnum, Van Norman, Vanorman), John: warned rebels at Oakland of MacNab's approach, jailed Hamilton 23 Dec. 1837, bailed 20 Feb. 1838, indicted, absconded, named in 22 Oct. 1838 Proclamation. American, 15 years in province, innkeeper, Brantford township, 100 patented and 174 unpatented acres, married.
153 Vanduzen, Abraham (Abram): jailed Hamilton 15 Dec. 1837, not indicted, freed 20 March 1838. American, doctor (unlicensed), Oakland, married.
154 Vincent, Martin: bailed 18 Dec. 1837. Farmer, Dumfries, politics 1.
155 Walrath (Walrod), Charles P.: drilled rebels at Scotland, jailed Hamilton 15 Dec. 1837, tried, found guilty, to be transported for 14 years, escaped from

231 The Rebels

Toronto jail 7 Nov. 1838. Age 26, American, eight months in province, farm labourer, Windham, no property, single, no politics.
156 *Watts, William: jailed London 30 Dec. 1837, petitioned, bailed 9 June 1838. Age 21, English, at least eight years in province, Yarmouth, single, politics 1.
157 Webb, William: jailed Hamilton 17 Dec. 1837, tried found guilty, ordered bailed 13 Aug. 1838. Age 50, American, 12 years in province, farmer, Dumfries, property (unknown amount), married, politics 2.
158 Westbrook, William: examined 16 Dec. 1837 and freed. Farmer, Oakland.
159 Wethy (Withy, Withey), Mire (Myre, Morey): jailed London 15 Dec. 1837, petitioned, freed 1 June 1838. Age 28, American, farmer, Oxfords.
160 Wilson, Clarke: bailed 20 Dec. 1837. Oxfords.
161 Winegarden, Henry: jailed Hamilton 15 Dec. 1837, petitioned, bailed 6 June 1838. Upper Canadian, Blenheim, married, politics 1.
162 Wood (Woods), Isaiah (Josiah, Israel): jailed London 21 Dec. 1837, bailed 3 Jan. 1838. Age 16, Norwich, single, politics 1.
163 Wood, James: adjutant in rebel 'army,' jailed 15 Dec. 1837, bailed 4 Jan. 1838, jailed 7 July 1838 in Norwich scare, bailed Sept. 1838. Age 48, New Brunswicker, 38 years in province, farmer, East Oxford, 200 patented acres and squatted on 200, married, politics 1.
164 Yeigh, Adam: jailed Hamilton 23 Jan. 1838, tried, acquitted, freed 31 March 1838. Age 49, American, 37 years in province, farmer, Burford, 418 patented acres, married.
165 Yeigh, Jacob: absconded, indicted, allowed to return in fall of 1838 (?). Age 53, American, 37 years in province, farmer, Burford, 600 patented and 50 unpatented acres and rented 200, married, politics 1.
166 Bartlett. Windham.
167 Beamer (Beemer, Bemer), David. Upper Canadian (American), Oakland.
168 Bentley, Hiram: ensign in rebel 'army.' Norwich.
169 *Burgess, Nelson. Yarmouth.
170 Dennis, John: jailed Sodom June 1838 in Norwich scare. Age 25, American, 17 years in province, Regular Baptist, farmer's son, Norwich, no property, single.
171 Eastling: led a company of men from the Oxfords. Oxfords.
172 *Fisher, Isaac. Yarmouth.
173 Goodin (Goodwin). Innkeeper, West Oxford, married.
174 Horton, Emos. Dumfries.
175 Hughes, John. Norwich.
176 Kelly, John. Age 19, Upper Canadian, Congregationalist, farmer's son, Burford, no property, single, politics 1.
177 Lemons, Hiram. Labourer, Burford.

232 Appendix 1

178 McGuire, William: ensign in rebel 'army,' very active at Oakland. Teacher, Oakland, politics 1 and 2.
179 Malcolm, Charles: jailed Hamilton 17 July 1838 on suspicion of being a Short Hills raider, freed 21 July 1838. Age 33, Upper Canadian (American), farmer, Windham, 200 patented acres, married, politics 2.
180 Malcolm, Duncan. Age 39, Upper Canadian (American), farmer, Oakland, married, politics 1.
181 Malcolm, George: jailed Hamilton 17 July 1838 on suspicion of being a Short Hills raider, freed 21 July 1838. Age 31, Upper Canadian (American), Congregationalist, farmer, Oakland, 299 patented acres, married, politics 1.
182 Marvel (Marble), Dudley: captained those collecting arms in Dumfries and Blenheim. Dumfries, married, politics 1.
183 Mathews, William: officer in rebel 'army,' very active at Oakland. Irish, auctioneer, Brantford town, 1 patented town lot.
184 *Moore, Elias. Canadian (American), Quaker, farmer's son, Yarmouth, no property, single.
185 Nicholls, Harmon (Hermon). American, Norwich, single, politics 1.
186 Raymond, Cyrenus (Cyrenius). Age 23, Upper Canadian, Windham, single.
187 Silverthorne (Silverthorn), Richard. Farmer, Burford, 100 patented acres, married.
188 Silverthorne (Silverthorn), Thomas. Age 24, Upper Canadian, farmer, Windham, rented 100 acres, married, politics 2.
189 *Smith, Benjamin J. Yarmouth.
190 Sprague, Harlow. Blenheim, politics 1.
191 Steinhoff (Steinhoof, Stenhoff), Levi. Congregationalist, farmer, Burford, married, politics 1.
192 Stewart (Stuart), Daniel. Dumfries.
193 Stewart (Stuart), John. Dumfries.
194 Stover, Adam. Age 39, American, 26 years in province, Methodist, Norwich, rented 175 acres, single.
195 Thompson, Joseph. Norwich, politics 1.
196 Van Camp (Van Campin), Garrett (Jared): arrested as a Short Hills raider 25 June 1838, tried, found guilty, transported for life. Age 28, American, labourer, Burford, married.
197 Wrigley, Silvanus (Sylvanus) Fearns: jailed Hamilton 25 Jan. 1838 after being taken aboard the *Caroline*, not indicted, freed 31 March 1838. Age 23, English, 20 years in province, labourer, Dumfries, single, politics 1.

APPENDIX 2

Those who Aided the Rebels

1 Amy, Henry: helped intimidate loyalists in Norwich. Norwich, politics 1.
2 Anderson, John: spoke at Waterford meeting of 12 Dec. 1837. Blacksmith, Woodhouse, politics 1.
3 Brown, Hiram James: chaired Malahide meeting 11 Dec. 1837. American, 17 years in province, millwright, Malahide, 50 patented acres, married, politics 1 and 2.
4 Brown, James: gave money to Yarmouth rebels, jailed at London n.d., bailed 13 Jan. 1838. Yarmouth.
5 Brown, John D.: urged rebellion in Yarmouth, jailed London 21 Dec. 1837, tried, acquitted, freed 8 May 1838. American, at least 21 years in province, Regular Baptist, Malahide, rented 100 acres, married, politics 1.
6 Bryant (Briant), Harvey (Harry): warned Yarmouth rebels they were being pursued, jailed London 22 Dec. 1837, tried, found guilty, bailed 25 Sept. 1838. Age 40, American, at least 12 years in province, farmer, Yarmouth, 200 unpatented acres, married.
7 Clark, Orsimus (Osmus, Orsamus, Orasmus, Orson) B.: commissary for Norwich rebels, remained in Norwich, absconded, indicted, named in 22 Oct. 1838 Proclamation. Merchant, Norwich, married, politics 1.
8 Connors (Connor), Albus: urged son Andrew to join rebels. Age 40, Irish, at least 21 years in province, farmer, Bayham, married, politics 2.
9 Conrad (Conrade, Coonrod, Conrod), Charles H.: gave supplies to Yarmouth rebels, jailed London 17 Dec. 1837, bailed 18 Jan. 1838. Upper Canadian, farmer, Yarmouth, 300 patented acres, politics 1 and 2.
10 Cook, Abraham: supplied rebels from his store, examined n.d., freed. Age 44, American, 32 years in province, supported an interdenominational church, merchant, Brantford township, 700 patented acres and 1 patented town lot, married.

234 Appendix 2

11 DeLong (Delong), Garry (Gorry) V.: very active in helping foment revolt in Norwich, jailed Hamilton 23 Dec. 1837, bailed 28 Feb. 1838, absconded. Age 26, Upper Canadian (American), innkeeper, Norwich, 49 patented acres, married, politics 1 and 2.
12 DeLong (Delong), Peter: on 'Home Committee' of Norwich rebels, absconded, indicted, named in 22 Oct. 1838 Proclamation. Age 60, American, 27 years in province, Quaker, farmer, Norwich, 1,619 patented acres, married.
13 Goucher, Western: gave gun to a rebel. Dereham.
14 Green, James L.: chaired Waterford meeting 12 Dec. 1837, bailed 23 Dec. 1837. American, nine years in province, merchant, Townsend, married, politics 1 and 2.
15 Hagle (Hagel, Hogel), Peter: urged sons and others to rebel. Age 45, American, at least 13 years in province, Dereham, married, politics 1.
16 Harvy (Hervey), David: gave money to Yarmouth rebels. Age 28, American, 20 years in province, Hicksite Quaker, farmer's son, Yarmouth, no property, single.
17 Headman (Herdman, Hardman, Heardman, Herdsman), Thomas: urged others to rebel, jailed London 17 Dec. 1837, bailed 18 Jan. 1838. English, 21 years in province, farmer, Bayham, 80 unpatented acres, married.
18 Hitchcock, Artemas (Almos, Hartimus): active in fomenting revolt in Yarmouth. Innkeeper, Yarmouth, patented town lot, married, politics 1.
19 Hoskins (Hoskin), Calvin: urged others to rebel, bailed 20 Dec. 1837. Age 19, Upper Canadian, farmer, West Oxford, 185 patented acres, single, politics 1.
20 Humphrey (Umphrey), George: supplied Bayham rebels with supper at a tavern, bailed 3 Feb. 1838. Upper Canadian, innkeeper, Bayham, three patented acres.
21 Hussey (Huzey), Walter: helped intimidate loyalists in Norwich. Age 28, English, Norwich, married.
22 Kenny (Kinney), Franklyn: collecting arms in Dumfries for rebels. Dumfries, married.
23 Knight, Silas: supplying rebels. Woodhouse, married.
24 Lawton, George: active in fomenting revolt in Yarmouth, absconded, indicted, named in 22 Oct. 1838 Proclamation. Age 51, English, 20 years in province, Quaker, farmer, Yarmouth, 200 patented acres, married, politics 1 and 2.
25 Lossing, Augustus: helped supply rebels with flour. Age 18, Upper Canadian (American), Conservative Quaker, miller, Norwich.
26 Lossing, Solomon: sold flour to rebels, urged others to rebel, jailed Hamilton 23 Dec. 1837, tried, acquitted, freed 3 April 1838. Age 56, American, 26 years

235 Those who Aided the Rebels

in province, Conservative Quaker, flour mill owner, Norwich, 200 patented acres, married, politics 2.
27 McKee (McKay, McFee), Hugh: helped supply rebels with flour. Norwich.
28 McQueen, Alexander: supplying rebels, bailed 23 Dec. 1837. Age 35, Upper Canadian, farmer, Woodhouse, 100 patented acres, married, politics 2.
29 Malcolm, Daniel: urged others to rebel. Age 63, American, 42 years in province, farmer, Bayham, 100 patented acres, married.
30 Massacre (Massecar, Massacar, Messacar, Masacar), John: active at Townsend meeting 12 Dec. 1837, bailed 26 Dec. 1837, indicted, absconded, named in 22 Oct. 1838 Proclamation. Upper Canadian (American), farmer, Townsend, property (unknown amount), married, politics 1.
31 Massacre (Massecar, Massacar, Messacar, Masacar), William: supplying rebels, bailed 23 Dec. 1837. Innkeeper, Woodhouse.
32 Moore, Andrew: urged others to rebel, warned Yarmouth rebels they were being pursued. Age 31, American, 15 years in province, farmer, Bayham, 370 patented acres, married.
33 Moore, Elias: active in fomenting revolt in Yarmouth, jailed London 21 Dec. 1837, bailed 19 Feb. 1838, indicted but not tried. Age 61, American, 25 years in province, Quaker, farmer, Yarmouth, 699 patented acres and rented 200, married, politics 1 and 2.
34 Moore, Enoch: appointed captain of defence force organized at Malahide meeting of 11 Dec. 1837, jailed London 21 Dec. 1837, tried, found guilty, bailed 5 Oct. 1838. Age 67, American, 25 years in province, farmer, Malahide, 300 patented acres and property (unknown amount), married, politics 1 and 2.
35 Moore, John: chaired Sparta meetings 9 and 11 Dec. 1837, warned Yarmouth rebels they were being pursued, jailed London 22 Dec. 1837, tried, found guilty, ordered bailed 13 Aug. 1838. Age 67, American, 25 years in province, Conservative Quaker, farmer, Yarmouth, 300 unpatented acres, married, politics 1 and 2.
36 Mott, Moses: on 'Home Committee' of Norwich rebels. Age 39, American, 27 years in province, Quaker, farmer, Norwich, rented 100 acres, married, politics 2.
37 Nevers, Samuel: collected arms in Dumfries and Blenheim for rebels, examined 14 Dec. 1837, freed. New Brunswicker, farmer, Blenheim.
38 Pearce (Prince), Noble: collected arms in Dumfries and Blenheim for rebels. Dumfries, politics 1.
39 Peasley (Peasly, Peaslee, Peasle), Luke: helped intimidate loyalists in Norwich. Age 36, Upper Canadian, farmer, Norwich, 100 unpatented acres, married, politics 1 and 2.

236 Appendix 2

40 Putnam, Thomas: urged people in West Oxford to rebel, bailed 21 Dec. 1837.
41 Showers, Michael: urged others to rebel, jailed Hamilton 2 Jan. 1838, not indicted, freed 17 March 1838. Age 69, American, 59 years in province, farmer, Burford, 232 patented acres, married, politics 2.
42 Simons, Descom (Descomb, Desmond): urged others to rebel, jailed London 22 Dec. 1837, indictment ignored, freed 26 April 1838. American, at least 15 years in province, tailor, Yarmouth, 100 unpatented acres, married, politics 1 and 2.
43 Smith, Stephen: collected arms in Norwich for rebels, jailed Hamilton 23 Dec. 1837, tried, found guilty, bailed Sept. 1838. Age 24, American, two years in province, tradesman, Norwich, married, no politics.
44 Stockton (Stockden, Stocton), William: chaired meeting 12 Dec. 1837 in Dumfries, collected weapons. Age 45, New Brunswicker, at least nine years in province, farmer, Dumfries, 200 unpatented acres, married, politics 1 and 2.
45 Strobridge, Richard Ransom: supplied ammunition to the rebels. Age 21, American, Wesleyan Methodist, merchant, Brantford township, 5 patented acres, politics 1.
46 Sutton, Abraham: on 'Home Committee' of Norwich rebels, absconded, indicted, named in 22 Oct. 1838 Proclamation. American, Norwich, 200 unpatented acres, politics 1.
47 Tilden, Charles: circulated letter from Duncombe in Dorchester and Westminster urging others to rebel, jailed London 15 Feb. 1838, indicted, bailed April (?) 1838. Age 30, Lower Canadian (American), carpenter, Dereham, 100 patented and 200 unpatented acres, married.
48 Town, Nathan: on 'Home Committee' of Norwich rebels, jailed London 24 Dec. 1837, tried, found guilty, bailed Sept. 1838. Age 50, American (?), doctor (unlicensed), Norwich, property (unknown amount), married, politics 2.
49 Tripp (Trip), Job (Joab, Jacob): helped rebels obtain powder, bailed 22 Dec. 1837. Age 28, American, store clerk, Brantford township, politics 1.
50 Wilcox (Willcox), Ebenezer: organized and addressed Malahide meeting 11 Dec. 1837, jailed London 21 Dec. 1837, tried, found guilty, ordered bailed 11 Oct. 1838. American, 18 years in province, Baptist, Malahide, 359 patented acres, married, politics 1 and 2.
51 Wilson (Willson), David D.: urged others to rebel, jailed London 26 Dec. 1837, bailed 26 Feb. 1838. Age 34, American, at least 13 years in province, Conservative Quaker, farmer, Norwich, 190 patented acres, married, politics 1 and 2.
52 Wilson (Willson), Duncan: gave money to Yarmouth rebels, jailed London 30 Dec. 1837, bailed 26 Jan. 1838, recommitted, not indicted, freed 7 April 1838, arrested in June as a Short Hills raider, ordered freed 19 Nov. 1838. Age 36,

237 Those who Aided the Rebels

   American, two years in province, Quaker, doctor (unlicensed), Yarmouth, single, politics 1.
53 Winegarden, Adam: collected arms in Blenheim and Dumfries for rebels, jailed Hamilton 17 Dec. 1837, petitioned, bailed 6 June 1838. American, at least 23 years in province, farmer, Dumfries, 100 patented acres, married, politics 1 and 2.
54 Winegarden, Isaac Brock: collected arms in Blenheim and Dumfries for the rebels. Age 24, Upper Canadian (American), Blenheim, single.
55 Winegarden, Morris: collected arms in Blenheim and Dumfries for rebels. Upper Canadian (American), Blenheim, single.
56 Winegarden, Lord Wellington: collected arms in Blenheim and Dumfries for rebels, jailed Hamilton 21 Dec. 1837, petitioned, bailed 6 June 1838. Upper Canadian (American), Blenheim.
57 Winegarden, William: collected arms in Blenheim and Dumfries for rebels, jailed Hamilton 21 Dec. 1837, petitioned, bailed 6 June 1838. Age 56, American, 38 years in province, farmer, Blenheim, 300 patented acres, married.

APPENDIX 3

Suspected Traitors

Each of these individuals was cited by only one contemporary source as having been in arms or having aided the rebels. None were apprehended by the authorities. An asterisk indicates those cited by secondary authorities as having been involved in the rebellion but for whom no such evidence could be found. It has been thought necessary to cite only their residences, real or supposed.

1. Anderson, Robert.*
2. Baker.
3. Baker, Hiram: Windham.
4. Ball, Joseph: Dumfries.
5. Ball, Peter.
6. Blake.
7. Burns, Thomas.
8. Chaseman, Robert: Bayham?
9. Clarke, James: Norwich?
10. Coho, Andrew B.: Bayham? Middleton?
11. Coho, William L.: Bayham? Middleton?
12. Colman brothers: Dumfries?
13. Condon, Jeremiah: Norwich?
14. Cromwell, James: Norwich.
15. Cromwell, William: Norwich.
16. Curlis: Dumfries?
17. Davis, Elijah: Malahide?
18. Duncombe, Wheeler.
19. DeLong, Albert: Norwich.
20. Dodge.

Suspected Traitors

21 Doel: Yarmouth?
22 Doyle, Pat: Norwich.
23 Durfee, Elisha: Norwich.
24 Elsworth, Aaron.
25 Elsworth, Justus.
26 Emigh, John C.: Norwich?
27 Emigh, King: Norwich?
28 Fox: Oxfords?
29 Hagle, Josiah:* Yarmouth.
30 Hazen, William.
31 Hodges, Samuel and brother.
32 Johnston, F.C.:* Yarmouth.
33 Keeler: Brantford.
34 Kelly, Jacob.
35 Kett, Thomas.
36 Landon, Stephen: Burford.
37 Leach, Joab: Yarmouth?
38 Lemons (?), Joseph.
39 Luce, Alfred: Dumfries?
40 McBain, David: Dumfries?
41 M'Combs, George.
42 McCool, Robert: Townsend.
43 McCool, William: Townsend?
44 McMaster, Caleb E.:* Yarmouth.
45 Malcolm, Wheeler.
46 Merritt, Edward:* Oakland.
47 Mills, Samuel:* Yarmouth?
48 Moore, John: Yarmouth.
49 Moot, Rosel:* Malahide.
50 Moses, John: Norwich.
51 Mott, Enoch:* Norwich.
52 Mott, Reuben:* Norwich.
53 Nicholls, James: Norwich?
54 Ostrander, Henry: Bayham.
55 Ostrander, Isaac: Bayham.
56 Raymond, Timothy.
57 Ryckman, Charles: Yarmouth?
58 Scott, Enos: Yarmouth?
59 Showers, Alexander: Burford.
60 Smith, Justus: Oakland?

240 Appendix 3

61 Smith, Montgomery: Southwold.
62 Smith, Oliver (son): Bayham? Townsend?
63 Smith, Oliver: Townsend.
64 Smith, Thomas: Yarmouth.
65 Snider, Lawrence: Norwich?
66 Tompkins, Caleb: Norwich.
67 Trouss (?), John: Norwich?
68 Vanalstine: Brantford?
69 Walker, Joseph: Townsend?
70 Whalon, Thomas: Oakland.
71 White, Washington: Dumfries? Blenheim?
72 Winegarden, George: Dumfries? Blenheim?
73 Woodworth, Solomon: Malahide?
74 Wilson, Dr John T.: Yarmouth.
75 Yirks, William: Townsend.

APPENDIX 4

Bayham Loyalists

1 Allen, Thomas: Age 26, English, two years in province, Anglican, labourer, no property, married.
2 Anderson, John: Bayham.
3 Bain, James: Age 17, Nova Scotian, Anglican.
4 Bain, John.
5 Blaney, John: Upper Canadian, Bayham, 200 patented acres.
6 Brown, Peter.
7 Burwell, John: Age 41, Upper Canadian (American), Anglican, gentleman, Bayham, married, politics 2.
8 Carns (Carnes, Cerns), Peter: Age 51, Upper Canadian, Baptist, blacksmith, Bayham, 200 unpatented acres, married.
9 Cascadden, Thomas: Age 23, Upper Canadian, farmer, Malahide, 100 unpatented acres, single.
10 Clifford, John: clerk, Bayham.
11 Code, George: Age 25, Irish, Anglican, Bayham.
12 Cook, Ira: Age 33, Upper Canadian (American), farmer, Bayham, 175 patented and 100 unpatented acres.
13 Culp, Jacob: Age 30, Upper Canadian, lumberman, Bayham, married.
14 Culton, Edward S.: shoemaker, Bayham, no property.
15 Cutter (Colton), David: Age 26, English, Anglican, Bayham, single.
16 Draper, Isaac: Age 46, English, 20 years in province, Anglican, sawmill owner, Bayham, 200 unpatented acres, married, politics 2.
17 Ellsworth, William: Age 24, New Brunswicker, Anglican.
18 Fall, Phillip.
19 Ford, Alexander: British, 21 years in province, Middleton, 200 unpatented acres.
20 Foster, David: Canadian, Bayham.

242 Appendix 4

21 Francis, John: Age 34, Irish, Anglican.
22 Gibbs, John H.
23 Gilbert, George: Age 19, Irish, Anglican, Bayham, single.
24 Griffin, David.
25 Griffin, Sanders (Saunders): Age 20, Upper Canadian, Baptist, Malahide, 100 unpatented acres.
26 Harris, Nelson: Age 20, Upper Canadian, Anglican.
27 Hepburne, William.
28 Hepburne, William (son).
29 Hewer (Hure), John.
30 Hollowood, Amos: Age 32, Canadian, innkeeper, Bayham, 1 patented town lot, single.
31 Hollowood, George William: Age 23, Upper Canadian, Regular Baptist, gentleman, Bayham, 100 unpatented acres, 1 patented town lot.
32 Hollowood, Samuel.
33 Hollowood, Solomon: Age 18, Upper Canadian, Baptist, Bayham.
34 Hutchinson, Alexander: Age 20, Canadian, Bayham, single.
35 Hutchinson, Thomas H.: Age 20, Upper Canadian, Bayham.
36 Livingston, Benjamin.
37 Livingston, Samuel: Irish, 13 years in province, Bayham.
38 McDonell (McDonel), Peter: Age 38, Upper Canadian, carpenter, Bayham, 1 patented town lot.
39 McDormand, Nelson (Elson): Canadian, weaver, Bayham, married.
40 McGuire, Thomas.
41 McKenny (MacKenny), Doyle: Age 40, Canadian, farmer, Malahide, 300 patented and 1,000 unpatented acres, rented 200 acres, married, politics 2.
42 Mabee (Maby), Pickney (Pinkney): Upper Canadian, Anglican.
43 Mack, John: 20, English, Bayham, single.
44 Martin, James: Bayham, married.
45 Medcalf (Medcalfe), Henry: Age 59, Irish, 31 years in province, Anglican, clothier, Bayham, 200 patented and 200 unpatented acres, married, politics 2.
46 Mitchell, Ephraim Cole: Age 50, American, 45 years in province, farmer, Bayham, 234 patented acres, married.
47 Mitchell, George: Age 19, Upper Canadian, Anglican.
48 Mitchell, Simpson: Age 23, Upper Canadian, Bayham, married.
49 Moore, John.
50 Moore, Solomon: Age 39, Upper Canadian (American), farmer, Bayham, 200 patented acres, married, politics 2.
51 Murphy, William: British, one year in province, saddler, Bayham.

243 Bayham Loyalists

52 Neville, James: Age 22, Upper Canadian, Anglican, Bayham, single.
53 Panell, Charles.
54 Panell, George.
55 Rees, David.
56 Richards, R.G.: Bayham.
57 Rumell, George.
58 Sampson, William.
59 Saxton, Alexander: Age 36, Nova Scotian, 26 years in province, farmer, Bayham, property (unknown amount), married, politics 2.
60 Saxton, William: Age 48, Nova Scotian, 26 years in province, Regular Baptist, farmer, Bayham, 470 patented acres, married, politics 2.
61 Sheldon, Elihu: Age 25, Upper Canadian.
62 Sibley, John: Age 36, Nova Scotian, at least 19 years in province, Regular Baptist, farmer, Bayham, married.
63 Smith, Benjamin.
64 Sweetlow, Elias.
65 Taylor, James: Age 20, English, Baptist, Bayham, married.
66 Taylor, John.
67 Taylor, Samuel: Age 18, English, Anglican.
68 Thompson, John.
69 Thompson, William.
70 Titus, Isaac: Nova Scotian, at least 10 years in province, Regular Baptist, blacksmith, Bayham, 200 patented acres, married.
71 Titus, Lewis: Age 18, Nova Scotian, Regular Baptist, Bayham.
72 Turnbull, James.
73 Tyrell (Tyrrell), Miles: Upper Canadian, Malahide, 250 patented acres, married.
74 Tyrell (Tyrrell), Noah: Age 32, Upper Canadian, farmer, Dereham, 100 unpatented acres, married.
75 Vance, Alexander: Age 49, Nova Scotian, 5 years in province, Anglican, farmer, Houghton, 100 unpatented acres, married, politics 2.
76 Walker, George: Anglican, labourer, Bayham, married.
77 Walker, John.
78 Westin (Weston), Joseph: Age 39, Irish, farmer, Bayham, 100 unpatented acres, married.
79 Westover, William: Age 38, Upper Canadian, Anglican, ship's carpenter, Bayham, married.
80 Woodman, E.B.
81 Wright, John: Anglican, merchant, Bayham, married.

APPENDIX 5

Bayham Rebels

1 Anderson, William A.: Bayham.
2 Bell, James: Age 45, English, 20 years in province, farmer, Bayham, 100 unpatented acres, married, politics 1 and 2.
3 Berry, Matthew (Mathew): Bayham.
4 Bowes (Bower, Boaz), Joseph: 40, American, three years in province, farmer's son, Bayham, no property, married.
5 Cheeseman, William: Age 21, English, 18 years in province, farmer's son, Bayham, no property, single.
6 Connors (Connor, Conners, Conner), Andrew: Age 21, Upper Canadian, farmer's son, Bayham.
7 Cook, Moses: Age 42, Upper Canadian (American), farmer, Bayham, 200 unpatented acres.
8 Cook, Robert: Age 39, Upper Canadian (American), 'no particular religion,' farmer, Bayham, 250 patented acres, married, politics 1.
9 Denton, Losee (Loce): Age 25, Upper Canadian, Bayham, single.
10 Edison, Samuel: Age 33, Nova Scotian (American), 26 years in province, Regular Baptist, innkeeper, Bayham, married.
11 Fisher, Henry: English, farmer, Bayham, 100 unpatented acres, married, politics 2.
12 Herrington, William: Age 25, tailor, Bayham, married.
13 Hill, George: Age 38, American, blacksmith, Bayham.
14 Humphrey (Humphries), Norris (Noris): Upper Canadian, merchant, Bayham, 1 patented acre, 1 patented lot and property (unknown amount), married, politics 2.
15 Leach (Leitch), Nelson: Age 19, American, labourer, Bayham, no property.
16 Malcolm, Finlay (Findlay, Finley): Age 38, Upper Canadian (American), farmer, Bayham, 200 unpatented acres, married.

245 Bayham Rebels

17 Medcalf (Medcalfe, Metcalf), John: Age 30, Irish, 15 years in province, farmer, Malahide, 100 unpatented acres, married.
18 Paulding (Pauling), Jesse: innkeeper, Bayham, 110 patented acres, married, politics 1.
19 Ribble (Ribball), George: Bayham.
20 Sands, Samuel: Age 58, Nova Scotian, farmer, Bayham, property (unknown amount), married.
21 Smith, Oliver: American, doctor, Bayham, married, politics 1.
22 Storey (Story), William: Age 32, English, 21 years in province, farmer, Bayham, 50 patented acres, married.

APPENDIX 6

Those Bound Over in the Rebel Area in December 1837 for Reasons Unknown

An asterisk indicates bound over in Norwich on 17 Dec. 1837.

1. Avery, Orin:* bailed 17 Dec. 1837. Age 23, American, at least three years in province, Norwich, married, politics 2.
2. Boman, George:* bailed 17 Dec. 1837.
3. Boyce, Efremitus:* bailed 17 Dec. 1837. Age 17, American, single.
4. Clause, George: bailed 23 Dec. 1837. Age 17, Upper Canadian, farmer, Townsend, 250 patented acres, single.
5. Corbin, Aaron L.:* bailed 17 Dec. 1837. Age 37, American, at least 17 years in province, Quaker, Norwich, 100 patented acres, married.
6. Enrigh (Emigh?), Henry:* bailed 17 Dec. 1837.
7. Flueln (Flewellen, Flewelling), Benjamin: bailed 23 Dec. 1837. Labourer, Townsend, single.
8. Mercer, Richard:* bailed 17 Dec. 1837.
9. Mills, David: bailed 20 Dec. 1837. American, at least 19 years in province, Hicksite Quaker, farmer, Yarmouth, 200 patented acres, married.
10. Mills, Stephen: bailed 20 Dec. 1837. Yarmouth.
11. Moore, Daniel B.:* bailed 17 Dec. 1837.
12. Moyer, Joseph:* bailed 17 Dec. 1837. Age 25, American, Norwich, single.
13. Odell, John Henry:* bailed 17 Dec. 1837. Norwich.
14. Peasley, Samuel:* bailed 17 Dec. 1837.
15. Shattick, Hiram:* bailed 17 Dec. 1837. Age 21, American, Norwich, single.
16. Spencer, Henry:* bailed 17 Dec. 1837.
17. Swayzie, Caleb: bailed 26 Dec. 1837. Age 49, American, Hicksite Quaker, farmer, Norwich, property (unknown amount), married.

APPENDIX 7

Those Charged with Offences Unconnected with the Duncombe Rising

1 Beamer (Beemer, Bemer), Philip: aided William Lount's attempt to escape, bailed 27 Dec. 1837. Farmer, Townsend.
2 Clarke, George Washington: after revolt suppressed, posted notices calling out the rebels about Woodstock, bailed 23 Dec. 1837. Merchant, East Oxford, married.
3 Dace (Dease, Deese, Dees), James: aided William Lount's attempt to escape, jailed Hamilton 25 Jan. 1838, bailed 15 Feb. 1838. Upper Canadian, Regular Baptist, labourer at Long Point Furnace, Charlotteville, married.
4 McLean (McLane), Hector: landed arms in Queenston Nov. 1837, bailed 23 Dec. 1837. Dumfries.
5 Malcolm, Norman: threatened Tories for arresting his father, jailed Hamilton 23 Dec. 1837, indicted, bill ignored, freed 31 March 1838. Age 18, Upper Canadian (American), Episcopal Methodist, farmer's son, Oakland, no property, single.

APPENDIX 8

Those Bailed or Imprisoned Suspected of Being Implicated in the Duncombe Rising on Evidence that Now Seems Insufficient or Contradictory

The activities described for each are alleged, not proven.

1 Adkins (Atkins): rebel, jailed London 20 Dec. 1837, bailed 6 Jan. 1838.
2 Alway, Robert: urged others to rebel, jailed Hamilton 17 Dec. 1837, indicted, bill ignored, bailed 28 March 1838 (to appear at London). Age 47, English, 21 years in province, Anglican, Assemblyman, West Oxford, leased 200 acres, married, politics 2.
3 Blakey (Blakie), James: urged others to rebel, bailed 27 Dec. 1838. Labourer, Townsend.
4 Canfield (Campfield), James: rebel, urged others to rebel, jailed London 15 Dec. 1837, bailed 4 Jan. 1838. London township, 100 patented acres, married, politics 1 and 2.
5 Charles, Lewis: gave money to rebels, urged others to rebel, bailed 26(?) Dec. 1837. Age 46, France, innkeeper, Blenheim, 114 patented acres, married.
6 Clark (Clarke), George Alexander: in contact with the rebels, persuaded militia not to turn out against them, bailed 26 Jan. 1838, indicted, absconded, named in 22 Oct. 1838 Proclamation. Age 40, Upper Canadian (American), merchant, Brantford town, 300 patented acres, married, politics 2.
7 Coho, Nathan J.: rebel, bailed 28 Dec. 1837.
8 Crable, John: rebel, bailed 28 Dec. 1837. American, 10 years in province, Quaker, carpenter, Yarmouth, 100 patented acres, married.
9 Curtis, David: rebel, jailed London 20 Dec. 1837, bailed 12 Feb. 1838. Age 59, American, 43 years in province, Open Communion Baptist, innkeeper,

249 Those Bailed or Imprisoned on Suspicion

West Oxford, 150 patented and 200 unpatented acres, married, politics 1 and 2.

10 Doxie (Doxy, Doxey, Doxsie), Enoch D.: rebel, jailed London 20 Dec. 1837, bailed 26 Dec. 1837 or 3 Jan. 1838, jailed in Norwich scare 29 June 1838, bailed Oct. 1838. Age 30, Upper Canadian, shoemaker, Norwich, no property, married.

11 Edison, Marcellus (Marsella, Marsellah, Mersellah, Merselles): rebel, bailed 21 Dec. 1837. Age 43, Nova Scotian (American), 26 years in province, innkeeper, Bayham, 200 patented acres, married.

12 Edmonds, Oliver: rebel, jailed London 16 Dec. 1837, not indicted, freed 15 March 1838. Age 42, American, at least 15 years in province, farmer, Windham, 200 patented and 200 unpatented acres, married, politics 1 and 2.

13 Emigh, Henry: rebel(?), jailed London 16 Dec. 1837, freed 29 Dec. 1837. American, Norwich.

14 Esmond (Esmon, Esmonds), Jacob S.: rebel, jailed London 17 Dec. 1837, bailed 2 Jan. 1838. Norwich, married.

15 Goff, Henry: rebel, jailed Hamilton 16 Dec. 1837, not indicted, freed 20 March 1838. Age 53, Irish, at least eight years in province, teacher, Windham.

16 Gould, Anson: urged others to rebel, jailed London 24 Dec. 1837, indicted, bill ignored, freed 26 April 1838. Age 32, American, eight years in province, carder and fuller, Yarmouth, 10 patented acres, married, politics 1.

17 Graham, David: rebel, bailed 21 Dec. 1837. Oxfords, married, politics 1.

18 Hammill, John: told rebels how to attack Brantford, jailed Hamilton 9 March 1838, tried, found guilty, bailed 17 Aug. 1838. Age 46, Upper Canadian, Regular Baptist, carpenter, Brantford (town?), married.

19 Heap, John: rebel, jailed Hamilton 15 Dec. 1837, not indicted, freed 20 March 1838. English, labourer, Oakland.

20 Hogan, Harry (Harvey): rebel, bailed 22 Dec. 1837. Age 26, American, labourer, Dereham.

21 Kenny (Kinney), John: rebel, jailed London 20 Dec. 1837, bailed 23 Dec. 1837. Norwich, rented 100 acres.

22 Lymburner (Limburner), William: rebel (?), jailed London 20 Dec. 1837, bailed 14 Feb. 1838. Age 51, Nova Scotian, 31 years in province, Burford, 100 patented acres, married, politics 1 and 2.

23 McLees (McClees, McLeese), James: rebel, jailed London 17 Dec. 1837, bailed 26 Jan. 1838. Age 27, American, 26 years in province, Conservative Quaker, farmer, Norwich, property (unknown amount), married, politics 2.

24 Murray (Murry), Philip: rebel, bailed 27 Dec. 1837. Labourer, Townsend.

250 Appendix 8

25 Reid (Reed), George Stephen: rebel, jailed London n.d., bailed 22 Jan. 1838. Yarmouth, politics 1.
26 Secord, Asa: rebel, bailed 27 Dec. 1837. Farmer, Oakland, 200 patented acres.
27 Secord (Sechord), Stephen A. (H.): spread news of the rebellion among the disaffected, jailed London 21 Dec. 1837, not indicted (?), bailed 16 April 1838. Age 36, Upper Canadian (American), Yarmouth, 21 patented acres, single, politics 1.
28 Sirpell (Serpell), Thomas: rebel(?), jailed Hamilton 3 Jan. 1838, freed 6 Feb. 1838. English, Burford.
29 Shaw, Bela: urged others to rebel, bailed 26 Dec. 1837. American, 14 years in province, merchant, Yarmouth, 85 patented acres and 4 patented town lots, married, politics 1 and 2.
30 Stants (Stantz, Statts), William: rebel, jailed Hamilton 15 Dec. 1837, freed 15 March 1838. Upper Canadian.
31 Sturgess (Sturges, Sturgis), David: rebel, jailed Simcoe Dec. 1837, escaped. Merchant, Bayham.
32 Sumner (Summers), Alexander: urged others to rebel, jailed London 15 Dec. 1837, bailed 20 Feb. 1838. Age 36, Upper Canadian (British), farmer, Bayham, 100 patented and 200 unpatented acres.
33 Talbot, John: planned rebellion, at Flannagan's meeting, absconded, indicted, named in 22 Oct. 1838 Proclamation. Age 40, Irish, 19 years in province, Anglican, newspaper editor, Yarmouth, rented 200 acres, single, politics 1 and 2.
34 Teckling (Jeckling, Jacklin), John: rebel(?), jailed Hamilton 16 Dec. 1837, not indicted, freed 15 March 1838. English, cordwainer, Oakland.
35 Tillson, George B.: rebel, bailed 27 Dec. 1837. Age 22, American, 15 years in province, Dereham, single.
36 Tillson, Henry (Harry): rebel, bailed 27 Dec. 1837. American, Dereham, politics 2.
37 Tripp, Michael: rebel, bailed 3 Feb. 1838. East Oxford, married, politics 1.
38 Walker, Baldwin: subscribed to rebel document at Waterford meeting 12 Dec. 1837, bailed 23 Dec. 1837. Age 28, Upper Canadian (American), farmer, Townsend, 100 patented acres, single, politics 1.
39 Walker, John: subscribed to rebel document at Waterford meeting 12 Dec. 1837, bailed 23 Dec. 1837. Age 26, Upper Canadian (American), farmer's son, Townsend, politics 1.
40 Walker, Ralph: subscribed to rebel document at Waterford meeting 12 Dec. 1837, bailed 23 Dec. 1837. Townsend, politics 1.
41 Wilson, John: agreed to lead rebels to Hamilton, jailed Hamilton n.d. (in jail on 12 Feb. 1838), freed n.d. Oakland, married.

APPENDIX 9

Norwich Men

1 Austin, Calvin: jailed Hamilton 8 July 1838, bailed Sept. 1838. Age 38, American, at least 17 years in province, Methodist, watchmaker and gunsmith, Brantford town, unpatented town lot, married.
2 Dennis, John: jailed London 7 July 1838, freed n.d. Age 25, American, 17 years in province, Regular Baptist, farmer's son, Norwich, no property, single.
3 Doxie (Doxey, Doxy, Doxsie), Enoch D.: jailed London 26 July 1838, bailed Oct. 1838. Age 30, Upper Canadian shoemaker, Norwich, no property, married.
4 Fish, John: jailed Hamilton 8 July 1838, freed n.d. American, Norwich, married.
5 Hatcock (Hadcock), Daniel: jailed Sodom 2 July 1838, bailed 7(?) July 1838. American, at least two years in province, farmer, Norwich, 190 patented acres, married.
6 Hillaker (Hallaker), Benjamin: jailed London 7 July 1838, freed n.d. Age 51, American, 20 years in province, Methodist, sawmill owner, Norwich, 100 patented acres, married, politics 2.
7 Hillaker (Hallaker), William: jailed London 7 July 1838, freed n.d. Age 24, American, 20 years in province, Methodist, miller, Norwich, no property, married.
8 Lossing, Horace: jailed Hamilton 8 July 1838, freed n.d. Age 18, Upper Canadian (American), Conservative Quaker, miller, no property, single.
9 Matthews (Mathews), Jesse: jailed Hamilton 8 July 1838, ordered freed 7 Feb. 1839. Age 35, American, millwright, Norwich.
10 Scott, Enos: jailed Toronto 20 July 1838, tried London in fall 1838, found guilty, to be imprisoned for three years. Age 20, Quaker, Norwich, single.
11 Scott, Job (John): jailed Toronto 20 July 1838, tried London in fall 1838,

found guilty, to be imprisoned for three years. Age 19, Quaker, Norwich.
12 Smith, Isaac L.: jailed London 13 July 1838, bailed 20 July 1838. At least seven years in province, Norwich, rented 200 acres, married, politics 2.
13 Wilson, Andrew: jailed Sodom 29 June 1838, freed n.d. Age 25, American, 16 years in province, Quaker, Norwich 200 patented acres, married.
14 Wood, James: jailed London 7 July 1838, bailed Sept. 1838. Age 48, New Brunswicker, 38 years in province, farmer, East Oxford, 200 patented acres and squatted on 200, married, politics 1.

Notes

ABBREVIATIONS

AGOC Adjutant General's Office, Correspondence, Public Archives of Canada
AHMSC American Home Missionary Society Congregational, United Church Archives
CAAC Catholic Archdiocesan Archives (Toronto) Collection, Archives of Ontario
CGCS Correspondence of the Glasgow Colonial Society, United Church Archives
CMS Correspondence of the Military Secretary of the Commander of the Forces, Public Archives of Canada
CO 42 Colonial Office 42 Series, Archives of Ontario
DCB Dictionary of Canadian Biography
HPL Hamilton Public Library
L-G LB Lieutenant-Governor's Letter Books, Archives of Ontario
LPL London Public Library
MLB Military Letter Books, Public Archives of Canada
MLC Mackenzie-Lindsey Clippings, Archives of Ontario
NCPSO Numbered Correspondence of the Provincial Secretary's Office, Public Archives of Canada
PAC Public Archives of Canada
PAO Archives of Ontario
RLDM Records of the London District Magistrates, Public Archives of Canada
SPG Records of the Society for the Propagation of the Gospel in Foreign Parts, Public Archives of Canada
TPL Toronto Public Library
UCA United Church Archives
UCS Upper Canada Sundries
UCSP Upper Canada State Papers, Archives of Ontario
UWO University of Western Ontario Library, Regional History Collection

254 Notes to pp. 6–19

CHAPTER 1

1 Norfolk county had been settled primarily by Americans. In 1812 the militia of that county refused to move beyond the boundary of Norfolk. In May 1814 fifteen people were convicted as traitors at Ancaster, eight of whom were hanged. All of those executed came from the Niagara and London districts, which were heavily settled by Americans.
2 Craig, *Upper Canada: The Formative Years, 1784–1841* 218
3 See, for example, Mackenzie, *Sketches of Canada and the United States* 158–72.
4 Stagg, 'The Yonge Street Rebellion of 1837' (PH D diss.)
5 Landon, *Western Ontario and the American Frontier* 166

CHAPTER 2

1 The boundaries of the various time zones are only approximations. In choosing the years assigned to each area, I was guided by the dates of the establishment of the first sizable and permanent settlements.
2 See PAO, Abstract Index to Deeds.
3 'Estimate of the Lands in the Province of Upper Canada ...,' Sept. 1838, PAO, Crown Lands Papers, Series A-IV, 56
4 Evidence of John Radenhurst, PAC, Durham Papers, Series 2, 49, 'Evidence for the Durham Report' 141
5 *Appendix to the Journal of the House of Assembly of Upper Canada*, 1836, I, App. 22, 24
6 See Guillet, *Early Life in Upper Canada* 121.
7 Gourlay, *Statistical Account of Upper Canada* I, 304–83
8 'Statement of Clergy Reserves of Upper Canada,' Sanderson, ed., *The Arthur Papers* I, 13–14
9 Evidence of Sullivan, PAC, Durham Papers, Series 2, 49, 'Evidence for the Durham Report' 206
10 Ibid.
11 Lucas, ed., *Lord Durham's Report* II, 220
12 Wilson, *The Clergy Reserves of Upper Canada* 134
13 'Estimate of the Lands ...,' Sept. 1838, PAO, Crown Lands Papers, Series A-IV, 56
14 Gates, *Land Policies of Upper Canada* 199
15 See Book D, 10, PAO, Talbot Maps.
16 UWO, Copy of Assessment Roll from 1839 to 1843 inclusive, London district
17 Return of John Strachan, 7 May 1838, Sanderson, ed., *The Arthur Papers* I, 110

Notes to pp. 19–27

18 Carruthers, *Retrospect of Thirty-Six Years' Residence in Canada West* 53–4
19 See Evidence of Samuel P. Jarvis, PAC, Indian Affairs, 717, Six Nations Indians, 1830–45, 105–6.
20 Petrie to W.J.D. Waddilove, Burford, 1 Oct. 1839, Hanshaw, ed., *The Late Bishop of Quebec's Upper Canadian Travelling Mission Fund* 80
21 Memorial of Marcus Blair, enclosed in Petition of Blair to Sir George Arthur, 28 Aug. 1838, PAC, Indian Affairs, 69
22 Ibid.
23 Carruthers, *Retrospect* 55
24 Numerical Return of Resident Indians in Canada, Waddilove, *The Stewart Missions* 227
25 Flood to W.J.D. Waddilove, Carradoc, 9 March 1841, Hanshaw, ed., *The Late Bishop* 184
26 Those being admitted to the rights of citizenship under this legislation had to take the oath of allegiance if they had not already done so.
27 Gates, *Land Policies* 121–2. Gates provides an excellent discussion of the entire alien controversy.
28 Lucas, ed., *Lord Durham's Report* II, 173
29 Memorandum [Colborne] to [Arthur], Sorel, 10 Oct. 1838, Sanderson, ed., *The Arthur Papers* I, 298
30 The Scots appear to have been dominant in Mosa and Westminster.
31 PAC, Durham Papers, Series 2, 49, 'Evidence for the Durham Report' 212–14
32 Miller to Dr Burns, Ancaster, 1 Feb. 1833, CGCS, 4, no. 20
33 Bettridge Manuscript, 24, PAO, Bettridge Papers
34 Shirreff, *A Tour through North America* 396
35 Martin to R.B. Sullivan, Vienna, 4 Jan. 1837, PAO, Township Papers, Bayham, folder for concession 5
36 *Constitution* (Toronto), 4 Oct. 1837
37 There is some controversy whether or not the Burwells could legitimately be considered Loyalists.
38 Bettridge Manuscript, 6, PAO, Bettridge Papers
39 *Canada in the Years 1832, 1833 and 1834* 24, 61
40 Marchen to Peter Robinson, Townsend, 15 Jan. 1833, PAO, Township Papers, Windham, folders for concessions 5 and 6
41 John Ryerson to Egerton Ryerson, Toronto, 2 Jan. 1837, UCA, Ryerson Papers
42 Elmsley to Talbot, Clover Hill, 24 May 1838, UWO, Talbot Papers, Box 1
43 Proudfoot Diary, 127, 164–5 (typescript), UWO, Proudfoot Family Papers
44 Ibid. 29, 27 Oct. 1838
45 Samuel Rose to John Rose, 21 Nov. 1833, PAO, Rose Papers

46 See *Appendix to the Journal of the House of Assembly of Upper Canada*, 1839–40, I, Pt. I, 148, 151–3. The 1839 returns for Brantford were omitted here but can be found in CO 42, 476/223
47 T.R. Preston noted the lack of uniformity and system in the taking of the census. Preston, *Three Years' Residence in Canada* II, 115
48 Romanes to Dr Burns, Hamilton, 25 June 1833, CGCS, 4, no. 159
49 *Quarterly Record of the ... United Secession Church* VII (1839) 535
50 John B. Askin to Colonel Rowan, London, 18 Dec. 1835, UCS, 159/87441
51 The church's statistics can be found in a letter of Wm. Proudfoot, London, 27 April 1839, *Quarterly Record of the ... United Secession Church* VII (1839) 535
52 Gregg, *Short History of the Presbyterian Church in Canada* 51
53 Session Book, Communion Roll, 27 March 1837, First United Church, Galt, Congregational Records
54 UCA, 'Associated Synod of North America, Presbytery of Stamford, Extract from the Minutes of Associate,' XI, 1835–6
55 An itinerant from the Associate Reformed Church (another American Presbyterian Church) had been active in Yarmouth at some time during the years from 1834 to 1837.
56 W.F. Curry to Milton Badge, Montreal, 27 Sept. 1827, AHMSC
57 Furman and Marsh to Absalom Peters, Hamilton, 14 Nov. 1836, AHMSC
58 Missionary Report of Daniel Allan, London, 22 Aug. 1837, *Canadian Christian Examiner and Presbyterian Review* I (1837) 292
59 Romanes to Dr Burns, Hamilton, 25 June 1833, CGCS, 4, no. 159
60 Clark, *Church and Sect in Canada* 202
61 UCA, Minutes of the Ninth Canadian Wesleyan Conference, 1837, 5
62 UCA, Minutes of the Seventh Canadian Wesleyan Conference, 1835, 8
63 *The Minutes of the Annual Conferences of the Wesleyan-Methodist Church* 56
64 Webster, *History of the Methodist Episcopal Church in Canada* 323, 335
65 Carroll, *Case and His Contemporaries* I, 17
66 Clark, *Church and Sect* 126
67 Green to W.J.D. Waddilove, London, 23 Nov. 1837, Waddilove, *The Stewart Missions* 180
68 Lucas, ed., *Lord Durham's Report* II, 176. Durham felt that, even admitting the validity of this questionable procedure, the Anglicans probably constituted less than one-quarter of the province's population. In 1838 supporters of the church claimed it had 150,000 adherents, about 40 per cent of the province's population. Mountain, *Canadian Church Destitution* 5
69 Gilmore to the editor, Montreal, 7 July 1837, *Baptist Magazine* XXIX (1837) 404. In 1837 the Canada Baptist Missionary Society was organized to recruit British missionaries.

Notes to pp. 35–8

70 Letter from Fraser, Breadalbane, 24 Oct. 1834, *Baptist Magazine* XXVII (1835) 147
71 One 1835 estimate was that there might be as many as 14,000 members of the Baptist Church in the province. *Baptist Magazine* XXVII (1835) 147
72 Baptist Archives, Minute Book of Baptist Church organized 22 April 1822 in the town of Oxford, entry for 28 Aug. 1837, 84
73 Hotson, *Pioneer Baptist Work in Oxford County* 43
74 See Clark, *Church and Sect* 300.
75 The Toronto *Mirror* claimed on 14 July 1838 that there were 85,000 Catholics in the province.
76 Downie to Alexander Macdonell, St Thomas, 5 March 1835, CAAC, AB 11
77 Proudfoot Diary, 286, UWO, Proudfoot Papers. Dorland says that Hicks' views about Christ were peculiar, but maintains that Hicks still felt Christ to be divine. In any event, says Dorland, Hicks' views of Christ and the Scriptures were not widely shared by his followers. Dorland, *A History of the Society of Friends* 120, 154
78 This is part of the mast-head of the *Christian Palladium*. A copy of its 15 December 1837 issue is in UCA, Christian Connection Records.
79 *Evangelical Magazine and Gospel Advocate* II (1831) 21
80 In 1839 eleven of the thirty-five townships dealt with here reported high percentages of people professing no religious persuasions. In descending order they were: Nissouri 66 per cent, Malahide 60, North and West Oxford combined 51, Yarmouth 51, Dorchester and Dunwich 48 each, Burford 32, Bayham 23, Dumfries 11, and London township 5.5.
81 Letter of Daniel Allan, London, 8 Jan. 1838, *Canadian Christian Examiner* II (1838) 119
82 Proudfoot Diary, 24, UWO, Proudfoot Papers
83 *Appendix to the Journal of the House of Assembly of Upper Canada*, 1839–40, I, Pt. I, 151
84 Address of the Synod Committee, *Canadian Christian Examiner* II (1838) 84
85 Ibid. 88
86 O'Meara's Journal, no. 1, 10 July 1838, SPG, Series X 7
87 Letter of Wm. Proudfoot, London, 6 Nov. 1834, *United Secession Magazine* III (1835) 286
88 J. Rothwell to C.H. Minchin, Oxford, 22 March 1836, SPG, Series C, Section 477
89 Robert Thornton to Wm. Proudfoot, Dundas, 16 Aug. 1833, Knox College, Proudfoot Papers
90 Anna R. Dickson to Sir Walter Farquhar, St Martin's near Paris, 12 May 1838, SPG, Series C, Section 498

91 Joseph Maria Burke to Alexander Macdonell, London, 18 Oct. 1837, CAAC, AB05, 6
92 James O'Flynn to Benjamin Gaulin, St Thomas, 4 Dec. 1839, CAAC, BB15, 2
93 Ryerson to Robert Alder, private, New York, 25 Nov. 1837 (copy), UCA, Ryerson Papers
94 O'Neill's Journal, no. 8, 16 July, 165, SPG, Series X 7
95 Mackintosh to Mathew Montgomery, Thorold, 22 Oct. 1836, CGCS, 6, no. 205
96 Thomson, 'Proudfoot and the Secession Churches' 37
97 Norwich Monthly Meeting, Men, 1822–34, 13 May 1829, UWO, Quaker Records
98 *British, Irish and Canadian Gazette*, 22 Dec. 1838, MLC, item 6098
99 Samuel Rose to John Rose, 21 Nov. 1833, PAO, Rose Papers
100 In the following survey of topography and soil types numerous sources were consulted. The two most useful were Gourlay, *Statistical Account* I, 308–83, and Picken, *The Canadas* 192–5.
101 Report of the Bishop of Quebec, 25 March 1829, SPG *Report ... for the Year 1828* 122–3
102 Gourlay, *Statistical Account* I, 322
103 Ibid. 315
104 PAO, 'A Few Remarks on a Tour in Upper Canada,' 1837, 9
105 Proudfoot Diary, 18, UWO, Proudfoot Papers
106 Brydone, *Narrative of a Voyage* 38
107 Proudfoot Diary, 25, 239, UWO, Proudfoot Papers
108 PAO, 'A Few Remarks ...,' 1837, 9
109 Murray, *An Historical and Descriptive Account* I, 324
110 Shirreff, *A Tour* 182
111 Brydone, *Narrative* 38
112 Horsman and Benson, eds., *The Canadian Journal of Alfred Domett* 34
113 Murray, *An Historical and Descriptive Account* I, 323
114 Proudfoot Diary, 27–8, UWO, Proudfoot Papers
115 Adam Hope to Robert Hope, Hamilton, 26 Feb. 1837, 5–6, HPL, Hope Letters
116 [Dunlop], *Statistical Sketches of Upper Canada* 26
117 The preceding discussion is based on Hoffman et al., *Soil Associations of Southern Ontario*.
118 See Finch et al., *Elements of Geography* 454.
119 Wicklund and Richards, *The Soil Survey of Oxford County* 37–8
120 PAO, 'A Few Remarks ...,' 1837, 11
121 Adam Hope to Robert Hope, Hamilton, 26 Feb. 1837, 5–6, HPL, Hope Letters

Notes to pp. 42–6

122 Report of John Strachan, SPG *Report ... for the Year 1828* 150
123 PAC, Leith Diary, 17
124 Adam Hope to Robert Hope, St Thomas, 24 Dec. 1837, 4, HPL, Hope Letters
125 Bettridge Manuscript, 24, PAO, Bettridge Papers
126 PAO, 'A Few Remarks ...,' 1837, 8–9
127 Letter of 'Brother' Tapscott, Colborne, 30 Aug. 1838, *Canada Baptist Magazine, and Missionary Register* II (1838) 114
128 Picken, *The Canadas* 300–1
129 Samuel Rose to John Rose, 21 Nov. 1833, PAO, Rose Papers
130 Proudfoot Diary, 17, UWO, Proudfoot Papers
131 Brydone, *Narrative* 39
132 Proudfoot Diary, 18–19, 239, UWO, Proudfoot Papers
133 Lower, *Settlement and the Forest Frontier in Eastern Canada* 41
134 Petition of various Bayham inhabitants, 8 Feb. 1833, UCSP, 44/44
135 Leonard, *The Honourable Elijah Leonard – A Memoir* 7
136 Jameson, *Winter Studies and Summer Rambles in Canada* 145
137 *A Concise Description of Canada* 105
138 Jameson, *Winter Studies* 141, 145–6
139 Adam Hope to Robert Hope, Hamilton, 26 Feb. 1837, 4, HPL, Hope Letters
140 TPL, Diary 1838–40 of a soldier in the [34th] regiment, 3
141 PAO, 'A Few Remarks ...,' 1837, 10. Jameson, *Winter Studies* 159. Shirreff, *A Tour* 181
142 J. Algar to Sec. S.P.G., Frome, Somerset, 28 Sept. 1837, from *Church Messenger* of November 1937, Anglican Diocese of Toronto Archives, Canon Allan Notes. *The History of the County of Brant, Ontario* 468–75
143 Rolph, *A Brief Account ... together with a Statistical Account of Upper Canada* 229. PAO, Smith reminiscences, 176
144 Petition to the Bank of Upper Canada, 11 March 1837, UCS, 185/103612
145 See Samuel Rose to John Rose, 21 Nov. 1833, PAO, Rose Papers.
146 Petition to the Bank of Upper Canada, 11 March 1837, UCS, 185/103612
147 Daniel Allan to Dr Burns, London, 1 July 1837, CGCS, 6, no. 173
148 PAO, Macdonald Diary, 11
149 Green to W.J.D. Waddilove, London, 23 Nov. 1837, Waddilove, *The Stewart Missions* 175
150 PAC, Leith Diary, 18
151 Extract of a letter from Skinner, *United Secession Magazine* IV (1836) 187
152 Adam Hope to Robert Hope, Hamilton, 26 Feb. 1837, 3, HPL, Hope Letters
153 Jones, *History of Agriculture in Ontario, 1613–1880* 107

CHAPTER 3

1 Patterson, 'Studies in Elections and Public Opinion in Upper Canada' (PH D diss.), 34–5
2 Talman, 'John Baptist Askin' *DCB* IX, 8
3 See PAO, Abstract Index to Deeds.
4 See *Liberal* (St Thomas), 15 Sept. 1836.
5 Burwell to John Joseph, Port Talbot, 15 Oct. 1836, UCS, 172/93956
6 Talman, 'Askin' 8. Westminster Town Council Minutes, 17, PAO, Municipal Records
7 Sheriff Cameron, 'Old Court House Papers Tell of Early Politics' No. 2, 34, LPL, Local History Scrapbooks
8 Talman, 'Askin' 9
9 Campbell, 'The Settlement of London' 15
10 Wise, 'Upper Canada and the Conservative Tradition,' in *Profiles of a Province* 21–2
11 Landon, '1837 Letter Gives Indication of Alarm ...' No. 37, LPL, Local History Scrapbooks
12 Shirreff, *A Tour through North America* 104
13 Marsh to Absalom Peters, Barton, 21 Sept. 1836 (draft), AHMS
14 PAC, Teeple Diary, 9
15 Clark, *Movements of Political Protest in Canada, 1640–1840* 418
16 *Liberal* (St Thomas), 15 Nov. 1832, 4 April 1833
17 See *St Thomas Journal*, 30 Aug. 1832.
18 *Liberal* (St Thomas), 24 Jan. 1833
19 Ibid. Thomas Talbot to Peter Robinson, Port Talbot, 26 Jan. 1833, private, Coyne, ed., 'The Talbot Papers,' 151
20 For Duncombe's early life see 'A Short Sketch of the Life and Times of Dr. Chas. Duncombe by his eldest daughter Eliza J. Tufford' 18–19, PAC, Duncombe Papers. Cross, 'Charles Duncombe' *DCB* IX, 228. Wilkinson, *Duncombes in America* 32–3, 39
21 Canniff, *The Medical Profession in Upper Canada, 1783–1850* 347
22 Craig, 'John Rolph' *DCB* IX, 683. Patterson, 'Studies in Elections' 64
23 Cross, 'Duncombe' 228. Wilkinson, *Duncombes in America* 44
24 Charles Duncombe to Lt. Col. Rowan, Burford, 6 Aug. 1834, UCS, 144/78510. Duncombe to R.B. Sullivan, Burford, 16 May 1837, PAO, Crown Lands Correspondence, 16. James McMillan to S.B. Harrison, Brantford, 27 Aug. 1842, PAO, Brantford Township Papers, folder for concessions 4 and 5. Affidavit of Charles Duncombe, Brantford, 10 June 1836, PAC, Executive Council Petitions, 'T' Bundle 22, 1839–41, 9f

261 Notes to pp. 53–8

25 *The History of the County of Brant, Ontario* 379
26 Duncombe to Lt Col Rowan, Burford, 6 Aug. 1834, UCS, 144/78510
27 Canniff, *The Medical Profession in Upper Canada* 79, 347
28 Duncombe to Lt Col Rowan, Burford, 6 Aug. 1834, UCS, 144/78510
29 Letter of Fitzgibbon, Toronto, 6 Nov. 1837, *London Gazette*, 18 Nov. 1837. Robertson, *The History of Freemasonry in Canada* I, 1159
30 Petition of Charles Duncombe to Glenelg, n.d., PAC, Executive Council Petitions, 'D' Bundle 19, 1832–5, 46f-i
31 Cross, 'Duncombe' 229
32 Aitchison, 'Development of Local Government in Upper Canada, 1783–1850' (PH D diss.) II, 460. *History of the County of Middlesex, Canada* 195. Seaborn, *The March of Medicine in Western Ontario* 73. 'A Short Sketch ... by ... Eliza J. Tufford,' 21, PAC, Duncombe Papers
33 Aitken, *The Welland Canal Company* 122
34 Cross, 'Duncombe' 229
35 *Liberal* (St Thomas), 13 Dec. 1832
36 *Sun*, UCS, 118/66250
37 Cross, 'Duncombe' 229. *Liberal* (St Thomas), 3 Oct. 1833
38 Address to the Electors of Oxford, PAC, Duncombe Papers
39 Petition of Charles Duncombe to Glenelg, n.d., PAC, Executive Council Petitions, 'D' Bundle 19, 1832–5, 46f–i
40 A Canadian to the Colonial Secretary, 24 Aug. 1836 [Ryerson] *The Affairs of the Canadas* 57
41 *Liberal* (St Thomas), 29 Jan. 1835
42 Ibid. 4 Feb. 1836
43 Charles Duncombe to Elijah Duncombe, Westminster, 25 Dec. 1835 (typescript), LPL, Seaborn Collection, Diaries, 1135
44 PAC, Executive Council Minute Books, Book R, 195–7. Petition of Charles Duncombe to Glenelg, n.d., PAC, Executive Council Petitions, 'D' Bundle 19, 1832–5, 46f–i
45 Canniff, *The Medical Profession in Upper Canada* 84
46 Robertson, *The History of Freemasonry in Canada* II, 187–9. Cross, 'Duncombe' 229
47 Cross, 'Duncombe' 229–30
48 Baehre, 'Origins of the Penitentiary System in Upper Canada,' 197
49 Aitchison, 'Development of Local Government' II, 736
50 Letters from Campbell, Elizabethtown, 3 May 1836, CGCS, 6, no. 52
51 *Correspondent and Advocate* (Toronto), 28 March 1836, MLC, item 2877
52 See *Liberal* (St Thomas), 25 Feb. 1836.
53 Simpson McCall to John Joseph, Vittoria, 2 April 1836, UCS, 165/89812. Isaac Draper and John Burwell to Joseph, Port Burwell, 21 April 1836,

UCS, 202/112122–32. Mahlon Burwell to John Strachan, 12 April 1836, PAO, Strachan Papers
54 Burn to ———, Dereham, 19 July 1838, UCS, 199/110452–3
55 Landon, 'The Common Man in the Era of the Rebellion in Upper Canada,' 88
56 Ross to Sir F.B. Head, St Thomas, 22 June 1836, UCS, 167/91476–9. J.B. Askin to J. Joseph, London, 22 Sept. 1836, UCS, 172/93964
57 Macdonell, *A Sketch of ... Alexander Macdonell* 38–9
58 Letter of Thomas Rolph to the editor, *Hamilton Gazette*, 18 Jan. 1837
59 John Ryerson to Egerton Ryerson, Toronto, 25 Sept. 1836, UCA, Ryerson Papers. Clark, *Church and Sect in Canada* 269. Sissons, *Egerton Ryerson* I, 346–7
60 Lucas, ed., *Lord Durham's Report* II, 157–8
61 *The Speech of the Hon. John Rolph* 37–8
62 Evans to the Bishop of Quebec, 6 July 1836, Waddilove, *The Stewart Missions* 152
63 Proceedings of St Thomas meeting, 6 May 1836, UCS, 166/90541. John Burwell to John Joseph, Port Burwell, 11 May 1836, UCS, 166/90628. Loyal Address from Woodstock, 14 May 1836, UCS, 166/90678
64 Ingersoll to John Joseph, Ingersoll, 4 June 1836, UCS, 167/91098
65 Askin to Joseph, London, 6 June 1838, UCS, 167/91110
66 Henry Becher to John Harris, 21 June (1836), 1–2 (typescript), Robin Harris, Harris Papers
67 Patterson, 'Studies in Elections' 125–6
68 Return of the Patents, CO 42, 440/53–64
69 Burwell to Joseph, Port Talbot, 11 June 1836, Confidential, UCS, 167/91306–7
70 Return of the Patents, CO 42, 440/53–64
71 Young to Robinson, Hamilton, 29 June 1836, PAO, Township Papers, Brantford town, folder S–Y
72 Return of the Patents, CO 42, 440/64
73 Gates, *Land Policies* 188
74 UWO, Woodman Diary and Letters, 4 (typescript)
75 Talbot to J.B. Robinson, 10 July 1836, Careless, ed., 'Letters from Thomas Talbot to John Beverley Robinson' 29
76 Lucas, ed., *Lord Durham's Report* II, 181
77 The election returns can be found in CO 42, 440/96–7.
78 MLC, item 404A
79 Petition of Duncombe, CO 42, 437/31–40
80 Head to Glenelg, Toronto, 16 July 1836, Head, *A Narrative*, ed. Wise, 61–2

263 Notes to pp. 63–7

81 Duncombe to Glenelg, 20 Sept. 1836, CO 42, 440/4
82 Duncombe to Baldwin, Charing Cross, 15 Sept. 1836, TPL, Robert Baldwin Papers, Section I
83 Petition of Duncombe to Glenelg, PAC, Executive Council Petitions, 'D' Bundle 19, 1832–5, 46f–i
84 James Stephen to Duncombe, Downing Street, 21 Sept. 1836, PAC, Executive Council Petitions, 'D' Bundle 19, 1832–5, 46ppp-aaaa. The subsequent history of this dispute is cloudy, but Duncombe was never granted any patents for any lands in Brantford township where the Mallory lands lay.
85 A copy of the assembly's report can be found in CO 42, 437/31–40
86 Cross, 'Duncombe' 230
87 *The Speech of the Hon. John Rolph* 4–10
88 John Burwell to John Joseph, Port Burwell, 18 June 1836, UCS, 167/91439. Burwell to Joseph, Port Burwell, 18 July 1836, UCS, 168/91975–7. J.B. Askin to Joseph, London, 9 Nov. 1836, UCS, 172/93967. Askin to Joseph, London, 21 Nov. 1836, Confidential, UCS, 172/94188. John Burwell to Joseph, Port Burwell, 31 Oct. 1836, UCS, 171/93777–8
89 Adam Hope to Robert Hope, Hamilton, 26 Feb. 1837, 3, HPL, Hope Letters
90 Letter from Proudfoot, London, 1 Jan. 1838, *Quarterly Record of the Missions in Connexion with the United Secession Church* II (1838) 211
91 Robinson, 'A Study of Agriculture in Upper Canada between 1830 and 1850' (Master's thesis), 147, 215
92 *Liberal, St Catharines Journal*, 20 July 1837
93 Adam Hope to Robert Hope, Hamilton, 26 Feb. 1837, 3, HPL, Hope Letters
94 UWO, Wood Diary, 16 and 17 Aug. 1837, 19. Wood turned out with the Woodhouse loyalists to suppress the revolt.
95 Daniel Allan to Dr Burns, London, 1 July 1837, CGCS, 6, no. 173
96 See Petition of various inhabitants of Hamilton to Sir F.B. Head (n.d.), PAC, Petitions and Addresses, 9.
97 W.A. Howard to John A. Macdonald, Belleville, 16 June 1837, UCS, 176/97164
98 Proudfoot Diary, 301, UWO, Proudfoot Papers
99 Rudé, *The Crowd in History* 21–2, 35–7
100 Darvall, *Popular Disturbances and Public Order in Regency England* 6
101 Hobsbawm and Rudé, *Captain Swing* 30–52, 72–86, 195. Rudé, *The Crowd* 182
102 See *Constitution* (Toronto), 5 July 1837.
103 Ibid. 19 July 1837
104 Ibid. 2 Aug. 1837

105 *Liberal*, 30 Aug. 1837
106 Aitchison, 'Development of Local Government' I, 209
107 Statement of fees due Township and Parish Officers in the London District, 1837, UWO, Harris Family Papers, John Harris. This document provides the names of the district's clerks, collectors, and assessors.
108 Petition of Finlay Malcolm, Niagara, 10 May 1796, Executive Council Petitions, 'M' Bundle 2, 1795–6, 122
109 Patterson, 'Studies in Elections' 15–16
110 Muir, *The Early Political and Military History of Burford* 264
111 *Colonial Advocate, Liberal* (St Thomas), 3 Oct. 1833
112 Petition of Samantha Malcolm, 23 Jan. 1840, UCSP, 52/229
113 Waldie, 'Malcolm Folk Made Presence Felt in Brant,' *London Free Press*, 1 July 1939
114 PAO, John Arthur Tidey Memoranda. A survey Malcolm ran in East Oxford also caused discontent there.
115 Burwell to Z. Mudge, Port Talbot, 13 June 1831, UCS, 208/70876
116 Askin to John Joseph, London, Confidential, UCS, 177/97746
117 *Constitution* (Toronto), 11 Jan. 1837
118 Ibid. 13 Sept. 1837
119 *Patriot* (Toronto), 6 Oct. 1837
120 *Liberal, Constitution* (Toronto), 27 Sept. 1837
121 Ibid.
122 *London Gazette, Patriot* (Toronto), 6 Oct. 1837
123 *Liberal, Constitution* (Toronto), 4 Oct. 1837. Three Reformers were arrested for assaulting McKenny and Medcalf. True bills were found against them and they were released on bail prior to the revolt. It appears that the matter was dropped after the rebellion.
124 *Liberal, Constitution* (Toronto), 18 Oct. 1837
125 *Liberal, Constitution* (Toronto), 2 Aug. 1837
126 Grieve to Talbot, London, Sept. 1837, Gray, ed., 'The Letters of John Talbot' 146
127 Examination of Shubal Nicholls, 19 Jan. 1838, RLDM, I/92. Examination of Calvin Birch, 23 Jan. 1838, RLDM, I/101
128 *London Gazette, Patriot* (Toronto), 13 Oct. 1837
129 *Liberal*, MLC, item 479f
130 *London Gazette, Patriot* (Toronto), 13 Oct. 1837
131 *Hamilton Gazette*, 11 Oct. 1837
132 *Liberal*, MLC, item 479f
133 *Constitution* (Toronto), 25 Oct. 1837
134 *Quarterly Record of the ... United Secession Church* II (1838) 211

265 Notes to pp. 72–9

135 *Constitution* (Toronto), 25 Oct. 1837
136 *London Gazette*, 18 Oct. 1837
137 *Liberal*, MLC, item 2388
138 *Patriot* (Toronto), 3 Nov. 1837
139 John Joseph to J.B. Askin et al., 1 Nov. 1837 (copy), *Liberal*, MLC, item 2388
140 Askin to John Joseph, London, 12 Nov. 1837, NCPSO, 8, file 1088
141 Latimer to John Talbot, 5 Nov. 1837, RLDM, II
142 *Constitution* (Toronto), 15 Nov. 1837
143 See the journals of the assembly for daily attendance.
144 John George Bridges to John Joseph, London, 4 Sept. 1837, NCPSO, 7, file 899
145 Duncombe to [Davis], 24 Oct. 1837, Muir, *The Early Political and Military History of Burford* 157–8
146 *Constitution* (Toronto), 15 Nov. 1837
147 Deposition of Cyrus Moore, 7 March 1838, UCS, 187/104603
148 *Constitution* (Toronto), 15 Nov. 1837
149 Graham to John Joseph, North Oxford, 13 Nov. 1837, NCPSO, 8, file 1093
150 *Liberal* (St Thomas), 2 Nov. 1837
151 Resolutions and note intended for publication in the *Liberal*, UCS, 179/98935–58
152 Philip Graham to John Joseph, North Oxford, 13 Nov. 1837, NCPSO, 8, file 1092
153 *Liberal*, MLC, item 479f
154 *London Gazette*, 18 Nov. 1837
155 Deposition of John McKenzie, n.d., RLDM, II
156 List of members of St Thomas political union, UCS, 179/98854–5
157 *Constitution* (Toronto), 25 Oct. 1837
158 Examination of Joseph Seabrook, 26 Dec. 1837, RLDM, I/13
159 Deposition of Alvaro Ladd, 27 Dec. 1837, RLDM, II
160 Deposition of Joseph Seabrook, n.d., RLDM, II
161 Examination of David Johnston, 26 Dec. 1837, RLDM, I/16. Examination of Gideon Tiffany, 27 Dec. 1837, RLDM, I/30
162 Evidence of Joseph Seabrook, UCS, 204/112788–9
163 See Guillet, *The Lives and Times of the Patriots* 10.
164 Parker to Henry Lasker, 6 Nov. 1837, CO 42, 467/10
165 *Constitution* (Toronto), 6 Dec. 1837. *Hamilton Gazette*, 28 Nov. 1837
166 Deposition of John S. McCollom, 29 Dec. 1837, UCS, 185/103594. Deposition of Henry Brinton, 31 Dec. 1837, UCS, 185/103599
167 *St Catharines Journal*, 16 Nov. 1837

168 Deposition of Solomon Camp, 26 Feb. 1838, AGOC, 36
169 *Constitution* (Toronto), 18 Oct. 1837
170 Talbot to Mackenzie, St Thomas, 21 Nov. 1837, UCS, 179/98852
171 Colborne to Sir F.B. Head, Sorel, 6 Nov. 1837, MLB, 1272/26–7
172 A.K. McKenzie to W.L. Mackenzie, Lockport, 25 April 1838, private, PAO, Lindsey Collection, Mackenzie Correspondence
173 Petition of Duncombe to Sir Charles Metcalfe [1843] (photostat), PAO, Dent Scrapbook
174 W.L. Mackenzie, 'Account of the Rebellion near Toronto' in a letter to the *Jeffersonian*, PAC, Rebellion Exiles
175 A.K. McKenzie to W.L. Mackenzie, Lockport, 25 April 1838, private, PAO, Lindsey Collection, Mackenzie Correspondence
176 Draper's memorandum on the rebellion, 28 May 1838, CO 42, 447/133–4. Despite the available evidence, Draper still could not bring himself to believe that the leaders of the two revolts were not 'in correspondence with each other.'
177 Askin to John Joseph, London, 12 Nov. 1837, NCPSO, 8, file 1088
178 Adam Hope to Robert Hope, St Thomas, 24 Dec. 1837, 6, HPL, Hope Letters

CHAPTER 4

1 C.A. Hagerman to John Joseph, 30 Nov. 1837, UCS, 179/98925
2 Militia General Order, 4 Dec. 1837, CO 42, 439/428
3 'Sullivan's Report on the State of the Province 1838,' Sanderson, ed., *The Arthur Papers* I, 170
4 Baskerville, 'Sir Allan Napier MacNab,' *DCB* IX 519–22
5 Deposition of Thomas Chase Patrick, 3 March 1838, UCS, 187/104411
6 Proudfoot Diary, 302, UWO, Proudfoot Papers
7 Catharine R. Merritt to Jediah Prendergast, St Catharines, 8 Dec. 1837, PAC, Merritt Papers, Correspondence W.H. Merritt, 13/002031
8 Proudfoot Diary, 302, UWO, Proudfoot Papers
9 Deposition of Duncan Cameron, n.d., UCS, 195/108709–10
10 John Tufford to ———, n.d., UCS, 205/113448. For other evidence that Duncombe felt personally threatened see Deposition of John Kelly, 26 Jan. 1838, UCS, 195/108699.
11 Examination of John Tidey, 9 Feb. 1838, RLDM, I/126
12 Examination of Daniel Bedford, 26 Jan. 1838, RLDM, I/121
13 Petition of John Tidey, London Gaol, 9 March 1838, UCS, 203/112555–6
14 Petition of Paul Bedford, 19 March 1838, UCS, 194/107986

Notes to pp. 86–9

15 Deposition of Joseph J. Lancaster, 18 Dec. 1837, RLDM, II. John Haycock to John Joseph, Ingersoll, 11 Dec. 1837, NCPSO, 9, file 1172
16 Deposition of Joseph J. Lancaster, 20 Dec. 1837, *Appendix to the Journal of the House of Assembly*, 1837–8, 404–5
17 Report of J.B. Macaulay, Toronto, 6 April 1838, CO 42, 447/239
18 Requisition Order of Norwich Committee, 13 Dec. 1837, PAO, MacNab Papers. George W. Whitehead to A.N. MacNab, 13 Dec. 1837, UCS, 180/99169
19 Deposition of Joseph J. Lancaster, 18 Dec. 1837, RLDM, II
20 John Treffry to George Treffry, Summerville, 24 June 1838, UWO, Treffry Letters
21 Ibid.
22 Deposition of Lyman Chapin, 4 March 1838, UCS, 193/107829
23 Deposition of Peter Coon, 17 Dec. 1837, in Guillet, *The Lives and Times of the Patriots* 250
24 Guillet, *Lives and Times* 48
25 Deposition of James Oswald, 18 Dec. 1837, *Appendix to the Journal of the House of Assembly*, 1837–8, 405
26 Deposition of Duncan Cameron, n.d., UCS, 195/108709–10
27 Deposition of Joseph N. Smith, 7 March 1838, UCS, 187/104607. Deposition of Mahlon Roberts, 12 March 1838, UCS, 188/104819
28 Deposition of Duncan McDermid, 14 Dec. 1837, UCS, 187/104471
29 Evidence of Book, UCS, 189/105540
30 Deposition of Duncan McDermid, 14 Dec. 1837, UCS, 187/104471
31 Evidence of Richard Ransom Strobridge, UCS, 187/104505
32 Deposition of Joseph N. Smith, 7 March 1838, UCS, 187/104507
33 Deposition of Robert Cook, 25 Dec. 1837, UCS, 193/107632. Deposition of Thomas W. Clark, 22 Dec. 1837, UCS, 187/104623
34 Deposition of Baldwin Walker, 2 [8?] Dec. 1837, UCS, 181/99805. Deposition of Thomas W. Clark, 22 Dec. 1837, UCS, 187/104623
35 Deposition of Peter Coon, 17 Dec. 1837, in Guillet, *Lives and Times* 249
36 Copy of a letter of a militia officer, Burford, 15 Dec. 1837, *Patriot* (Toronto), 15 Dec. 1837
37 Deposition of Moore, n.d., UCS, 187/104605
38 Deposition of Finlay Malcolm, 23 Dec. 1837, RLDM, II. Deposition of George Hill, 28 Dec. 1837, RLDM, II
39 Evidence of Doyle McKenny, UCS, 193/107352–3
40 Deposition of William Darrow, n.d., UCS, 181/99991
41 Examination of Isaac Moore, 12 Jan. 1838, RLDM, I/73. Deposition of Stephen Secord, 19 Dec. 1837, RLDM, II

42 Deposition of Samuel Sands, 21 Dec. 1837, RLDM, II
43 Deposition of William Storey [27?] Dec. 1837, RLDM, II
44 Evidence of William A. Anderson, CO 42, 447/261–2. It may be that a second and smaller group also left Bayham for Oakland.
45 Deposition of Stevens Newell, 21 Dec. 1837, UCS, 181/99979
46 John Burn to ———, Dereham, 19 July 1838, UCS, 199/110454
47 Statement of John Hawk in Dent, *The Story of the Upper Canadian Rebellion* II, 41n. *The History of the County of Brant* 441
48 John Burwell to R.S. Jameson, Port Burwell, 8 Jan. 1838, UCS, 184/102968
49 Deposition of Duncan Wilson, 19 Jan. 1838, UCS, 196/109205–6. Deposition of Wilson, 23 Jan. 1838, UCS, 196/109200–1
50 Examination of Lewis Norton, 26 Jan. 1838, RLDM, I/112. Deposition of Levi Heaton, 20 Dec. 1837, RLDM, II
51 Deposition of Levi Heaton, 20 Dec. 1837, RLDM, II. Deposition of Jonathan Steele, 20 Dec. 1837, RLDM, II. One rebel said that Switzer assured the rebels that Toronto would fall to Mackenzie and that the governor had already sent out a flag of truce and was prepared to capitulate. Examination of Andrew McLure, 1 Jan. 1838, PAC, RLDM, I/39. The flag incident occurred on 5 Dec.; thus Switzer must have left after that date.
52 Deposition of Hosea Van Potter, 23 Dec. 1837, RLDM, II. Examination of Anson Gould, 1 Feb. 1838, RLDM, I/125. Deposition of Lyman Davis, 28 Dec. 1837, UCS, 181/100013
53 Adam Hope to Robert Hope, St Thomas, 24 Dec. 1837, 1, HPL, Hope Letters
54 Deposition of Jonathan Steele, 20 Dec. 1837, RLDM, II. Examination of Charles Conrad, 11 Jan. 1838, RLDM, I/69
55 Deposition of John Johnson, 18 Dec. 1837, UCS, 205/113453
56 John Burwell to R.S. Jameson, Port Burwell, 8 Jan. 1838, UCS, 184/102968
57 Deposition of Elisha Hall, 18 Dec. 1837, UCS, 180/99432
58 Examination of Mark Hagel, 29 Dec. 1837, RLDM, I/32
59 Deposition of Myre Wethy, 15 March 1838, RLDM, II
60 Deposition of Thomas Putnam, 20 Dec. 1837, UCS, 180/99607. Deposition of Finlay McFee, 20 Dec. 1837, UCS, 180/99607
61 Deposition of John Grieve, 16 Feb. 1838, UCS, 192/106740. Deposition of Amos Wheeler, 21 April 1838, UCS, 192/106724–5
62 Hall to Charles Duncombe, Oxford, 6 Dec. 1837 (typescript), LPL, Seaborn Collection, Medical Doctors, 891R
63 John Haycock to John Joseph, Ingersoll, 11 Dec. 1837, NCPSO, 9, item 1172
64 Deposition of Charles Travers, 29 Dec. 1837, RLDM, I/35. Two small groups may have left the West Oxford area for Oakland, Teeple's being one.

Notes to pp. 93–7

65 Deposition of William Stockton, 16 Dec. 1837, UCS, 180/99353. Deposition of John Dumon, 16 Dec. 1837, UCS, 180/99355
66 Deposition of Samuel Nevers, 15 Dec. 1837, UCS, 200/110864
67 Deposition of Alexander Sprague, 18 Dec. 1837, UCS, 187/104487
68 Deposition of Henry Herskins, 16 Dec. 1837, UCS, 180/99336
69 Deposition of Winegarden, 18 Dec. 1837, UCS, 180/99464
70 Deposition of Grigg, 16 Dec. 1837, UCS, 200/110848
71 Head to Glenelg, 13 Dec. 1837, CO 42, 439/459
72 Deposition of Peter Coon, 17 Dec. 1837, in Guillet, *Lives and Times* 250
73 Deposition of William Storey, 2 [7?] Dec. 1837, RLDM, II
74 Deposition of Marlatt, 16 Dec. 1837, UCS, 180/99370
75 AGO, Toronto, 7 Dec. 1837, no. 2, PAC, Militia General Orders, 5
76 Evidence of Wallace, UCSP, 45/148–9
77 Racey to Coffin, Brantford, 8 Dec. 1837, AGOC, 34
78 Deposition of Perley, 10 Dec. 1837, NCPSO, 9, file 1170
79 Samuel Ryckman to Land et al., 10 Dec. 1837, UCS, 180/99073
80 Edmund Ritchie to Alexander Hamilton, 7 Dec. 1837, PAC, Hamilton Papers, 65, 150
81 McKenny to Burwell, Malahide, 9 Dec. 1837, AGOC, 34
82 Burwell to Joseph, Port Burwell, 10 Dec. 1837, AGOC, 34
83 McKenny to Ermatinger, Malahide, 11 Dec. 1837, Ermatinger, *The Talbot Régime* 357
84 Affadavit of William Murphy et al., UWO, Harris Family Papers, John Harris, Rebellion Losses Papers, 7, no. 271
85 Regimental Order of the Second Middlesex, 7 Jan. 1839, UCS, 214/117209. Afterwards Lewis Norton claimed erroneously that Anderson's party had been attacked crossing the bridge at Otter Creek. Norton, *Life and Adventures of Col. L.A. Norton* 32
86 List of Burwell's volunteers, AGOC, 36
87 List of Medcalf's volunteers, AGOC, 38
88 Deposition of John Caswell, n.d., 190/106126. Evidence of John Burwell, CO 42, 447/249–50
89 Deposition of Page, 16 Dec. 1837, UCS, 181/99924. Examination of Page, 6 Jan. 1838, RLDM, I/60–1
90 Deposition of Davis, 28 Dec. 1836, UCS, 181/100014
91 Deposition of Edward Carman, 2 Jan. 1838, RLDM, II
92 Deposition of Lewis Burwell, 22 Jan. 1838, UCS, 187/104400. Complaints were laid against Clark in January 1838 for having been in league with the rebels. He fled the province and, embittered by these accusations, joined the 'patriots.'

270 Notes to pp. 97–101

93 UWO, Wood Diary, 22
94 Duncan Campbell to [James?] Richardson, Simcoe, 13 Dec. 1837, UCS, 180/99167
95 Evans to Sir George Arthur, 14 April 1838, UCS, 204/112711
96 *Upper Canada Gazette* (Toronto), 7 Dec. 1837
97 Petition of John Van Arnam, 4 Jan. 1839, UCSP, 75/97–8
98 MacNab to Sir F.B. Head, Scotland, 14 Dec. 1837, *Patriot* (Toronto), 22 Dec. 1837. Other sources gave other figures for the size of MacNab's force.
99 Duncombe reportedly sent a dispatch to Toronto on 8 December. Deposition of James Kinney, 21 Dec. 1837, RLDM, II. What became of this message or the messenger is not known.
100 Amelia Harris to Henry Becher, 14 Dec. 1837, UWO, Harris Family Papers
101 Ranald McKinnon to Marcus Blair, Oneda Mills, 14 Dec. 1837, HPL, Land Papers, 142–3
102 Deposition of Joseph J. Lancaster, 18 Dec. 1837, RLDM, II
103 Deposition of William Storey, 27 Dec. 1837, RLDM, II. George W. Whitehead to A.N. MacNab, Brantford, 13 Dec. 1837, UCS, 180/99169. Deposition of A. Vanduzen, 17 Dec. 1837, UCS, 180/103589. Deposition of Preserved Thompson, 17 Dec. 1837, UCS, 180/99402
104 Deposition of Finlay Malcolm, 23 Dec. 1837, RLDM, II. Deposition of William Storey, 2 [7?] Dec. 1837, RLDM, II
105 Deposition of Augustus Chaple, 29 Dec. 1837, RLDM, II
106 Deposition of Malcolm, 23 Dec. 1837, RLDM, II
107 Deposition of Joseph J. Lancaster, 18 Dec. 1837, RLDM, II
108 MacNab to Sir F.B. Head, Scotland, 14 Dec. 1837, *Patriot* (Toronto), 22 Dec. 1837
109 Adam Hope to Robert Hope, St Thomas, 24 Dec. 1837, 4, HPL, Hope Letters
110 Letter of 17 Dec. 1837 to the *Rochester Democrat*, MLC, item 6017
111 John Joseph to W.J. Kerr, 19 Dec. 1837, L-G LB, 3, no. 78
112 Ranald McKinnon to Marcus Blair, Oneda Mills, 14 Dec. 1837, HPL, Land Papers, 143. J.B. Askin to Jonas Jones, London, 22 Dec. 1837, Sanderson, ed., *The Arthur Papers* I, 35–6
113 Deposition of John Dumon, 16 Dec. 1837, UCS, 180/99355
114 Deposition of Marcus Holmes, 21 Dec. 1837, RLDM, II. Deposition of William Niles, 10 Jan. 1838, RLDM, II. Deposition of David O. Marsh, 15 Jan. 1838, RLDM, II. Deposition of Joshua Putnam, 17 Jan. 1838, RLDM, II
115 Askin to Jonas Jones, London, 22 Dec. 1837, Sanderson, ed., *The Arthur Papers* I, 35–6

Notes to pp. 101-4

116 MacNab to Col Halkett, Scotland, 15 Dec. 1837, *Patriot* (Toronto), 22 Dec. 1837
117 Petition of Lossing, 12 July 1838, UCSP, 45/138
118 See Landon, 'The Duncombe Uprising of 1837 and Some of Its Consequences' 86–7; Guillet, *Lives and Times* 50–1, 58.
119 Letter to the *Rochester Democrat*, Brantford, 17 Dec. 1837, *Palladium ... Extra* (Toronto), 8 Jan. 1838. Several excerpted versions of this letter exist.
120 Adam Hope to Robert Hope, St Thomas, 24 Dec. 1837, 4, HPL, Hope Letters. Hope provides an excellent account of all the activities of the Yarmouth volunteers.
121 John Haycock to John Joseph, Ingersoll, 11 Dec. 1837, NCPSO, 9, file 1172
122 P.B. de Blaquiere to A.N. MacNab, Norwich, 15 Dec. 1837, UCS, 180/99384–6
123 Petition of 103 Norwich inhabitants, *Patriot* (Toronto), 22 Dec. 1837
124 MacNab to ———, Hamilton, 6 Aug. 1838, UCSP, 45/144, 144B
125 MacNab to ———, Sodom, 18 Dec. 1837, *Patriot* (Toronto), 22 Dec. 1837. MacNab asserted that the rebels had assembled at Sodom on the seventeenth.
126 MacNab to Jonas Jones, Sodom, 18 Dec. 1837, *Extra to the Hamilton Gazette*, 2 Jan. 1838
127 See J.W. Wilson to John Joseph, Toronto, 14 June 1838, UCS, 195/108825.
128 *Upper Canada Gazette* (Toronto), 14 Dec. 1837
129 Jonas Jones to ———, Toronto, 14 Dec. 1837, L-G LB, 3, no. 39
130 John Joseph to MacNab, 18 Dec. 1837, *Patriot* (Toronto), 22 Dec. 1837. Henceforth, MacNab in his dealings with captives paid strict attention to the general principles established by Head's instructions.
131 MacNab to Jonas Jones, Sodom, 18 Dec. 1837, *Extra to the Hamilton Gazette*, 2 Jan. 1838
132 Young, *Reminiscences of the Early History of Galt and the Settlement of Dumfries* 155
133 Colin McNeilledge Diaries, 19 Dec. 1837, PAC, Norfolk Historical Society Papers
134 Adam Hope to Robert Hope, St Thomas, 24 Dec. 1837, 5, HPL, Hope Letters
135 Ibid.
136 J.B. Askin to Jonas Jones, London, 22 Dec. 1837, Sanderson, ed., *The Arthur Papers* I, 36
137 Evidence of Philo Bennett, CO 42, 447/277–8
138 Askin to Jonas Jones, London, 22 Dec. 1837, Sanderson, ed., *The Arthur Papers* I, 35

272 Notes to pp. 105–111

139 Edward Ermatinger to John Joseph, St Thomas, 16 Dec. 1837, NCPSO, 9, file 1211. Hamilton to J.B. Askin, London, 13 Dec. 1837, UCS, 180/99181
140 Deposition of John Burgess, 18 Dec. 1837, UCS, 180/99468
141 Petition of Nathaniel Deo, n.d., RLDM, II
142 Deposition of Alvaro Ladd, 27 Dec. 1837, RLDM, II. Schedule of London Prisoners, UCS, 191/106678
143 Deposition of Joseph Hendershot, 20 Dec. 1837, RLDM, II. Deposition of James Edwards, 22 Dec. 1837, RLDM, II. Deposition of Richard Neale, 22 Dec. 1837, RLDM, II. Deposition of Adam Hatelie, 22 Dec. 1837, RLDM, II. Deposition of William Gardiner, 23 Dec. 1837, RLDM, II
144 Head to MacNab, 18 Dec. 1837, PAO, MacNab Papers. This letter also authorized MacNab to allow some of his men to return home and bore the news of Navy Island.
145 Petition of John Wilson, Saltfleet, 15 April 1838, UCS, 191/106343
146 Burwell to James Fitzgibbon, private, Port Talbot, 18 Dec. 1837, AGOC, 34
147 Proclamation of 16 Dec. 1837, CO 42, 439/430
148 Draper's memorandum on the rebellion, 28 May 1838, CO 42, 447/142, 147

CHAPTER 5

1 Askin to John Joseph, London, 22 Dec. 1837, UCS, 180/99759
2 Deposition of John George Bridges, 2 Jan. 1838, RLDM, II. Deposition of Robert Mackey, 2 Jan. 1838, RLDM, II
3 J.B. Askin to James Hamilton, London, 20 Dec. 1837, TPL, Hamilton Papers
4 Draper's memorandum on the rebellion, 28 May 1838, CO 42, 447/136
5 [W.H. Draper?] to [John Joseph?], Hamilton, 11 March 1838, UCS, 188/104814
6 Deposition of Robert Armstrong, 11 Dec. 1837, UCS, 187/104647
7 Deposition of William Armstrong, n.d., UCS, 186/103777. Deposition of Robert Grindall, 28 Dec. 1837, UCS, 186/103777
8 Deposition of Duncan McPhederain, 13 Dec. 1837, UCS, 180/99239–40
9 Duncan Wilson to the Toronto *Mirror*, Yarmouth, 24 Jan. 1840, MLC, item 3006
10 Recognizance of Bela Shaw, 26 Dec. 1837, UCS, 181/99918
11 See appendix 1.
12 See appendix 2.
13 Recognizance of Joseph Bowes et al., 17 Dec. 1837, UCS, 180/99397–8
14 Schedule of prisoners in London jail, UCS, 181/99857

Notes to pp. 111–14

15 'List of prisoners as per Comm*r* Book,' RLDM, II
16 Deposition of William Storey, 27 Dec. 1837, RLDM, II
17 K.G. Kirbury to John Prince, Bayham, 17 July 1838, UCS, 199/110370
18 Philip Hodgkinson to Mahlon Burwell, Aylmer, 18 July 1838, UCS, 199/110368
19 Norton, *Life and Adventures of Col. L.A. Norton* 38
20 This does not include John Tidey, jailed on 17 February.
21 This does not include Charles Tilden, jailed on 15 February.
22 'Reminiscences by Judge William Elliott' 26
23 PAO, Municipal Records, London District Court of Quarter Sessions, 65, 14 Jan. 1837, 14 July 1837
24 Hamilton to Mahlon Burwell, 27 Oct. 1837, *Constitution* (Toronto), 22 Nov. 1837
25 John Grieve to his wife, 22 March 1838, Miller, ed., 'The Letters of Rebels and Loyalists' 72–3
26 Entry of 6 Jan. 1838, RLDM, I/54
27 See appendix 1.
28 See appendix 2.
29 See appendix 8.
30 Thomas Headman, Patrick Malada, Alexander Sumner
31 David Curtis, William Lymburner, David D. Wilson
32 J.B. Askin to Allan [MacNab?], 9 Feb. 1838, RLDM, II
33 Matthew Berry, Sobiske Brown, Augustus Chaple, Levi Heaton, John James Jolly, Joseph Lancaster, George Ribble, William Storey, Charles Conrad, Jacob Esmond. Brown fled the province and did not testify at the spring trials.
34 Deposition of Riley, n.d., RLDM, II. Mire Wethy also indicated his willingness to be a Crown witness, but he was not granted bail.
35 Petition of Travers, 30 Jan. 1838, UCS, 185/103643
36 Examination of Emmons, 4 Jan. 1838, RLDM, I/49
37 Schedule of those proceeded against for treason, 20 April 1843, PAC, State Book B, 368
38 Examination of Charles Scrivener, 26 Jan. 1838, RLDM, I/119
39 William Jarvis to Lt Col Rowan, Hamilton, 31 Aug. 1835, UCS, 156/85898
40 Report of Duncan Campbell, 31 Dec. 1837, HPL, Land Papers, 3068–70
41 See the various requisitions in the Land Papers.
42 MLC, item 453
43 Malcolm Brown, Peter Coon, John Heap, John Johnson, Dudley Newton, Abraham Vanduzen. It is not certain that Brown and Newton were, in fact, questioned at Hamilton.

44 Petition of Stephen Smith, n.d., UCS, 194/108091
45 Petition of Henry Goff, Pelham, 16 June 1838, UCS, 196/109138
46 Ephraim Cook, Thomas Sirpell, Garry V. DeLong, John Van Arnam. The last two fled.
47 *Patriot* (Toronto), 22 Dec. 1837
48 J.B. Askin to John Douglas, London, 27 Dec. 1837, TPL, Hamilton Papers
49 Henry Becher to Amelia Harris, Chippawa, 6 Jan. 1838 (typescript), Robin Harris, Harris Papers
50 Martyn, 'Upper Canada and Border Incidents, 1837–38' (Master's thesis), 104. Chisholm, *Annals of Canada for 1837–38* 64
51 Adam Hope to Robert Hope, St Thomas, 24 Dec. 1837, 7, Hamilton, Hope Letters. Mahlon Burwell to John Joseph, Port Talbot, 30 Dec. 1837, UCS, 181/100117–8
52 Talbot to Hugh O'Brien, 14 Jan. 1837 [1838], RLDM, II
53 John Prince et al. to Sir George Arthur, Toronto, 1 April 1838, NCPSO, 10, file 1370
54 *Scotsman* (Toronto), 8 Feb. 1838. On 15 February the *Scotsman* became the *British Colonist*.
55 Jameson, *Winter Studies and Summer Rambles* 237
56 Thomas Radcliffe to ———, Amherstburg, 9 Jan. 1838, UCS, 184/102987–8. J.B. Robinson to Sir John Colborne, Toronto, 16 Jan. 1838, PAC, Colborne Papers, 13/003701. Wm. H. Draper to Sir John Colborne, Toronto, 16 Jan. 1838, PAC, Colborne Papers, 13/003704
57 John Prince to the Attorney General, Park Farm, 3 Aug. 1838, UCS, 201/111098
58 Charles Hagerman to Sir John Colborne, Toronto, 13 Jan. 1838, PAC, Colborne Papers, 13/003618
59 J.B. Askin to John Douglas, London, 16 Jan. 1838, TPL, Hamilton Papers
60 John Colborne to Sir F.B. Head, 6 Jan. 1838, MLB, 1272/64
61 Laurence Laurason to James Ingersoll, London, 29 Jan. 1838, HPL, Land Papers, 313
62 Askin to John Douglas, London, 27 Dec. 1837, TPL, Hamilton Papers
63 Militia Return in B.B. Brigham to Richard Bullock, Ingersoll, 24 Jan. 1838, AGOC, 36
64 Arnold Burrowes to Col. Foster, Brantford, 27 Jan. 1838, AGOC, 38. J.B. Askin to John Joseph, London, 16 Jan. 1838, NCPSO, 9, file 1299. Major Magrath to John Maitland, Brantford, 28 May 1838, CMS, 608/222
65 Adam Hope to Robert Hope, St Thomas, 24 Dec. 1837, 8, HPL, Hope Letters
66 See the statements of the township officers' fees for 1837 and 1838, UWO, Harris Family Papers, John Harris.

Notes to pp. 118–23

67 See PAO, Municipal Records, London District Court of Quarter Sessions, 66.
68 Landon, *Western Ontario and the American Frontier* 166
69 UWO, Harris Family Papers, John Harris, Rebellion Losses Papers, 2, no. 51
70 Waldie, 'Pioneer Days in Brant County' 59
71 TPL, Diary of a soldier in the [34th] regiment, 2 July 1838
72 John Carey to Mahlon Burwell, 10 Jan. 1838, PAC, Indian Affairs Correspondence, 68
73 Lucas, ed., *Lord Durham's Report on the Affairs of British North America* II, 165
74 Deposition of Thomas Higginson, 20 July 1838, UCSP, 5/5. Deposition of W.B.H. Stone, 28 July 1838, UCSP, 5/34. Copy of Complaint of James Merrill, 12 May 1838, UCSP, 5/34. Deposition of Anselm Foster, 20 June 1838, UCSP, 5/15
75 Deposition of W.B.H. Stone, 20 June 1838, UCSP, 5/19
76 Deposition of Anselm Foster, 20 June 1838, UCSP, 5/18
77 Report of Magistrates, UCSP, 5/55
78 Executive council minute, 25 July 1839, UCSP, 8/29–30
79 Leonard, *The Honourable Elijah Leonard – A Memoir* 10
80 Adam Yeigh and John Tidey were the rebels, George Humphrey and Charles Tilden the accomplices, and George Alexander Clark the accused accomplice.
81 Deposition of Joseph Bowes, 31 Jan. 1838, UCS, 196/109196–7
82 *Patriot* (Toronto), 30 Jan. 1838
83 Ibid. 6 March 1838
84 *Upper Canada Gazette* (Toronto), 15 March 1838
85 Ibid. 18 Jan. 1838
86 Ibid. 15 March 1838
87 Address of R. Rollo Hunter, 5 Feb. 1838, PAO, Snyder Papers
88 *Journal of the House of Assembly*, 1837–8, 374–5, 431
89 Ibid. 64
90 Ibid. 138
91 Hitsman, *Safeguarding Canada, 1763–1871* 113
92 John Colborne to Sir Colin Campbell, Montreal, 16 Feb. 1838, MLB, 1272/88–9
93 *St Catharines Journal*, 1 Feb. 1838
94 Malcolm to Mackenzie, Buffalo, 29 Dec. 1837, PAO, Lindsey Collection, Mackenzie Correspondence
95 *St Catharines Journal*, 29 March 1838
96 Martyn, 'Upper Canada and Border Incidents, 1837–38' 194. Ross, 'The Patriot War' 534

97 Martyn, 'Upper Canada and Border Incidents, 1837–38' 203–8. Guillet, *The Lives and Times of the Patriots* 101. David Iler to Samuel Iler, Colchester, n.d., Hiram Walker Museum, Military Papers
98 M. Salmon to Geoff Hall, 17 Jan. 1838, PAO, MacNab Papers
99 Deposition of W.B.H. Stone, 28 July 1838, UCSP, 5/16
100 Deposition of Andrew Connors, 26 Feb. 1838, UCS, 186/104246
101 Bostwick et al. to Head, St Thomas, 12 March 1838, AGOC, 40
102 Burwell to Colonel L. Foster, Port Burwell, 12 March 1838, AGOC, 40
103 Burwell to John Joseph, Port Burwell, 12 March 1838, UCS, 188/104844. Note, Attorney General's Office, 26 March 1838, UCS, 188/104847
104 Burwell to Col Foster, Port Talbot, 16 March 1838, AGOC, 40
105 Salmon to ———, Simcoe, 17 March 1838, AGOC, 40
106 Rapelje to Richard Bullock, Vittoria, 17 March 1838, AGOC, 40
107 Meade to Col Foster, Port Dover, 19 March 1838, AGOC, 40
108 The eight rebels were Joseph Beamer, Peter Coon, Alonzo Foster, John Johnson, Peter Ladon, Dudley Newton, Joseph N. Smith, and Abraham Vanduzen. The two accomplices were Albus Connors and Michael Showers, and the five accused accomplices were Oliver Edmonds, Henry Goff, John Heap, John Teckling, and William Stants.
109 UWO, Harris Family Papers, John Harris, Rebellion Losses Papers, 2, no. 56
110 Ibid. no. 36
111 The five arrested for unknown reasons were Thomas Balls, Isaac Edmunds, James Johnson, Charles McIntosh, and John Whalen. The four arrested near Hamilton were Jonathan Bishop, Joshua Lind, Andrew Miller, and Robert Armstrong.
112 Schedule of indictments, UCS, 190/106180–3
113 Sir George Arthur to Glenelg, 23 April 1838, CO 42, 446/112
114 See Schedule of indictments, UCS, 190/106180–3. By this time Parker had been transferred to the Home district jail from where he petitioned on 10 April.
115 The two Nassagaweya men were Robert Laing and Duncan McPhederain. The nine rebels were Malcolm Brown, Philip Henry, Charles Chapin, Lyman Chapin, Robert Elliott, Isaac Brock Malcolm, George Roberts, William Thompson, and Henry Winegarden. The three accomplices were Adam, Lord Wellington, and William Winegarden.
116 Petition of John Tufford, May 1838, UCS, 194/108341
117 Draper to John Joseph, Hamilton, 19 March 1838, UCS, 108/105165–6
118 Draper to John Joseph, Hamilton, 19 March 1838, UCS, 188/105177–8
119 UWO, Harris Family Papers, John Harris, Rebellion Losses Papers, 2, no. 63
120 Schedule of indictments, UCS, 190/106180–3. On this return Robert Armstrong's name was incorrectly inserted for Robert Alway's.

Notes to pp. 126–9

121 Riddell, 'A Trial for High Treason in 1838' 51
122 *St Catharines Journal*, 5 April 1838
123 Ibid. 12 April 1838
124 Draper to John Joseph, Hamilton, 28 March 1838, UCSP, 45/6–7
125 *St Catharines Journal*, 12 April 1838
126 *Hamilton Express, Mirror* (Toronto), 14 April 1838. The trial records are in UCSP, 45/145–61.
127 Note by Macaulay, Toronto, 5 Oct. 1838, UCSP, 45/161
128 MacNab to ———, Hamilton, 6 Aug. 1838, UCSP, 45/144B
129 UWO, Harris Family Papers, John Harris, Rebellion Losses Papers, 3, no. 139
130 Schedule of indictments, UCS, 190/106183
131 Draper to John Joseph, Hamilton, 30 March 1838, UCSP, 45/11. Draper to John Joseph, Hamilton, 2 April 1838, UCSP, 45/14–17
132 *St Catharines Journal*, 12 April 1838
133 Minute read before the executive council, 31 March 1838, UCSP, 50/3–11
134 Executive council minute, 3 April 1838, CO 42, 446/56
135 Arthur to Glenelg, 14 April 1838, CO 42, 446/53
136 Col Halkett to Robert Land, Toronto, 18 April 1838, HPL, Land Papers, 455
137 Robert Land to Col Halkett, Hamilton, 20 April 1838, CMS, 608/132
138 C.A. Hagerman to Robert Land, Toronto, 1 May 1838, HPL, Land Papers, 464
139 Miller, *Notes of an Exile to Van Diemen's Land* 5–16
140 Watt, 'The Political Prisoners in Upper Canada' 540
141 Robert Cavanaugh, William Cheeseman, James Coleman, Andrew Connors, Moses Cook, Robert Cook, Losee Denton, Robert Franey, Luther Hoskins, Caleb Kipp, Nelson Leach, Andrew McLure, John Medcalf, Isaac Moore, Benjamin Page, Jonathan Steele
142 The three rebels were George Blake, William Childs, and Charles Travers, the two accomplices, Elias Moore and David D. Wilson. The three accused were William Lymburner, Stephen Secord, and Alexander Sumner. The five arrested for activities unconnected with the Duncombe revolt were John Grieve, Orlando Inglis, Cyrus McCartney, Joshua Moore, and James Nash. The last prisoner was Thomas Herman.
143 Thomas Arker, Daniel Bedford, Paul Bedford, James Bell, Joseph Bowes, Amos Bradshaw, Stephen Bronger, Edward Carman, Dennis Cavanaugh, James Coville, Uriah Emmons, Horatio Fowler, Joseph Hart, George Hill, Charles Lawrence, Patrick Malada, Finlay Malcolm (of Bayham), Ezekiel Manns, Alexander Neilly, Lewis A. Norton, John Riley, Abraham Sackrider, William Watts, Mire Wethy

144 Wm. Cheeseman, James Coleman, Andrew Connors, Moses Cook, Losee Denton, Robert Franey, Caleb Kipp, Nelson Leach, Andrew McLure, John Medcalf, Isaac Moore, Benjamin Page, Jonathan Steele
145 Luther Hoskins, John Kelly, Samuel Sands, John Tidey
146 Schedule of indictments, UCS, 190/106181-2
147 Draper to John Joseph, London, 24 April 1838, UCS, 192/106861
148 Petition of Daniel Davis and Charles Tozer, 8 Sept. 1838, UCSP, 22/22-4. Executive council minute, 8 Nov. 1838, UCSP, 22/25
149 Petition of James McLees, n.d. and note by Draper, 17 Nov. 1838, UCSP, 54/86-8
150 Draper to Sir George Arthur, Toronto, 31 Aug. 1838, UCSP, 54/93-5
151 Schedule of indictments, UCS, 190/106181-2
152 PAC, RLDM, I/128
153 W.H. Draper to ———, London, 23 April 1838, UCS, 192/106820
154 Sherwood to John Joseph, Toronto, 16 May 1838, UCS, 194/107966
155 Ibid.
156 *London Gazette, Patriot* (Toronto), 18 May 1838
157 Draper to John Joseph, London, 10 May 1838, UCS, 193/107741
158 *Regina v. Isaac Moore and Harvey Bryant*, CO 42, 447/273-9
159 Draper to John Joseph, London, 2 May 1838, UCS, 193/107231
160 Sherwood to John Joseph, Toronto, 16 May 1838, UCS, 194/107964
161 James Hamilton to John Joseph, London, 21 May 1838, UCS, 194/108069
162 Hobsbawm and Rudé, *Captain Swing* 262
163 Draper's memorandum on the rebellion, 28 May 1838, CO 42, 447/148-9

CHAPTER 6

1 Burwell to Richard Bullock, Port Talbot, 21 April 1838, AGOC, 42
2 Fuller to Sullivan, Port Dover, 23 April 1838, NCPSO, 10, file 1374
3 Salmon to the Military Secretary, Simcoe, 24 April 1838, CMS, 608/141
4 Ibid. 140-1
5 Colin McNeilledge Diaries, 14 April to 6 May, PAC, Norfolk Historical Society Papers
6 Magrath to John Maitland, Brantford, 1 May 1838, Sanderson, ed., *The Arthur Papers* I, 95
7 Ibid. 96
8 Ibid.
9 Major Magrath to Col Halkett, Brantford, 11 May 1838, CMS, 608/180
10 Major Magrath to John Maitland, Brantford, 28 May 1838, CMS, 608/220-2. C. Foster to John ———, Toronto, 17 May 1838, CMS, 610/46

11 Thomas Leigh Goldie to Captain Sandom, Montreal, 4 May 1838, MLB, 1273/141
12 Memorandum of 29 March 1838, attached to A.K. McKenzie to C.H. Graham, Lockport, 13 April 1838, UWO, Graham Papers
13 Duncombe to Benjamin Fuller, 28 May 1838 (typescript), LPL, Seaborn Collection, Diaries, 1132
14 UWO, Harris Family Papers, John Harris, Rebellion Losses Papers, 6, no. 300
15 Duncombe to Benjamin Fuller, 28 May 1838 (typescript), LPL, Seaborn Collection, Diaries, 1132-4
16 Burwell to Joseph, Port Burwell, 3 June 1838, UCS, 195/108460
17 Burwell to Joseph, Port Burwell, 12 June 1838, UCS, 195/108670
18 Ermatinger to John Joseph, St Thomas, 6 June 1838, UCS, 195/108458-62
19 Worthington to John Joseph, Burford Town line, 5 July 1838, UCS, 198/110001
20 Ibid. 198/110001-2
21 Catherine ———, to 'My Dear Mother,' Burford, 11 June 1838, Luard, 'Oxen, Candles and Homespun' 20
22 Johnson to Joseph, Blenheim, 5 June 1838, UCS, 193/108440
23 Brearley to Col Halkett, Toronto, 9 June 1838, UCS, 195/108604-5
24 William Holcroft to Richard Bullock, West Oxford, 30 June 1838, AGOC, 43
25 Memorandum by F. Halkett, Toronto, 11 June 1838, UCS, 195/108639. *Niagara Reporter, London Gazette*, 26 May 1838
26 Ross, 'The Patriot War' 542. For the events of the Short Hills raid see Read, 'The Short Hills Raid of June, 1838.'
27 William J. Kerr to Col Halkett, Wellington Square, 30 June 1838, CMS, 610/105-16
28 Laurence Laurason to Edward Ermatinger, 26 June 1838; Ermatinger, *The Talbot Régime* 361
29 *Examiner, St Catharines Journal*, 26 July 1838
30 *London Gazette, Patriot* (Toronto), 3 July 1838
31 Eliza McKenny to Richard McKenny, Malahide, 3 July 1838, UCS, 198/110126-7
32 Ibid. 110128-9
33 Riddell to John Macaulay, Woodstock, 28 June 1838, UCS, 198/109590-1
34 Light to Richard Bullock, Woodstock, 6 July 1838, UCS, 197/109678-82
35 Cruikshank, 'A Twice-Told Tale (The Insurrection in the Short Hills in 1838)' 210
36 A.W. Light to Richard Bullock, Woodstock, 6 July 1838, UCS, 197/109678

280 Notes to pp. 140-6

37 P.B. de Blaquiere to Richard Bullock, Woodstock, 30 June 1838, AGOC, 43
38 Light to Richard Bullock, Woodstock, 6 July 1838, UCS, 197/109678
39 Cruikshank, 'A Twice-Told Tale' 210
40 Ibid. 210-11
41 George W. Whitehead to the Attorney or Solicitor General, Burford, 10 Aug. 1838, UCS, 201/111448
42 Burn to ———, Dereham, 19 July 1838, UCS, 199/110455
43 Kinchen, *The Rise and Fall of the Patriot Hunters* 49
44 Tiffany, 'Relations of the United States to the Canadian Rebellion of 1837-38' 62-3
45 Mott, 'Rebellion of 1837. Norwich' 9, UWO, Landon papers, Correspondence
46 Light to Bullock, Woodstock, 6 July 1838, UCS, 197/109679-80
47 Fuller to John Macaulay, Port Dover, 10 July 1838, UCS, 198/110148-51
48 Executive council minute, 10 Jan. 1839, UCSP, 52/60
49 William Holcroft to Richard Bullock, Ingersoll, 6 July 1838, AGOC, 44
50 William Brearley to Richard Bullock, Norwich, 16 July 1838, AGOC, 43
51 Ibid.
52 UWO, Harris Family Papers, John Harris, Rebellion Losses Claims, 2, no. 91
53 Ibid. no. 43
54 Deposition of Russel Babbit, 28 July 1838, UCS, 208/114610
55 Throckmorton to Sir George Arthur, n.d., UCS, 208/114634-5
56 Treffry to Sir George Arthur, Otterville, 2 Aug. 1838, UCS, 201/111028-9
57 Letter to Sir George Arthur, Norwich, 15 July 1838, UCS, 200/110690-3
58 John Macaulay to Maitland, 2 Aug. 1838, L-G LB, 45/227-8
59 Report of Committee of Court of Quarter Sessions, UCS, 208/114565-76
60 Deposition of Hatcock, n.d., UCS, 208/114628. Although Hatcock said that his two sons were detained for a few days, their names have not been included because there is no other evidence that they were jailed.
61 Deposition of Wilson, 26 July 1838, UCS, 208/114595
62 Petition of John G. Losee et al., n.d., UCS, 203/112444
63 Petiton of various people on behalf of Benjamin and William Hillaker, n.d., UCS, 207/144425
64 Petition of Solomon Lossing, n.d., UCS, 208/114780. George W. Whitehead to Solomon Lossing, Burford, 20 Oct. 1838, UCS, 208/114697
65 William Brearley to John Macaulay, Norwich, 26 Jan. 1839, UCSP, 52/84
66 Deposition of Gardiner, 25 June 1838, UCS, 197/109717-A
67 W. Wright to Sir George Arthur, 29 June 1838, UCS, 197/109746-7
68 *Western Herald* (Sandwich), 17 July 1838

281 Notes to pp. 146–9

69 Clench to Jarvis, Colborne on Thames, 27 June 1838, PAC, Indian Affairs, Correspondence, 25, no. 267
70 UWO, Woodman Diary and Letters (typescript), 19. Alex. D. Ward to John Maitland, Mosa, 29 June 1838, UCS, 197/109772
71 Arthur to Sir John Colborne, Toronto, 30 June 1838, Sanderson, ed., *The Arthur Papers* I, 214. Allan MacNab to W.J. Kerr, Hamilton, 2 July 1838, CMS, 611/4. The warriors were never sent because the situation improved.
72 See Grogan to John Maitland, Chatham, 2 July 1838, CMS, 610/221.
73 John Maitland to Col Foster, London, 1 July 1838, CMS, 610/167. *London Gazette*, *Western Herald* (Sandwich), 17 July 1838
74 William McVity to W.W. Baldwin, Chatham, 3 July 1838, TPL, W.W. Baldwin Papers, sec. I, 102
75 Extract from a letter of Thomas Fuller to Thomas Street, Chatham, 30 June 1838, UCS, 197/109819–20
76 Deposition of John Murdaugh, 3 July 1838, CMS, 610/216–17
77 John Maitland to Col Foster, London, 3 July 1838 (copy), CMS, 610/219
78 TPL, Diary of a soldier in the [34th] regiment, 3
79 Kinchen, *The Rise and Fall of the Patriot Hunters* 35–6. See also Tiffany, 'Relations of the United States to the Canadian Rebellion of 1837–38' 56–60.
80 *London Gazette*, *Western Herald* (Sandwich), 17 July 1838
81 James Everett to W.L. Mackenzie, Ypsilanti, 1 Sept. 1838, PAC, Mackenzie Papers
82 *London Gazette*, *Western Herald* (Sandwich), 17 July 1838
83 W.H. Draper to Henry Sherwood, Toronto, 13 July 1838, UCS, 199/110221–2
84 *London Gazette*, *Mirror* (Toronto), 4 Aug. 1838
85 Affidavit of Laurence Laurason, 14 June 1839, UCSP, 52/145
86 Evidence of Caleb Kipp, CO 42, 477/254–5
87 William Proudfoot to William Peddie, London, Aug. 1839, UWO, Proudfoot Papers
88 The three accomplices were Adam, Lord Wellington, and William Winegarden. The six rebels were Malcolm Brown, Lyman Chapin, Robert Elliott, Isaac Brock Malcolm, George Roberts, and Henry Winegarden.
89 Thomas Arker, Daniel Bedford, Stephen Bronger, Dennis and Robert Cavanaugh, William Cheeseman, James Coleman, Andrew Connors, Moses Cook, Losee Denton, Robert Franey, Charles Lawrence, Nelson Leach, Andrew McLure, Patrick Malada, Ezekiel Manns, John Medcalf, Alexander Neilly, Benjamin Page, John Riley, Abraham Sackrider, Samuel Sands, William Watts, Mire Wethy

282 Notes to pp. 149–53

90 *London Gazette, St Catharines Journal*, 21 June 1838
91 Norton, *Life and Adventures of Col. L.A. Norton* 66
92 Executive council minute, 21 May 1838, UCS, 187/104453. The six Americans were Joseph Bowes, Amos Bradshaw, James Coville, George Hill, Caleb Kipp, and Lewis Norton.
93 Schedule of petitioners at London, UCS, 191/106670–2. Return of J.B. Robinson, n.d., Sanderson, ed., *The Arthur Papers* I, 131
94 Petition of John Tidey et al., Fort Henry, 19 July 1838, UCS, 203/112570–3
95 Petition of Deo, RLDM, II
96 John Joseph to W.H. Draper, Hamilton, 21 March 1838, L-G LB, 44/45
97 Schedule of petitioners at London, UCS, 191/106670–2. Return of J.B. Robinson, n.d., Sanderson, ed., *The Arthur Papers* I, 131. Executive council minute, 21 May 1838, UCS, 194/108097
98 Diary of Robert Gilkison, 30 July 1838, PAC, Gilkison Papers, 2
99 Report by Laidlaw, 21 July 1838 and 17 Aug. 1838, PAC, Hamilton Papers, 65
100 *Niagara Reporter, St Catharines Journal*, 23 Aug. 1838
101 Report by Laidlaw, 2 Aug. 1838, marginal note, PAC, Hamilton Papers, 65
102 *London Gazette, British Colonist* (Toronto), 4 Oct. 1838
103 Executive council minute, 30 Aug. 1838, UCSP, 64/90–2
104 John Macaulay to W.H. Draper, 13 Aug. 1838, L-G LB, 46/16–17
105 Executive council minute, 30 Aug. 1838, UCSP, 64/90–2. The six rebels were James Bell, Horatio Fowler, Joseph Hart, Philip Henry, Luther Hoskins, John Tidey.
106 PAO, Tidey Diary, 12 Nov. 1838
107 *Hamilton Express, St Catharines Journal*, 12 April 1838
108 Evans to the *Examiner, Church* (Coburg), 3 Nov. 1838. George W. Whitehead to James Winniet, Brantford, 19 Oct. 1838, AGOC, 45
109 Evans to John Macaulay, Woodhouse, 18 Oct. 1838, UCS, 208/114638–40
110 C.A. Hagerman to Allan Macdonnell, Toronto, 3 Nov. 1838, PAC, Macdonnell Papers, 37/45
111 Convicted prisoners undisposed of, UCS, 207/114181
112 Sheriff W.B. Jarvis to John Macaulay, Toronto, 7 Nov. 1838, UCS, 209/115187
113 Guillet, *The Lives and Times of the Patriots* 115–18
114 Report of Peter Diehl, Surgeon, 12 Nov. 1838, UCS, 209/115453
115 John Macaulay to Allan Cameron, 26 Sept. 1838, L-G LB, 46/184
116 *Upper Canada Gazette* (Toronto), 25 Oct. 1838

283 Notes to pp. 153–6

117 McKenny to John Joseph, Malahide, 28 Dec. 1837 and note of C.A. Hagerman, UCS, 181/100074–7
118 Note of Attorney General's Office, Toronto, 6 Sept. 1838, UCSP, 50/319–20
119 Burwell to Richard Bullock, 2 Aug. 1838, AGOC, 44
120 John Macaulay to William Collins, 1 Aug. 1838, L-G LB, 45/211–12
121 Sir George Arthur to Glenelg, 14 April 1838, CO 42, 446/53
122 Askin to John Douglas, London, 30 Dec. 1837, TPL, Hamilton Papers
123 Elijah Duncombe to Benjamin Fuller, 28 May 1838 (typescript), LPL, Seaborn Collection, Diaries, 1133
124 Executive council minute, 22 Aug. 1839, PAC, Executive council petitions, 'T' Bundle 22, 8A
125 J. Sheridan Hogan to R.B. Sullivan, Hamilton, 16 April 1839, PAO, Township Papers, Brantford Township, folder for concessions 4 and 5
126 Executive council minute, 16 July 1839, UCSP, 24/86–7
127 Bridges to John Macaulay, Malahide, 11 Sept. 1838, UCS, 205/113413–14. Bridges to [Sir George Arthur], Norwichville, 30 Oct. 1838, UCS, 208/115015–18
128 Petition of various inhabitants of Norwich and Dereham, answered 27 Nov. 1838, UCS, 210/115818–19
129 Arnold Burrowes to Richard Bullock, Brantford, 10 Oct. 1838, Sanderson, ed., *The Arthur Papers* I, 299
130 H.V.A. Rapelje to John Macaulay, Talbot District, 31 Oct. 1838, UCS, 208/115021–2
131 Simpson McCall to R.A. Tucker, Vittoria, 24 Nov. 1838, UCS, 210/115748
132 William J. Kerr to A.N. MacNab, 6 Dec. 1838, NCPSO, 14, file 1731
133 Arthur to P.B. de Blaquiere, Toronto, n.d., Sanderson, ed., *The Arthur Papers* I, 385
134 Lindsey, *The Life and Times of William Lyon Mackenzie* II, 199–201. Corey, *The Crisis of 1830–42 in Canadian-American Relations* 78
135 George C. Salmon to Richard Bullock, Simcoe, 29 Oct. 1838, AGOC, 45
136 Henry Evilegh to James Winniet, Simcoe, 24 Oct. 1838, AGOC, 45. Richard Bullock to George C. Salmon, Toronto, 26 Oct. 1838, AGOC, 69. Bullock to James Winniet, Toronto, 26 Oct. 1838, AGOC, 69. This episode led to Colonel Salmon's resignation and retirement.
137 Evilegh to Col Foster, Simcoe, 24 Oct. 1838 (copy), CMS, 611/229–31
138 PAC, Militia Orders, 10
139 John George Bridges to John Macaulay, Norwich, 22 Nov. 1838, UCS, 210/115662–3

284 Notes to pp. 156–9

140 Adjutant General's Office, Toronto, 13 June 1838, PAC, Militia Orders, 10
141 Proceedings of a public meeting at Brantford, 11 July 1838, UCS, 199/110164–6
142 Petition of Mosa militiamen, received 16 Dec. 1838, AGOC, 36
143 Proudfoot Diary, 312, UWO, Proudfoot Papers
144 John Cameron to John Macaulay, Ingersoll, 10 Nov. 1838, UCS, 209/115319–20. Not until 24 October was a schedule of rates established throughout the province for goods and services provided.
145 Cruikshank, *A Memoir of Colonel the Honourable James Kerby* 246
146 T.H. Ball to Richard Bullock, London, 6 Nov. 1838, AGOC, 46. C. Chichester to the Ass*t* Ad*nt* General, Chatham, 7 Nov. 1838, CMS, 707/308
147 Arthur to Sir John Colborne, Toronto, 24 Oct. 1838, Sanderson, ed., *The Arthur Papers* I, 317, 318, nos. 375, 377
148 L. Wallbridge to Mrs Howard, Toronto, 31 Dec. 1838, PAC, Wallbridge Papers
149 Proudfoot Diary, 322–3, UWO, Proudfoot Papers
150 Arthur to Sir John Colborne, London, 18 Jan. 1839, Sanderson, ed., *The Arthur Papers* II, 20
151 Executive council minute, 25 July 1839, UCSP, 90/3. J.B. Clench to Col Land, 14 Aug. 1839, CMS, 615/59. Doyle McKenny to J.B. Clench, Malahide, 12 Aug. 1839, CMS, 615/58
152 William Brearley to Col Love, Norwich, 20 Aug. 1839, CMS, 615/61
153 Col Love to Sir George Arthur, 22 Aug. 1839, CMS, 615/63–5
154 Robert Johnston to Richard Bullock, nr Katesville, 28 Jan. 1838, UCS, 185/103306
155 Duncombe to Benjamin Fuller, 28 May 1838, LPL, Seaborn Collection, Diaries, 1132
156 Deposition of George C. Salmon, n.d., CMS, 608/137
157 T.W. Magrath to Colonel Halkett, Brantford, 11 May 1838, CMS, 608/180A
158 Jane O'Brien to Isabella Crichton, London, 31 May 1838, UWO, O'Brien Papers
159 *Hamilton Express, Mackenzie's Gazette*, 30 June 1838
160 John Burn to ———, Dereham, 19 July 1838, UCS, 199/110454
161 Proudfoot Diary, 316, UWO, Proudfoot Papers
162 Proudfoot to ———, 3 Dec. 1838, PAO, Proudfoot Papers
163 W.M. McKillican to ———, London, 8 Dec. 1838, UCS, 211/116169
164 Holcroft to A.W. Light, West Oxford, 12 Dec. 1838, AGOC, 47
165 Van Arnam to Arthur, Lockport, 22 March 1838, UCS, 189/105268
166 Daubigny to Samuel Street, Brantford, 26 Oct. 1836, PAO, Street Papers

285 Notes to pp. 159–63

167 Proudfoot Diary 27, 5 Oct. 1837, UWO, Proudfoot Papers
168 Duncombe to Benjamin Fuller, 28 May 1838 (typescript), LPL, Seaborn Collection, Diaries, 1134
169 Proudfoot to ———, 14 Aug. 1838, Draft, PAO, Proudfoot Papers
170 Woodman to his sister (typescript), Woodman Diary and Letters, 47
171 Longley, 'Emigration and the Crisis of 1837 in Upper Canada' 33–4
172 Guillet, *Lives and Times* 59
173 Graham, *The Tiger of Canada West* 173
174 The censuses up to 1834 were published in the *Journals of the House of Assembly of Upper Canada*. After that they were published in the *Appendices* to the *Journals*.
175 The five rebel townships were Dereham, Norwich, Southwold, West Oxford and Yarmouth. The three non-rebel ones were Charlotteville, Houghton, and Nissouri.
176 The three rebel townships were Blenheim, Burford, and Norwich. The three non-rebel ones were Adelaide, Middleton, and Zorra.
177 PAO, Canada West Census 1841–2, Yarmouth
178 C.H.P. Normanby to Sir George Arthur, CO 42, 458/150A, 150B
179 L.M. Phillips to James Stephen, 13 July 1838, CO 42, 465/235
180 PAO, Canada West Census, 1851–2, Norwich and Dereham
181 PAO, John Arthur Tidey Memoranda, 298. Canniff, *The Medical Profession in Upper Canada, 1783–1850* 306
182 David Beamer, Charles Christie, Henry Merwin, Garrett Tuttle, Sobiske Brown, Garry V. DeLong, William McGuire, Andrew Moore, Moses Mott, Asa Secord, James Tuttle. The last seven were those who returned.
183 Deposition of Israel and Margaret Titus (copy), UCSP, 88/130
184 Return of traitors, 20 April 1843, PAC, State Book B, 381
185 W.L. Mackenzie to James Mackenzie, New York, 9 Jan. 1838 [1839], PAC, Mackenzie Papers, 10
186 James Mackenzie to W.L. Mackenzie, Lockport, 13 Jan. 1839, PAO, Lindsey Collection, Mackenzie Correspondence
187 Duncombe to Mackenzie, Hartford, 8 March 1839, PAO, Lindsey Collection, Mackenzie Correspondence
188 Hugh Carmichael to W.L. Mackenzie, Cincinnati, 12 Dec. 1839, PAO, Lindsey Collection, Mackenzie Correspondence
189 Petition of Duncombe to Sir Charles Metcalfe [1843], PAO, Dent Scrapbook
190 Return of traitors, 20 April 1843, PAC, State Book B, 381
191 Duncombe to T. Barthellier, Rochester, 19 July 1844, PAO, Township Papers, Brantford, folder for concession 2

192 Charles Duncombe to Elijah Duncombe, Hicksville, 27 June 1865 (typescript), LPL, Seaborn Collection, Diaries, 1140
193 Ibid.

CHAPTER 7

1 Prisoner list, CO 42, 452/383
2 This group includes Elisha Hall, who would have gone to Oakland had he not hurt himself in a fall, and young John Riley of Yarmouth, who set off for Scotland with Anderson's men but claimed that he did not complete the journey.
3 Longley, *Sir Francis Hincks* 30
4 Martin Switzer of Streetsville and George Case of Hamilton
5 The 1837 census for the area is to be found in *Appendix to the Journal of the House of Assembly of Upper Canada*, 1837–38, 251. Populations of the larger towns were omitted from the calculations in order to show the distribution of the rural population. The 1837 census listed London's population, but other contemporary evidence was used for the populations of Brantford (1200), Paris (800), St Thomas (700), Simcoe (600), Galt (500), Woodstock (300), and Ingersoll (200).
6 The area of each township under cultivation was calculated by taking the 1836 assessment figures for rateable cultivated acres. They are to be found in *Appendix to the Journal of the House of Assembly of Upper Canada*, 1836–37, App. 9/2, 5. It was necessary to use the 1835 figures for the Norfolk townships. They are to be found in *Appendix to the Journal of the House of Assembly of Upper Canada*, I, 1836, App. 45/11.
7 The individuals and debts are Norris Humphrey, £468; Charles Duncombe, £183; Walter Chase, £172; Jacob Yeigh, £165; Elisha Hall, £183; William Mathews, £103; John Van Arnam, £38; Samuel Edison, £34; Henry Merwin, £17; Eliakim Malcolm, £15; James Malcolm, £12; George Malcolm, £6.
8 Petition of Lyman Chapin, Hamilton, 14 March 1838, UCS, 193/107830. Petition of Clarissa Hart, 18 April 1838, UCS, 204/113067. Petition of Finlay Malcolm, n.d., received 3 July 1838, UCS, 198/109933. Petition of Philip Henry, 5 May 1838, UCS, 193/107572. Petition of Henry Winegarden, 24 March 1838, UCS, 187/105326
9 Petition of William Thompson and Charles Chapin, 3 May 1838, UCS, 193/107839
10 W.H. Draper's report on Gore jail petitioners, 16 May 1838, CO 42, 447/294

Notes to pp. 169–81

11 Executive council proceedings concerning those to be transported, 29 May 1838, CO 42, 447/152
12 They are George Lawton, Solomon Lossing, and Elias, Enoch, and John Moore.
13 Deposition of Nevers, 15 Dec. 1837, UCS, 200/110846
14 PAO, Abstract Index to Deeds, Blenheim, 165
15 For the purpose of this study, one was considered a landholder if he owned land either patented or unpatented, or if he leased a Clergy Reserve or land from private individuals, or indeed simply stated that he owned property.
16 Theller, *Canada in 1837–38* I, 158
17 John Treffry to George Treffry, Norwich, 24 June 1838, UWO, Treffry Letters
18 Bettridge Manuscript, 139, PAO, Bettridge Papers
19 Petition of Thompson and Chapin, n.d., UCS, 193/107824
20 Wood, 'The Historical Geography of Dumfries Township, Upper Canada: 1816 to 1852' (Master's thesis) 72A
21 *Richmond Compiler*, MLC, item 3147
22 Fred Landon, 'Bitterness of Troubles in 1830's ... ,' LPL, Seaborn Collection, Medical History, 1096
23 Coventry, 'A Concise History of the Late Rebellion in Upper Canada' 127
24 Adam Hope to Robert Hope, St Thomas, 24 Dec. 1837, 6, HPL, Hope Letters
25 John Treffry to George Treffry, Norwich, 24 June 1838, UWO, Treffry Letters
26 Burwell to James Fitzgibbon, private, Port Talbot, 18 Dec. 1837, AGOC, 34
27 Deposition of Lewis Norton, 29 Dec. 1837, RLDM, II
28 Deposition of Conrad, 29 Dec. 1837, RLDM, II
29 Adam Hope to Robert Hope, St Thomas, 24 Dec. 1837, 1, HPL, Hope Letters
30 John Medcalf of Malahide did not join Anderson's group; he is not one of the thirty-six rebels discussed.
31 Adam Hope to Robert Hope, St Thomas, 24 Dec. 1837, 8, HPL, Hope Letters
32 Montreal *Herald, Mackenzie's Gazette*, 30 March 1838
33 Bettridge Manuscript, 139, PAO, Bettridge Papers
34 Bettridge Manuscript, 139–40, PAO, Bettridge Papers
35 Burn to ———, Dereham, 19 July 1838, UCS, 110452–5

288 Notes to pp. 181–7

36 Lucas, ed., *Lord Durham's Report* II, 172–3. Durham thought the Americans were disaffected because of the insecurity of their land tenure.
37 Arthur to the Archbishop of Canterbury, Toronto, 11 Aug. 1838, Sanderson, ed., *The Arthur Papers* I, 254–5
38 Confidential report on the political state of the districts, Sanderson, ed., *The Arthur Papers* I, 141
39 Lucas, ed., *Lord Durham's Report* II, 163–4
40 Preston, *Three Years' Residence in Canada* II, 25
41 Letter from Augmentation of Grenville, 9 March 1838, University of Toronto, Robarts Library, Rare Books, Commonplace Book, 1838
42 P.B. de Blaquiere to Sir F.B. Head, Woodstock, 15 Jan. 1838, NCPSO, 9, file 1298
43 Askin to John Douglas, London, 27 Dec. 1837, TPL, Hamilton Papers
44 George Phillpotts to Sir John Colborne, Cornwall, 20 Nov. 1837, PAC, Colborne Papers, 002969–70
45 Idem ———, Preston, Waterloo township, 23 June 1838, UCS, 196/109225. Some of the Scots of Eramosa attended a meeting that was considered by the local Tories to be treasonable.
46 *British Colonist* (Toronto), 10 May 1838. The *Colonist* fiercely denied the validity of this claim.
47 Erin to the *Constitution*, 6 Nov. 1837, *Mirror* (Toronto), 25 Nov. 1837
48 Buchanan to Sir George Arthur, New York, 12 July 1838, PAO, Lindsey Collection, Mackenzie Correspondence
49 Report of Dr Alling to the Canada Company, Guelph, 16 Dec. 1840, *A Statement of the Satisfactory Results which Have Attended Emigration to Upper Canada* 65
50 Powell to George William Murphy, Toronto, 7 March 1838, TPL, Powell Papers, A97
51 *Mirror* (Toronto), 30 Dec. 1837
52 *Canada Baptist Magazine and Missionary Register* II (1838) 59
53 Ibid. 75–6
54 O'Neill's Journal, Aug. 1837, no. 5, 120, SPG, Series x7
55 Taken from *Appendix to the Journal of the House of Assembly of Upper Canada*, 1839–40, I, Pt. I, 148, 151–3. The 1839 returns for Brantford were omitted here but can be found in CO 42, 476/223.
56 First Parish Register of St Thomas, 130, St Thomas Trinity Church
57 Bonnycastle and Alexander, *Canada, as It Was, Is, and May Be* 196
58 James Durand to Robert Baldwin, Toronto, 26 Feb. 1840, TPL, Robert Baldwin Papers, Sec. I
59 Green to W.J.D. Waddilove, London, 19 Feb. 1838, Waddilove, *The Stewart Missions* 248

Notes to pp. 187–92

60 Norwich Monthly Meeting, Men, 1834–52, 10 Jan. 1838, UWO, Quaker Records
61 *Second Annual Report of the Colonial Missionary Society* (1838) 22
62 Ibid. 22–3
63 They were the largest in East Oxford, West Oxford, Malahide, Oakland, and Townsend, and second or third in Bayham, Blenheim, Burford, Dereham, and Norwich.
64 Burford, East Oxford, Southwold
65 Green to W.J.D. Waddilove, London, 19 Feb. 1838, Waddilove, *The Stewart Missions* 248
66 *Canada Baptist Magazine and Missionary Register* (1838) 59
67 Ibid.
68 Baptist Archives, First Yarmouth Church, Minutes 1832–52, 7 April 1838
69 W.M. McKillican to J.B. Harrison, St Thomas, 6 Oct. 1840, UCSP, 9/74
70 O'Neill's Journal, Aug. 1837, no. 5, 118, SPG, Series x7
71 Baptist Archives, St George Church Records, 1
72 Carpenter to Glenelg, 2 June 1838, CO 42, 454/67
73 Burwell to John Macaulay, Port Talbot, 29 Dec. 1838, UCS, 212/116859
74 Baptist Archives, Port Burwell Baptist Church Minute Book, 1819–72, 11
75 *Canada Baptist Magazine and Missionary Register* I (1838) 192. *Upper Canada Baptist Missionary Magazine* II (1838) 73–4, 77
76 Downie to Alexander Macdonell, St Thomas, 24 Dec. 1837, CAAC, AB11
77 Bayham, Blenheim, Burford, Dereham
78 Bayham, Burford, Dereham, East Oxford, West Oxford, Oakland, Southwold, Townsend, Windham, Woodhouse
79 Bayham, Burford, Malahide, and possibly Townsend
80 Blenheim, Norwich, Townsend, Woodhouse
81 Examination of Sackrider, 17 Jan. 1838, RLDM, I, 88
82 Deposition of Sackrider, 27 Jan. 1838, RLDM, II
83 UCA, Minutes of the 1837 conference of the Methodist Episcopal Church, 5. Minutes of the 1838 conference of the Methodist Episcopal Church, 4
84 Hodgins, ed., *The Story of My Life* 178. Harvard to Robert Alder, Toronto, 15 Dec. 1837, UCA, Methodist Missionary Correspondence
85 UCA, Minutes of the 1838 conference of the Methodist Episcopal Church, 5
86 Macdonell to Lord Durham, 14 June 1838, PAO, Macdonnell Papers
87 Burn to ———, Dereham, 19 July 1838, UCS, 199/110453
88 *The Minutes of the Annual Conference of the Wesleyan-Methodist Church* 197
89 Green to W.J.D. Waddilove, London, 19 Feb. 1838, Waddilove, *The Stewart Missions* 248

90 Extract from a letter of Thornton, Whitby, 28 April 1838, *Quarterly Record of ... The United Secession Church* II (1838) 382
91 G. Mor [mutilated] to Absalom Peters, Beamsville, 8 Dec. 1837, AHMSC. R.H. Close to Milton Badger, St Catharines, 13 Jan. 1838, AHMSC
92 Joseph Maria Burke to Alexander Macdonell, 29 Feb. 1838, CAAC, AB05
93 H. Fitzpatrick to Macdonell, Adjala, 11 June 1838, PAO, AB19
94 Macdonell to Anthony Manahan, Kingston, 24 Feb. 1838, PAO, Macdonnell Papers
95 Bayham, Blenheim, Burford, East Oxford, West Oxford, Malahide, Oakland, Southwold
96 Green to W.J.D. Waddilove, London, 19 Feb. 1838, Waddilove, *The Stewart Missions* 248
97 O'Neill's Journal, no. 7, Toronto, 1 April 1838, 118, SPG, Series X7
98 Tidey to John Strachan, Kingston, 8 Aug. 1838, UCS, 203/112560. After his release, however, he did not rejoin the Church of England, in which he had been raised.
99 *Second Annual Report of the Colonial Missionary Society* (1838) 22
100 *Examiner*, 26 Dec. 1838, MLC, item 6188
101 W.H. Allworth, 'Congregational Church At Southwold, Ontario,' *Canadian Independent* (1867) 161–3, UCA, Church Histories
102 *Third Annual Report of the Colonial Missionary Society* (1839) 18
103 Ibid. 19
104 *Fourth Annual Report of the Colonial Missionary Society* (1840) 11
105 Burn to ———, Dereham, 19 July 1838, UCS, 199/110453
106 Address to Arthur from ministers and officials of Wesleyan Methodist Church, n.d., UCS, 212/116599
107 *The Minutes of the Annual Conference of the Wesleyan-Methodist Church* 150, 192
108 UCA, Minutes of the 1838 conference of the Methodist Episcopal Church, 4. Minutes of the 1839 conference of the Methodist Episcopal Church, 3
109 UCA, Minutes of the 1839 conference of the Methodist Episcopal Church, 4–5
110 Baptist Archives, Records of the First Regular Baptist Church in Norwich
111 Letter of 'Brother' Tapscott, Colborne, 30 Aug. 1838, *Canada Baptist Magazine and Missionary Register* II (1838) 14
112 McKillican to ———, London, 8 Dec. 1838, UCS, 211/116169
113 Proudfoot to ———, 14 Aug. 1838, draft, PAO, Proudfoot Papers
114 Skinner's statement for 1838 [?] of the Union road congregation, PAO, Proudfoot Papers

Notes to pp. 195–8

115 Proudfoot Diary, 322–3, UWO, Proudfoot Papers
116 George J. Ryerse to R.A. Tucker, Woodhouse, 19 Nov. 1838, UCS, 210/115504
117 Census of Missionary Presbytery for 1840, Knox College, Proudfoot Papers
118 W.F. Curry to Milton Badge, Montreal, 27 Sept. 1837, AHMSC
119 Marr to Absalom Peters, St Thomas, 5 July 1838, AHMSC
120 Ibid. 7 Sept. 1838, AHMSC
121 Upper Canada Conference, 1839, UCA, Christian Connection Records
122 J. Melville to Fred Landon, Corunna, Mrs Phelps, Smythe Collection
123 After January 1838 the Universalist journal, the *Evangelical Magazine and Gospel Advocate*, published in Utica, New York, ceased comment about Universalist activity in Upper Canada.
124 Petrie to W.J.D. Waddilove, Burford, 23 Dec. 1839, Waddilove, *The Late Bishop of Quebec's Upper Canadian Travelling Mission Fund* 99
125 Bettridge Manuscript, 31, PAO, Bettridge Papers
126 Burwell to Richard Bullock, Port Burwell, 5 Jan. 1838, AGOC, 36
127 List of Medcalf's volunteers, 26 June 1838, AGOC, 38
128 Of the eighty-one loyalists, the townships of forty-seven have been identified. Forty lived in Bayham. One came from Dereham, though he appears to have moved there from Bayham just prior to the revolt. Four came from areas of Malahide contiguous to Bayham. Another lived in Houghton and another in Middleton. These seven people have been included where possible in the calculations for the Bayham loyalists. The rebels of Dereham and Malahide (none came from Houghton or Middleton) have not been added to the Bayham rebels, however, as it was felt that the addition of the seven known 'outsiders' to the eighty-one loyalists would not seriously distort the loyalists' statistics but that the addition of two Malahide and eight Dereham rebels to Bayham's twenty would affect the calculations of the number of Bayham rebels. John Medcalf of Malahide was included with the Bayham rebels because he set out with them on their trek to Oakland, the other two Malahide insurgents going with the Yarmouth party. Medcalf also lived close to the Malahide-Bayham town line. See appendix 5 for the information on the rebels and appendix 4 for that on the loyalists.
129 Petition of Burwell, Port Burwell, 20 Jan. 1836, PAC, Norfolk Historical Society Papers, F.L. Walsh Papers, 3656
130 Luther Line to D. McCurdy, 18 Sept. 1835, enclosed in Doyle McKenny to Col Rowan, 24 Nov. 1835, PAO, Crown Lands Papers, A-I-6, Correspondence

131 Ibid.
132 Titus to Robinson, Bayham, 6 July 1836, PAO, Township Papers, Bayham, folder for concession 1
133 Draper and Burwell to John Joseph, Port Burwell, 21 April 1836, UCS, 202/112128
134 Burwell to Col Foster, Port Talbot, 16 March 1838, AGOC, 40. It was not possible to find any Bayham rebels positively identified as being in the timber trade.
135 Ontario, *Otter Valley Conservation Report* Pt. I, 59
136 Petition of various people from Bayham, 8 Feb. 1833, UCSP, 44/155–7
137 Ontario, *Otter Valley Conservation Report* Pt. I, 52
138 Burwell to Col Foster, Port Talbot, 16 March 1838, AGOC, 40
139 By 1833 eleven ships averaging fifty tons each had been built at the port. Petition of various people from Bayham, 8 Feb. 1833, UCSP, 44/155–7
140 Creighton, *The Empire of the St Lawrence* 316
141 Note, however, that two London district justices, Eliakim Malcolm of Scotland and Solomon Lossing of Norwich, were implicated in the revolt.
142 Eleven more of those known to have gathered at Oakland held or had held minor government appointments.
143 Schedule of the 206 volunteers of the Second Middlesex Militia serving for six months after 31 Oct. 1838, PAC, Militia Nominal Rolls, 13
144 No significant data are available about the family origins of those born in British North America in the two sample populations. The family origins of only three of the thirty-four relevant loyalists have been established. The families of all were American in origin, as were the families of the corresponding four rebels. Eight rebels were born in British North America.

CHAPTER 8

1 Askin to John Joseph, London, 22 Dec. 1837, Sanderson, ed., *The Arthur Papers* I, 34
2 Dispatch from MacNab, Sodom, 18 Dec. 1837, *Patriot* (Toronto), 22 Dec. 1837
3 Petition of 103 Norwich inhabitants, *Patriot* (Toronto), 22 Dec. 1837
4 Ibid.
5 McKenny to Edward Ermatinger, 11 Dec. 1837, Ermatinger, *The Talbot Régime* 357
6 Catherine ——— to 'My Dear Mother,' Burford, 11 June 1838, Luard, 'Oxen, Candles and Homespun' 20–1

Notes to pp. 207–12

7   Deposition of Chaple, 15 Dec. 1837, UCS, 181/99925–6. Deposition of Conklin, 21 Dec. 1837, UCS, 180/99727
8   Petition of Jacob S. Esmond et al., n.d., PAC, Petitions and Addresses, 9
9   Deposition of Sackrider, 27 Jan. 1838, RLDM, II
10 John Treffry to George Treffry, Norwich, 24 June 1838, UWO, Treffry Letters
11 See evidence of Joseph J. Lancaster, UCSP, 45/146
12 Deposition of Sackrider, 16 Dec. 1837, Muir, *The Early Political and Military History of Burford* 14
13 Deposition of Peter Coon, 17 Dec. 1837, in Guillet, *The Lives and Times of the Patriots* 250
14 Deposition of John Beard, 10 Dec. 1837, PAO, Snyder Papers
15 Deposition of Nicholls, 17 Dec. 1837, UCS, 180/99400. Deposition of Thompson, 17 Dec. 1837, UCS, 180/99402
16 Strachan to Durham, Hamilton, 30 Aug. 1838, UCS, 204/113343–4
17 Petition of Bedford, 19 March 1838, UCS, 194/107986
18 Petition of Brown, Hamilton Gaol, 20 March 1838, UCS, 189/105538, 105541
19 Regimental Order of Burwell to the Second Middlesex, *Patriot* (Toronto), 30 Jan. 1838
20 This happened to accused rebel Michael Tripp of West Oxford in 1832. PAO, Township Papers, West Oxford, documents for lot 16, Broken Front, and lots 10 to 16, concession 1
21 In 1831 John Malcolm lost lot 1, concession 14 of Walsingham for non-payment of taxes. PAO, Abstract Index to Deeds for Walsingham, 917
22 Proudfoot to William Peddie, London, August 1839, UWO, Proudfoot Papers
23 James Hunter to W.L. Mackenzie, 18 Oct. 1839, PAO, Lindsey Collection, Mackenzie Correspondence
24 Hall to W.L. Mackenzie, Lewiston, 10 May [1839?], PAO, Lindsey Collection, Mackenzie Correspondence
25 PAO, Tidey Diary no. 2, 11 May 1839
26 James Durand to Robert Baldwin, Toronto, 26 Feb. 1840, TPL, Robert Baldwin Papers, sec. 1
27 Ibid.
28 *Oxford Star and Woodstock Advertiser*, 15 Dec. 1848
29 Landon, *Western Ontario and the American Frontier* 232

Bibliography

UNPUBLISHED PRIMARY SOURCES

GOVERNMENT RECORDS

Archives of Ontario, Toronto
Canada West Census, 1842 (microfilm)
Canada West Census, 1851–2 (microfilm)
Colonial Office 42 Series, vols. 437–76 (microfilm)
Courts of Oyer and Terminer and General Gaol Delivery, vol. 167
Crown Lands Papers
    Correspondence A-1-6; Series A-IV, vol. 56; Series A-VI-10, vol. 2; Series B-II, vols. 1, 7, 15, 19; Series C-I-4, vols. 4, 14, 17; Series C-III-3, vols. 1, 7; Series C-III-5, vols. 1, 5, 6, 7; Series C-III-7, vols. 1, 2; Township Papers
Department of the Provincial Secretary, Index to Land Patents (microfilm)
Governor General's Office, Lieutenant Governor's Internal Letter Books, 1805–6, 1818–41 (RG7, G-16A), vols. 2–15 (microfilm)
Land Registry Offices, Abstract Indexes to the Deeds (microfilm)
Map Collection, Talbot Maps, Books C, D, E
Municipal Records (RG21)
Records of Courts of General Quarter Sessions Prior to 1842, London District, vols. 63–6; Township Minute Books (microfilm)
Upper Canada State Papers, vols. 3–10, 18–19, 22, 24, 29, 31, 34, 36, 41, 43–6, 50–4, 57, 63–4, 75, 84–91, 97 (microfilm)

Public Archives of Canada, Ottawa
Adjutant General's Office, Correspondence (RG9, I B-1), vols. 33–47, 68–9
Colonial Office 47 Series, vols. 116–17, 153–4 (microfilm)

Correspondence of the Military Secretary of the Commander of the Forces, 1767–1870 (RG8, I C Series A-1), vols. 95, 173, 608–15, 707
Executive Council Minute Books (RG1, L-1) (microfilm)
Executive Council Petitions (RG1, L-3) (microfilm)
Indian Affairs (RG10, A-7), vols. 5, 66–9, 124–8, 717
Militia General Orders (RG9, I B-3), vols. 5, 10
Military Letter Books (RG8, I C Series A-2), vols. 1271–3, 1292–3
Numbered Correspondence of the Provincial Secretary's Office (RG5, C-1), vols. 7–14
Petitions and Addresses (RG5, B-3), vols. 9–10
Records of the London District Magistrates Relating to the Treason Hearings, 1837–8 (RG5, B-36), vols. I-II
State Book B, 1841–3 (RG1, E-1)
Upper Canada Militia Nominal Rolls (RG9, I B-2), vol. 30
Upper Canada Sundries (RG5, A-1), vols. 99–221

University of Western Ontario Library, Regional History Collection, London
Copy of Assessment Roll from 1839 to 1843 inclusive, London District
London District Surrogate Registry, no. 294

MANUSCRIPTS

Archives of Ontario, Toronto
Anonymous Diary, 'A Few Remarks on a Tour in Upper Canada,' 1837 (typescript)
Bishop Alexander Macdonnell Papers
Diary of John Sandfield Macdonald (typescript)
John Arthur Tidey Memoranda and Diary
John Strachan Papers
J.M. Snyder Papers
Lindsey Collection, Mackenzie Section, General Correspondence
Mackenzie-Lindsey Clippings
Proudfoot Papers (microfilm)
Rev. William Bettridge Papers, Bettridge Manuscript (typescript)
Rev. William W. Smith, unpublished reminiscences
Samuel Rose Papers
Samuel Street Papers
Scrapbook donated by Mrs Lucy Dent
Sir A.N. MacNab Papers

Bibliography

Dundas Historical Society Museum, Dundas
Lesslie Diaries (typescripts)

Hamilton Public Library, Hamilton
Adam Hope Letters (typescripts)
Land Family Papers

Hiram Walker Museum, Windsor
Military Papers

London Public Library, London
Dr. Edwin Seaborn Collection
Local History Scrapbooks

Mrs Phelps, Mount Pleasant
Miss Margaret Smythe Collection

Norwich District Museum and Archives, Norwich
Diary of William F. Barns
Throckmorton Diary

Presbyterian Church in Canada Archives, Knox College, University of Toronto, Toronto
Proudfoot Papers (microfilm)

Public Archives of Canada, Ottawa
Allan Macdonnell Papers (MG24, I-8 3)
Colborne Papers (MG24, A-40) (xeroxes)
Diary of Colonel A.W. Light (MG24, I-74)
Diary of George Leith (MG24, H-17)
Diary of Pelham C. Teeple (MG24, H-5)
Doctor Charles Duncombe Family Papers (MG24, B-38)
Durham Papers (MG24, A-47), Series 2, vol. 49
Gilkison Family Papers (MG24, I-25)
Merritt Family Papers (MG24, E-1)
Norfolk Historical Society Papers (MG9, D-8 24) (microfilm)
Rebellion Exiles (MG24, A-43)
Sheriff Alexander Hamilton Papers (MG24, I-26)
Wallbridge Family Papers (MG24, B-124)
William Lyon Mackenzie Papers (MG24, B-18)

Robin Harris, Toronto
Harris Papers

Toronto Public Library, Baldwin Room, Toronto
Diary 1838–40 of a soldier in the [34th] regiment
James Hamilton Papers
Robert Baldwin Papers
William Dummer Powell Papers
W.W. Baldwin Papers

United Church Archives, Victoria College, University of Toronto, Toronto
Ryerson Papers (microfilm)

University of Toronto, Robarts Library, Rare Books Room, Toronto
Commonplace Book, 1838

University of Western Ontario Library, Regional History Collection, London
C.H. Graham Papers (photostats)
Dennis O'Brien Papers
Diary of William Wood (typescript)
Elijah C. Woodman Diary and Letters
Fred Landon Papers
Harris Papers
John Treffry Letters
Proudfoot Family Papers
Thomas Talbot Papers

CHURCH RECORDS

Anglican Diocese of Toronto Archives, Toronto
Canon Allan Notes

Archives of Ontario, Toronto
Catholic Archdiocesan Archives (Toronto) Collection (microfilm)
Vital Statistics Collection, Church Records

Baptist Archives, McMaster University, Hamilton
Burgessville Church Minute Book, 1837–9
First Baptist Church, Simcoe, Minute Book, 1836–1941
First Regular Baptist Church, Norwich, Records
First Yarmouth Church Records

Bibliography

Minute Book of Baptist Church organized 22 April 1822 in Oxford
New Sarum Church Minute Book, 1838-62
Oxford Church Minute Book, 1808-59
Port Burwell Baptist Church Minute Book, 1819-72 (typescript)
St George Church Records, vol. I
Vittoria Church Minute Book, 1820-53

Diocese of Huron Archives (Anglican), London
Port Burwell Trinity Church Records

First United Church, Galt
Congregational Records

Guest, Mrs William, Mount Pleasant
All Saints Church, Mount Pleasant, Records

Paris Presbyterian Church
Dumfries Street Presbyterian Church Records

Public Archives of Canada, Ottawa
Baptist Church, Boston, Ontario, Minute Book (MG9, D7-2)
St Paul's Church, London, Parish Register No. 1 (MG9, D7-8)
Society for the Propagation of the Gospel in Foreign Parts (MG17, B-1), Series C (microfilm), Series X7 (microfilm)

St Thomas Trinity Anglican Church
First Parish Register

Taylor, Senator W.H., Brantford
Congregational Church of Scotland Records

Toronto Public Library, Baldwin Room, Toronto
First Baptist Church, Brantford, Minutes, vol. I

United Church Archives, Victoria College, University of Toronto, Toronto
American Home Missionary Society Congregational (microfilm)
Associated Synod of North America, Presbytery of Stamford, Extract from the Minutes of Associate, vol. XI
Canadian Wesleyan Methodist Church Annual Minutes, 1835-9
Church Histories
Christian Connection Records

Correspondence of the Glasgow Colonial Society, vols. 4–7 (microfilm)
Methodist Missionary Correspondence, Canada West, 1830–50 (microfilm)
Wellington Street Church, Brantford, Minutes of the Quarterly Board, vol. I

University of Western Ontario Library, Regional History Collection, London
Church of England, Delaware, Records
Quaker Records

PRINTED PRIMARY SOURCES

CHURCH AND GOVERNMENT PUBLICATIONS

Annual Report of the Colonial Missionary Society, in Connexion with the Congregational Union of England and Wales, 1837–1841
Appendix to the Journal of the House of Assembly of Upper Canada, Session of 1835 to Session of 1839–40
Baptist Magazine, XXIV (April 1832) – XXX (Nov. 1838)
Canada Baptist Magazine, and Missionary Register, I, 1 (June 1837) – II, 5 (Oct. 1838)
Canadian Christian Examiner and Presbyterian Review, I, 1 (March 1837) – II, 4 (April 1838)
Evangelical Magazine and Gospel Advocate, I, 1 (2 Jan. 1830) – X, 26 (28 June 1839)
Journal of the House of Assembly of Upper Canada, Session of 1828 to Session of 1839–40
The Minutes of the Annual Conferences of the Wesleyan-Methodist Church in Canada, from 1824 to 1845, Inclusive ... Toronto 1846
Quarterly Record of the Missions in Connexion with the United Secession Church II (April 1838) – VII (July 1839)
Report of the Incorporated Society for the Propagation of the Gospel in Foreign Parts for the Year 1828
United Secession Magazine, III (1835) – V (1837)

CONTEMPORARY NEWSPAPERS

British Colonist (Toronto), 1 Feb. 1838 – 27 Dec. 1838
Christian Guardian (Toronto), 7 June 1837 – 26 Dec. 1838
Church (Coburg), 6 May 1837 – 29 Dec. 1838
Constitution (Toronto), 11 Jan. 1837 – 6 Dec. 1837
Hamilton Gazette, and Gore District General and Commercial Advertiser, 4 Jan. 1837 – 16 Jan. 1838
Liberal (St Thomas), 20 Sept. 1832 – 10 Oct. 1833; various issues 1834, 1835, 1836, 1837

London Gazette, 28 Oct. 1837, 18 Nov. 1837, 19 May 1838, 26 May 1838
Mackenzie's Gazette (New York State), 17 April 1838 – 23 Dec. 1840
Mirror (Toronto), 28 Oct. 1837 – 21 Dec. 1838
Oxford Star and Woodstock Advertiser, 15 Dec. 1848
Patriot (Toronto), 2 June 1837 – 4 Sept. 1838
Palladium of British America, and Upper Canada Mercantile Advertiser (Toronto), various issues from 20 Dec. 1837 – 27 June 1838
St Catharines Journal, and Welland Canal (Niagara District) General Advertiser, 1 June 1837 – 1 Nov. 1838
Upper Canada Gazette (Toronto), 6 July 1837 – 28 Dec. 1838
Western Herald and Farmer's Magazine (Sandwich), 3 Jan. 1838 – 6 Nov. 1838

AUTOBIOGRAPHIES AND REMINISCENCES

Brown, Thomas Storrow. *1837 – My Connection with It.* Quebec 1898
Carruthers, J. *Retrospect of Thirty-Six Years' Residence in Canada West: Being a Christian Journal and Narrative.* Hamilton 1861
Hincks, Sir Francis. *Reminiscences of His Public Life.* Montreal 1884
Hodgins, J.G., ed. *The Story of My Life.* Toronto 1883
Leonard, Elijah. *The Honourable Elijah Leonard – A Memoir.* London 1894
Norton, L.A. *Life and Adventures of Col. L.A. Norton, Written by Himself.* Oakland, California 1887
'Reminiscences by Judge William Elliott.' *Transactions of the London and Middlesex Historical Society* IX (1918): 26–9
Young, James. *Reminiscences of the Early History of Galt and the Settlement of Dumfries.* Toronto 1880

PAMPHLETS, TRAVELLERS' AND SETTLERS' ACCOUNTS, ETC.

A Concise Description of Canada (n.p., n.d.)
A Statement of the Satisfactory Results which Have Attended Emigration to Upper Canada ... London 1842
Bonnycastle, Richard H., and James Edward Alexander. *Canada, as it Was, Is, and May Be.* London 1852
Brydone, James Marr. *Narrative of a Voyage; A Party of Emigrants Sent out from Sussex, in 1834, by the Petworth Emigration Committee ...* Petworth 1834
Canada in the Years 1832, 1833, and 1834. Containing Important Information and Instructions ... Dublin 1835
Chisholm, David. *Annals of Canada for 1837–38* (n.p., n.d.)
Davis, Robert. *The Canadian Farmer's Travels in the United States of America ...* Buffalo 1837

[Dunlop, William.] *Statistical Sketches of Upper Canada, for the Use of Emigrants: By a Backwoodsman.* London 1832

Gourlay, Robert. *Statistical Account of Upper Canada, Compiled with a View to a Grand System of Emigration, by Robert Gourlay.* 2 vols. London 1822

Hanshaw, John P.K., ed. *The Late Bishop of Quebec's Upper Canadian Travelling Mission Fund ...* Piccadilly (1840?)

Horsman, E.A., and Lillian Rea Benson, eds. *The Canadian Journal of Alfred Domett ... 1833–35.* London, Ontario: University of Western Ontario 1955

Jameson, Anna. *Winter Studies and Summer Rambles in Canada.* Toronto: McClelland and Stewart Ltd. 1923

Mackenzie, William L. *Sketches of Canada and the United States.* London 1833

Mountain, George Jehosophat. *Canadian Church Destitution ...* Hexam 1839

Murray, Hugh. *An Historical and Descriptive Account of British America ...* vol. I. Edinburgh 1839

Picken, Andrew. *The Canadas: Comprehending Topographical Information ... and the Fullest General Information ...* London 1836

Preston, T.R. *Three Years' Residence in Canada, from 1837 to 1839 ...* 2 vols. London 1840

Rolph, Dr Thomas. *A Brief Account, Observations Made During a Visit in the West Indies ... Together with a Statistical Account of Upper Canada.* Dundas 1836

[Ryerson, Egerton.] *The Affairs of the Canadas. In a Series of Letters. By a Canadian.* London 1837

Shirreff, Patrick. *A Tour through North America: Together with a Comprehensive View of the Canadas and United States as Adapted for Agricultural Emigration.* Edinburgh 1835

The Speech of the Hon. John Rolph, MPP. Delivered on the Occasion of the Late Inquiry into Charges of High Misdemeanours at the Late Elections ... Toronto 1837

Theller, E.A. *Canada in 1837–38: Showing by Historical Facts, the Causes of the Late Attempted Revolution, and of Its Failure ...* 2 vols. Philadelphia 1841

Waddilove, W.J.D. *The Stewart Missions: A Series of Letters and Journals Calculated to Exhibit to British Christians the Spiritual Destitution of the Emigrants Settled in the Remote Parts of Upper Canada.* London 1838

CONTEMPORARY MATERIAL OF LATER PRINTING

Careless, J.M.S., ed. 'Letters from Thomas Talbot to John Beverley Robinson.' *Ontario History* LXIX (1957): 25–41

Coventry, George. 'A Concise History of the Late Rebellion in Upper Canada to the Evacuation of Navy Island 1838.' Notes by W.R. Riddell. *Ontario Historical Society Papers and Records* XVII (1919): 113–74

303 Bibliography

Coyne, James H., ed. 'The Talbot Papers.' *Proceedings and Transactions of the Royal Society of Canada* I (1907) sec. II, 15–210
Gray, Leslie R., ed. 'The Letters of John Talbot.' *Ontario History* XLIV (1952): 139–64
Head, Sir Francis Bond. *A Narrative, with Notes by William Lyon Mackenzie.* Edited by S.F. Wise. Toronto: McClelland and Stewart Ltd. 1969
Lucas, Sir C.P., ed. *Lord Durham's Report on the Affairs of British North America.* 3 vols. Oxford: Clarendon Press 1912
Miller, H. Orlo, ed. 'The Letters of Rebels and Loyalists.' *Canadian Science Digest* 1 (Jan. 1938): 70–8
Miller, Linus W. *Notes of an Exile to Van Diemen's Land ...* East Ardsley: S.R. Publishers Ltd., Johnson Reprint Corporation 1968
Sanderson, Charles R., ed. *The Arthur Papers.* 2 vols. Toronto: Toronto Public Libraries and University of Toronto Press 1957

SECONDARY SOURCES

BOOKS, THESES, GENEALOGIES, PAMPHLETS

Aitchison, J.H. 'Development of Local Government in Upper Canada, 1783–1850,' PH D dissertation, University of Toronto, 1953
Aitken, Hugh G.J. *The Welland Canal Company: A Study in Canadian Enterprise.* Cambridge Massachusetts: Harvard University Press 1954
Canniff, William. *The Medical Profession in Upper Canada, 1783–1850 ...* Toronto 1894
Carroll, John. *Case and His Contemporaries or, the Canadian Itinerants' Memorial ...* vol. I. Toronto 1874
Chadwick, Edward Marion. *Ontarian Families, Genealogies of United Empire Loyalist and Other Pioneer Families of Upper Canada.* New Jersey: Hunterdon House 1970
Clark, Samuel Delbert. *Church and Sect in Canada.* Toronto: University of Toronto Press 1948
– *Movements of Political Protest in Canada, 1640–1840.* Toronto: University of Toronto Press 1959
Corey, Albert B. *The Crisis of 1830–42 in Canadian-American Relations.* New Haven: Yale University Press 1941
Craig, Gerald M. *Upper Canada: The Formative Years, 1784–1841.* Toronto: McClelland and Stewart Ltd. 1963
Creighton, Donald G. *The Empire of the St Lawrence.* Toronto: Macmillan Co. of Canada Ltd. 1956

Cruikshank, E.A. *A Memoir of Colonel the Honourable James Kerby, Welland County Historical Society Papers and Records*, vol. IV. Welland: Welland County Historical Society 1931

Darvall, Frank Ongley. *Popular Disturbances and Public Order in Regency England ...* London: Oxford University Press 1934

Dent, J.C. *The Story of the Upper Canadian Rebellion.* 2 vols. Toronto 1885

Dorland, Arthur Garratt. *A History of the Society of Friends (Quakers) in Canada.* Toronto: Macmillan Co. of Canada Ltd. 1927

Dunham, Aileen. *Political Unrest in Upper Canada, 1815–36.* London: McClelland and Stewart Ltd. 1927

Ermatinger, C.O. *The Talbot Régime – or the First Half Century of the Talbot Settlement.* St Thomas: Municipal World Ltd. 1904

Finch, Vernor C. et al. *Elements of Geography: Physical and Cultural.* 4th ed. New York, Toronto, London: McGraw-Hill Book Co. Inc. 1957

Gates, Lillian F. *Land Policies of Upper Canada.* Canadian Studies in History and Government, vol. IX. Toronto: University of Toronto Press 1968

Graham, W.H. *The Tiger of Canada West.* Toronto: Clarke, Irwin and Co. Ltd. 1962

Gregg, William. *Short History of the Presbyterian Church in Canada from the Earliest to the Present Time.* Toronto 1892

Guillet, E.C. *Early Life in Upper Canada.* Toronto: University of Toronto Press 1963

– *The Lives and Times of the Patriots ...* Toronto: University of Toronto Press 1968

Hamil, Fred Coyne. *Lake Erie Baron.* Toronto: Macmillan Co. of Canada Ltd. 1955

The History of the County of Brant, Ontario. Toronto: Warner, Beers and Co. 1883

History of the County of Middlesex, Canada. Toronto: W.A. & C.L. Goodspeed 1889

Hitsman, J. Mackay. *Safeguarding Canada, 1763–1871.* Toronto: University of Toronto Press 1968

Hobsbawm, E.J., and George Rudé. *Captain Swing.* London: Lawrence and Wishart 1969

Hoffman, D.W., B.C. Matthews, and R.E. Wicklund. *Soil Associations of Southern Ontario.* Ottawa: Canada, Department of Agriculture 1964

Hotson, Zella M. *Pioneer Baptist Work in Oxford County.* Woodstock: [By the Author?] [1939]

Jones, Robert Leslie. *History of Agriculture in Ontario, 1613–1880.* University of Toronto Studies, History and Economics Series, vol. IX. Toronto: University of Toronto Press 1946

Bibliography

Kinchen, Oscar A. *The Rise and Fall of the Patriot Hunters.* New York: Bookman Associates 1956
Landon, Fred. *An Exile from Canada to Van Diemen's Land ...* Toronto: Longmans, Green and Co. 1960
- *Western Ontario and the American Frontier.* Toronto: McClelland and Stewart Ltd. 1941
Lindsey, Charles. *The Life and Times of William Lyon Mackenzie ...* 2 vols. Toronto 1862
Longley, R.S. *Sir Francis Hincks.* Toronto: University of Toronto Press 1943
Lower, A.R.M. *Settlement and the Forest Frontier in Eastern Canada.* Canadian Frontiers and Settlement Series, vol. IX. Toronto: Macmillan Co. of Canada Ltd. 1936
McCready, H.W., ed. *Lord Durham's Mission to Canada; An Abridgement of Lord Durham ... by Chester New.* Toronto: McClelland and Stewart Ltd. 1963
Macdonell, John Alexander. *A Sketch of the Life of the Honourable and Right Reverend Alexander Macdonell ...* Alexandria 1890
Malcolm, John Karl. *The History and Genealogy of the Malcolm Family of the United States and Canada.* Ann Arbor: By the Author 1950
Martyn, John Parks. 'Upper Canada and Border Incidents, 1837-38, A Study of the Troubles on the American Frontier Following the Rebellion of 1837.' Master's thesis, University of Toronto, 1962
Merritt, J.P. *Biography of the Hon. W.H. Merritt ...* St Catharines 1875
Muir, R. Cuthbertson. *The Early Political and Military History of Burford.* Quebec: La Cie D'Imprimerie Commerciale 1913
Ontario, Department of Planning and Development, *Otter Valley Conservation Report.* 1957
Patterson, Graeme H. 'Studies in Elections and Public Opinion in Upper Canada.' PH D dissertation, University of Toronto, 1969
Reville, F.D. *History of the County of Brant.* 2 vols. Brantford: Hurly Publishing Co. Ltd., Published under the Auspices of the Brant Historical Society 1920
Robertson, J. Ross. *The History of Freemasonry in Canada.* 2 vols. Toronto 1899
Robinson, Fred. V. 'A Study of Agriculture in Upper Canada between 1830 and 1850.' Master's thesis, University of Western Ontario, 1939
Rudé, George. *The Crowd in History, A Study of Popular Disturbances in France and England, 1730-1848.* New York: John Wiley & Sons, Inc. 1964
Seaborn, Edwin. *The March of Medicine in Western Ontario.* Toronto: Ryerson Press 1944
Sissons, C.B. *Egerton Ryerson, His Life and Letters,* vol. I. Toronto: Clarke, Irwin and Co. Ltd. 1948

Stagg, Ronald J. 'The Yonge Street Rebellion of 1837: An Examination of the Social Background and a Re-assessment of the Events.' PH D dissertation, University of Toronto, 1976
Webster, Thomas. *History of the Methodist Episcopal Church in Canada.* Hamilton (n.d.)
Wicklund, R.E., and N.R. Richards. *The Soil Survey of Oxford County.* Ontario Soil Survey, Report No. 28. Guelph: Canada and Ontario Departments of Agriculture 1961
Wilkinson, Kathryn Morris. *Duncombes in America, with Some Collateral Lineages.* Milwaukee: By the Author 1965
Wilson, Alan. *The Clergy Reserves of Upper Canada: A Canadian Mortmain.* Canadian Studies in History and Government, vol. IX. Toronto: University of Toronto Press 1968
Wood, John David. 'The Historical Geography of Dumfries Township, Upper Canada: 1816 to 1852.' Master's thesis, University of Toronto, 1958

ARTICLES

Baehre, Rainer. 'Origins of the Penitentiary System in Upper Canada.' *Ontario History* LXIX (1977): 185–207
Baskerville, Peter. 'Sir Allan Napier MacNab.' *Dictionary of Canadian Biography* IX (Toronto: University of Toronto Press 1976): 519–27
Campbell, Cl. T. 'The Settlement of London.' *Transactions of the London and Middlesex Historical Society* (1909–11): 9–51
Craig, G.M. 'John Rolph.' *Dictionary of Canadian Biography* IX (Toronto: University of Toronto Press 1976): 683–90
Cross, Michael S. 'Charles Duncombe.' *Dictionary of Canadian Biography* IX (Toronto: University of Toronto Press 1976): 228–32
Cruikshank, E.A. 'A Twice-Told Tale (The Insurrection in the Short Hills in 1838).' *Ontario Historical Society Papers and Records* XXIII (1926): 180–222
Landon, Fred. 'The Common Man in the Era of the Rebellion in Upper Canada.' *Canadian Historical Association Report* (1937): 76–91
– 'The Duncombe Uprising of 1837 and Some of Its Consequences.' *Proceedings and Transactions of the Royal Society of Canada* XXV (1931) sec. II, 83–98
– 'London and Its Vicinity, 1837–38' *Ontario Historical Society Papers and Records* XXIV (1927): 410–38
Longley, R.S. 'Emigration and the Crisis of 1837 in Upper Canada.' *Canadian Historical Review* XVII (1936): 29–40
Luard, Mrs Peter D. 'Oxen, Candles and Homespun. In *'A Glimpse of the Past': A*

307 Bibliography

Centennial History of Brantford and Brant County. Compiled by the Brant Historical Society (Brantford: Brant Historical Society 1966): 10–21

Read, Colin. 'The Duncombe Rising, Its Aftermath, Anti-Americanism, and Sectarianism,' *Histoire sociale – Social History* IX (1976): 47–69

– 'The Short Hills Raid of June, 1838, and Its Aftermath.' *Ontario History* LXVIII (1976): 93–115

Riddell, W.R. 'A Trial for High Treason in 1838.' *Ontario Historical Society Papers and Records* XVIII (1920): 50–8

Ross, Robert B. 'The Patriot War.' *Collections and Researches Made by the Michigan Pioneer and Historical Society* XXI (1894): 509–608

Talman, J.J. 'John Baptist Askin.' *Dictionary of Canadian Biography* IX (Toronto: University of Toronto Press 1976): 8–9

Thomson, James A. 'Proudfoot and the Secession Churches.' In *Enkindled by the Word, Essays on Presbyterianism in Canada.* Compiled by the Centennial Committee of the Presbyterian Church in Canada (Toronto: Presbyterian Publications 1966): 31–41

Tiffany, Orrin Edward. 'Relations of the United States to the Canadian Rebellion of 1837–38.' *Publications of the Buffalo Historical Society* VIII (1905): 1–118

Waldie, Jean H. 'Malcolm Folk Made Presence Felt in Brant.' *London Free Press* (1 July 1939)

– 'Pioneer Days in Brant County.' *Ontario Historical Society Papers and Records* XXXV (1943): 56–43

Watt, R.C. 'The Political Prisoners in Upper Canada.' *English Historical Review* LXI (1926): 526–55

Wise, S.F. 'Upper Canada and the Conservative Tradition.' In *Profiles of a Province: Studies in the History of Ontario* ... Compiled by the Ontario Historical Society (Toronto: Ontario Historical Society 1967): 20–33

Index

Adelaide township 12, 39, 159; settlement 15, 16, 22, 24, 44, 45, 168, 285 n176; religion 28, 29, 30, 36; politics 61; militia 119
Adelaide (village) 45
agriculture 38–43, 44, 198; harvests 65, 72, 160
Aikman, Michael 62
Aitchison, James 157, 195
Aitchison, J.H. 57
Aldborough township 12, 39, 40; settlement 15, 16, 17, 22, 23, 26, 42–3, 182; religion 28, 29, 30, 36, 59; politics 50; in rebellion 183
alien question 6, 21, 178
Allan, Rev Daniel 37
Allan, Nathan 147
Alway, Robert 54, 62, 68, 69, 79, 121, 126, 193, 248, 276 n120; in rebellion 90, 92, 106
Amherstburg 116, 122, 123
Anderson, Anthony 83
Anderson, David 70, 116, 218–19, 220; in rebellion 91, 96–7, 104, 106, 184, 197
Armstrong, Robert 109, 276 n111, 276 n120

'Army of the North-West' 116
Arthur, Sir George 139, 153, 157–8, 159, 162, 181, 195; policy towards prisoners 127–8, 131, 148, 149–50, 152, 158; in patriot troubles 134, 138, 143–4, 146, 155, 156, 157
Askin, John 48
Askin, Col John Baptist 48–9; politics in 1836–7 61, 68–9, 74, 80; in rebellion 100–1, 103–4, 108; on militia 115, 117; on rebellion 154, 183, 206
assembly 5, 8, 65, 66, 72, 74, 75, 77; elections to in 1828–36 7, 8, 54, 57–65; reports to 56, 58, 64; in 1838 120–1, 125
Associate Reformed Church 192, 256 n55
Associated Synod 32, 38
Austin, Calvin 144, 145, 220, 251
Aylmer 45

Babbit, Russel 142–3
Baldwin Robert 8, 57–8, 63
Baldwin, William Warren 8, 57, 64
Bank of Upper Canada 7
Baptist Missionary Magazine 190
Baptists 27, 35, 37, 38; in study area

23, 27, 31, 35–6, 185, 186, 189, 198, 211; among rebels 187, 189–90, 201; loyalty 190, 201, 203; effects of rebellion on 194–5, 196
- Closed Communion 35–6; in study area 3, 35, 186, 189, 198; among rebels 187, 189, 190; loyalty 190, 201; effects of rebellion on 195
- Free Will 31, 36, 186, 189
- Open Communion 35–6; in study area 31, 35–6, 186, 189; among rebels 187, 189; effects of rebellion on 195
- Scotch 36, 195

Bathurst, Lord 21
Bayham township 12, 39, 40, 166; settlement 15, 17, 18, 22, 23, 24, 25, 42, 43, 45, 179, 183, 197–9; religion 28, 29, 30, 32, 37, 38, 187, 189, 191, 193, 198, 257 n80, 289 n63, n77, n78, n79, 290 n95; politics 51, 58, 61, 70–1, 73, 75, 199; in rebellion 89, 91, 95–7, 104, 119, 164, 170, 181, 197, 199–201, 206, 268 n44; post-rebellion 119–20, 124, 136, 160, 190; rebels from 170, 181, 189, 198, 200, 201–4; loyalists from 197, 199–204
Beachville 45, 193
Beamer, Jacob 137, 151, 220
Bedford, Daniel 157, 158, 220–1, 277 n143, 281 n89
Bedford, Paul 149, 161, 209, 221, 277 n143
Bell, James 149, 221, 277 n143, 282 n105
Bennett, Philo 104, 138, 144, 151
Bethune, Rev A.N. 205
Bidwell, Marshall Spring 8, 55, 63
Big Creek 155

Bird, Rev Francis 191–2
Bishop, Jonathan 109, 276 n111
Bishopsgate 45, 52
blacks 19, 62, 71, 73, 134, 136
Blair, Marcus 20
Blandford township 12, 139; settlement 15, 16, 22, 23, 45; religion 28, 29, 30
Blaquiere, Col P.B. de 102, 139–40, 183
Blenheim township 12, 20, 39, 165, 169; settlement 14, 15, 16, 20, 22, 24, 168, 179, 286 n176; religion 28, 29, 30, 32, 189, 191, 195, 289 n63, n77, n80, 290 n95; in rebellion 93, 94, 170; post-rebellion 117, 139, 140, 141
Bois-Blanc 116–17
Book, John 88
Bostwick, Col John 49, 100–1, 123
Bowes, Joseph 119, 221, 244, 277 n143, 282 n92
Bradshaw, Amos S. 113, 221, 277 n143, 282 n92
Brantford Sentinel 71
Brantford (town) 9, 44, 45, 46, 53; settlement 24, 182, 183, 286 n5; religion 27, 28, 29, 30, 32, 33, 35, 37, 50, 188, 189, 193, 194; in rebellion 84, 87, 88, 92, 94–5, 97, 98, 99, 100, 105, 126, 182, 183; post-rebellion 117, 120, 134–5, 138, 155, 156
Brantford township 11, 12, 40, 154, 165; settlement 14, 15, 20, 22, 23, 41, 45, 179; religion 27, 28, 29, 30, 32, 35, 37; politics 75; in rebellion 88, 92, 103, 170, 181, 191; post-rebellion 157
Brearley, Col William 136, 142, 158
Bridges, John George 154–5, 211

311 Index

British Colonial Society 33
British Constitutional Society 61
Brown, John D. 131, 233
Brown, Malcolm 209, 221, 273 n43, 276 n115, 281 n88
Brown, Sobiske 129, 221, 273 n33, 285 n182
Bryant, Harvey 131, 150, 152, 233
Brydone, James Marr 40, 42
Buchanan, James 184
Buffalo 91, 115, 122, 134, 199
Bull, G.P. 184
Bullock, Col Richard 139, 141, 155
Burford township 12, 39, 165; settlement 14, 15, 17, 20, 22, 24, 42, 45, 168, 179, 183, 285 n176; religion 28, 29, 30, 188, 189, 193, 194, 257 n80, 289 n63, n64, n77, n78, n79, 290 n95; politics 75; in rebellion 85, 88, 170, 188; post-rebellion 117, 118, 136–41 passim, 152, 155
Burford (village) 45
Burlington Bay 46
Burn, John 59, 140, 181, 192, 194
Burwell, Col John 158, 198, 201, 241; politics 64–5, 70, 199; in rebellion 95–6, 197, 199, 201; post-rebellion 119, 123–4
Burwell, Col Mahlon 25, 49, 64, 68, 154, 158, 190, 199, 203; politics 61, 62; on rebels 106, 175, 199, 209; post-rebellion 124, 133

Camden township 148
Campbell, Rev Dugald 195
Campbell, Rev P.C. 57
Canada Baptist Magazine and Missionary Register 184–5, 190
Canada Company 7, 17–18, 50, 76–7, 78

Canadian Christian Examiner and Presbyterian Review 37
Canadian Farmer's Travels, The 75
Canadian Missionary Society 190
Canadian Refugee Relief Association 135, 137
Caradoc township 12, 39; settlement 15, 16, 19, 20, 22, 23, 24, 182; religion 28, 29, 30, 36; politics 73, 77; post-rebellion 119
Carman, Edward 149, 161, 221, 277 n143
Carmichael, Hugh 77
Carpenter, Rev Charles 190
Case, George Washington 85, 137, 157, 162, 221, 286 n4
Cayuga township 103
census 172, 173; of 1839 27, 160–1, 185, 188, 191, 193, 256 n47; of 1841–2 162, 185
Chapin, Charles 149, 151, 171, 222, 276 n115
Chaple, Augustus 207, 222, 273 n33
Charlotteville township 12, 39, 40, 43; settlement 14, 15, 16, 17, 20, 22, 45, 166, 285 n175; religion 28, 29, 30; politics 58; post-rebellion 124, 155
Chatham 146
Chippawa 115
Chisholm, William 62
Christian Guardian 60
Christian Palladium 257 n78
Christians 37, 59, 192, 196
Church, The 205
Church of England 5, 6, 34, 49, 190; in study area 20, 27, 31, 34–5, 185, 186, 193, 198; politics 50, 59; among rebels 187, 193; post-rebellion 152, 193, 195, 196, 197; loyalty 193, 201, 203, 210

Church of Scotland 27, 32; in study area 31, 186, 192; politics 59, 77, 183; effects of rebellion on 196, 197
Cincinnati 163
Clark, George Alexander 97, 162, 248, 269 n92, 275 n80
Clench, J.B. 146
Clergy Reserves 5, 6, 51, 59, 76, 77; effects on settlement 5–6, 17, 18–19
Cleveland 122, 123, 134, 140, 147, 155, 199
Cleveland Herald 122
Coffin, Col (Nathaniel) 165
Colborne 45
Colborne, Sir John 21–3, 55, 57, 59, 63, 73, 79, 117, 156
Colonial Missionary Society 188
Colonial Office 21, 47, 64, 75, 211
Congregationalists 32; in study area 31, 32–3, 186, 188; politics, among rebels 187, 188–9; effects of rebellion on 194
Conklin, George 207, 222
Conneaut, Ohio 122
Connors, Andrew 123, 222, 244, 277 n141, 278 n144, 281 n89
Conrad, Charles 175, 233, 273 n33
Conservatives 49–50, 60–1; *see also* Tories
Constitutional Act 4, 5
Constitutional Reform Society 63
Cook, Abraham 88, 233
Cook, Ephraim 127, 150, 151, 161–2, 222, 274 n46
Cook, Harry 108
Cook, Ira 197, 241
Cook, Robert 128, 131, 150, 152, 197, 223, 244, 277 n141
Court of Oyer and Terminer and General Gaol Delivery 103, 110, 112, 120, 124, 129; *see also* Treason, trials for
Court of Quarter Sessions 47, 124
Coventry, George 173
Craig, Col 156
Craig, Gerald M. 4
Cronyn, Rev Benjamin 59
Crown Reserves 5–6, 17, 18
Crown witnesses 113, 129, 132, 133, 151
Cunningham, Cornelius 158
Curtis, David 111, 112–13, 248–9, 273 n31

Daubigny, William 159
Davis, Lyman 96–7, 130, 162, 223
Davis, Robert 75, 105, 116
Dawn township 146
deaths 135; in rebellion 99–100, 154; in patriot troubles 123, 146, 147, 157; executions 127, 129, 132, 150, 151, 158, 162; among state prisoners 148, 149, 153
Delaware township 12, 39, 52; settlement 14, 15, 16, 17, 20, 22, 45; religion 28, 29, 30; politics 67, 72, 74, 77; in rebellion 105, 108, 128, 130, 150; post-rebellion 146
Delaware (village) 45
DeLong, Peter 162, 188, 234
Dennis, James 162, 223
Dennis, John 144, 231, 251
Dent, J.C. 9
Deo, Nathaniel 129, 149–50, 152
depression 60, 65–6, 72, 135, 159–60, 168, 188, 198, 205
Dereham Forge 43, 45, 89–90, 123, 155
Dereham township 12, 20, 39, 43, 59, 166; settlement 14, 15, 16, 22, 23,

24, 45, 179, 285 n175; religion 28, 29, 30, 35, 189, 193, 289 n63, n77, n78; politics 76; in rebellion 86, 89–90, 92, 93, 103, 181, 182; post-rebellion 123, 124, 137, 139, 142, 154–5, 159, 181
Detroit 111, 116, 117, 122, 134; frontier 117, 122, 156
Detroit River 45, 46, 116, 157
Dickson, William 16
Doan, Joel P. 162, 223
Doan, Joshua 106, 157, 158, 162, 223
Doel's brewery 67, 69
Domett, Alfred 40
Dorchester township 12; settlement 14, 15, 16, 17, 21, 22; religion 28, 29, 30, 257 n80; politics 67, 72, 74; in rebellion 92, 105, 108, 129, 130, 149; post-rebellion 142, 147
Downie, Rev Daniel 36, 191
Doxie, Enoch D. 144, 249, 251
Draper, Isaac 198, 201, 241
Draper, William H. 148, 150; on rebellion 80, 106, 109; at Hamilton trials 125–7, 130; at London trials 129–32 passim
Drew, Capt Andrew 115
Dumfries township 11, 12, 39, 40, 41, 165; settlement 15, 16, 17, 22, 23, 24, 41, 45, 172, 180, 182; religion 28, 29, 30, 31, 32, 33, 34, 36, 37, 189, 191, 193, 257 n80; politics 50; in rebellion 93, 94, 103, 170, 181, 182; post-rebellion 140, 157
Duncombe, Charles 3, 62, 69, 125, 286 n7; relations with Mackenzie 8, 54, 63, 79–80, 90, 115, 162–3, 266 n176; reasons for rebelling 9, 85, 163, 208; biography 52–3, 163, 186, 223; early political career 53–5, 63, 68;

radicalized 55–7; mission to England 63–4, 67; in 1837, 74–5, 76; organizes rebellion 85–7, 90, 92, 93, 95, 97, 99, 100, 173, 189, 197, 205, 206, 207, 209, 210, 270 n99; escape 98–9, 106; and patriots 116–17, 122, 135, 137, 142, 147, 155, 162–3; retaliation against 118–19, 121, 153, 154, 162; pardon 163
Duncombe, Charles (son) 64
Duncombe, David 52, 62, 63, 78, 99, 186, 211; in assembly 54, 55, 74, 121
Duncombe, Elijah 52, 55, 77, 135, 154, 159, 160, 163
Duncombe, Huldah 52
Dunham, Aileen 4
Dunlop, William 41, 160
Dunwich township 12, 39, 40; settlement 14, 15, 16, 17, 22, 23, 26, 182; religion 28, 29, 30, 257 n80; politics 50, 61; in rebellion 183
Durand, James 54
Durham, Lord 18, 21, 35, 60, 62, 119, 153, 181, 182, 211, 256 n68

East Oxford township 12, 39, 165; settlement 14, 15, 16, 20, 22, 42, 179; religion 28, 29, 30, 189, 193, 289 n63, n64, n78, 290 n95; politics 76; in rebellion 86, 181; post-rebellion 137, 139, 142–3
Ekfrid township 12, 39, 40; settlement 15, 16, 19, 22, 23, 183; religion 28, 29, 30, 36
Elmsley, John 26
Embro 45, 77
emigration, in 1838 118, 135, 159–61, 193–4, 195, 196, 210
Emmons, Uriah 113, 149, 151, 152, 224, 277 n143

314 Index

England 23, 24, 26, 39, 42, 51, 63, 66, 113, 132, 161, 196; *see also* Colonial Office, Great Britain, Immigration
Eramosa township 109, 126, 288 n45
Ermatinger, C.O. 9
Ermatinger, Edward 96, 136
Esquesing township 183
Evangelical Magazine and Gospel Advocate 291 n123
Evans, Rev Francis 60, 97, 152
Evelegh, Capt J.H. 155
executive council 4, 8, 47, 69, 82; and Duncombe 55, 63, 86, 154; in 1836 crisis 57–8; and prisoners 126, 127, 128, 129, 149, 150, 151–2; *see also* Prisoners, state
executions 127–8, 129, 131–2, 150, 151, 158, 162

Family Compact 3, 4–5, 7, 48, 75, 76, 84, 211
farmers 38, 42–6 passim, 65, 72, 157, 198; in rebellion 170–1, 172, 173, 175, 177, 178, 201, 202
Fergus 103
Fighting Island 122–3
Fish, John 144, 145, 251
Fisher, Henry 153, 162, 224, 244
Fitzgibbon, Col James 53, 84
Five Stakes 45
Flannagan's tavern 100, 130, 146
Flood, Rev Richard 20, 71
Fort Erie 45
Fort Malden 116
Foster, Alonzo 125, 224, 276 n108
Fowler, Horatio 149, 224, 277 n143, 282 n105
Fuller, Stephen 133, 142
Furman, Rev C.E. 32

Galt 28, 29, 30, 32, 38, 44–5, 93, 103, 193, 286 n4
Gardiner, William 145, 146
Gilmore, Rev John 35
Glenelg, Lord 63–4, 67, 75, 93, 127
Glengarry 183
Goff, Henry P. 114, 249, 276 n108
Gore district 11, 65, 78–9, 106, 147; settlement 15, 22; religion 27, 28, 29, 30; rebels 124, 127, 153, 162; *see also* Brantford township, Dumfries township
Gould, Anson 130, 249
Gourlay, Robert 6, 17, 74
Government
 – local 4, 47–8; 1835 act 58–9; elections 67, 118, 181
 – responsible 8, 57, 58, 69, 72, 86, 211
Governor's road 45, 46, 101
Graham, Philip 76, 102
Graham, W.H. 160
Grand Jury 47, 48; and Hamilton prisoners 111, 114, 125, 126, 130; and London prisoners 112, 128–9
Grand River 53, 103, 138
Great Britain 4, 6, 8, 60, 77, 160, 161, 181; and Upper Canada Reformers 8, 55, 57, 58, 67, 69, 72, 74, 75, 78, 80; British Radicals 55, 166; and Upper Canada Tories 61, 70, 212; and rebels 87, 163, 208, 210; *see also* Colonial Office, England, Immigration
Great Western Railroad 46
Green, James L. 88, 234
Green, Rev Thomas 34–5, 45–6, 187, 190, 192, 193
Grieve, John 71, 148, 277 n142
Grigg, James 93

Grogan, Lieut 146
Guelph 79, 109, 184
Guillet, E.C. 9, 88, 160

Hackstaff, George 211
Hagerman, Christopher 55, 63, 100, 129
Hagerman, David 131, 224
Haldimand county 62
Hale, William 130
Hall, Elisha 76, 92–3, 153, 162, 211, 224, 286 n2, n7
Halton county 11, 15, 22, 28, 29, 30, 54, 62; *see also* Dumfries township
Hamilton 11, 45, 46, 78, 192; in rebellion 85, 86, 88, 89, 91, 92, 94, 95, 96, 97, 98, 109, 164, 184, 196, 206; post-rebellion 113–14, 115, 124, 125, 128, 152, 194
Hamilton, James 49, 73, 104, 112
Hamilton, Alexander 150
Hamilton and Brantford road 45
Hamilton Express 78, 159
Hamilton Free Press 78
Hamilton Gazette 184
Hamilton jail 109, 111, 113–14, 128, 145, 148, 149, 150, 185, 210
Hammill, John 126, 150, 151, 249
Harris, John 49
Hart, Joseph 149, 224, 277 n143, 282 n105
Harvard, Rev William 192
Hatcock, Daniel 144, 251
Head, Sir Francis 56, 57, 69; in 1836 crisis 57–8, 60, 61, 63, 64–5; in 1837 69, 73, 74, 75; in rebellion 83, 84, 86, 93, 95, 96, 97, 100, 102, 103, 104, 105, 108; post-rebellion 123, 124, 127

Henry, Philip 149, 225, 276 n115, 282 n105
Herrington, William 198, 225, 244
Hicks, Elias 36, 38
Hill, George 129, 225, 244, 277 n143, 282 n92
Hillaker, Benjamin 144, 251
Hillaker, William 144, 251
Hills, Horatio 93, 127, 150, 153, 225
Holcroft, Col William 136–7, 142, 159
Home district 147; *see also* Toronto, in rebellion
Hope, Adam 41, 42, 65, 104, 118, 173, 175, 177
Hopkins, Caleb 54
Hoskins, Luther 149, 225, 277 n141, 278 n145, 282 n105
Houghton township 12, 39, 40, 43, 201; settlement 15, 16, 19, 22, 23, 43, 285 n175; religion 28, 29, 30
Howard township 148
Howes, Nancy (Mrs Charles Duncombe) 52
Hume, Joseph 55, 75
Humphrey, Norris 153, 168, 225, 244, 286 n7
Hunter, Roger Rollo 121
Hunters, the 140–1, 142, 145, 146, 155, 157; *see also* Patriots
Huron county 12, 117
Huron Tract 17, 78, 105

immigration 6, 7, 20–4 passim, 46, 71, 157, 160, 181; *see also* Settlers
Indians 19–20, 22, 34, 75–6
– Chippewas, Munceys, and Delawares 20, 105, 130, 146, 147
– Six Nations 19–20; reserve 12, 19–20; in rebellion 87, 99–100, 169,

206; post-rebellion 138, 139, 142, 146, 155
Ingersoll 28, 29, 30, 45, 97, 102, 142, 193, 286 n4
Ingersoll, James 61

Jameson (R.S.) 55, 63
Jameson, Anna 43, 44
Jamestown 45, 175
Jarvis, S.P. 146
Jedburgh 45
Johnson, Capt Moses 136
Joseph, John 61, 64, 95, 103, 129, 136
justices of the peace 25, 47, 58–9, 62, 165, 185, 206, 207, 209; dismissals 65, 69; appointments 68; in 1837 70, 73, 74; in rebellion 95, 96, 102, 173, 188, 199, 201; jailing rebels 103, 108, 170, 176; empanelled at London 108, 109; actions at London 108–9, 110, 112–13, 114, 120, 128, 131, 192; examinations at Hamilton 109, 114; post-rebellion arrests and examinations 110–11, 119–20, 123, 144–5, 146–7, 148; post-rebellion activities 119, 120, 134, 136, 137, 139, 140, 141, 142, 143, 155, 194

Katesville 45
Kelly, John 149, 225–6, 278 n145
Kenny, Franklyn 182, 234
Kent, John 55, 58
Kerr, William Johnson 138
Kerry, Capt 146, 147
Kettle Creek 46
Kinchen, Oscar 147
Kingston 123, 194; penitentiary 56, 149, 150, 151, 152, 158

labourers 43, 198, 217; in rebellion 172, 173, 174, 175, 176, 177, 178, 198, 202
Ladd, Alvaro 77, 78, 128, 130, 150, 152
Laing, Robert 149, 218, 276 n115
Lake Erie 43, 45, 122
Lancaster, Joseph 143, 226, 273 n33
Land: patents 14; frauds 61–2; policies 12–19, 76
Land, Col Robert 95, 128
Landon, Fred 9–10, 118
Lang, Christopher 145
Latimer, Charles 74, 130
Laurason, Laurence 108
Lawton, George 91, 162, 234, 287 n12
legislative council 4, 5, 21, 47, 57; legislation in 1838 120–1
Leith, George 42, 46
Leonard, Elijah 119
Lewis, Asahel 54, 55
Lewiston 92
Liberals 51; *see also* Reformers
Light, Col Alexander Whalley 24–5, 42, 139, 140, 141, 171, 181, 196–7
Lillie, Rev David 194
Lindsey, Charles 3, 7, 9
Line, Luther 198
Lloydtown 193
Lobo township 12, 15, 22, 39, 40; settlement 23, 24, 182; religion 28, 29, 30, 36, 195; politics 67, 72, 74, 77; post-rebellion 159; in rebellion 183
Lockport 135, 140, 163
London and Gore Railroad 53
London district 11, 43, 50, 153, 162, 172, 201; settlement 15, 16, 22, 23, 254 n1; religion 28, 29, 30, 37; oligarchy 48–9; politics 58–62,

317 Index

70–1, 72–3, 79, 80–1, 82; in rebellion 94, 105, 106, 192, 212; post-rebellion 115, 116, 117, 118, 122, 124, 128, 129, 131, 132, 133, 138, 140, 146, 147, 156, 157, 159, 160
London Gazette 71, 73, 77, 131, 148, 149
London Sun 54
London (town) 43, 44, 45, 46, 48, 56, 168, 171, 172; religion 26, 28, 29, 30, 32, 33, 36, 37, 192, 194, 195; politics 51, 61, 62, 73, 74, 77; in rebellion 84, 92, 97, 99, 100, 104–5, 108, 130, 192; jail 102, 104, 108, 111–12, 113, 137, 147, 148, 149, 150, 154, 158; post-rebellion 108–9, 111–13, 115, 122, 123, 124, 128, 129, 130, 139, 144, 146–8, 151, 158, 159, 211
London township 12, 39, 40; settlement 15, 16, 22, 23, 24, 58, 71, 182; religion 28, 29, 30, 32, 33, 36, 257 n80; politics 71, 72, 74; in rebellion 184
Longley, R.S. 160, 165
Long Point 40, 41, 42, 134, 139, 142
Long Point Furnace 43, 212
Lossing, Horace 144–5, 251
Lossing, Solomon 85, 101, 102, 126–7, 144–5, 188, 234–5, 287 n12, 292 n141
Lount, Samuel 63, 83, 127, 129, 132
Lower Canada 117; agitation in 1837 65, 67, 73, 74, 79, 183; Reform resolutions on 67, 69, 72, 76; Tory resolution on 71; rebellion in 80, 83, 85, 87, 88, 89, 95
Loyalists: during rebellion 95–6, 99, 101–2, 104–5, 164, 188, 190, 210; post-rebellion 115–21 passim, 132, 133, 136, 139, 140, 142, 143, 145, 146, 147, 154, 157, 158, 196–7, 210; loyalist-rebel dichotomy 164, 197, 199–204, 207; *see also* Tories
Lyons, William 88, 127, 226

Macaulay, James Buchanan 126
Macaulay, John 143, 152, 154
McConnell, Rev Shook 190
McDermid, Duncan 88
Macdonald, John A. 212
Macdonald, John Sandfield 45
Macdonell, Bishop Alexander 59, 72, 192, 193
McGuire, William 87–8, 208, 232, 285 n182
McKenny, Doyle 70, 95–6, 123, 153, 201, 206, 242
McKenny, Eliza 139
McKenny, Richard 139
Mackenzie, A.K. 137
McKenzie, Rev Donald 59
Mackenzie, James 163
Mackenzie, William Lyon 3, 122; political career 7–8, 57, 60, 63, 75, 84, 205; organizes rebellion 8–9, 79, 80, 82–3, 86–92 passim, 109, 125, 183, 189, 205; relations with Duncombe 8–9, 54, 63, 79–80, 85, 86, 97, 115, 162, 266 n176; in 1837 agitation 66–7, 69, 70–1, 72, 75; at Navy Island 115–16, 117
Mackenzie Rebellion 3, 8, 11, 79, 80, 82–3, 84, 97, 98, 106, 109, 127, 183; rumours about 9, 84–92 passim, 100, 109, 205, 206, 210
McKillican, Rev W.M. 159, 190, 195
McLeod (Donald) 142
McLure, Andrew 190, 226, 277 n141, 278 n144, 281 n89
MacNab, Col Allan 62, 83, 206; in Toronto rebellion 83–4; in

Duncombe rebellion 98, 99, 100, 101–3, 105–6, 114, 119, 206; at Navy Island 115; at treason trials 149, 218, 276 n115
McPhederain, Duncan 149, 218, 276 n115
magistrates. *See* Justices of the peace
Magrath, Major T.W. 134–5
Maitland, Col John 122, 123, 141, 143, 146, 147
Maitland, Thomas 143
Malahide township 12, 39, 166; settlement 14, 15, 21, 22, 23, 24, 42, 43, 45, 179; religion 28, 29, 30, 37, 186, 189, 191, 193, 257 n80, 289 n63, n79, 290 n95; politics 51, 73; in rebellion 91, 95–6, 104, 170, 175, 182; post-rebellion 139, 147; rebels from 170, 171, 175–7, 183–4, 189
Malcolm, Daniel 89, 235
Malcolm, Eliakim 67, 208, 286 n7; biography 68–9, 163, 227; politics 69, 74, 75, 79; organizes rebellion 85, 86, 87–9, 95, 97, 98, 100, 206, 210, 292 n141; actions against 106, 118, 153–4; with patriots 122, 142; pardon 162
Malcolm, Finlay (father) 67–8, 89, 227
Malcolm, Finlay (of Bayham) 89–90, 91, 98, 149, 161, 168, 210, 227, 244, 277 n143
Malcolm, Finlay (of Oakland) 67–8, 106, 127
Malcolm, James 88, 89, 118, 153, 162, 206, 208, 227, 286 n7
Malcolm, John 68, 126, 191, 227, 293 n20
Malcolm, Norman 126, 191, 247
Malcolm, Peter 127, 150, 152, 227
Malcolm, Samantha 153–4

Malcolm, Tryphena 67
Malcolm's Mills (Oakland village) 45, 93, 134
Malloch (Edward) 121
Mallory, Benajah 55, 63, 68
Marchen, Rev George 26
Marlatt, Samuel 94, 127, 227
Marr, Rev J. 196
Marsh, Rev Edward 32, 50
Martin, James 25, 242
Mason (Stevens Thomson, Governor of Michigan) 116–17
Masons 53, 56, 140, 186
Massacre, John 130, 142, 162, 235
Matthews, Capt (John) 7
Matthews, Jesse 144, 145, 251
Matthews, Peter 127, 129, 132
Meade, Benjamin 124
Medcalf, Capt Henry 70, 95–6, 197, 201, 242
Mennonites 12, 22, 24–5
merchants 43–4, 66, 72; in rebellion 172, 199, 201, 202
Merwin, Henry 88, 228, 285 n182, 286 n7
Methodists 33, 35, 37, 38, 196; in study area 31, 33–4, 185, 186, 191, 198; politics 57; among rebels 187, 191, 192
– Episcopal 34, 38; in study area 31, 33, 34, 38, 186, 191, 198; politics 59; among rebels 187, 191–2; effects of rebellion on 194
– Ryanite 33; in study area 31, 33–4, 38, 186, 191, 198
– Wesleyan 26, 34, 38; in study area 20, 31, 33, 38, 186, 191, 198; politics 59–60; among rebels 187, 191, 192, 194; loyalty 192; effects of rebellion on 194

Michigan 52, 98, 105, 140, 159
Middlesex county 11, 12, 41, 46; settlement 15, 22, 42, 166, 182; religion 28, 29, 30, 31, 33, 34; politics 48, 54, 59, 62, 90; 1837 agitation in 74-9 passim; rebellion in 103, 107, 170; post-rebellion 107-8, 116, 117, 123, 160
Middleton township 12, 39, 43; settlement 15, 16, 17, 19, 22, 23, 40, 43, 168, 285 n176; religion 28, 29, 30, 37
military
- militia: in rebellion 82, 84, 94-6, 99, 100-2, 103-6, 109, 170, 190, 197, 272 n144; organization 94; post-rebellion 115-16, 117-18, 122, 123, 133-8 passim, 146, 154, 155-7, 161, 203, 211; in second Norwich rebellion 139-41, 142-4, 145, 146; discontent in 155-7, 159
- Regulars: withdrawn from Upper Canada 73, 115; returned 117; post-rebellion 122, 123, 124, 134, 135, 137, 146, 147, 155
Miller, Linus 128
Mills, M.M. 162
Mitchell, Ephraim Cole 203-4, 242
Montreal Herald 181
Moore, Cyrus 75, 89
Moore, Elias 91, 235, 287 n12; politics 54, 62; in rebellion 90, 188; post-rebellion 121, 130, 277 n142
Moore, Enoch 91, 131, 150, 152, 235, 287 n12
Moore, Isaac 129, 131, 228, 277 n141, 278 n144
Moore, James 169, 228
Moore, John 131, 148, 150, 151, 235, 287 n12

Moore, Joseph 148, 228
Moore, W.S. 141
Mormons 37, 38, 108, 192, 193, 196
Morreau, James 137, 138, 150, 151
Mosa township 12, 39; settlement 14, 15, 16, 19, 21, 22, 23, 24, 45, 182, 255 n30; religion 28, 29, 30, 36; politics 67; in rebellion 105, 108, 145; post-rebellion 146, 148, 156, 158
Mount Pleasant 45, 138
Muir, R.C. 9
Murray, Hugh 40

Nall, Rev 152, 194
Nassagaweya township 109, 125, 149, 183
Navy Island 115-16, 117, 120, 133, 272 n144
Nevers, Samuel (father) 169-70, 235
Nevers, Samuel (son) 169-70, 235
New Fairfield 20
New Sarum 45
New York (state) 137
Niagara 80, 150, 151; district 37, 38, 79, 110, 115, 137, 147, 153, 192, 254 n1; frontier 115, 117, 122, 123, 173
Niagara Presbytery 32, 38, 59, 192, 195-6
Niagara Reporter 151
Niagara River 115
Nicholls, David 208, 228
Nickerson, Moses Chapman 133-4, 162, 193
Nissouri township 12, 45-6; settlement 15, 22, 23, 182, 285 n175; religion 28, 29, 30, 34, 37, 257 n80; politics 67, 76; in rebellion 105, 183; post-rebellion 120, 139, 142
Nithvale 45
Norfolk county 11, 12, 40, 41; settle-

ment 15, 22, 42, 166, 254 n1; religion 27, 28, 29, 30, 33, 34, 35; lumbering 43; politics 48, 54, 59, 62, 63, 75, 78, 79; in rebellion 103, 107; post-rebellion 117, 121, 138, 156, 158, 159, 160, 211

Normandale 43

North Oxford township 12; settlement 14, 15, 16, 20, 22; religion 28, 29, 30, 257 n80; politics 76; post-rebellion 139, 142

Norton, Lewis Adelbert 9, 228, 277 n143, 282 n92

Norwich township 12, 20, 39, 43, 68, 162, 165; settlement 14, 15, 16, 17, 21, 22, 24, 42, 45, 160, 168, 179, 183, 285 n175, n176; religion 28, 29, 30, 34, 35, 37, 38, 137, 186, 189, 191, 193, 195, 289 n63, n80; politics 59, 67, 69, 74, 81; in rebellion 85–7, 90, 92, 94, 95, 98, 99, 101–3, 104, 105, 182, 191–2, 206; post-rebellion 117, 118, 123, 124, 129, 136, 137, 138, 139–45, 154–5, 156, 158, 162, 174, 181, 211; second Norwich rebellion 139–45; rebels from 170, 171, 174, 181, 183, 189, 191

Oakland (Malcolm's Mills) 45, 93, 134

Oakland township 12, 39, 40, 67, 68, 165; settlement 14, 15, 20, 22, 45, 179; religion 28, 29, 30, 32–3, 35, 188, 189, 193, 194, 289 n63, n78, 290 n95; politics 67, 75, 76, 81; in rebellion 85, 87–8, 89, 91–6 passim, 97–8, 99–101, 105, 197, 207; post-rebellion 111, 117, 118, 123, 124, 128, 134, 138, 139, 140, 142, 156, 159; rebels from 170, 171, 181, 183, 188, 189, 191

O'Brien (O'Beirne), John 61

Ohio 74, 122, 123, 155

O'Neill, Rev 185, 190, 193

Orangemen 51, 62, 70, 71, 75, 76

Otter Creek 43, 96, 104, 198, 199

Otterville 45

Oxford-Burford road 138

Oxford county 11, 12, 41, 65; settlement 15, 22, 41–2, 166; religion 28, 29, 30, 33, 34, 35, 36; politics 53, 54, 59, 61, 62, 63, 68, 72, 74, 75–6, 78, 81; in rebellion 92, 103, 107, 182; post-rebellion 117, 121, 123, 136–7, 139, 155, 159, 160, 162, 171

pacifism 36, 87, 187, 188, 190, 207

Page, Benjamin 96–7, 193, 277 n141, 278 n144, 281 n89

Papineau (Louis Joseph) 75

Paris 41, 44, 53, 138; settlement 24, 182, 183, 286 n4; religion 28, 29, 30, 33, 188

Parke, Thomas 54, 62, 90, 121, 211

Parker, John G. 78, 85, 149, 153, 161, 276 n114; as symbol for rebels 88, 89, 95, 97, 206

patriots 10, 162–3; raids 107, 114–17, 122–3, 128, 136, 146, 157, 210, 212; legislation against 120; threats and fears 121, 122, 123–4, 128, 132, 133–7, 139–42, 145–8, 151, 154–6, 158

Pelee Island 122, 123

Perley, Amos 158

Perley, Charles Strange 95, 158

Perry, Peter 54, 63

petitions: for clemency 154; statute concerning 120, 125, 128, 129, 131, 148–50

Petrie, Rev George 20, 196

Petworth emigration committee 23
Picken, Samuel 42
Pond's Mill 45
Port Burwell 43, 45; in rebellion 95, 96, 201; post-rebellion 117, 123–4, 133, 136, 146, 156, 160; settlement 198–9
Port Dover 43, 45; post-rebellion 117, 124, 133–4, 135, 155, 156
Port Rowan 45, 156
Port Ryerse 155
Port Sarnia 146
Port Stanley 45, 46, 193; post-rebellion 117, 123, 135, 136, 146, 156
Port Talbot 51
Powell, Anne 184
Presbyterians: in study area 23, 31–2, 38, 185, 186, 192; and rebellion 192
Prescott 157
Preston, T.R. 182
Prince, John 157
prisoners, state 123, 157; captures of 102–4, 107–8, 110; at London 108–9, 111–13, 114; at Hamilton 109, 114, 124, 210; at Simcoe 111; legislation about 120; trials of 124–32, 148, 158; bail for 108, 109, 110, 112–13, 114, 119, 123, 126, 128, 129–30, 148, 149, 151, 152; other dispositions 108, 109, 113, 119–20, 125, 126–7, 129, 130–1, 133, 149–50, 151–2, 161–2; from second Norwich rebellion 141, 144–5; from Chatham 146–8; from Short Hills 150–1; escapes of 152–3, 162; from Windsor 157–8; list of 164–5, 171–2
proclamations: of government 97, 102–3, 104, 153, 162; of Mackenzie 115; of Duncombe 122
Proudfoot, Rev William 37, 71; on settlers and settlement 26–7, 40–1, 42–3; on depression 65, 66, 72; on Reformers 67, 211; on militia 156–7; loyalty 157–8, 195; on emigration 159, 160
Putnam, Thomas 92, 236
Putnam, William 130, 146, 157

Quakers 36, 38, 137; in study area 31, 36–7, 186–7; politics 56, 69; post-rebellion 143, 194–5; among rebels 186–7; in rebellion 186–8
– Conservative 36–7, 38, 187
– Hicksite 36–7, 38, 187

Racey, Col James 84, 95
Rapelje, Col A.A. 53, 124
rebellion: historiography 3–4, 9–10; effects of 106, 159, 161, 193–7, 210–12
rebels
– accomplices 111, 165–6, 167, 174, 200, 233–7; legal disposition of 110, 112, 113, 125, 126, 127, 128, 130–1, 149, 150, 151, 152, 162; identification of 165, 166, 169–70; background 169, 174, 175, 177; nationalities 169, 178, 179, 181, 182, 184; religion 169, 186, 187, 189, 191
– Duncombe 111, 136–7, 165–6, 167, 220–32; mustering 85–94, 96–7, 109; rewards promised to 89, 91, 206–7; number 94, 164; proclamations about 97, 102–3, 104; dispersing of 98–9, 101, 106; surrenders and arrests 102–5, 107, 110, 119–20; legal disposition of 102,

322 Index

103, 110, 112, 113, 119–20, 123, 125–31 passim, 148–52 passim, 153, 158, 161, 162, 210; rewards offered for 106; property confiscations of 153–4, 177; leaders' aims 163, 208, 209; identification of 165, 166, 169–70, 171; prosperity of 165–9, 170, 173, 174; propertyholdings 169, 170–1; occupations 169, 171–3, 176–8, 201; ages 169, 173–4, 175, 176–7, 201, 202; marital status 169, 174, 175–6, 201, 203; nationalities 169, 178–84, 192, 203–4, 208, 209, 210; religion 169, 184–93, 194, 201, 203, 204; political activities 169, 209, 210; rebel-loyalist dichotomy 197, 199–204, 207; reasons for rebelling 204, 206–10
- Mackenzie 97, 102–3, 149, 165, 173, 193
- suspected 111, 165, 174, 246–50; legal disposition of 110, 111, 112, 113, 125, 126, 128, 130, 150, 151, 162, 174, 175; character 174, 175, 178, 179, 184, 186, 187, 189, 191, 193

Rees, Rev (William) 190
Reformers 51, 54, 55; grievances 3–7, 49, 50, 64–5, 66; rise of 7, 51–2, 54; post-rebellion 10, 107–8, 110, 115, 118–21 passim, 133, 147, 159, 160, 161, 211; in 1836 crisis 58–9, 60, 62, 63–4; in 1837, 67, 68–81; proposed convention of 67, 69, 74, 78, 80, 205; involvement in rebellion 82, 85–90 passim, 90, 94, 106, 113, 183, 210; meetings of 100, 105, 106, 108, 126, 130, 183
- moderate 8, 57, 205

- radicals 51, 68, 73, 74, 77; rise of 8, 57, 205; in rebellion 80, 82, 85, 89, 90, 95, 99, 104, 184, 197, 199, 206; post-rebellion 115, 118, 124, 133, 136, 147, 211
religion: in study area 27–38, 186–7, 188, 189, 191, 192, 193; 1839 census of 27, 31, 185, 188, 191, 193; sectarian animosities 38, 46, 184; rebels' affiliations 169, 184–93; effects of rebellion on 193–7; Bayham loyalists and rebels 201, 203
Reville, F.D. 9
Richmond 45, 70–1, 89, 198–9
Riddell, Robert 139
Riley, John 113, 129, 229, 277 n143, 281 n89, 286 n2
riots 66, 70, 71, 132
Roaf, Rev John 188–9
Roberts, Alexander 105
Robinson, John Beverley 5, 125
Robinson, Peter 62, 198
Rochester 140
Rochester Democrat 99, 101
Rolph, John 52, 57, 60, 62, 64, 80, 82–3, 91, 121
Roman Catholics 38; in study area 24, 31, 36, 186; politics 59, 72; in rebellion 183, 184, 193
Rose, Rev Samuel 27, 39, 42
Ross, Rev Alexander 59
Rothwell, Capt (William) 102
Round Plains 97, 101
Rouse, George 127, 229
Ryan, Rev Henry 33
Ryerson, Rev Egerton 26, 38, 192
Ryerson, Rev John 26
Ryerson, Rev William 26
Rymal, Jacob 54

Sackrider, Abraham 129, 191, 207, 208, 229, 277 n143, 281 n89
St Catharines 79, 84, 137
St Catharines Journal 79, 94, 106
St Clair frontier 145, 146
St George 45, 190
St Johns 137, 138
St Thomas 9, 42, 44, 45, 52; settlement 24, 183, 286 n4; religion 28, 29, 30, 189, 193, 196; politics 51, 58, 61, 77, 79; in rebellion 96, 100–1, 104, 105; cavalry 123, 146; post-rebellion 135, 156
St Thomas Liberal 110; before 1837 51, 54, 55, 57, 58, 61; in 1837 65, 67, 71, 72, 73–4, 76, 118
St Thomas Table of Events 118
Salmon, Col George C. 49, 100, 124, 134, 283 n136
Salmon, William 121
Sandwich 116, 122
Scatcherd, John 65
Scotland (village) 45; in rebellion 87–8, 94, 95, 98, 99–101; post-rebellion 123, 124, 159
Scott, Enos 144, 151, 251
Scott, Job 144, 151, 251–2
Scrivener, Charles 113, 229
Seabrooke, M.A. 50
Selborne 45
settlers
– American: alien question 6, 21, 178; in study area 20–3, 178–80, 198; loyalty 21, 132, 141, 171, 181, 203–4, 212; and British settlers 25–6, 32, 44, 46, 59, 136, 156, 181; religion 33, 35, 36; politics 50, 51, 57, 72; emigration 159; among rebels 178–81, 184, 192, 203–4, 208, 209, 210
– British 23, 216; politics 7, 50, 60; and American settlers 25–6, 32, 44, 46, 59, 136, 156, 181; religion 33, 34, 35, 36; loyalty 137, 182, 203, 208; among rebels 180, 182, 184, 208
– 'Canadian' 179, 203, 216
– Dutch 12, 22, 24–5
– English: in study area 22, 23–4, 180, 198; pretensions 24; and American settlers 32, 181; religion 33; politics 60; among rebels 179, 181, 182, 203; loyalty 181–2, 203, 204
– French 179
– French Canadian 36, 116
– Irish 23; in study area 22, 24, 58, 198; religion 33, 36; politics 60, 71; among rebels 179, 183–4, 203; loyalty 182, 184, 203, 204
– Lower Canadian 179
– Maritime 22, 203, 204
– New Brunswick 179, 182, 198
– Nova Scotian 24, 179, 198
– Scots: in study area 22, 23, 255 n30; religion 23, 36; politics 50, 59, 60; in rebellion 109, 182–3; loyalty 158, 182–3, 195
  – Highlanders 26–7; in study area 22, 23, 24, 42–3, 180; religion 23, 31, 36, 77; politics 76–7; in rebellion 102, 182–3; post-rebellion 117
  – Lowlanders 22, 23, 26–7, 32, 180, 182
– Upper Canadians 23, 198; in study area 22; and British settlers 25–6, 44, 46, 156; religion 36; politics 50, 60; loyalty 141, 171, 203; among rebels 178–81, 182, 184, 203, 208, 209, 210

– Welsh 22, 24, 182
Shade, Absalom 62, 63, 103
Shaw, Bela 58, 64–5, 73, 77, 90, 110, 118, 250
Sherman, Willard 126
Sherwood, Henry 130, 131
Shirreff, Patrick 25, 40, 50
Short Hills 79, 151; raid 137–8, 141, 150–1
Showers, Michael 126, 236, 276 n108
Simcoe 43, 44, 45, 286 n4; in rebellion 96–101 passim, 105, 197; jail 103, 111; post-rebellion 118, 134–5, 155, 156
Simons, Descom 130, 236
Skinner, Rev James 46, 195
Smith, Harmannus 54
Smith, Isaac L. 144, 252
Smith, Joseph N. 125, 229, 276 n108
Smith, Oliver 127, 229, 245
Smith, Stephen 114, 127, 150, 152, 236
Snider, Elias 90, 127, 150, 152, 229
Sodom 45, 98; politics 69; in rebellion 85–7, 101, 102, 103, 126, 191–2, 206; post-rebellion 139, 140, 141, 144
Sons of Liberty 140, 147
Southwold township 11, 12, 39, 45, 46, 166; settlement 15, 16, 17, 22, 23, 24, 42, 45, 180, 182, 285 n175; religion 28, 29, 30, 32, 33, 36, 188, 189, 194, 195, 289 n64, n78, 290 n95; in rebellion 89, 91, 105, 182; rebels from 170, 171, 175–7, 181, 183–4, 189
Sparta 69; politics 69–70, 73, 90, 91; in rebellion 90–2, 104, 170, 175, 177
Spragge (William) 61
Springfield 45

Steele, Jonathan 149, 151, 229, 277 n141, 278 n144
Steer, Rev 26
Stephens, John 130
Stephens, Moore 128, 130
Stewart, Daniel 182, 232
Stewart, John 182, 232
Stewart, Rt Rev Charles James (Lord Bishop of Quebec) 39
Strachan, John (barrister) 209
Strachan, Rev John 5, 42
Strang, Rev J. 38
Sturgis, David 111, 250
Sugar Island 117
Sullivan, Robert Baldwin 18, 83, 119, 133
Sumner, Cyrus 138
Swing riots 66, 132
Switzer, Martin 90–2, 106, 152, 175, 217, 230, 286 n4

Talbot, John 58, 193, 250; in 1837, 70, 71, 77, 79; in rebellion 90, 100; post-rebellion 116, 118
Talbot, Col Thomas 52, 53; settlement activities 16–17, 21, 26, 181; politics 49, 51, 62
Talbot, Richard 24, 58
Talbot Dispensatory 52
Talbot road 45, 96, 104
Tapscott, Rev 42
Teeple, Pelham C. 50, 93, 106, 113, 153, 162, 230
temperance 32, 51, 59
Temperanceville 45
Thames River 146
Theller, Edward 171
Thompson, Preserved 208, 230
Thompson, William 149, 151, 171, 230, 276 n115

Thornton, Rev Robert 192
Throckmorton, Joseph 143
Tidey, John Arthur 68, 69, 149, 152, 193, 230, 273 n20, 275 n80, 278 n145, 282 n105
Tiffany, Gideon 77–8, 130
Tiffany, Orrin Edward 147
Tilden, Charles 130, 273 n20, 275 n80
Tillson, George 90
Titus, Isaac 198, 243
Tories 10, 51, 53–56 passim, 163, 199; in 1828–36 7, 8, 58, 59–62, 63, 64; constituency 49–51; in 1837 67, 70–2, 73, 74, 76, 181; in rebellion 86, 91, 97, 100, 184, 191, 206, 207; post-rebellion 107, 118–21 passim, 135, 157, 159, 195, 205, 210; effects of rebellion on 159, 211–12
Toronto 32, 44, 66, 79; in rebellion 80, 82, 83, 84, 86–92 passim, 94, 95, 109, 115, 183, 205; post-rebellion 118, 119, 123, 127, 129, 148, 151, 159, 194; jail 149, 152, 153, 171
Toronto Constitution 66, 69, 80, 82, 183
Toronto Examiner 194
Toronto Mirror 184
Toronto Patriot 173
Town, Nathan 127, 150, 152, 236
Townsend township 12, 39, 166; settlement 14, 15, 20, 22, 24, 26, 42, 45, 179; religion 28, 29, 30, 36, 37, 189, 193, 289 n63, n78, n79, n80; politics 67; in rebellion 88–9, 111, 170
Townships: 'non-rebel' 12, 15, 16, 18, 28, 29, 30, 160, 166–8, 182; 'rebel' 12, 117, 165–6, 209; settlement 15, 18, 22, 160, 166–8, 178–80, 210; religion 28, 29, 30, 36–7, 186–7, 188, 189, 191, 192, 193
Travers, Charles 113, 230, 277 n142

Treason: acts against 120; trials for 107, 124–32, 133, 148, 158
Treffry, John 87, 143, 171, 174, 207
Tripp, Job 88, 236
Tufford, Eliza 53
Tufford, John 99, 125, 127, 150, 152, 154, 230
Turkey, Rufus 135
Tyrell, John Burwell 158

Uline, John L. 127, 230
unions, political: in 1832 51–2, 54; in 1837 8, 67, 69, 71, 74, 77–9, 80, 81, 90, 91
United Associate Synod 192
United Empire Loyalists 4, 6, 14, 24, 50, 60, 67
United Secession Church 26, 31–2, 38, 59, 192, 195–6
United States 60, 178, 181, 196, 199; and Reformers 50, 56; help for rebels 87, 91, 105, 196; and escaped rebels 106, 125, 153, 162, 163; and patriots 107, 115, 116, 117, 122, 123, 128, 137, 141, 142, 145, 147, 155, 158, 163, 212; 1838 emigration to 135, 139, 141, 159–61, 194, 195; *see also* Patriots
United Synod 31–2, 192
Universalists 37, 38, 59, 196
Upper Canada Gazette 168

Van Allen, Eliza (Mrs John B. Askin) 48
Van Arnam, John 130, 159, 230, 274 n46, 286 n7
Van Camp, Garrett 137, 151, 232
Vance, Alexander 201, 243
Van Diemen's Land 149, 158, 161
Vanduzen, Abraham 126, 230, 273 n43, 276 n108

Van Egmond, Anthony 12, 78
Van Norman, Benjamin 211–12
Vienna 32, 38, 45, 160, 198, 199, 201
Vittoria 45, 48, 124, 155, 156
voluntaryism 32, 34, 59, 60, 189, 195

Wallace, Thomas 95, 142
Walrath, Charles P. 127, 150, 152, 162, 230
Walsh, Francis Leigh 54
Walsingham township 12, 39, 155; settlement 14, 15, 16, 17, 20, 22, 24, 25; religion 28, 29, 30
Wardsville 45
War of 1812 6; claims from 68
Waterford 45, 88–9, 97, 98, 111, 118, 193
Waterloo county 24
Watts, William 149, 231, 277 n143, 281 n89
Webb, William 127, 150, 151, 231
Welland Canal Company 7, 53–4, 80
Wellington 45
Wellington Square 79
Wentworth county 11; politics 54, 62
Western district 11, 16, 37, 116, 122, 146, 147, 148, 171
Western road 97, 146
Westminster township 12, 39; settlement 14, 15, 21, 22, 23, 24, 42, 45, 182, 255 n30; religion 28, 29, 30, 32, 33, 194; politics 67, 71–3, 74, 75, 77; in rebellion 92, 130, 182; post-rebellion 140, 147
West Oxford township 12, 165; settlement 14, 15, 16, 20, 22, 42, 45, 179, 182, 285 n175; religion 28, 29, 30, 36, 189, 257 n80, 289 n63, n78, 290 n95; in rebellion 86, 92–3, 94, 102, 181, 189; post-rebellion 137, 139, 142
Wethy, Mire 129, 231, 273 n34, 277 n143, 281 n89
White, John 105
Whitehead, Col George Washington 139, 140
Wilberforce 71, 73
Wilcox, Ebenezer 91, 131, 150, 152, 236
Wilkes, Rev Henry 188–9
Willey, Jeremiah 108
Wilmot township 12
Wilson, Alan 18
Wilson, Andrew 144, 252
Wilson, David 138, 236, 273 n31, 277 n142
Wilson, Duncan 110, 128, 137, 138–9, 141, 144, 150–1, 216, 236–7
Wilson, Jeremiah 96
Wilson, John 106
Wilson, Justus 138
Windham township 12, 20, 39, 40, 43, 155, 166; settlement 14, 15, 20, 22, 42, 43, 45, 179; religion 28, 29, 30, 36, 37, 189, 193, 289 n78; in rebellion 88, 170
Windsor 116, 157, 160, 171
Winegarden, John 93
Wood, James 144, 231, 252
Wood, William 65
Woodhouse township 12, 39, 166; settlement 14, 15, 17, 20, 22, 42, 45, 179; religion 28, 29, 30, 60, 193, 289 n78, n80; in rebellion 97, 100, 103, 170; post-rebellion 124
Woodman, Elijah 160
Woodstock 45, 138; settlement 24, 44, 286 n4; politics 61; in rebellion 99, 102, 105, 182; post-rebellion 117

Woodstock British American 211
Worthington, Warren 136

Yarmouth township 12, 39, 40, 46, 166; settlement 14, 15, 16, 17, 21, 22, 23, 42, 43, 45, 179, 182, 285 n175; religion 28, 29, 30, 36, 37, 137, 186, 189, 191, 193, 256 n55, 257 n80; politics 51, 61, 67, 69–70, 72, 73, 74, 81, 90, 91; in rebellion 89, 90–2, 94, 95, 96, 100–1, 104, 149, 183; post-rebellion 129, 136, 138–9, 140, 158, 190; rebels from 170, 171, 175–7, 181, 183–4, 197, 208

Yeigh, Adam 127, 231, 275 n80
Yeigh, Jacob 153, 231, 286 n7
Yeomans, Michael 108
Young, James 9
Young, John 62

Zorra township 12, 20, 76; settlement 15, 16, 22, 23, 45, 65, 168, 182, 285 n176; religion 28, 29, 30, 31, 59; politics 50, 76, 77; in rebellion 102, 183; post-rebellion 117, 139, 140

www.ingramcontent.com/pod-product-compliance
Lightning Source LLC
Chambersburg PA
CBHW070247010526
44107CB00056B/2373